FROM THE

SOUTHERN CROSS

A View of World Art

c. 1940 – 88

Presented by

THE BIENNALE OF SYDNEY, 7th, 1988

in association with

THE AUSTRALIAN BICENTENNIAL AUTHORITY

Indemnified in part by the Commonwealth Government of Australia
through the Department of Arts, Sport, Environment and Territories

ART GALLERY OF NEW SOUTH WALES and PIER 2/3, WALSH BAY, SYDNEY
18 May — 3 July 1988

NATIONAL GALLERY OF VICTORIA, MELBOURNE
4 August — 18 September 1988

This publication is a co-production of
THE BIENNALE OF SYDNEY and
THE AUSTRALIAN BROADCASTING CORPORATION

 The Seventh Biennale of Sydney

Australia
1788-1988
arts

COMPILER'S NOTE

Artists participating in the 1988 Australian Biennale are listed alphabetically in this catalogue and appear in the order given on page 57.

Critical and/or artists' statements were received from each artist or artist's representative. In instances where information was not received in time for printing, other publications were consulted. Wherever possible, the Biennale of Sydney has ensured that copyright clearance has been obtained.

Details of works included in the exhibition and selected bibliographies for artists are listed in separate sections at the end of the catalogue. Credits for photography appear on each artist's page. Credits for loans and collections appear in the list of works.

All dimensions are for unframed works except in instances where no other dimensions have been available. All dimensions are in centimetres. Dimensions are shown in this sequence: height × width × depth.

Published by ABC Enterprises for the
AUSTRALIAN BROADCASTING CORPORATION
20 Atchison Street (Box 4444) Crows Nest NSW 2065
and The Biennale of Sydney Limited
100 George Street Sydney NSW 2000

National Library of Australia
Cataloguing-in-Publication entry
Biennale of Sydney (7th: 1988)
   The 1988 Australian Biennale: From the Southern
   Cross: a view of world art c. 1940–88
   Bibliography
   ISBN 0 642 53094 7.
   1. Art, Modern—20th century—Exhibitions.
   I. Australian Bicentennial Authority.
   II. Australian Broadcasting Corporation.
   III. Title
709′ 04′074099441

CATALOGUE PRODUCTION

Compiled by Josephine Heitter
Edited by Bryony Cosgrove
Designed by Helen Semmler
Set in 8/10 Century Schoolbook by Caxtons Pty Ltd, Adelaide
Printed and bound in Australia by Griffin Press, Adelaide
13-2495

CONTENTS

FROM THE SOUTHERN CROSS

A View of World Art c. 1940 – 88

COMMISSIONERS

We should like to thank the following commissioners and national co-ordinators for their assistance in assembling works and catalogue material:

AUSTRALIA: Frances Lindsay, Director, University Gallery, University of Melbourne
AUSTRIA: Angelica Bäumer, Vienna
BRITAIN: Julia Little, London (Co-ordinator)
FEDERAL REPUBLIC OF GERMANY: René Block, Gallery Director, DAAD
    (German Academic Exchange Service), Berlin
FRANCE: Bernard Blistène, Senior Curator, Musée National d'Art Moderne,
    Centre Georges Pompidou, Paris
ITALY: Professor Flavio Caroli, Milan
JAPAN: Fumio Matsunaga, Japan Foundation, Tokyo
NETHERLANDS: Gijs van Tuyl, Director, Visual Arts, Rijksdienst Beeldende Kunst,
    Amsterdam
NEW ZEALAND: John McCormack, Manager, Visual Arts Program, Queen Elizabeth II
    Arts Council, Wellington
POLAND: Ryszard Stanislawski, Director, Museum Sztuki, Lodz
SWITZERLAND: Dr César Menz, Chief, Service des Beaux Arts, Office Fédéral de la
Culture, Berne
UNITED STATES OF AMERICA: Diane Waldman, Deputy Director, Solomon R.
    Guggenheim Museum, New York; Assistant to the Commissioner, Clare Bell

OVERSEAS FUNDING AND SUPPORT

AUSTRIA: Bundesministerium für Unterricht, Kunst und Sport (Mag. Joseph Secky)
BELGIUM: The Flemish Council
BRITAIN: The British Council, (Henry Meyric Hughes, London; Ray Newberry and
    Patricia Zeppel, Sydney)
CANADA: The Canada Council (Edythe Goodridge); Department of External Affairs
    (Arts Promotion Division) (Yves Pépin)
FEDERAL REPUBLIC OF GERMANY: Institut für Auslandsbeziehungen
    (Dr Hermann Pollig); Goethe Institute, Munich and Australia (Susanna Abegg and
    Dagmar James, Sydney; Monique Phillips, Melbourne)
FRANCE: Association Française d'Action Artistique (Marie-Claude Collette)
ITALY: Comune di Milano (Dr Luigi Corbani and Dr Anna Sansuini):
    Ministero degli Affari Esteri
JAPAN: The Japan Foundation
NETHERLANDS: Rijksdienst Beeldende Kunst
NEW ZEALAND: Queen Elizabeth II Arts Council
POLAND: Ministry of Culture and Fine Arts
SWITZERLAND: Office Fédéral de la Culture; Pro Helvetia (Luc Boissonnas)
UNITED STATES OF AMERICA: Arts America, United States Information Service
    (Susan Stirn); National Endowment for the Arts (Dr Ruth Berenson,
    Beverly Kratochvil)
YUGOSLAVIA: Yugoslav Airlines

SPONSORS AND DONORS

ANSETT AIRLINES LTD (domestic freight and travel)

AUSTRALIAN BROADCASTING CORPORATION (visit of Bill Fontana)

DIGITAL EQUIPMENT CORPORATION (AUSTRALIA) PTY LTD (provision of computers and software)

GADENS – Solicitors

KUMAGAI–GUMI PTY LTD

MERLIN INTERNATIONAL PROPERTIES (AUSTRALIA) PTY LTD

MITSUI PUBLIC RELATIONS COMMITTEE (Close-up of Japan)

QANTAS AIRWAYS LTD (international travel and Qantas Art Apprenticeship Program)

SAIPEM AUSTRALIA PTY LTD

WARGON CHAPMAN PARTNERS PTY LTD

Government Support

THE VISUAL ARTS & CRAFTS BOARD OF THE AUSTRALIA COUNCIL,

the FEDERAL GOVERNMENT'S ART FUNDING AND ADVISORY BODY

the ABORIGINAL ARTS BOARD OF THE AUSTRALIA COUNCIL

NEW SOUTH WALES GOVERNMENT: OFFICE OF THE MINISTER FOR THE ARTS

THE COUNCIL OF THE CITY OF SYDNEY

THE MARITIME SERVICES BOARD

Major Donors

AUSTRALIAN GUARANTEE CORPORATION LTD

BROKEN HILL PROPRIETARY CO LTD

COLES MYER LTD

COMMONWEALTH BANKING CORPORATION

CONCRETE CONSTRUCTIONS (NSW) PTY LTD

SIR WILLIAM DOBELL ART FOUNDATION

DOMINGUEZ BARRY SAMUEL MONTAGU LTD

JOHN FAIRFAX LTD

FOLLOW ME TRAVEL

WILLIS FABER JOHNSON & HIGGINS PTY LTD

Donors

BONDS INDUSTRIES LTD

SIR DAVID GRIFFIN

MR MICHAEL HOBBS

JOHNSON & JOHNSON AUSTRALIA PTY LTD

PERMANENT TRUSTEE COMPANY LTD

The Biennale of Sydney is one of the most significant events in Australia's art calendar and the Australian Bicentennial Authority is delighted to be able to join forces to make the 1988 Australian Biennale a national event.

Australia's bicentennial celebrations reflect the many ways in which individuals, organisations and governments believe it appropriate to recognise two hundred years of settlement.

The arts community has developed its own approach for involvement in the Bicentenary, one that is possibly a more objective and distanced view but also one that is telling and relevant. In this context the impact of a Biennale during the celebrations is exciting, providing an opportunity for the exhibition of Australian artists together with a fascinating range of visiting artists.

We look forward to the Biennale with all its various components, two large exhibitions plus a rich series of lectures, performances and seminars which we know will be stimulating, provocative and powerful.

The opportunity for the Bicentennial Authority to co-present the Biennale not only in Sydney but also in Melbourne is an important first and an exciting development, which we hope will be continued well beyond 1988.

National celebrations of all kinds are organised by governments and countries of many persuasions and in such celebrations the arts must play a central and vital role. The Bicentennial Arts Program of which the Biennale is a highlight is making its contribution to the broader bicentennial statement about Australia, a contribution variously perceptive, stimulating, irreverent, reassuring and critical. The opportunity for a heightened and more telling role for the arts in this Bicentennial year should not be missed.

PETER SARAH
Director, Arts & Entertainment

Over fifteen years ago a small group perceived the need for a regular major exhibition of international contemporary art in Sydney. We took our inspiration and our model from the famous Venice Biennale. The first exhibition—the first Biennale of Sydney—was held in the Sydney Opera House in 1973. Each of the following Sydney Biennales has marked an ever-enlarging dimension.

Due to continuing dedicated work and support over those fifteen years, the stature of the Sydney Biennale has grown almost beyond our hopes and expectations. And with it has grown also the reputation of Sydney and the Art Gallery of New South Wales as a focal centre for the whole of Australia for the display and development of understanding and appreciation of contemporary art from all over the world.

The Sixth Biennale in 1986 contained works by over a hundred artists from twenty-one countries. Our Bicentennial Biennale includes works by over 110 from fifteen countries. It rightfully stands among the foremost of the outstanding events of our Bicentennial year. The Sydney Biennale of 1988 will be shown for the first time at the National Gallery of Victoria. Visiting artists, critics and curators will travel throughout Australia to make this a truly national event. The range of artists, countries and cultures represented makes it unique as an exhibition in Australia of contemporary art both from here and overseas. Sydney can be justly proud of the achievement of all who have worked so hard and who have contributed so generously to bring it all together. It does more than justice to the importance of the 200th anniversary of the creation of the British colony out of which modern Australia has grown and includes a truly significant Aboriginal work.

There are many to whom, on behalf of the Board of Directors of the Biennale, I should like to make sincere and grateful acknowledgement.

First, the Art Gallery of New South Wales has been generous in agreeing to display a substantial part of the exhibition in its own premises. We gratefully acknowledge also the Maritime Services Board for providing space for us at Pier 2/3. There are many others to be included in this message of appreciation for their financial contributions, great and small. Without this sponsorship we could not have presented this exhibition on such a grand scale.

We are also grateful to the Commonwealth Government of Australia, through the Department of Arts, Sport, Environment and Territories, for indemnifying certain key works that play an integral part in the theme of this exhibition.

Over and above the provision of exhibition space and the provision of financial support, the Biennale is essentially the product of the inspiration and dedicated work of those who have carried out the broad as well as the detailed planning. They are the ones who have, in effect, made the exhibition for us.

I have left until last two special matters. Firstly, I should like to welcome the many visitors both from overseas and from Australia who have come to share this Biennale with us. They include eminent artists and distinguished critics as well as thousands whose personal interests include the study and appreciation of contemporary art. Their participation is, perhaps, the most convincing evidence of the importance of this Biennale.

Finally, on behalf of all connected with the Biennale, I should like to say to His Excellency Sir Ninian Stephen, Governor General of Australia, how much we value his gracious acceptance of the office of our Patron. We are grateful for this mark of confidence and for his encouragement to us in our endeavours.

FRANCO BELGIORNO-NETTIS, CBE, AM
Chairman
The Biennale of Sydney

ACKNOWLEDGEMENTS

Our thanks go to:

Peter Sarah, Judy Annear, Jan Ross and Tom Thompson (Australian Bicentennial Authority)

John Gooch (Department of Foreign Affairs, Canberra), Georges Zask (French Embassy),
Connie Watkin (Canadian Consulate-General), Heather Stewart (United States Information
Service), Clelia March (Australian Embassy, Rome), Elsa Fischer (Australian Embassy, Berne)

The British Council, Sydney, for assistance with the visits of Lynne Cooke, Hannah Collins,
Gary Stevens and Caroline Wilkinson. The Goethe Institute for assistance with the visit of
Dr Ernst Busche. The Power Gallery of Contemporary Art for assistance with the visit of
Hermann Nitsch.

The Comune di Milano, without whose assistance the participation of Italian artists would not have
been possible.

Bruce Adams, Jan Minchin, Dr Ursula Hoff, Murray Bail, Janine Burke, Patrick McCaughey,
Linda Hicks-Williams, Elwyn Lynn, James Gleeson, Elizabeth Butel, Daniel Thomas, Ian North,
John Mundine, Elizabeth Cross, Terence Maloon, Tony Bond, David Brown, Lynne Cooke,
Jonathan Watkins, David Sylvester, Dan Cameron, Jeanne Siegel, Edward F. Fry, Donald B. Kuspit,
Dore Ashton, Arthur C. Danto, Thomas Lawson, Richard Armstrong, Pat Steir, Dena Shottenkirk,
Henry Geldzahler, Anne d'Harnoncourt, Joshua Decter, Wieland Schmied

Dr Richard Haese, Ray Hughes, Albert Tucker, Henry Jolles, Sylvana Scannapiego, Lyn Williams,
Lady Drysdale, Rosemary Waters, Mike Parr, Susan Schmocker

Gretchen Cook, Angela Kerley, David McClintock

The Arts Law Centre of Australia, the Australian Elizabethan Theatre Trust, the Volunteer
Association of NSW

Rodney Swan, Barry Wright, Graham Moon, Ken Garthwaite (Maritime Services Board)

Denis Crawford (Qantas), Jennifer McNamara (Mitsui & Co.), Adriano Vicari (Follow Me Travel),
Marco Belgiorno-Zegna, Penny Ferguson, Tony Winterbotham, Joe Bollen, Sue Douglas,
Rocco Tallarida and Jim Smith (Transfield), Sir David Griffin. Special thanks to Montrose Wines

Clare O'Brien, Lindsay Somerville (ABC Enterprises); Bryony Cosgrove, Helen Semmler;
Brian Kench and Tony Hackemer (Bloxham and Chambers)

Maggie Gilchrist (Ivan Dougherty Gallery), Neil Godfrey (Sydney Theatre Company),
John Borthwick (Sydney College of the Arts)

Neil Wilson (Panalpina World Transport Pty Ltd), Great Northern Industries, The Jackson Hotel

Mark Davoren, Roxanne De Luca, Lindsay Moloney, Barry Anderson, Di Henry, Bill Beattie,
Antonia Lomny, Mila Gelvezon, Sylvia Tropiano

All the students from Nepean College of Advanced Education, Sydney College of the Arts, City Art
Institute and Canberra School of Art who helped with preparation and installation at Pier 2/3.

Bridget Battersby and Members of the Task Force of the Art Gallery Society, Art Gallery of
New South Wales.

Special thanks to the many volunteers who have helped with administration, installation and
manning of the exhibition.

NICK WATERLOW

I

The 1988 Australian Biennale will present a view of art today expanded by the inclusion of key Australian, European and American precursors. It will, wherever possible, present works in the light of an Australian context, appropriate in the year of the bicentenary, and in relation to this context overseas work will come from the major arenas of creative inter-communication since settlement, namely Britain, New Zealand, Europe, North America and Japan.

For the first time, a small number of key Australian antecedents will be shown side by side with their peers from other countries. This should have occurred years ago but did not, because until the 1970s the Australian art world was extraordinarily isolated and diffident in its relationship to modernist culture. It was only occasionally relieved by an experience of someone else's reality, such as the 1939 Herald Exhibition of *French and British Contemporary Art*, the *Two Decades of American Art* in 1964, or Christo's wrapping of Little Bay, Sydney, in 1969.

This isolation, however, did not impair the production of remarkable work by a small band of artists such as Margaret Preston, Joy Hester, Ralph Balson, Tony Tuckson, Ian Fairweather and Fred Williams, although it did necessitate a mass exodus overseas of artists, writers, musicians and other creative souls in the 1950s and 60s. Today it is possible to live in Australia as an artist and exhibit with one's peers in other countries fairly frequently, and while this may not be often enough, it is still a great advance on the previous situation.

The purpose of referring to the work of this particular group of Australian artists is that their concerns remain absolutely valid for our contemporary artists, since Australia in 1988 demands a comprehensive understanding of the particularities of context more than ever before. We must learn from our history rather than repeatedly trying to rewrite it.

The attempt to view key developments in world art since 1940 from an Australian perspective must be made if we are, both collectively and individually, to come to grips with crucial problems of identity and creativity. No Australian has ever doubted his or her prowess in the arena of world sport; no cringe has ever been manifested there. Why not? Largely because sport has never suffered, apart from during the war years, the isolation that has been the lot of art.

This exhibition will, I hope, contribute further significant evidence of the essential role artists have played and continue to play in expressing, for those of us fortunate enough to live here, the reality of existence as Australians. 'They give birth astride of a grave, the light gleams an instant, then it's night once more.' The darkness of Samuel Beckett is pierced by their illumination.

This exhibition will make it possible for viewers to form a first-hand and more complete picture of the art of Australia as it has emerged since about 1940. My intention is not to provide a total picture, but rather to concentrate on particular strengths, on certain neglected areas of work that originate a perception forged here.

The period on which I have chosen to focus emerges around 1940. It was then that a specifically antipodean imagery began to emerge, one with its own symbols, mythology and metaphorical representations of this land. Despite the arguments raging between nationalists and internationalists, between figuration and abstraction, what was at stake was the way Australians perceived themselves and their habitat and the projection of that understanding both here and abroad. As a movement it was the expression of an intuitive urge amongst a group of Victorians to enlarge a national experience and to forge a visual culture that could build on the tentative origins of the Heidelberg School three generations before. In contrast to the Heidelberg School the Antipodeans, as they would come to be called, had not travelled abroad to witness at first-hand the giants of European art. In a perverse way this was their strength and, unawed, they pillaged and utilised whatever they could glean from text, reproduction and hearsay. Such was their success and their influence on others that Nolan, Williams and Boyd created the context for perceiving this continent. This influence remains pervasive and it is against this background that our best contemporary artists work, as do Americans in tension with the New York School.

II

In the mid 1960s I remember favourably reviewing Ian Fairweather's retrospective at the Art Gallery of New South Wales for the *Nation*, soon to become *Nation Review*, 'lean and nosey like a ferret'. 'But how good is he?' someone asked. 'Probably better than Mark Tobey,' I replied, having seen a show of his in London earlier that year. 'Mark who?' they said. Imagine the loss to Britain's understanding of not just Australian cricket but cricket per se if Don Bradman had never toured. I was not interested in rating Fairweather but he revealed uniquely something that would otherwise have remained hidden about the experience of living in this part of the world and at that particular moment. Like Bradman, whom I had been fortunate enough to see play, they both contributed something essential to one's global understanding and appreciation of these two very different intuitive languages of painting and batting.

People in the United States who did not see Fairweather's paintings, or for that matter Tuckson's, would have had a broader grasp of the etymology of Klein, Rothko, Pollock, De Kooning and Tobey's art if they had. Australia, artists and public alike, was for too long disadvantaged by the inability to see 'a full picture'. None of Fairweather's generation was well known beyond this country, as indeed were few of the next generation apart from Boyd and Nolan. The view of Australian art beyond this country remained fragmentary.

This exhibition deals with an 'extended' present. Art opens our eyes to dimensions of human consciousness previously unexplored, dimensions that are timeless and which make art such a crucial ingredient of the humanist tradition. It remains one of the few areas of the psyche, individually or collectively conceived, that is unexpurgated, whole and without censorship.

Alexander Solzhenitsyn, in his acceptance speech for the Nobel Literature Prize in 1970, put his finger on it:

. . . the genuinely artistic work is utterly, irrefutably convincing, and even the resisting heart surrenders to it. A political speech, a piece of assertive propaganda, a plan for a new society, or a philosophical system can all be built with apparent harmony and consistency even on an error, on a lie; and what has been hidden or distorted will not be immediately apparent. And then a diametrically opposite speech, piece of propaganda or plan, a differently constructed philosophy, may emerge looking just as smooth and consistent, with no visible flaw. That is why they inspire trust—and distrust too.

It is useless to assert what one's heart does not believe.

A work of art carries its proof in itself. Artificial, strained concepts do not withstand the image-test; all such concepts crumble, they are revealed as puny and colourless, they convince nobody. But works which have drawn on truth and presented it to us in live, concentrated form, grip us and communicate themselves to us compellingly—and nobody, even centuries later, will ever be able to refute them.

III

In addition to the work of Preston, Williams, Boyd and Nolan, which is essentially moulded by visual experience in Australia, this exhibition will show works by the artists Fairweather and Tuckson whose sensory experience could only have been derived more widely from Oceania and its surrounds, but whose expression of place was even more crucially inclusive. Both these artists produced work that could only have emerged from Terra Australis, seen in a wider regional context inclusive of Chinese, Japanese, New

MAX BECKMANN
Soldatenkneipe (Soldiers' Pub), 1948
Oil on canvas
55.5 ×85
Collection: Staatsgalerie, Stuttgart

Guinean and Aboriginal influences. The most effective art-making here has, I repeat, often been plundered, plucked and pillaged as the need arose. This 'mother of invention' is the muse of some of the finest artists and artwork to arise in this country. Explicably enough, one 'ism here has not led inexorably to the next, if only because our relationship to modernism is not an originatory one. However, like a desert flower our major artists emerged from the most unexpected terrain. This is a peculiarly Australian condition and is common to many different fields of activity . . . the music of Percy Grainger, the opera of Melba and Sutherland, the poetry of Christopher Brennan and the images in extremis of Joy Hester and the lonely constructivism of Ralph Balson.

There is, of course, a particular curatorial reason for the inclusion not only of the six Australian precursors (Nolan and Boyd being current practitioners) but of their foreign counterparts, which I hope will become apparent within the hanging of the exhibition. Occasionally it has been necessary to show a pre-1940 work, as in the case of Bonnard's *La Sieste* of 1900, which is the only major painting by this artist in Australia with subject matter relevant to this Biennale as none such was available for us from France. Necessity, again, is the mother of our invention.

The exhibition puts forward five specific avenues for exploration: landscape as metaphor, the figure and its psyche, the non-objective, myth and allegory, intervention and de-construction. With landscape we see approaches from Braque to Fred Williams to American video artist Bill Viola; in figure, from Bonnard to Balthus to Hester to Julie Brown-Rrap; in myth and allegory, from Beckmann to Anselm Kiefer to Peter Booth.

IV

Where does Australian art come from? This is a vexing question since, placed in the context of my own feelings, I see the single most important statement in this Biennale as being the Aboriginal Memorial of two hundred burial poles, one for each of the two hundred years of white culture. Aborigines have always been more concerned with spirit than matter, and it says much about the materialist, possession-based nature of our own society that for so long it was almost blind to a culture intangible but so crucially present. 'Time is money' and 'the Dreamtime' are worlds apart and yet for many artists, particularly in this century, the Aboriginal presence is the most civilising and creatively challenging element in our world.

Although intellectual nourishment has always been available from Europe, Britain, North and South America or elsewhere, it is the Aboriginal presence that nourishes our spirit. Herein lies the divided nature of the non-Aboriginal artist, which makes inevitable our hybrid art, straddling a consciousness of two worlds. But at its best, in the hands of a Fairweather, a Tuckson or a Peter Booth, it lacks little by comparison with a mono-cultural or purist expression.

Let me say by way of conclusion that I value my experience of the world as one of change and development. It is an approach that is suspicious of the stereotypical and I find that this exhibition has already altered my attitudes, which I hope will also be the case for its audience.

Neither perception of a pear nor perception of a painting requires faculties beyond those of an average man. Perception through vision is a highly accelerated response, so fast, so complex, so free that it cannot be pinned down by the very recent limited science of word communication. To understand a work of art, it must be seen and perceived, not worded. Words can be used to place art historically, to set it in social context, to describe the movements, to relate it to other works, to state individual preferences, and to set the scene all around it. But the actual understanding of a work of art only comes through the process by which it was created—and that was by perception.[1]

1. David Smith, 'Perception and Reality', delivered at Williams College, Williamstown, Massachusetts, 17 December 1951.

ANTIPODEAN ANTECEDENTS:

AN ACCENT ON THE PRESENT

FRANCES LINDSAY

The 1988 Australian Biennale is the first Biennale to have a Commissioner to assist with the representation of Australian artists. The idea for such a Commissioner was first mooted in 1979 at the time of *European Dialogue*, Nick Waterlow's first Biennale.[1] It was this Biennale that also firmly established Nick Waterlow's commitment, as Director of the 1986 and 1988 Biennales, to having a generous representation of Australian artists (including a fair proportion of women) and to seeking the advice and assistance of artists, curators, dealers and arts administrators around Australia in order to arrive at a consensus. However, this 1988 Biennale has provided the Curatorium, to use Nick Waterlow's description of the group that contributes to discussions, with a much wider brief for the Australian selection than was possible with previous Biennales, which had a more prescriptive theme. Its aim of presenting the best contemporary art while focusing on key historical artists since the 1940s has enabled a diverse selection to be made of artists working in Australia in a wide range of styles. The criterion for inclusion was excellence, not geographical location, gender or media. The Australian component thus in no way intends to serve as a general survey of everything that is happening in Australian art today, rather it highlights certain key artists whose contribution to the art of this country is significant.

Australian Aboriginal art is represented in this Biennale by the Aboriginal memorial created by the Ramingining Arts Community from Arnhemland. An age-old ceremonial tradition, involving the placing of bones into decorated hollow log coffins, is recalled by the 'forest' of two hundred specially commissioned hollow logs. This 'forest' symbolically represents a large burial ground: a memorial to all the Aborigines who died after the white man's occupation of Australia.

Of the twenty-six European Australian artists, six are historical figures: Margaret Preston, Ralph Balson, Joy Hester, Ian Fairweather, Tony Tuckson and Fred Williams. They have been chosen because of their relevance to the artistic concerns of today, not because of their importance in the history of Australian art. Joy Hester and Tony Tuckson were virtually unknown in their day outside a small coterie of admirers, but are now universally recognised in Australia as being major figures. The feminist movement of the 1970s brought Hester's seminal work of the 1940s into consideration, while the new expressionists of the 1980s found much to admire in the late gestural works of Tony Tuckson. Let it not be forgotten that we choose our artistic antecedents in accordance with the necessities of our own time, and while these artists provide us with a focus of interest, no direct lineage or influence from the earlier artists to those of the present is suggested. For example, Hester's immediacy, her psychologically loaded and expressive images, her invention and distortion within a self-imposed parameter, and the power of her gestural drawings in ink on paper which are all metaphorical self-portraits, find parallels today in the work of Mike Parr who works in a similar medium, albeit on a much larger scale, with an equally intense penetration of the psychological inner self. In all other respects they are the most opposite of artists. Hester was an intensely private artist whose status and recognition were limited by her choice of medium.[2] Parr is one of Australia's most acclaimed contemporary artists whose work has been included in a large number of international exhibitions. Parr's work, from his performance works of the 1970s to his current large-scale anamorphic works, is also concerned with self-portraiture, self scrutiny, identity, fragmentation, metamorphosis, loss. As with Hester's work the autobiographical quality of his self-portrait drawings is distanced by the repetition of seemingly similar images. Bernice Murphy has written recently that Parr's works 'embody a diversified, fragmented, multiple identity, breaking beyond individual status and thereby revising the impetus of self-portraiture as traditionally regarded'.[3]

If Joy Hester needed the feminist movement of the 1970s for her work to be re-assessed and re-valued, Margaret Preston's work has been held in high esteem in Australia almost continuously since the 1920s when she painted bold Modernist still-life compositions, often of Australian native flowers, and led a revival of printmaking in Sydney with her stylised woodblock prints. Nevertheless, it is Preston's work of the 1940s, in which she adapted Aboriginal motifs and designs to the decorative geometry of her own style, that in the 1980s has become the focus of increased attention and admiration. Margaret Preston was one of the first white Australian artists to appreciate Aboriginal art and to explore the possibilities of appropriating its compositional qualities, decorative elements and abstracted symbolism. Her work had received some international recognition during the 1930s, and in 1941 three of her paintings were included in an exhibition of Australian art that toured the United States and Canada under the auspices of the Carnegie Corporation. This exhibition was also one of the first international exhibitions to include bark paintings and drawings by Aboriginal artists, and the catalogue essays on these artists were contributed by Margaret Preston.[4]

Preston's admiration for Aboriginal art first emerged in the 1920s with a strongly espoused belief that its characteristics should be adapted by Australia in order to develop an endemic or truly national art.[5] However, it was not until the 1940s when her knowledge of Aboriginal art had increased after many trips to Aboriginal sites in New South Wales, Queensland and the Northern Territory, that she began putting this theory into practice. In 1941 she wrote, 'The art of the aborigine has for too long been neglected. The attention of Australian people must be drawn to the fact that it is a great art and the foundation of a national culture for this country.'[6]

Sadly it has taken some forty years or more for Margaret Preston's views about Aboriginal art to find universal acceptance, although she is not alone among white artists in Australia in recognising its unique beauty and significance. Both Ian Fairweather in the 1950s and 1960s, and Tony Tuckson in the 1970s incorporated elements of Aboriginal art into their work. Fairweather's personal calligraphic gestural style in which the painted line implants the outline of the figure upon a field of abstraction relates to Aboriginal art, especially to the outline drawings of the Oenpelli painters, although it is not so central to his work as either Chinese art or European Cubism.[7] Tony Tuckson also assimilated references to tribal art into his work which in its early stages owed much to Picasso and Dubuffet, and later to the American Abstract Expressionists. Tuckson was extremely knowledgeable about Aboriginal art; as Deputy Director at the Art Gallery of New South Wales he made trips to Melville Island and Yirrkalla to acquire the grave posts and bark paintings which form the basis of the gallery's Tribal Art collection. His late expressionist paintings, with their bold slashes of colour on raw unprimed sheets of hardboard, immediately bring to mind Aboriginal bark paintings—a feature that was more apparent when these late works were first exhibited in 1973, unfettered by frames, the sheets of hardboard hanging free and curving inward like large sheets of bark. Other artists in Australia have more recently used images from Australian Aboriginal art or Oceanic art to enrich the traditions of Western Modernism. John Walker, who has been resident in Australia since the late 1970s, has incorporated images of tribal artefacts into the abstract forms of his paintings with their references to Goya. His works are profound expressions of Oceania united with the greatest traditions of Western painting. Tim Johnson has spent time studying Aboriginal art with the Papunya painters, discovering similarities between their complex abstraction and layering of imagery with both Eastern and Western art. Both these artists were represented in previous Biennales. Imants Tillers, too, has used images of Aboriginal art, but in his case they are images from contemporary Aboriginal painting appropriated by him for incorporation into works composed of juxtaposed pre-existing images, deconstructed and displaced from their original sources.

Ralph Balson, a pioneer in Australia of non-objective geometric abstraction, is a precursor in this exhibition for contemporary non-figurative systemic painters, although his direct influence on their work is negligible. Balson held the first exhibition of entirely non-figurative painting in Australia in 1941. His Constructive paintings of the 1950s with their blocks of solid colour have their origins in his admiration for Mondrian. In his later works these geometric constructions gave way to a more expressionistic abstraction in which the paint was dabbed onto the surface. In later paintings it was poured and allowed to flow freely before congealing in a thick, painterly abstraction.

Ralph Balson died in 1964. The only artist in this Biennale with whom he had a real link is Robert Klippel, Australia's foremost sculptor of this century who has been producing abstract assemblages of found parts since the late 1940s. Klippel's early sculptures were composed of machinery components such as parts of old typewriters, and his recent works are assembled from the wooden templates used for the construction of factory machines. While his sculptures are constructed from the material elements of an industrial society, Rosalie Gascoigne collects and gathers junk such as discarded road signs, weathered packing cases and natural materials from the countryside near her Canberra home. her assemblages and installations evoke the feeling and environmental processes of the Australian landscape.

Abstraction, as a continuing force in Australian art, is also represented in this Biennale by Robert Hunter, whose paintings since the late 1960s have employed minimal variations of subtle colour relationships within complex geometric structures, and by Lesley Dumbrell, whose work over a similar period has been concerned with vibrant colour sequences, overlapping and receding in a controlled ordering of harmony and discord. Both artists have sustained the Modernist belief in pure non-representational art. Other artists have used abstraction as a way into another level of meaning, either conceptual or symbolic. For example Hilarie Mais's geometric abstractions have a metaphorical content contained within their grid constructions and Victor Meertens' towering configurations evoke references to Giotto and Goya despite being made of that most Australian of materials, galvanised corrugated iron. For over twenty years John Nixon has used the vocabulary of Malevich's Suprematist cross in works and installations that he has now collectively titled *Non-Objective Self-Portrait*.

It is tempting to look for references to the landscape in the recent paintings of Michael Johnson with their exuberant use of colour and thickly applied paint. However, his painting of 1968, which is also included in this exhibition, reminds us that his work has its origins in the pure colour abstraction of the New York School and owes its allegiance to artists such as Mark Rothko and Barnett Newman.[8]

The importance of the tradition of the landscape to Australian art is recognised by the inclusion of Fred Williams, Arthur Boyd and Sidney Nolan—a triumvirate of outstanding innovative Australian painters who, as individual artists, have changed our perceptions of the Australian landscape.

Sidney Nolan's paintings of the 1940s produced in the Wimmera district of north-eastern Victoria are now recognised as representing a pivotal and crucial moment for Australian art when the fundamental changes to Western art wrought by Modernism were relocated in the antipodes of the Australian landscape. Nolan's intense involvement with the landscape produced a vision in which the horizon line could be tilted and emphasised, and the vegetation and foliage abstracted into a series of gestures and dots. According to Richard Haese, 'What Nolan brought to the Australian experience above all else was a recognition of the momentous changes that had taken place in European—and especially French—art at the end of the nineteenth and in the first years of the twentieth centuries. Nolan was not alone in responding to these changes, but his particular direction and his grasp of what they signified were unique, as was his overriding and profound involvement with landscape after 1942. His impact on later painters—and one thinks especially of Fred Williams who looked closely at the Wimmera and Kelly paintings of the 1940s—has been an immensely liberating one'.[9] Nolan's achievement was not only to fuse Modernism with a new vision of the Australian landscape, but also to provide insight into the great underlying concern of the Australian psyche with the inevitability of catastrophes and with the outsider in society who is doomed, like the outlaw Ned Kelly, the luckless explorers Burke and Wills, the ill-fated Mrs Fraser, and the Australian soldiers at Gallipoli.

If Nolan paved the way for a new vision of man in the Australian landscape, it is Fred Williams who has contributed most in the twentieth century to developing a unique vernacular for the Australian landscape which conveys direct observation, form and feeling. When Williams returned to Australia in 1957, after studying and working in England, he took up the challenge of confronting the past masters of Australian art by painting the landscape and creating a new mode of expression for it. In doing this Williams merged the experience of Cézanne and the French masters with the gestural painterly forms of the American Abstract Expressionists. He developed a unique artistic calligraphy whereby the vegetation of the Australian bush could be interpreted as a series of dots and painterly marks within the abstracted schematised compositional format of the landscape.

The Australian landscape has also provided the setting for the central themes of Arthur Boyd's art, especially that of metamorphosis—humans and beasts changing from one physical state to another—which in Boyd's art is used as a metaphor for man's emergence from cruelty and primordial bestiality to a higher spiritual reality. Boyd draws on Classical sources, myths, religious legends and his own imagination to produce a humanist art that expresses through allegory and metaphor some of the most powerful emotions in the history of Australian art. Like Sidney Nolan his career spans the 1940s to the 1980s and his recent work continues to be enriched by the recurrent iconography and themes of his oeuvre. Grazia Gunn writes, 'Boyd's work expresses a range of social and psychological realities which project a variety of meanings: conflict and order, cruelty and compassion, sin and innocence, passion and resignation. The work is figural representation, but it does not hold to the principles of realism; rather it is analogous to the reality it expresses.'[10]

Spirituality and humanism, metamorphosis and transformation, are also the essence of Peter Booth's art. In his paintings and drawings the cycle of birth, death and resurrection appears in a number of different guises. His figurative paintings focus intently on the inner world of the subconscious and the outer world of reality. Images from the world of appearances intermingle with those produced in his dreams. Booth's recent paintings have shifted from apocalyptic landscapes with scenes of destruction, where man is seemingly doomed by his own violence, to idyllic dream-like landscapes of hope and renewal where man, beast and organic life co-exist among the fossils and skeletal remains of the past.[11] Jan Minchin has recently suggested that these primordial landscapes are Booth's version 'perhaps of the Dreaming when, in Aboriginal mythology, landscapes and living things came into being'.[12]

It is perhaps not co-incidental that both Boyd and Booth are Melbourne artists. Melbourne has a long tradition of producing strong painters, such as Gareth Sansom who, since the 1960s, has pursued a highly idiosyncratic and individual path for his art. His paradoxical paintings contain a powerful counterbalance between abstraction and figuration. Multi-layered in meaning, they are masked with disguise and ambivalence. On the other hand, perhaps partly as a result of the Sydney Biennale, theory-based art has had greater impact in Sydney, as evidenced in this Biennale by the works of Richard Dunn, Julie Brown-Rrap and Jacky Redgate. Dunn's work, to quote Rob Horne, 'seeks to be engaged in an arena with wider social and cultural—ultimately political—possibilities, an arena where the problematic of imaging intersects a certain problematic of modern society in general'.[13] Julie Brown-Rrap poses her own body in photographic constructs in which iconic images from the traditional male history of art are deconstructed from their known context and re-worked as radical statements within the cultural context of feminism. Jacky Redgate's cibachrome photographs *Taming the Spectrum* (1987) present us with a series of portraits of family groups taken at the turn of the century. Though each was found independently by the artist, the seven photographs are arranged in a numerical sequence so that a mathematical system has been imposed. Her *Work to Rule* photographs have a formalist quality, but in spirit are closer to John Nixon's artistic stance in their use and glorification of humble crafted objects which are essentially anachronistic but endowed with associated meaning. They present us with three-dimensional tableaux rendered photographically into two-dimensional form. By way of contrast Tom Arthur's installations occupy real space, but paradoxically have a cinematic 'freeze frame' quality. The viewer confronts Arthur's installations with an air of expectancy, conscious that something has just happened, or is about to happen. They are mysterious, on-going narratives with a Proustian quality—of memory, of associated meanings attached to individual elements—which resonates throughout.

A remembrance of things past is to be found in the allegorical paintings of Vivienne Shark LeWitt. Her paintings, with their references to Medieval and Renaissance models, seduce us with their beauty and apparent familiarity, then disturb us with the contemporaneity of their meaning. We are at once charmed and yet uneasy. Disquiet is also the feeling we get when looking at Caroline Williams' landscapes. Her intention is to subvert the conventions that focus our perceptions into predictable readings of images. The enigmatic monoliths and imaginary edifices in her landscapes substitute as the sublime element in the eighteenth century picturesque convention. Their surrealistic incongruity deconstructs the comfortable and immediate recognition of the Romantic landscape. It is the disquiet produced by the artist's awareness and manipulation of contradictions. Here we are aptly reminded that art continually re-stages and re-enacts the past and the present. And so it does in this Biennale.

1. *Sydney Biennale: White Elephant or Red Herring?*, Alexander Mackie CAE, Sydney, 1979.
2. Janine Burke, *Joy Hester*, National Gallery of Victoria, 1981.
3. Bernice Murphy, 'Mike Parr', *The Australian Bicentennial Perspecta*, Art Gallery of New South Wales, Sydney, 1987.
4. Roger Butler, *The Prints of Margaret Preston*, Australian National Gallery, Canberra, Oxford University Press, 1987.
5. Margaret Preston, 'The Indigenous Art of Australia', *Art in Australia*, 3rd series, no 11, March 1925.
6. Margaret Preston, 'Aboriginal Art', *Art in Australia*, 4th series, no 2, June 1941.
7. Murray Bail, *Ian Fairweather*, Bay Books, Sydney, 1981.
8. Terence Maloon, 'Michael Johnson', *Michael Johnson Paintings 1968–86*, University Gallery, The University of Melbourne, 1986.
9. Richard Haese, 'The Wimmera Paintings of Sidney Nolan 1942–44', *Sidney Nolan: The City and The Plain*, National Gallery of Victoria, 1983.
10. Grazia Gunn, *Arthur Boyd: Seven Persistent Images*, Australian National Gallery, Canberra, 1985.
11. Frances Lindsay, Foreword to *Peter Booth: Works on Paper*, University Gallery, The University of Melbourne, 1985.
12. Jan Minchin, 'Peter Booth', *The ANZ Bicentennial Art Commissions*, ANZ Banking Group Ltd, Melbourne 1987.
13. Rob Horne, 'Art and Possibility: Regarding Some Recent Work by Richard Dunn', *The Australian Bicentennial Perspecta*, Art Gallery of New South Wales, Sydney, 1987.

THE BIENNALE: HOW AUSTRALIAN ART

ESCAPED PROVINCIAL INTERNATIONALISM

AND JOINED THE WORLD IN ITS OWN RIGHT

DANIEL THOMAS

The first Biennale of Sydney was a small exhibition of forty-six paintings and sculptures by thirty-six artists and, because it was shown in November 1973 in the Sydney Opera House as one of several fringe events during the opening festivities for that building, it did not receive much attention. The work was new but not avant-garde. Most of the artists were Australian, two were from New Zealand, seven from the east Asian regions, and one each came from Mexico, the United States, England, West Germany and Italy. A larger exhibition of 'Recent Australian Art' at the Art Gallery of New South Wales in the preceding month was also part of the official opening celebrations for the Opera House.

Subsequent Biennales were shown in the Art Gallery of New South Wales and soon gave Sydney's principal art museum very high international visibility, albeit for an initiative of Mr Franco Belgiorno-Nettis of the Transfield engineering and construction company and for an event which continues to be organised from outside the Gallery.

The 1973 association with the Sydney Opera House opening was nevertheless appropriately symbolic. That building has become Australia's principal tourist attraction. And, even in its first months of existence, we became aware that visitors who had never previously found any reason to come to Australia were re-routing their flights to take in Sydney and see its new architectural wonder. The construction of Sydney Opera House conspicuously signalled new art-based contributions to the Australian economy.

Similarly, the Biennales of Sydney have become the principal international marketing device for Australian art, and hence an extremely significant contribution to international awareness of Australia—an advertisement not merely for Australia's existence but also for its creativity and inventiveness.

The artists, critics, curators and dealers who in 1976 came to the second Biennale (or during its lead-up or follow-up) were conscious that it was a major occasion, comparable with the established international surveys of contemporary art in Venice, São Paulo, Paris, New York, New Delhi. Some were a little apologetic about inadequate effort from their own countries. In April 1977 *Data* published Tommaso Trini's article 'Domani l'Australia (Australia next)'.

But by the time of the third Biennale, in 1979, the slight note of surprise had disappeared. The world's experts in contemporary art by then took it for granted that Australia was a significant producer. In the 1980s they would organise their own exhibits of Australian art, in London, Paris, New York, Germany.

International promotion and marketing of Australian art had not really been the intention behind the Biennale of Sydney or of most previous art patronage.

Australian artists and consumers of art had always felt isolated from the stimulus of the new and deprived of the example of excellence from the past as well as the present. John Power was an expatriate painter whose will in 1939 endowed the University of Sydney with substantial funds to establish a faculty of fine art and an art museum whose collections and programs would bring the most recent art of the world to the deprived people of Australia. His endowment became operative in 1968 and, although the department and collection have had less impact than the other forces behind Australia's new fruitful contact with the most recent art of the world, the impact has been real and the deferred timing was right; little could have been done in the 1940s or 1950s. However,

DONALD JUDD
Sculpture, 1974–75
Art Gallery of South Australia, Adelaide

I mention Dr Power chiefly as a reminder that already in the early twentieth century wealthy Australians were desperately conscious of the country's artistic isolation and provincialism and did something about it. And as a reminder of how pleased he would be with the now near-complete realisation of his wishes, even if largely done by others.

Since the 1880s Australian artists had been given many travelling scholarships for overseas study and stimulus. Exhibits of contemporary paintings and sculptures were regularly imported; from the 1880s as part of international trade fairs, from the 1920s usually as art museum exhibitions. They usually came through government agencies providing only moderately adventurous surveys of their national art; in the 1950s and 1960s such exhibitions were quite numerous, from Britain, France, Italy, Germany and Japan. However, the most vividly remembered were two non-government initiatives: Sir Keith Murdoch's Melbourne newspaper-sponsored *French and British Contemporary Art* (1939), a survey of modern masters from Cézanne to Dali, an Armory Show for Australia, and from the Museum of Modern Art, New York, its International Program's *Two Decades of American Painting* (1967).

One hundred years of outward flow of Australian artists and inward flow of non-Australian works of art were paralleled by one hundred years of art production that was largely a provincial reflection of new metropolitan styles (beginning with the 1880s exhibition in Melbourne of a group of young artists' *9 by 5 Impressions*). Much of it was excellent, as was that of the more isolated artists working prior to the 1880s, but it was probably best when most eccentric. From the 1880s Australian expatriates, for example Rupert Bunny or Bertram Mackennal, also maintained respected careers within French or British art.

The first Biennale of Sydney was just another attempt to stimulate Australian artists and their public by exposure to moderately new works of art from overseas—with the significant innovation of including Australian work in the same exhibition, for comparison. (And Robert Klippel, Fred Williams and John Brack compared well with Emil Schumacher, Clyfford Still and Renato Guttuso.)

Why did the second and third Biennales go beyond local stimulus for Australians to become the principal reason for the sudden international visibility of Australian art? It's partly because of institutionalisation, of continuity within an international program of art events. It's also partly because in the later 1970s Australia's new Federal Government arts-development agency, the Australia Council, was able to provide much more money than was available in 1973. In addition, the Australia Council began a more regular and better planned presence of Australian art in other Biennales throughout the world, Paris in 1977 and Venice in 1978 being especially significant.

But most of all it was because, from 1976, not only art objects but also art people were

NIKOLAUS LANG
Earth colour and paintings, 1979
Third Biennale of Sydney
Collection: Australian National Gallery,
Canberra

NAM JUNE PAIK
Video Garden, 1974
John Kaldor Art Project at Art Gallery
of New South Wales, Sydney

FUJIKO NAKAYA
Fog Sculpture, 1976
Second Biennale of Sydney
Collection: Australian National Gallery,
Canberra

regularly imported to accompany the objects. Artists, critics, curators and dealers ended up doing much more than supervising the installation of the art objects and assisting in their interpretation for an Australian audience. They ended up becoming very well-informed about Australia and Australian art, far beyond the limits of the particular Biennale exhibition they were servicing in Sydney. They also saw studios and exhibitions in Melbourne, Hobart or Adelaide. They wrote articles back home in Europe or America or Japan, planned exhibitions, spoke to others who had not been to Australia. They became an international network of friendship and professional information.

An earlier mass import of art people had been one of the first actions of the newly created Visual Arts Board of the Australia Council when, in 1974, it brought many American artists to Melbourne and elsewhere for the exhibition *Some Recent American Art*. They included Yvonne Rainer, William Wegman, Mel Bochner, Keith Sonnier, Robert Ryman, Lawrence Weiner and Donald Judd (who made an outdoor sculpture in Adelaide for the Art Gallery of South Australia). Artists participating in international exhibitions had begun to appreciate the professional networking benefits that came from accompanying their work, for example, Robert Hunter's meeting with Carl Andre at New Delhi in 1970, Imants Tillers' with Sigmar Polke at São Paulo in 1975.

Of course, there had always been occasional artist visitors to Australia independent of any Australian public support systems. They might have an Australian spouse in need of family reunion, like Richard Stankiewicz, who made and exhibited sculptures in Sydney in 1969. They might simply come as a private tourist, to see the Opera House and Ayers Rock, like Joseph Kosuth, who left a newspaper advertisement Conceptual Art ·piece here in the same year. Or they might have a passionate interest in Australian nature and in Aboriginal culture and come here specifically to make art, like Nikolaus Lang in 1979 (and again in 1986–88).

However, the systematic import of artists *plus* critics was pioneered in 1969 by the Sydney textile businessman John Kaldor. He decided that, instead of encouraging the development of Australian sculpture by the Alcorso-Sekers Travelling Scholarship

CHRISTO
Wrapped coast, 1969
John Kaldor Art Project,
Sydney

GILBERT & GEORGE
Singing Sculpture, 1973
John Kaldor Art Project at Art Gallery
of New South Wales, Sydney

JOSEPH BEUYS .
Eurasia, 1976
Second Biennale of Sydney,
Art Gallery of New South Wales

Award, which he had organised for three years, a reverse travelling scholarship might be more stimulating for more artists, and for the public as well. The first major artist to be flown in to make a work during a brief visit was Christo, whose *Wrapped Coast, Little Bay, Sydney* (1969) for long remained the best known work of art, old-master or avant-garde, among the mass public of Australia; it went beyond the world of art and became folklore. A then young student, Imants Tillers, now counts his three weeks' work helping Christo as the beginning of his art career, exactly as Kaldor hoped might occur by stimulus from the visit.

But besides the artist, Kaldor brought out a New York critic, David Bourdon, and a German team of television film-makers. Christo's *Wrapped Coast* thus signalled to the international art world that Australia had an unusually sophisticated commitment to the patronage of avant-garde art. Kaldor's subsequent visitor projects included Harald Szeemann, exhibition curator (1971), Gilbert & George, living sculptures (1973), Charlotte Moorman and Nam June Paik, performance and video artists (1976), Sol LeWitt, wall drawings (1977), and Richard Long, land art (1977).

In the end the enormous change from Australia's feeling of artistic isolation and inadequacy to a confident feeling of being part of an international art scene is a result of one particular change in the nature of art itself. It is not only that Mr Belgiorno-Nettis initiated a continuing, institutionalised Biennale, or that an upgraded Art Gallery of New South Wales was willing to house it, or that the Visual Arts Board of the Australia Council was able to assist and plan a general program of arts development. Nor even that John Kaldor had the vision to grasp the possibilities presented by the then new Global Village, serviced by jet aircraft, for reverse travelling scholarships, for brief visits to Australia by major artists in place of the previous hundred years of slow, seaborne visits to Europe by Australians in search of major art.

Art itself changed and was no longer embodied in paintings and sculptures. In the late 1960s avant-garde art became dematerialised, and the change was defined by Harald Szeemann's exhibition at the Kunsthalle Bern, Switzerland, in 1969 called *When Attitudes Become Form: Works, Concepts, Processes, Situations, Information*. In a post-object art world—or an art world that included ephemeral objects like outdoor wrapped coasts, indoor installations of heaped stones, body sculptures or performance pieces—the hitherto acceptable gap between avant-garde painting produced in, say, Paris, and long-delayed viewing of that painting in Australia or prompter viewing of weakened imitations, was no longer even possible. Australia would either see no new art at all, which would be unthinkable after a century of established import-systems, or else it would inadvertently find itself directly in touch with avant-garde art, for it was now embodied only in what an imported visiting artist might make in Australia. There were no longer any art objects to import separately from their makers.

The situation in the 1980s has again changed. Attention is again given to the production of new art objects such as paintings. But the welcome change forced on to Australia by the international situation of the 1960s and 1970s is unlikely to be reversed. We are unlikely to disengage from the research-and-development world of avant-garde art now that we have joined it and now that we have continuing support-structures to maintain the engagement.

The Biennale of Sydney in 1979 consummated the engagement, not only by the presence of European artists Marina Abramovic & Ulay, Daniel Buren, Hamish Fulton, Jürgen Klauke, Mario Merz, Daniel Spoerri, and again of work by Joseph Beuys, whose *Eurasia* was the key exhibit in 1976, but also by the presence, for the first time in such a context, of work by Australian Aboriginal artists. (The American and Japanese presence of earlier years, deliberately omitted in the European-Australian dialogue of 1979, of course reappeared in later Biennales.)

The anti-commodity attitudes of the 1960s and 1970s, with their post-object emphasis on concepts and processes, encouraged an acceptance of rough finish and of low-tech art, very appropriate for Australia with its relative shortage of high-art, high-finish example or training. Thus, they especially encouraged the liberation of (low-tech) Australian Aboriginal art from the worlds of ethnographic studies and low-priced marketing in souvenir shops—with the ironic result that rough-finish Aboriginal art is now less common and that all Aboriginal art is now tending towards high-priced marketing in art galleries.

The Biennale and its private enterprise predecessor John Kaldor were quick to grasp

the opportunities presented in the early 1970s by international art movements and by Australian social changes. They were the principal causes of the enormous shift, from an Australia which was provincial in its constant search for international styling to apply to art, to an Australia which, by operating confidently within an international network of personal contact and vigorous peer assessment of avant-garde production, is now relaxed enough to abandon an over-riding concern for international styling. Our new art is now free to concern itself with local (or personal) content in whatsoever style might be suitable.

All praise to all the admirers of innovation, invention and creativity, including the Biennale, who have begun the support systems and marketing that Australian art deserves. The artists—Aboriginal, Australian and European-Australian—have always been much better than their support systems.

HAMISH FULTON
Tasmania: A Slow Journey, 1979
Photograph and text piece, made after a visit to the Third Biennale of Sydney
Collection: Australian National Gallery, Canberra

MODERNISM — AN UNFINISHED PROJECT

JÜRGEN HABERMAS

The following text is the basis of the lecture I delivered in St Paul's Church in Frankfurt on 11 September 1980 on receiving the Adorno Prize.

After the painters and film-makers, the architects too have been admitted to the Venice Biennale. This first architectural Biennale has been greeted with disappointment. The exhibitors in Venice represent an avant-garde facing the wrong lines. Under the motto 'The Presence of the Past', they have sacrificed the tradition of modern art, which now makes way for a new historicism. W. Pehnt, writing in the *Frankfurter Allgemeine Zeitung* of 18 August 1980 ('Die Postmoderne als Lunapark') observes 'that the whole of modern art is nourished by its dialogue with the past, that Frank Lloyd Wright would have been inconceivable without Japan, Le Corbusier without antiquity and Mediter-ranean building, and Mies van der Rohe without Schinkel and Behrens'. With this commentary he supports his thesis, which has diagnostic significance for the age and goes far beyond the immediate occasion, that 'post-modernism is decidedly anti-modern in spirit'.

This statement relates to an affective current that has made deep inroads upon all intellectual fields, calling forth theories of post-enlightenment, post-modern, post-history etc—in short, a new conservatism. This is in marked contrast with Adorno and his work.

Adorno is so unreservedly committed to the spirit of modernism that in the very attempt to distinguish between authentic modern art and mere modernism he senses the kind of antagonism that is provoked by the affront of modern art. It may therefore not be entirely inappropriate for me to express my thanks for the award of the Adorno Prize by examining the present state of consciousness regarding modernism. Is modernism as passé as the post-moderns would have it? Or is the much-vaunted post-modernism itself simply phony? Is 'post-modern' a slogan under which the hostility provoked by cultural modernism since the mid-nineteenth century unobtrusively perpetuates itself?

THE ANCIENTS AND MODERNS

If one dates 'modernism' from about 1850, as Adorno does, one inevitably sees it through the eyes of Baudelaire and avant-garde art. Let me elucidate this concept of cultural modernism with a brief survey of its long prehistory, which has been illuminated by Hans Robert Jauss. The word 'modern' was first used in the late fifth century to distinguish the Christian present—Christianity having become the official religion of the Roman Empire—from the pagan past. Though the semantic content varies, 'modernity' repeatedly expresses the consciousness of an age that relates itself to the ancient world in order to understand itself as the outcome of a transition from the old to the new. This is true not only of the Renaissance, which *for us* marks the beginning of modern times: people thought of themselves as 'modern' even in the age of Charlemagne, in the twelfth century, and in the period of the Enlightenment—at any time, therefore, when a consciousness of a new epoch took shape in Europe through a renewed relationship with antiquity. Antiquity remained a normative model recommended for imitation right up to the famous quarrel of the ancients and moderns in seventeenth-century France—the former being the adherents of classical taste. Only the ideals of perfection conceived by the French Enlightenment, the notion, inspired by modern science, of the infinite advance of knowledge and progress towards social and moral improvement, gradually free men's minds from the spell cast by the works of classical antiquity on the spirit of the moderns at all periods. At last modern art, contrasting the classical with the romantic, sought its own past in an idealised vision of the Middle Ages. In the course of the nineteenth century *this* romanticism gave rise to a radicalised consciousness of modernity that freed itself from all specific historical links, contrasting itself only in abstract and generalised terms with tradition and history.

The term 'modern' now applies to anything that serves to give objective expression to the current spirit of the age, which spontaneously renews itself. Characteristic of modern works is their newness, a newness that is then overtaken and devalued by the next stylistic innovation. But whereas the merely fashionable, when once it is relegated to the past, becomes old-fashioned, the modern retains a secret link with the classical. 'Classical' is a term that has always been applied to works of enduring quality: what gives an emphatically modern work this enduring quality is of course not the authority of a past age, but the authenticity of past actuality. This switching from today's actuality to yesterday's is at once consuming and productive. As Jauss observes, modern art itself creates its own classicality; after all it has become normal to speak of classical modern art. Adorno opposes this distinction between modern art and modernism 'because without the subjective attitude provoked by the new, no objective modern art can crystallise'.[1]

THE SPIRIT OF AESTHETIC MODERNISM

This attitude of aesthetic modernism acquires more distinct contours with Baudelaire and his theory of art, influenced by Edgar Allan Poe. It develops in the avant-garde currents and finally culminates in the Café Voltaire of the Dadaists and surrealism. It can be characterised by attitudes which take shape around the focus of a changed consciousness of time. This finds expression in the spatial metaphor of the 'avant-garde'—that is to say, a vanguard that reconnoitres unknown territory, exposing itself to the risks of sudden and shocking encounters, conquering an as yet unoccupied future, being forced to orientate itself—to find a direction—in as yet uncharted terrain. But the forward orientation, the anticipation of an uncertain and contingent future, the cult of the new, really amount to the glorification of an actuality which repeatedly gives birth to subjectively conceived pasts. The new consciousness of time that finds its way into philosophy with Bergson not only expresses the experience of a mobilised society, an accelerated history, the discontinuity of everyday life, the positive evaluation of the transitory, the evanescent and the ephemeral, the celebration of the dynamic, it also articulates the longing for an immaculate and enduring present. Modernism, as a self-negating movement, is a 'longing for the true present'. This, in the opinion of Octavio Paz, 'is the covert theme of the best modernist poets'.

This also explains the abstract opposition to history, which thereby loses the structure of an articulated process of tradition that guarantees continuity. Individual periods of history lose their identity in favour of an heroic affinity between the present and both the remotest and the nearest: the decadent sees itself directly reflected in the barbaric, the savage, the primitive. The anarchistic intention of breaking up the continuum of history explains the subversive force of an aesthetic consciousness that rebels against the normalising functions of tradition and lives by the experience of the rebellion against everything normative, neutralising both the morally good and the practically useful, producing a continual dialectic of secret and scandal, longing for the fascination of the terror that results from the act of profanation—and at the same time seeking to escape its trivial results. Thus, according to Adorno, 'the signs of dissolution are the hallmarks of modern art, by which it desperately denies the solidity of the unchanging, explosion being one of its constant features. Anti-traditionalist energy becomes an all-destroying whirlwind. To this extent modern art is a myth turned against itself; the timelessness of the myth becomes the catastrophe of the moment, breaking up the temporal continuity.'[2]

The consciousness of time articulated in avant-garde art is not of course anti-historical in a simplistic sense: it is directed only against the false norms of a conception of history that relies on the imitation of models, a conception of history of which vestiges are to be found even in the philosophical hermeneutics of Gadamer. It draws upon periods of the past that have been made historically available and objectivised, but at the same time rebels against the neutralising of criteria that are embraced by historicism when it locks history up in the museum. It is this spirit that leads Walter Benjamin to construe the relation of modernism to history as 'post-historical'. He reminds us of the view that the French Revolution had of itself: 'It cited ancient Rome just as fashion cites ancient costumes. Fashion has a flair for the up-to-date wherever it sees it moving in the thicket of the past.' And just as Robespierre saw ancient Rome as a past that harboured essential elements of the present, so too the historian must grasp the relationship 'into which his own age has entered with a quite specific past age'. He thus justifies a concept of 'the present as the Now, interspersed with fragments of the messianic age'.

This spirit of aesthetic modernism has meantime become demoded. True, it was rehearsed once more in the sixties, but now, with the seventies behind us, we have to own that modernism calls forth hardly any echo today. Octavio Paz, a champion of modernism, noted at the time, not without a certain melancholy: 'The avant-garde of 1967 is repeating the deeds and gestures of the avant-garde of 1917. What we are seeing is the end of the idea of modernism'. Now, following the studies of Peter Bürger, we speak of 'post-avant-garde' art, which can no longer conceal the failure of the surrealist revolt. But what does this failure signify? Does it signal a turning away from modernism? Does 'post-avant-garde' already imply a transition to the 'post-modern'?

This is indeed how it is understood by Daniel Bell, the well-known social theorist and the most brilliant of the American neo-conservatives. In an interesting book, Bell develops the thesis that the phenomena of crisis in the developed societies of the west can be traced back to a rift between culture and society, between cultural modernism and the exigencies of the economic and administrative system. Avant-garde art penetrates into the value orientations of everyday life, infecting the world in which people live with the attitudes of modernism. Modernism is the great seducer, promoting the principle of unrestricted self-realisation, the demand for authentic experience, the subjectivism of an overwrought sensibility, and thus unleashing hedonistic motives that are incompatible with the discipline of professional life or, more generally, with the moral foundations of rational living. Thus, rather like Arnold Gehlen in Germany, Bell blames the dissolution of the protestant ethic, which disturbed Max Weber, on the 'adversary culture'—a culture whose modernism stirs up hostility to the conventions and virtues of everyday life, as rationalised by economics and administration.

On the other hand, according to this reading, the impulse of modernism is said to be exhausted and the avant-garde played out: though still spreading, it is no longer seen as creative. This leads the neo-conservatives to ask how norms can be established which will rein back permissiveness, restore discipline and the work ethic, and counter the levelling tendencies of the welfare state by emphasising the virtues of individual achievement and competition. The only solution that Bell sees is a religious revival or at any rate a link-up with organic traditions that are immune to criticism, making possible clear-cut identities and providing the individual with existential certitudes.

CULTURAL MODERNISM AND SOCIAL MODERNISATION

Naturally one cannot conjure authoritative beliefs out of thin air. Hence the only prescription for action that arises from such analyses is a postulate that has found favour here too—an intellectual and political confrontation with the intellectual representatives of cultural modernism. Here I should like to quote Peter Steinfels, a thoughtful observer of the new style which the neo-conservatives imposed on the intellectual scene in the seventies: 'The confrontation takes the form of representing everything that can be understood as expressing an adversary mentality in such a way that its consequences can be linked with this or that kind of extremism: in this way a connection is made between modernity and nihilism, between welfare programs and looting, between state intervention and totalitarianism, between criticism of defence expenditure and complicity with communism, between feminism and the fight for gay rights on the one hand and the destruction of the family on the other, between the left in general and terrorism, anti-semitism, or even fascism.' These observations relate solely to America, but there are obvious parallels. The bitter and personalised attacks on intellectuals fomented by our own anti-enlightenment intellectuals are to be explained not so much psychologically as by reference to the analytical weakness of the neo-conservative doctrines themselves.

Neo-conservatism shifts the blame for the uncomfortable consequences of a more or less successful capitalist modernisation of the economy and society on to cultural modernism. Choosing to disregard the links between the processes of social modernisation, which it welcomes, and the crisis of motivation, which it deplores with Catonian severity, and failing to reveal the socio-structural causes which underlie changes in attitudes to work, consumer habits, claims to standards, and the use of leisure, it is able to focus on what appears as hedonism and an unwillingness to identify and conform, as narcissism and a refusal to compete in matters of status and achievement, and to put the blame for all these directly on a culture which intervenes in these processes only very indirectly. Since the causes remain unanalysed, responsibility must lie with those intellectuals who remain committed to the project of modernism. It is true that Daniel Bell still sees a link between the erosion of middle-class values and the consumer habits of a society geared to mass production. However, even he is not much impressed by his own argument and ascribes the new permissiveness chiefly to the spread of a style of living that first arose in the élitist counter-cultures of the Bohemian world. This is merely a new variation on a misunderstanding to which the avant-garde itself fell prey—that it was the mission of art to make good its indirect promise of happiness by converting society to an alternative lifestyle based on one that was consciously cultivated by artists.

Looking back to the period which saw the emergence of aesthetic modernism, Bell remarks: 'While radical in economic matters, the bourgeois became conservative in matters of morality and taste'. If this were so one might see neo-conservatism as a reversion to a time-honoured *pattern* of bourgeois attitudes. But this is to oversimplify. For the sentiment on which neo-conservatism can rely *today* is by no means due to unease over the antinomistic consequences of a culture that has burst its banks and is flooding out of the museums into real life. This unease has not been produced by modernist intellectuals, but stems from more deep-seated reactions to a social modernisation which, responding to the imperative of economic growth, is penetrating farther and farther into the ecology of organic life forms and the communicative structure of the traditional world in which people live. The neo-populist protests thus merely give pointed expression to widespread anxieties about the destruction of the urban and natural environment and of existing modes of human interrelation. The many and varied causes of this unease—and the consequent protests—arise wherever a one-sided modernisation, geared to the criteria of economic and administrative efficiency, invades areas of life, which gives priority to the talks of handing down cultural traditions, of social integration and education, and hence applies different criteria, viz. those of communicative efficiency. Yet the neo-conservative doctrines divert attention from precisely these social processes, projecting the unanalysed causes on to the plane of a culture which is by its nature subversive and those who advocate such a culture.

Admittedly, cultural modernism also generates problems of its own. And these are the targets of those intellectual positions which proclaim post-modernism, or advocate a return to pre-modernism, or reject modernism altogether. Even from an *internal* view of cultural development—quite apart from the problems raised by *social* modernisation—there are grounds for doubt and even despair regarding the project of modernism.

THE PROJECT OF ENLIGHTENMENT

The idea of modernism is closely bound up with the development of European art; but what I have termed the project of modernism comes within our purview only when it ceases to be restricted to art, as it has been hitherto. Max Weber saw cultural modernism as characterised by the fragmentation of the substantial reason expressed in religious and metaphysical world views into three areas which cohere only in a formal way (by the form of justification by argument). When world views disintegrate and when the traditional problems can be compartmentalised under discrete viewpoints—those of truth, normative correctness, authenticity or beauty—and treated *as* questions of cognition, justice and taste, this leads today to the differentiation of science, morality and art. Scientific discourse, moral or legal theory, and artistic production and criticism become institutionalised as matters for experts. The professionalised handling of cultural tradition under different abstract headings focuses attention on the laws specific to different fields of knowledge—those of cognition, practical morality and aesthetic expression. From now on the sciences, moral and legal theory and art also have their own specific *internal* histories—not linear developments, of course, but at any rate learning processes. That is one side of the problem.

The other side of the problem is that the gap between the expert cultures and the public at large grows wider. What culture gains through specialist endeavour and reflection does not *automatically* pass into everyday practice. Rather, cultural rationalisation brings with it the danger that the world in which people live, devalued in its traditional substance, will become *impoverished*. The project of modernism, formulated by the eighteenth-century philosophers of the Enlightenment, consists only in resolutely developing the exact sciences, the universal foundations of morality and law, and autonomous art in their specific senses, but at the same time releasing the accumulated cognitive potential from their esoteric high forms and using it for practical ends, i.e. to the rational transformation of conditions of life. Representatives of the Enlightenment such as Condorcet still entertained the extravagant expectation that arts and sciences would promote not only man's control over the forces of nature, but our understanding of the world and ourselves, moral progress, the justice of social institutions, and even human happiness.

The twentieth century has largely discarded such optimism. But the problem has remained, and men are still divided as to whether they want to hold fast to the aims of the Enlightenment, however much they have been impaired, or whether they want to abandon the project of modernism altogether—whether, for instance, they want the cognitive potential, insofar as it does not contribute to technical progress, economic growth and administrative efficiency, to be so restricted that it should under no circumstances affect a form of practical living that is forced to rely on irrelevant traditions.

Even among those philosophers who today represent a rearguard of the Enlightenment, the project of modernism is curiously fragmented. They no longer put their trust in more than one of the areas into which reason has been divided. Popper—and I am referring to the theorist of the open society who has not yet let himself be taken over by the neo-conservatives—holds firm to the enlightening power of scientific criticism as it affects the political sphere, but he does so at the price of moral scepticism and a large measure of indifference towards aesthetics. Paul Lorenzen envisages a reform of the way we live that will be achieved through the methodical construction of an artistic language in which practical reason will assert itself, yet at the same time he relegates the sciences to the narrow confines of providing practical justifications analogous to those pertaining to morality; he too neglects the aesthetic dimension. With Adorno, by contrast, the emphatic claim to reason has withdrawn into the accusatory gesture of the esoteric work of art, while morality is no longer capable of being justified, and philosophy is left with the sole task of indicating, in reported speech, the covert critical content of art.

The differentiation of science, morality and art, which Max Weber saw as characteristic of the rationalism of western culture, means *at the same time* that specialist sectors become autonomous *and* that they are split off from a current of tradition which continues to develop unchecked in the hermeneutics of practical living. This separation is the problem that arises from the autonomy of the differentiated spheres of values; it has also produced the unsuccessful attempts to do away with the expert cultures. This can best be observed in art.

KANT AND THE SPECIAL QUALITY OF THE AESTHETIC

In the development of modern art one can, by somewhat oversimplifying, trace a progressive trend towards autonomy. The Renaissance witnessed the constitution of a particular sphere that was exclusively subject to categories of beauty. In the course of the eighteenth century, literature, the plastic arts and music then became institutionalised as an area of activity divorced from religious and courtly life. Finally, about the middle of the nineteenth century, there arose an aesthetic conception of art which encouraged the artist to produce his works in the spirit of 'art for art's sake'. This meant that the special quality of the aesthetic could become the goal of the artist.

The first phase of this process, then, saw the emergence of the cognitive structures of a new sphere which contrasted with those of science and morality. It later fell to philosophical aesthetics to clarify these structures. Kant devoted much effort to determining what characterised the sphere of aesthetic objects. He began with an analysis of aesthetic judgement, which, though concentrating on subjective factors, on the free play of the imagination, did not merely manifest personal preferences, but envisaged intersubjective agreement.

Though aesthetic objects belong neither to the sphere of those phenomena that can be recognised with the aid of the categories of cognition, nor to that of free actions subject to the laws of practical reason, works of art (and natural beauty) are susceptible to 'objective judgement'. Beside the spheres of truth and duty, the beautiful constitutes another area which justifies the *connection between art and art criticism*. 'Beauty is then spoken of as though it were a quality of the objects.'

Of course, beauty attaches only to the *conception of* an object, just as the aesthetic judgement relates only to the relation between the conception of an object and the feeling of pleasure or displeasure it evokes. Only in the *medium of appearance* can an object be perceived *as* an aesthetic object; only as a fictive object can it affect the senses in such a way that it comes to be represented; this does not apply to the concepts of objective thought and moral judgement. The frame of mind which is produced by the play of the imagination, stimulated aesthetically, is also described by Kant as *disinterested* pleasure. The quality of a *work* is thus determined independently of its relation to real life.

While the basic concepts of classical aesthetics, taste and criticism—beauty of appearance, disinterestedness and the transcendency of the work—serve primarily to delimit the aesthetic against other value spheres and practical living, the concept of the *genius* required for the creation of a work of art involves positive features. Kant describes genius as 'the exemplary originality of the natural gift of a subject freely using his faculty of cognition'. Detaching the concept of genius from its romantic origins, we can paraphrase this freely by saying that the gifted artist is able to give authentic expression to those experiences he has in his concentrated dealings with a decentred subjectivity freed from the compulsions of cognition and action.

This specific meaning of the aesthetic, i.e. the objectivisation of self-experiencing decentred subjectivity, detachment from the temporal and social structures of everyday life, the break with the conventions of perception and purposeful action, the dialectic of revelation and shock, could only emerge, with the gesture of modernism, as a consciousness of modern art, when two further conditions had been fulfilled. One was the institutionalising of artistic production, dependent on the market, and of a disinterested enjoyment of art provided by criticism. The other was that the artists should understand their role in aesthetic terms, and that the critics should see themselves less as advocates of the public than as interpreters who had their own part to play in the process of artistic production. It was now possible, in painting and literature, for a movement to be inaugurated which some see as having been anticipated in Baudelaire's critical writings on art: colours, lines, sounds and movements cease to have a primarily representational function; the media of representation and the techniques of production are themselves raised to the status of aesthetic objects. And Adorno is able to begin his 'Aesthetic Theory' with the proposition: 'It has become self-evident that nothing to do with art is any longer self-evident, either internally or in relation to the whole—not even its right to exist.'

THE FALSE REJECTION OF CULTURE

It is true that the right of art to exist would not have been questioned by surrealism had not modern art in particular also implied a promise of happiness which involves its 'relation to the whole'. For Schiller the promise that is given, but not fulfilled, by aesthetic contemplation still has the explicit form of a Utopia that points beyond art. This line of the aesthetic Utopia extends as far as Marcuse's anti-ideological complaint about the affirmative character of culture. But even in Baudelaire, who repeated the *promesse de bonheur*, the utopian notion of reconciliation had turned into a critical reflection of the unreconciled state of the social world. Consciousness of this becomes the more painful, the further art moves away from life and retreats into the fastness of total autonomy. This pain is reflected in the boundless *ennui* of an outcast who identifies himself with the rag and bone men of Paris.

In such affective channels there is a build-up of explosive energy which is finally discharged in revolt, in the violent attempt to destroy a sphere of art which only appears self-sufficient and to use this sacrifice in order to force a reconciliation. Adorno sees very clearly why the surrealist program 'rejects art without being able to shake it off'.[3] All attempts to bridge the gap between art and life, fiction and fact, appearance and reality, to remove the distinction between artefact and utensil, between product and natural object, between deliberate creation and spontaneous action—the attempts to declare everything to be art and everybody to be an artist, to eliminate all criteria and to equate aesthetic judgements with the expression of subjective experiences—all these endeavours, which have meanwhile been so well analysed, may today be seen as nonsense-experiments which unintentionally throw into greater relief the artistic structures that they were meant to impair—the medium of appearance, the transcendency of the work, the concentrated and purposeful nature of artistic production and the cognitive status of aesthetic judgement. Ironically, the radical attempt to put an end to art justifies those categories with which this particular sphere was encompassed by classical aesthetics, though of course these categories themselves have changed in the meantime.

The failure of the surrealist revolt sets the seal on the double error of a false rejection of art. In the first place, if one breaks the vessels of a cultural sphere that has evolved autonomously, their contents spill and are lost; nothing remains of the desublimated sense and the destructured form, and no liberation is achieved. Of greater consequence, however, is the other error. In everyday communication there must be an interpenetration of cognitive interpretations, moral expectations, expressions and evaluations. The processes of mutual understanding in the real world need a *comprehensive* cultural tradition. For this reason a rationalised everyday life could not be redeemed from the rigidity of cultural impoverishment by the violent splitting open of one cultural area—in this case art—and its annexation to one of the other specialised complexes of knowledge. This would at best lead to the replacement of one form of one-sidedness and one form of abstraction by one other.

The program and the unsuccessful practice of the false rejection of art has parallels also in the fields of theoretical cognition and morality, though these are admittedly less clear-cut. It is true that, not unlike art, both the sciences and moral and legal theory have become autonomous. Yet both these fields remain linked to specialised forms of practice— the former to scientific technology, the latter to a legally organised administrative practice which ultimately relies on moral justification. And yet both institutionalised science and the discussion of practical morality, compartmentalised as it is within the legal system, have become so far removed from everyday practice that here too it was possible for the program of *enlightenment* to turn into one of *rejection.*

Since the days of the Neo-Hegelians there has been talk of the overcoming of philosophy, and since Marx the question of the relation between theory and practice has been raised. In this case, of course, the intellectuals have allied themselves with the workers' movement. Only on the periphery of this social movement have sectarian groups found scope for their attempts to rehearse their program for the overcoming of philosophy in the same way as the Surrealists played the tune of the overcoming of art. Here too the same error is revealed in the consequences of dogmatism and moral rigorism: a reified everyday practice, which aims at an effortless interplay of the cognitive faculty with practical morality and aesthetic expression, cannot be cured by annexing it to one or other of the cultural spheres that have been violently split open. Moreover, the practical detachment and institutional embodiment of the knowledge accumulated in science, morality and art must not be confused with a copy of the lifestyle cultivated by outstanding representatives of these spheres—with the generalisation of the subversive forces to which the lives of Nietzsche, Bakunin and Baudelaire gave expression.

In certain situations, of course, terrorist activities may be connected with the overstretching of one of the cultural elements—with a tendency to aestheticise politics, to replace them by moral rigorism, or to subject them to the strict dogmatism of a particular doctrine.

These somewhat obscure connections should not, however, mislead us into defaming the intentions of unyielding enlightenment by labelling it as the product of a 'terrorist mentality'. To connect the project of modernism with the state of consciousness of individual terrorists and their spectacular public acts is just as irrational as it would be to maintain that the bureaucratic terror that is practised far more regularly and far more extensively in the cellars of the military and secret police, in camps and psychiatric institutions, was the *raison d'être* of the modern state (and its legal rule, subverted by positivist elements), simply because this form of terror employs the apparatus of state repression.

ALTERNATIVES TO THE FALSE REJECTION OF CULTURE

In my view we should learn from the aberrations accompanying the project of modernism, from the errors of exaggerated programs for the overcoming of culture, instead of giving up modernism and its project as a lost cause. It may be possible at least to *indicate* a way out of the *impasses* of cultural modernism by reference to the example of art reception. Since the development of art criticism in the Romantic period, there have been contrary trends, and these have become more polarised with the emergence of avant-garde currents: art criticism claims to supply both a productive complement to the work of art and a response to the public's need for interpretation. Bourgeois art directed *both* expectations to its addressees: the art-loving layman was at times expected to educate himself and become an expert, while at other times he was allowed to behave as a connoisseur, relating aesthetic experiences to the problems of his own life. Perhaps this second mode of reception, which is seemingly harmless, became less radical precisely because it retained obscure links with the first.

True, artistic production is bound to become semantically stunted if it is not carried out as a specialised approach to problems that are meaningful in themselves, as something purely for experts which pays no regard to esoteric needs. Everyone (including the critic, the trained recipient) agrees to sort out the problems in question under just one abstract aspect of application. However, this sharp differentiation, this exclusive concentration on one dimension, is lost as soon as the aesthetic experience is assimilated into the life-history of the individual or incorporated into collective experience. Reception by the layman (who ought rather to be called the expert on everyday life) acquires a *different direction* from the one it is given by the professional critic, whose attention is taken up with purely artistic developments. Albrecht Wellmer has drawn my attention to the way in which an aesthetic experience that is not converted primarily into aesthetic judgements changes its position in the scale of values. As soon as it is used exploratively to throw light on a real-life situation and related to real-life problems, it becomes involved in a word-game that is no longer that of aesthetic criticism. The aesthetic experience then not only alters the way we interpret those needs which inform our perception of the world: it also enters into the cognitive interpretations and normative expectations and changes the way in which all these factors *interrelate*.

Peter Weiss describes an example of this exploratory, life-orientating force, which can result from an encounter with a great painting at a crucial point in a person's life. In one of his works he makes his hero wander through Paris after returning in despair from the Spanish Civil War, and imaginatively anticipates the encounter that will take place later, in the Louvre, in front of Géricault's painting of the shipwrecked mariners. One variant of the mode of reception I am talking about is illustrated even more precisely by the heroic appropriation of culture which the same author describes in the first volume of *The Aesthetics of Resistance*. In the Berlin of 1937, a group of workers, young men who are politically motivated and eager to learn, attend night school and acquire the wherewithal to penetrate into the history of European painting, including its social history. From this tough objective rock they hack out fragments which they then assimilate and incorporate into the horizon of expectation of their own milieu, which is as far removed from educational tradition as it is from the existing régime. They move the fragments to and fro until they begin to shine: 'Our understanding of a culture only occasionally agreed with what presented itself to us as a gigantic reservoir of possessions, of accumulated inventions and illuminations. Having no property ourselves, we at first approached this reservoir with trepidation and reverence, until we realised that we had to fill it with our own evaluations, that the total concept could become usable only if it said something about the conditions of our own lives, the difficulties and peculiarities of our thinking.'

Such examples of the *appropriation of an expert culture from the viewpoint of real life* salvage something of the intention behind the hopeless surrealist revolt, and still more of Brecht's and even Benjamin's experimental reflections on the reception of non-auratic works of art. Similar reflections may be suggested by the spheres of science and morality when one considers that the human, social and behavioural sciences are not yet *completely* divorced from the structure of practical knowledge, and that the restriction of universalistic ethics to questions of justice is bought at the price of an abstraction which demands to be realigned with those questions of practical morality which were initially excluded.

A differentiated restoration of the link between modern culture and practical living, which relies on vital traditions but has been impoverished by mere traditionalism, will of course succeed only if social modernisation can also be directed into *other* non-capitalist channels, and if the world we live in can develop institutions that will impose limits on the autodynamism of the economic and administrative systems.

THREE VARIETIES OF CONSERVATISM

Unless I am mistaken, the prospects for this are not good. A climate has thus arisen, throughout virtually the whole of the western world, which favours currents critical of modernism. The disenchantment left behind by the failure of the programs for the false rejection of art and philosophy, as well as by the *impasses* into which cultural modernism has run, furnish pretexts for conservative positions. Allow me briefly to distinguish the anti-modernism of the young conservatives from the pre-modernism of the old conservatives and the post-modernism of the neo-conservatives.

The young conservatives appropriate the basic experience of aesthetic modernism, the revelation of a decentred subjectivity liberated from all the imperatives of work and usefulness—and use it as a means of escaping from the modern world. Adopting a modernist attitude, they make it a basis for an implacable anti-modernism. They locate the spontaneous forces of imagination, self-experience, and affectivity, in the remote and archaic, confronting instrumental reason with a principle that is accessible only to evocation—be it the will to power, sovereignty, true being, or the Dionysiac force of poetry. In France this line extends from George Bataille to Foucault and Derrida. And over all of them hovers the spirit of Nietzsche, conjured up afresh in the seventies.

The old conservatives do not even permit themselves to be infected by cultural modernism. They view with distrust the disintegration of substantial reason, the divorce between science, morality and art, the modern understanding of the world and its merely procedural rationality, and recommend a return to pre-modernist positions (what Max Weber regarded as a relapse into material rationality). A certain success has been achieved by neo-Aristotelianism, which allows itself to be stimulated by ecological problems into reviving a cosmological ethic. This line, begun by Leo Strauss, has produced interesting works by Robert Jonas and Robert Spaemann.

The neo-conservatives are the most positive in their attitude to the achievements of modernism. They welcome the development of modern science, insofar as it ventures beyond its own confines only in order to promote technological progress, capitalist growth, and rational administration. For the rest, they advocate a policy of defusing the explosive elements in cultural modernism. One of their theses is that science, if properly understood, has in any case lost its meaning as a force for orientation in the real world. Another thesis is that politics should as far as possible be exempt from demands for justification in terms of practical morality. And a third thesis asserts the pure immanence of art, disputes its utopian content and appeals to its illusory character in order to restrict aesthetic experience to the private sphere. As witnesses one might cite the early Wittgenstein, Carl Schmitt in his middle period, and the late Gottfried Benn. As a result of the definitive restriction of science, morality and art to their autonomous spheres, split off from the real world and left in the charge of specialists, all that is left of cultural modernism are those elements that are compatible with the rejection of the project of modernism. To fill the vacuum, traditions are proposed which are spared the demands for justification, though it is hard to see how such traditions are to survive in the modern world unless they have the support of the educational establishment.

This typology, like any other, is somewhat simplified, but for the analysis of today's intellectual and political controversies it may prove not altogether inept. I fear that the ideas of anti-modernism, with just a touch of pre-modernism, are gaining ground in the circles of the Greens and other alternative groups. In the changing consciousness of the main political parties, on the other hand, there seems to have been a partly successful change of tack, i.e. an alliance between the post-moderns and the pre-moderns. None of the parties, it seems to me, has a monopoly of neo-conservatism and anti-intellectualism. Therefore, my Lord Mayor, I have good reason, especially after the illuminating remarks contained in your introduction, to be grateful for the liberal spirit in which the city of Frankfurt is awarding me a prize associated with the name Adorno, the name of one of its sons who, as a philosopher and writer, has done almost as much as anyone in the Federal Republic to shape the image of the intellectual and become a model for all intellectuals.

Translated by David McClintock, London, 1987

1. Adorno, *Aesthetische Theorie*, p. 45.
2. *Ibid.*, p. 41.
3. *Ibid.*, p. 52.

THE ROPE, THE CLOCK & THE GIFT

TERENCE MALOON

A commodity appears at first sight an extremely obvious, trivial thing. But its analysis brings out that it is a very strange thing, abounding in metaphysical subtleties and theological niceties . . . In order to find an analogy we must take flight into the misty realm of religion. The products of the human brain appear as autonomous figures endowed with a life of their own, which enter into relations both with each other and with the human race. So it is in the world of commodities with the products of men's hands. I call this the fetishism which attaches itself to the products of labour as soon as they are produced as commodities.

Marx[1]

I A SCANDALOUS COMMODITY

The first volume of Marx's *Das Kapital* was published in 1867, a year of intriguing coincidences for the purposes of this essay, since it was the year that Manet began his famous *Portrait of Emile Zola*, the year Baudelaire died, and two years before Baudelaire's story 'The Rope' was anthologised in the posthumously published *Paris Spleen*. Baudelaire and Manet—two dandified apostles of art-for-art's sake, and Marx—an exiled revolutionary economic philosopher: what could they possibly have had in common? Two characteristics stand out, and these characteristics have singled them out for posterity as forerunners of the 'modern temper': their sceptical attitude towards authority, expressed either as a neurotic ambivalence or open revolt; and their awareness that the paramount authority in economics and the high culture of their time was vested in the *prestige of the commodity*.

Marx explained the fundamental role played by commodities in the first chapter of *Das Kapital*. This was the cornerstone of his theory of how the modern economy functioned. Furthermore, he noted that a process of commodification had begun to swallow up all the other forms of production and exchange and to alter the character of social relationships accordingly.

The universality of the commodity was a new and challenging fact of life for Baudelaire and Manet. It would be surprising if their art, consecrated to novelty and self-conscious modernity as it was, remained oblivious of this. Indeed a fruitful line of enquiry into the notorious peculiarities of Manet's style would proceed by linking these aberrations to what Marx termed 'the fetishism of the commodity'.

Manet's *Portrait of Emile Zola* suggests that commodities are not only things we possess, but things we can be possessed by in turn. It is the bric-a-brac rather than the figure of Zola that prepossessed the painter. As one of the earliest commentators on this painting noted in an 1869 review, it is more a still-life than a portrait: 'The main interest belongs not to the sitter but to certain Japanese drawings which cover the walls.' Zola's proprietary relation to his surroundings revealed more about his identity than his 'inert and vague' head: he *was* what he owned.[2]

Manet's tendency to see things as vignettes and his habit of plucking isolated figures and objects out of one context and transferring them into another led to alarming inconsistencies in the pictorial space in many of his compositions. Could Manet not see, was he not disturbed by the jarring dislocations in *View of the Universal Exhibition* (1867), *Music in the Tuileries* (1860) and other pictures from his hand? These are compilations rather than compositions: the seams are as glaringly obvious as in a cubist collage. The aforementioned paintings represent public spaces, and a sociologically-minded viewer might wonder if their incoherence is a symptom either of the embattled individualism of the modern artist (whose social standing, or lack of it, is expressed by a populace of literal misfits), or whether the awkwardly jostling and jibbing figures reflect an economic space—the competitive jockeying of goods on the open market perhaps.

Again, one of Manet's contemporaries comes to our assistance, reporting that Manet 'is pleased to dispense with composition'. His peculiar way of cropping his pictures 'gives to the frame all the charm of a merely financial boundary, such as that which is embraced at one glance of a scene framed by the hands, or at least all of it found worthy to preserve . . . For instance, what need is there to represent this arm, this hat, or that river bank, if they belong to someone or something exterior to the picture? The one thing to be attained is that the spectator accustomed among a crowd or in nature to isolate one bit which pleases him . . . shall not miss in the work of art one of his habitual enjoyments.'[3] This is also the way a window-shopper regards the merchandise displayed in such arcades and department stores as were newly established in Paris during the Second Empire.[4] Manet's recurrent allusions to shop-windows, fashion prints and high-class prostitutes underlines the fact that his paintings were also intended for the marketplace, and were destined to scandalise it.

The story 'The Rope' by Baudelaire was dedicated to Manet as a token of their friendship. It was based on a real-life incident that took place in Manet's studio. Since the story is clearly an allegory about commodification, it sheds a revealing light on Manet's and Baudelaire's scandalous disruptions of business-as-usual in their respective fields of art and literature.

'The Rope' tells of a young boy from a wretchedly poor family who is employed as an artist's studio assistant. The artist has no inkling of the wild despair he causes the boy when he scolds him for pilfering and threatens to return him to his parents. He enters the studio to find that the boy has hanged himself from a wardrobe. The boy's mother arrives shortly afterwards, impressing the artist by remaining stoically dry-eyed. Towards the end of the visit she makes a surprising request: she asks to be given the length of rope he had neglected to detach from the wardrobe when he cut down the body. The artist can make no sense of the request, but gives her the rope. The following day a bundle of letters arrives. Strangers in the neighbourhood have heard about the suicide. All of them ask if he will sell them a piece of the fatal rope. It occurs to him that the boy's mother was well aware of the demand for ghoulish souvenirs and that she planned to profit from her misfortune.[5]

The moral Baudelaire draws from this tale seems extraordinarily inadequate: mother-love is not innate whereas mercenary opportunism is, he concludes. For readers probably the most shocking part of the story is the discovery of a widespread appetite for macabre relics. Under the surface of a supposedly rational and respectable society, a 'barbaric' passion for such things still thrives. The rope has become a charismatic object, like the fetish objects in so-called primitive societies of the holy relics collected by the Catholic Church. The Melanesian word *mana* refers to the magical, spiritual power of inanimate objects and venerable leaders. Baudelaire's reader immediately realises that the rope's *mana* is contaminated by profanity—it is for sale to the highest bidder, hence the very epitome of a fetishised commodity. More disturbing yet, its contradictions are almost identical to the contradictions Manet and Baudelaire wrestled with in their art. Having turned into a fetishised commodity, the rope has come dangerously close to being . . . a work of art.

Let us attempt a concordance between the articles of faith of *l'art pour l'art* (art for art's sake) and the characteristics of the profaned rope:

1. (a) The highest goal of art is to be useless for all purposes other than pleasurable contemplation.
   (b) Cut into short lengths, the rope is rendered useless for all but contemplation.
2. (a) The 'pure' work aspires to an ideal impersonality. Its internal coherence and intense compression act to convince an audience of the autonomy of the object or test.
   (b) Rope is usually an agent of *relation*, used for linking, tying and wrapping other things. Here it has gained independence and self-sufficiency. Anonymous manufacture guarantees it the qualities of objectivity and otherness.
3. (a) The disinterested pursuit of beauty is a secular faith, born out of the failure of orthodox religions. Art is the 'last refuge of the sacred'.
   (b) The rope has usurped art's ancient, privileged relation to its historical origin in magic and religion. The true fetish's power of 'sanctification, fascination and psychological subjection' makes the modern artist's attempts at civilised magic seem merely decorative and effete by comparison.

Is it a coincidence that the motif in Manet's *Still life with asparagus* reminds us of a bundle of short lengths of rope? The modest vegetable has been elevated into an icon, isolated and made precious by its expensive frame. Obviously there is no intention to instruct or entertain viewers—Manet's moral indifference was one of the goading, galling things to his contemporaries. This still life was destined for the connoisseur, the epicurean collector of aesthetic sensations who would doubtless be amused at the fate of a 1-*franc* vegetable turning into a 1000-*franc* oil painting. The 999-*franc* difference was a steep price to pay for the artist's labour, materials, overheads and expertise, but the absurdity was beautiful: aesthetic value could no more be translated into monetary terms than moral and spiritual values. This pious truism of *l'art pour l'art* continues to fuel the world's dizzyingly inflated art market.[6]

Brush strokes (like ropes) are usually agents of relation, linking, wrapping or separating the items in a painting, and are subordinate to the composition as a whole. Here they have virtually won independence of descriptive and relational functions. They are estimable in their own right—as fresh and deliciously succulent as their real-life counterparts.

Taken in isolation, Manet's still life may seem innocuous enough, but not if we assume it a manifesto of *l'art pour l'art*, a forerunner of the Frenchified *petits riens* and *ridicules choses précieuses* shown in disproportionately large frames, submitted by students of von Guérard to the *9 × 5 Impressions* exhibition in Melbourne in 1889. These were understood (and were probably intended) as a calculated offence to professional etiquette (in the academic sense). The ensuing controversy (such as it was) indicated that an avant-garde had arrived on Australian shores, although perhaps only for a brief visit.

Manet's asparagus and the pieces of rope in Baudelaire's tale were also forerunners to Marcel Duchamp's famous *reductio ad absurdum* of *l'art pour l'art* in his 1916 *Fountain*. The autonomy and uselessness of the ideal work of art were rendered literally: *Fountain* consisted of an industrially manufactured porcelain urinal, detached from plumbing, turned upside-down, isolated on a plinth under the gallery spotlights, signed (pseudonymously) and dated. It insolently assumed the same rights that all art works have: to be reverently, devotedly contemplated.

The scandal surrounding the exhibition of *Fountain* was a reprise in many ways of the moral panic caused by Manet and Baudelaire when their work went into the public domain. The work's smuttiness was one thing, but the offence to the sacrosanct commodity was equally outrageous. If we accepted Duchamp's assurance and the exhibiting institution's endorsement that this was indeed a work of art, we could also assume it carried a price tag. What was the mark-up from the price of a common urinal? What justified the mark-up and assured the work its surplus value?

While *Fountain* upheld the letter of *l'art pour l'art* and exemplified a stereotype of the avant-garde work as a deviant, heretical commodity, it also played up to the philistines' hatred of modern art (the conviction that it was all sensation-seeking rubbish). However, Duchamp's most subversive innovation was to deny *Fountain* (and by implication all other works) any transcendental guarantee: the surplus value of the work was not a function of *mana*, but a mystique or mystification. The spotlights, the gallery, the plinth, the signature, the artist's fame and a speculative art market all shed their quota of radiance on to the object. The object itself was of no importance.

The avant-garde since Manet compulsively renewed this war against the commodity. It is easy to forget the ferocity of the battle in the light of modern art's Pyrrhic victory (a victory that we celebrate in this Biennale). The tactics artists developed to pre-empt, stave-off or delay the commodification of their work have become no more than an etiquette of late modernism or post-modernism (depending on the way you understand our epoch). Pulverising the object in painting, elevating the commonplace (Manet's asparagus, the junk in collages, Arte Povera), concealing signs of skill and professional competence, contradicting assumptions about the work's uniqueness and autonomy, displacing attention from the isolated object to a series of works or an installation, contravening 'taste' with something unpalatably ugly or provocatively ascetic, substituting documentation for an absent 'original' or offering ephemeral 'actions' in lieu of objects . . . the catalogue of insubordination is a long one, but what was the ultimate point of a century-long struggle where success could only be vouchsafed by failure?

The point was to maintain faith in an idealised 'other world' beyond the thrall of the commodity, a faith expressed by Adorno's aphorism that 'legitimate works of art are without exception socially undesired'.[7] For generations of artists, this other world was synonymous with purity, authenticity, spirituality and—above all—freedom.

The alienated or 'failed' commodity therefore took on a quality of intense pathos and made it the focus for a small minority's self-imaging. Most of the early supporters of the avant-garde were in some way deracinated and *déclassé*—new rich (infra-dig to the old rich), bohemians, migrants, homosexuals, Jews and 'progressives' of various shades. The symbolic efficacy, the pathos of the avant-garde work had been eerily foretold in the line from Shakespeare's *King Lear:* 'Thou art the thing itself—unaccommodated man.'

II SETTING THE CLOCKS FORWARD

All through the night-time, clock talked to clock,
In the captain's cabin, tock-tock-tock,
One ticked fast and one ticked slow,
And Time went over them a hundred years ago.

Kenneth Slessor: *Five Visions of Captain Cook.*

Modernism arrived in Australia with a cachet of smartness. The participants of the *9 × 5 Impressions* exhibition were well aware that 'in the formation of taste in this new country where art is so young and so tentative, every public expression of opinion and every show of works must have a more or less strong influence on the making of that taste'. For the occasion of the exhibition, Buxton's Gallery in Melbourne was fitted out in the latest Aesthetic fashion, with 'art' furniture and pottery, Japanese umbrellas, screens and swags of Liberty silks supplied free of charge by a local interior decorator. Twenty or so paintings were integrated into the decorator's ensemble, part of a package of furnishing and lifestyle.[8]

Modern art strengthened its connections with furnishing and lifestyle when Australian department stores took a great leap forward in the 1920s. All the major stores in Sydney (David Jones, Grace Bros, Farmer's and Anthony Hordern's) contained art galleries, and the elite lifestyle magazine *The Home* (1920–42) promoted some fairly adventurous local artists, commissioning original artwork by Margaret Preston, Thea Proctor, Adrian Feint and Hera Roberts for its covers and employing Harold Cazneaux, Max Dupain, Cecil Bostock and Olive Cotton as photographers. The tea-room coteries commemorated in paintings and prints by Preston, Proctor and Cossington Smith were an important component of this flourishing department-store subculture.

The stores introduced havens of simulated cosmopolitanism to Sydney and Melbourne, where you could get a whiff of London, Paris, Weimar, New York and Prague. The turnover of imported goods measured the tempo of modernity. In effect, these stores became chronometers of *world-time*: our slower colonial clocks periodically had to be corrected to their momentum.

Tom Roberts and Margaret Preston took a serious view of their social responsibilities as crusaders for 'taste' and advocates of advanced art. To their credit, both were also aware of the limitations of 'taste' (as a conventional marker of gentility more or less irrelevant to the concerns of ordinary people), and the folly of prostrating themselves before the *éclat* of imported artistic models. Their deliberately Australianised versions of modernism happened to accord with a spirit of nationalism: *l'art pour l'art* became fairly innocuous once it addressed the landscape and Australian wildflowers.

The attitude of neurotic ambivalence towards the commodity, which gave impetus to the avant-garde overseas, surfaced very belatedly in Australia. As was the case in England, Australian art tended to be affirmatively modern rather than negatively avant-garde. Modernism was understood in terms of style rather than as a strategy or praxis. However, Australian department stores were relatively progressive compared with the conservatism of the official cultural institutions. When the Melbourne *Herald* Exhibition of Modern British and French Art came to Australia in 1939, neither the National Gallery of Victoria nor the Art Gallery of New South Wales would have anything to do with it. In Sydney the exhibition took place in David Jones' department store. Whenever the occasion arose, State Gallery directors could be relied on to inveigh against dangerous extremism in art as the expression of sick minds and decadent civilisations, funda-mentally un-Australian.

Was it treasonable, then, for an Australian artist to deny or slight the robust health of our fine colonial stock, the prosperity of the nation, the glorious climate and exhilaratingly beautiful scenery? Only in the late 1930s, jolted by the Depression and impending war, did a mood of austerity and morbidity enter into Australian art, challenging the 'picture of health' that had been held up for admiration time and again.

Terry Smith has suggested that an avant-garde only emerged in Australia in the 1960s.[9] Rather, it was only then that Australians came into synch with the avant-garde in Europe and America. The resetting of Australian cultural clocks to *world-time* in the 1960s was possible because modernism, at that moment, had become an institution. Its history had consolidated into something like the standard versions available to us in textbooks today. The great names and breakthrough works of the avant-garde were given pride of place in museums of modern art mushrooming all over the world, from Los Angeles to Oslo, Teheran and Canberra.

These standard historical accounts of modernism had tremendous repercussions for the current generation of Australians, since they made any concordance with the history of modern art in Australia tenuous and obscure. Local art had been influenced by Bastien-Lepage, Sargent, André Lhote, Sickert, Graham Sutherland, Claude Flyte—to mention but a few names peripheral to or absent from the majority of books about modern art. Furthermore, Australians had felt the impact of Cézanne, Douanier, Rousseau, Léger and German expressionism between thirty and fifty years later than was 'relevant' in global terms.

The 'provincialism problem' Terry Smith diagnosed in his influential article became not so much a problem of space (the tyranny of distance), but a problem of time. Wherever art is produced, it corresponds to local conditions and circumstances: the momentum of change determines the local time sense. Local circumstances and conditions are linked to those elsewhere, but parts of the world do not change at the same rate.

To this day, Australian artists depend on foreign authority for legitimation and also, to a considerable extent, to complete the meanings of what they do. We continue to worry about provincialism even though we have shifted into such close synchronisation with international trends that Australian artists can anticipate and antedate major swings of fashion and contribute effectively to debates in international journals and forums. In one sense, our conversion to world-time represents progress; in another, it has not affected the fundamental condition of the provincialism problem; the role of time-keeper and pace-setter is still not ours.

Fernand Braudel proposed the idea of world-time in his ambitious history of Renaissance economics. According to Braudel, the pace of world-time is set by a world-city, a city absorbing and wielding the greatest concentration of capital, standing at the centre of a trading network and radiating cultural influence to its economic dependents far and wide.

The differences in the rates of change in various parts of the world are determined by their relation to the world-city, reflecting the region's status in the 'spatial arrangement of the world economy':

> The qualities and characteristics of the type of society, economy, technology, culture and political order necessarily alter as one moves from one zone to another . . . The centre or *core* contains everything that is most advanced and diversified. The next zone possesses only some of these benefits, although it has some share in them: it is the 'runner-up' zone. The huge periphery, with its scattered population, represents on the contrary backwardness, archaism and exploitation by others.[10]

Although Braudel's schema was developed to explain a world existing prior to the discovery and colonisation of Australia, it seems that the latter's role in the scheme of things had already been predetermined. Over the last two hundred years, Australia has evidently moved from the periphery of 'backwardness, archaism and exploitation by others' nearer the forefront of the 'runner-up' zone.

By and large, contemporary Australian artists accept the tradition of the avant-garde as their own, and in most cases identify more strongly with it than with the insular history of Australian art. Paradoxically, these displaced, off-centre affiliations *are* an Australian tradition, and an enduring feature of our art history. Braudel's schema is valuable, then, in explaining the ascendancy of avant-garde culture, how it has been universalised and how the world-cities maintain their control of the international art market and information networks.

A schizoid sense of time and place is the common lot of 'runner-up' zones, and the avant-garde culture that now flourishes in Australia compounds these traditional confusions with a schizoid attitude to the commodity as part of our dual inheritance.

The term 'fetishism' almost has a life of its own. Instead of functioning as a metalanguage for the magical thinking of others, it turns against those who use it, and surreptitiously exposes their own magical thinking.

Baudrillard[11]

Mana is a primitive abstraction, probably more primitive than numbers, but no more supernatural.

Martin Buber[12]

Fetishism. The word is rife in recent art criticism. As a term of abuse, it arraigns a modernism grown academic, robbed of moral force by its market success and celebrity, and fatally compromised, according to some, by its quest for autonomy. Autonomy, or the illusion of autonomy was one of the features that defined a fetishised commodity according to Marx. But did modernism fail in this quest, or did it succeed too well?

Used as a buzzword, *fetishism* tends to attach to some of the most contentious new art—notably the widely publicised, glitzy creations of Haim Steinbach and Jeff Koons. Steinbach and Koons share a pedigree that can be traced from Duchamp's readymades (cf. *Fountain*), through the specious glamour of Andy Warhol's paintings to the 'dumb' literalness of minimal sculpture. However, its other line of descent is not so exalted: it is pure American kitsch.

The ambience of the arcades evoked by Manet, the hardware stores by Duchamp, the department stores by Margaret Preston and the supermarkets by Warhol and the Pop generation have been updated to the shopping malls of the 1980s by Steinbach and Koons. The aura of the marketplace enforces a certain sense of 'the object' which is common to all these artists, probably for the reason Baudrillard gives: 'Fetishism is not the sanctification of a certain object or value . . . It is the sanctification of the system as such, of the commodity as system . . . The more the system is systematised, the more the fetishist fascination is reinforced.'[13]

So, when critics such as Hal Foster suggest that 'the work of art in capitalist society cannot escape the status of the commodity—that our adoration of the masterpiece is similar to our fetishism of the commodity',[14] Steinbach and Koons become prime examples of art's 'inescapable' fate. Does their work indicate a surrender to market values or is it a satire or travesty of the same? The question is undecidable or, rather, it ceases to matter, because the resoundingly successful promotion of their work seems to prove the irrelevance of moral positions and futility of criticism when confronted with an omnivorous, billion dollar business. Many artists—and I assume Steinbach and Koons are among them—react to the prospect of being devoured by the system by adopting a nihilist attitude. Nihilism flourishes best when it has an absolutist adversary, real or imagined, as a foil. When consumerism is understood to be an all-encompassing, omnipotent system, it serves very well as a foil.

I should point out, as an aside, that other artists have responded somewhat differently to the same ideas and have a similar historical understanding to Steinbach's and Koons'. The metaphors of incarceration (prisons, closed-circuitry) which occur in recent paintings by Peter Halley and Richard Dunn, the eerie frigidity of Jacky Redgate's *Work to Rule* photographs, the dismembered details in Juan Davila's giant canvases and Susan Norrie's claustrophobic still lifes from 1983–86 could all be discussed as inter-related 'symptoms' or various ways of looking at the effects of consumerism.

Koons and Steinbach occupy a position in contemporary art which in some respects is more limited, in another more extreme than the other artists I have mentioned—extreme, I think, because of an unmistakable streak of cruelty. They make a point of alienating viewers, repelling identification and empathy while exuding a perverse allure. They cannily anticipate a well-developed moral sense in their audience, a squeamishness which, rubbed the wrong way, gives their art its special *frisson*. Sophisticated viewers know full well that taking pleasure in inanimate objects is perverse, is *wrong*, and is also very American. The work's unspoken question is: 'Well, are you game?' The sadistic overtones here are obvious but should cause no surprise, for there is a close connection between sadism and fetishism.

Indeed, circling obsessively around the disreputable connotations of fetishism—

sexual perversion (Freud), money grubbing (Marx) and idol-worship (innumerable Christian anthropologists)—devolves into a kind of highbrow sado-masochism where art is shackled, gagged and thrashed to within an inch of its life. Likewise, viewers must be chastised for wanting to *like* art, for wanting to identify with it, not to speak of wanting to own it. How is it this sadistic aspect of our commodity-neurosis has attracted so little comment?

In the circumstances, we might welcome Baudrillard's warning that 'the term fetishism is dangerous . . . because it short-circuits analysis'. The term is most dangerous because, muddled-up in it is a factor I believe to be indispensable to any proper understanding of art. Baudrillard uses the Melanesian name for it: *mana*. *Mana* is the energy contained in animate objects, usually ascribed to a magical, religious or spiritual power. However, it is sufficient to define *mana* as a quality of *immanence* and *incommensurability*. The latter terms have the advantage of being relatively free from the taint of mysticism, or so one hopes.

Mana has passed into common usage among western writers. Baudrillard mentions it, Herbert Read uses the term to describe effects of sculpture,[15] and it occurs in Martin Buber's *I and Thou*, a book said to have influenced the painter Barnett Newman. Buber debunks *mana*'s supposed 'mystical potency'. His thesis begins with the premise that people have only two kinds of relationship—I/You and I/It. When human relations are marked by enmity, exploitation, contempt, etc., the It mode prevails. For Buber, art provides a vivid instance of the way an It can be transformed into a You. The difference between It and You is decided when we choose to consider something or someone an *object* or a *presence*: 'Presence is not what is evanescent and passes but confronts us, waiting and enduring. And the object is not duration but standing still, ceasing, breaking off, becoming rigid, standing out, the lack of relation, the lack of presence.'[16]

One of the weaknesses of Buber's argument is that his definition of the object is by no means universally valid, as he mistakenly supposes. His sense of objects is specifically western, defined by our economic and social history. In contrast, archaic societies such as those analysed in Marcel Mauss' book *The Gift* evidently hold a very different concept of objects, befitting the different way their economy functions. These archaic societies are bound together by obligations of exchange and by ceremonial gift-giving. Valuable objects are constantly in transit from one person to another. A valuable commodity cannot break off and separate itself out from the networks of exchange; it cannot be owned in the way that objects in our society are assumed to be exclusive property. Nonetheless, Buber's definition of the Western commodity as a thing broken-off, standing-out, lacking relation is relevant to any analysis of commodity fetishism.

His theory also highlights the fact that art works contradict their own objecthood by lapsing into the Thou mode. For anyone to achieve an imaginative rapport with a work of art, he or she has to defer to the work's emergent effects and meanings (to its quality of *immanence*) and recognise that the sense it precipitates is not finite, has no conclusion, no closure (the quality of *incommensurability*).

The anthropologist Claude Lévi-Strauss grasped that there were enormous implications in the 'primitive' concept of *mana*. His conjectures have a striking bearing on twentieth century art, abstract art in particular:

At one and the same time force and action, quality and state, noun and verb; abstract and concrete, omnipresent and localised—*Mana* is in effect all these things. But is it not precisely because it is none of these things that *mana* is a simple form, or more exactly, a symbol in the pure state, and therefore capable of becoming charged with any sort of symbolic content whatever? In the system of symbols constituted by all cosmologies, *mana* would simply be a zero symbolic value, that is to say, a sign marking the necessity of a symbolic content supplementary to that with which the signifier is already loaded.[17]

From this difficult explanation, I take it that Lévi-Strauss considers *mana* a sign-of-signs, a sort of prototype-symbol. When we assume art is not just, is more than an object, we implicitly acknowledge its *mana*.

As we unravel the implications of *mana*, we are led in a diametrically opposite direction to the implications of *fetishism*. The caricature of aesthetic experience as an idolatrous worship of 'masterpieces' and the failure to distinguish it from commodity fetishism as such, falls wide of the mark. Symbolic transactions do not demand belief, merely a willing suspension of disbelief, not blind faith but good faith.

However, a nihilistic reaction against consumerism is making a major impact centre-stage in the bizarre circus of contemporary art. This outbreak of nihilism is not an uninteresting phenomenon, nor is it uncritical of the world in which it finds itself, but it has an unfortunate enthusiasm for end-games. The 'end' is that art is laid bare and served up as a tautological commodity.

Mystification and self-deception play a negligible part in the conviction that the work of art is not just, is more than an object. We may detect in this conviction traces of pre-consumer, pre-industrial and pre-capitalist values, when 'things' were assumed to have communal and spiritual significance. In our living culture, art is unique in retaining these values. The etymologies of the European words for 'thing' reveal the pre-history of the modern commodity:

The Old High German word *thing* means a gathering, and specifically a gathering to deliberate on a matter under discussion, a contested matter. In consequence, the Old German words *thing* and *dinc* become the names for an affair or matter of pertinence. They denote anything that in any way bears upon men, concerns them, and that accordingly is a matter for discourse. The Romans called a matter for discourse *res*. The Greek *eiro* (*rhetos*, *rhetra*, *rhema*) means to speak about something, to deliberate on it.[18]

The *res* cannot originally have been the brute and tangible thing, the simple and passive object of transaction that it has become. The best etymology seems to be that which compares the word with the Sanskrit *rah*, *ratih*, meaning a gift or pleasant thing. The *res* must have meant that which gives a person pleasure.[19]

1. Karl Marx, *Capital*, Vol. 1, Penguin, London, 1976, pp. 163–5.
2. Phoebe Pool, *The Complete Paintings of Manet*, Abrams, New York, 1967, p. 97.
3. Stéphane Mallarmé, 'The Impressionists and Edouard Manet' in Francis Franscina and Charles Harrison (eds), *Modern Art and Modernism*, Harper and Row, London, 1982, pp. 42–3.
4. The arcades and department stores established during the Second Empire are discussed in Walter Benjamin, *Charles Baudelaire*, Verso, London, 1973, pp. 157–60; and T.J. Clark, *The Painting of Modern Life*, Alfred Knopf, New York, 1985, pp. 55–6.
5. Charles Baudelaire, *Paris Spleen*, New Directions, New York, 1970, pp. 64–7.
6. Hans Haacke has made an art work which documents the successive owners and increasing value of this particular painting. *See* Brian Walls (ed.), *Hans Haacke*, MIT Press, Cambridge Mass., 1987, pp. 119–34.
7. Theodor Adorno, *Minima Moralia*, NLB, London, 1974, p. 213.
8. Jane Clark and Bridget Whitelaw, *Golden Summers*, National Gallery of Victoria, Melbourne, 1985, pp. 112–17.
9. Terry Smith, 'The Provincialism Problem', in Paul Taylor (ed.), *Anything Goes*, Art & Text, Melbourne, 1984, p. 49.
10. Fernand Braudel, *The Perspective of the World*, Fontana, London, 1984, p. 39.
11. Jean Baudrillard, *For a Critique of the Political Economy of the Sign*, Telos, St Louis, 1981, p. 90.
12. Martin Buber, *I and Thou*, Y. & Y. Clark, Edinburgh, 1970, p.72.
13. Baudrillard, *op cit.*, p. 92.
14. Hal Foster, 'The Future of an Illusion' in *Endgame,* MIT Press, Cambridge Mass., 1986, p. 92.
15. Herbert Read, *The Art of Sculpture*, Faber & Faber, London, 1956, pp. 42–3.
16. Buber, *op cit.*, p. 64.
17. Quoted in Jacques Derrida, *Writing & Difference*.
18. Martin Heidegger, *Poetry, Language, Thought*, Harper, New York, 1975, p. 174.
19. Marcel Mauss, *The Gift*, Cohen & West Ltd, London, 1954, p. 49.

THE RE-APPROPRIATION

OF INFLUENCE

IAN BURN

Over the past two decades, conditions have been created which allow for a particular re-reading (and revaluing) of much of the art of the past century. This is especially significant for cultures at the periphery, that is, in places like Australia. Yet we are faced with a confusing situation. Historically, the uneven development of modernism has impinged on the kind (and the value) of art produced in this country; on the other hand there is a growing consensus today which casts modernism as the project of an era now past. At the periphery, both are experienced in terms of a 'distancing' effect and a structural equivalence appears between modernism in its *marginalised* forms and the *post-modernism* of today. It is as if the political-geographical condition of the one translates into the temporal space of the other. To make any sense of this, two tasks are demanded. Firstly, there is a need to analyse moments within Australian art which illuminate the relationship between centre and periphery. This entails a focus on the processes of influence and the way particular relations to the idea of modernism have been proposed—such as that which occurred in the early 1940s in Australian art. Secondly, there is a need to consider how particular historical circumstances have constructed the potential for a re-reading. This involves reassessing the artistic practices (including critical and theoretical writing) identified as sources for the attitudes prevalent at the end of the twentieth century.

As modernism evolved during the nineteenth century, the movement of ideas and stylistic tendencies multiplied and patterns of strong influence emerged bearing an approximate relation to the growth of various imperialisms. Which cultures competed as transmitters of influence, and which were receivers, seemed to be politically ordained at a global level. The compliant receivers drew their strength by strategies of dissidence, actively modifying and transforming the received influences. This phenomenon of mediated influence discovers its documentation in the separate histories of peripheral cultures.

A lot can be learned from the way a particular culture invokes and denies influences. Cultural boundaries both transcend and are embedded within national and political boundaries. Maybe the best one can say is that the relation between artistic practices and national entities is imprecise, despite many points of identification or commonality. However, on the level of individual practice, there are conflicting ideological pressures— on the one hand, to construct one's practice to conform to a national consensus; on the other, to arbitrarily isolate artistic practice from national form. While it may be true that the constitution of a (personal) cultural identity and the proposition of a 'national identity' are linked only as fiction, this can't mean that the contexts we work in are inter-changeable, as if some logical equivalence prevailed between different cultures. Those contexts are no more interchangeable than economies, no matter how interrelated they may be.

The diffusion of ideas or tendencies occurs not in isolation but in conjunction with political and economic forces. Thus what, in one context, may appear to offer a new freedom of expression can represent, in another, symbols of power or repression. Such a transformation is not exclusive of but is integral to, say, a particular style. The history of the dominant modes of modern art, regardless of national origins, includes their impact on an international scale—that is, the forms of imposition and impact on a local culture, the kinds of modifications they permit and the resistances they invoke. For example, the historical resistance, in Australia and elsewhere, to the picture-making techniques of Analytic Cubism is as important a factor of the history of Cubism as it is a (positive) feature of a history of Australian art.

SIDNEY NOLAN
Railway Guard, Dimboola, 1943
Ripolin enamel on canvas, 77 × 64
National Gallery of Victoria
Gift of Sir Sidney and Lady Nolan 1983

FERNAND LÉGER
The Mechanic, 1920
Oil on canvas, 115.5 × 88.3
National Gallery of Canada, Ottawa

The scene depicted in Nolan's *Railway Guard, Dimboola* (1943) is ordinary enough until we notice the underlying cubist strategies. The guard's face is locked into the vast landscape, coloured in as an extension of the golden wheatfields. The head is defined by the regulation blue of cap and uniform, symbolising the guard's job, and by the railway sheds, converging tracks and signals, symbols of transport and communication familiar in modern rural life. Many elements in the picture are rendered as flat, with edges parallel to the frame, emphasising their coincidence with the picture plane. Some areas are modulated and, in particular, the guard's face is noticeably modelled, which sets up a tension with the deliberately flattened areas. The face reads simultaneously as flat and voluminous, in a shallow space, with the sketchy black outlining of shapes mediating the spatial ambiguity.

An examination of the *mediation* of influence exposes both the technical or institutional processes which produce changes and the deliberate tactics of mediation which are historically distinct and specific to particular cultures. In the first instance, the changes are frequently the product of a particular mode of dissemination—for example, the institutional and educational structures of art, museums, exhibitions, publications, art schools, etc. In Australia, an often-remarked instance has been the reliance by artists on reproductions for their experience and visual knowledge of modern art, given a limited access to original examples. A not uncommon experience has been that of the young artist who, on arriving in Europe in the 1930s, was intensely disappointed at his first sighting of Cézanne's paintings, preferring instead the more unified and finished surfaces conveyed through reproductions. Such 'accidental' effects of printing technology and other forms of mechanical reproduction have since been turned to distinct advantage by a number of artists.

Another proof of mediation, however, emerged with certain American art of the sixties, which was conceived with a shrewd eye to its impact in reproduction on the pages of glossy art magazines. For instance, the success and influence of Minimal Art was assisted considerably by the style developed for photographing the work for reproduction; and the public impact and style of much Conceptual Art was created through its reproduced form which frequently was given an absolute priority over any exhibited appearance of the work. (Of course, access to internationally distributed art magazines was a not insignificant factor in the successful deployment of these tactics.) A different use again is the recent habit and passion for the reproduced image. A wide range of artists today exploit the familiarity derived from mass reproduction and, for example, deliberately treat the art historical image as having no more value than a Coke bottle.

However, for peripheral cultures, the mediation of influence may also be a constructed and self-conscious process. This may be taken as evidence of the acceptance but also a need to culturally *distance* the sources of influence. The forms of mediation, of distancing, are a means of self-affirmation and function as a critical space within the complex processes of influence. The points of mediation represent an intersection of different cultural histories and interests, a locus of strategies of exchange and transformation, of dominance and resistance. To encourage a dialectical exchange between discrete artistic cultures, no matter how similar, different, powerful or otherwise, the self-conscious process of negotiation and interruption of influence is vital. At the margins of modern art, this constructed mediation animates an important mode of *critical practice*.

Spatial ambiguity animates the picture surface, in a manner reminiscent of Léger's Cubism, but Nolan deliberately hasn't stopped there. Flat shapes reappear looking like naturalistic (or surrealist) cast shadows, introduced as if to make a trite joke about the shallowness of cubist space and to add a further layer of ambiguity. Then the railway signals, which are distant and small, have been painted in front of the guard's head, reversing the 'logical' reading of scale and recession and sandwiching those elements against the picture plane. Thus the clues to reading the pictorial space are interpenetrating and contradictory, and the different spaces collapse into each other around a reading of figure and ground.

In the late sixties, at a time when many of our armchair notions of the history of modern art were collapsing under siege (or was it exhaustion?), the processes of influence underwent a significant transformation in terms of structure and content. The consequences were intense—and intensely different—for artists at the centre and for those of the periphery.

Throughout the sixties, in advanced capitalist countries around the world, anti-authoritarian social movements demonstrated their power by occupation of the streets, buildings, universities. Artists of the (late) avant-garde asserted their power by creating an art which aggressively occupied the spaces of institutions, by intervening in the marketplace and by the contestation of the intellectual spaces of art. This revolt against the institutionality of modern art was conceived in a liberating spirit by the Pop artists and fuelled by moralistic acts of aesthetic self-determination by Minimal and Conceptual artists. Such art raised uneasy questions about the status and categorisation of works of art and our processes of perception. It emphasised that what we *saw*, and what we *knew* about what we saw, couldn't be taken for granted.

Late modernist art, reduced during the sixties to a rapid-fire succession of movements, of formal closures, was thus faced with a deregulated future. The simplistically ordered, non-hierarchical art shattered the illusion of its own rationality through visually articulated critiques of the conventionality of perception. Even the priority of perception itself was challenged by the transfiguratory claims of artists, offered in forms integral to practice. Meaning and complexity were reformulated and located within the 'social' and institutional relations of the object. Now simply an element within a system and with its autonomy dissipated, the art object was absorbed into a series of exhibition or presentational strategies conceived to convey its ordinariness and everyday-ness. Its status ('art-ness') was proposed speculatively and contingently, forcing new awarenesses (and prominence) on to the discursive conditions of art. Perception was accepted as a critical and reflexive process and institutional space redefined expansively (and more abstractly).

The consequence was that the relations between object and viewer underwent a complicated revaluation: notions about practice, about categories, style and skills, about the history and epistemology of art, had become unstable.

There are yet further instabilities. The predominantly shallow cubist space of the guard and landscape is contradicted by the strip of blue sky along the top edge. This blue aggressively registers as recession and tries to impose a naturalistic perspective over the entire picture. Its intensity establishes a colour key, visually unifying elements left at a spontaneous or awkwardly resolved stage. This well-worn pictorial device has been used to great effect by many artists, before and since. However, in this instance the artist appears to have been prompted by the need to retain a strong reference to naturalistic space in order to reiterate a certain specificity. Vastness, conveyed pictorially by an endless or sublime recession, has been a key signifier of an Australian-ness of landscape. The artist, forced to integrate cubist and naturalistic pictorial spaces, found a 'subversive' solution not in glossing over the contradictory spatial logics but rather by letting them co-exist, in temporally disjunctive readings.

Absorbed by these 'subversive' epistemological exercises, the circularity of the avant-garde strategy only became evident after the sixties. The break with the (modernist, formalist) conventionality of the object extended institutional power over the system of production (artistic practice itself) and not just over the product, the work of art. The strategy underestimated the ideological 'flexibility' of the institutions (to accommodate subversion) and the extent to which the viewer, as subject, had been constituted as a peripatetic agent of institutionality. It also underestimated the extent to which the institutionality being subverted was itself culturally and historically specific, as was its market apparatuses and even the contested intellectual space. And, despite characteristics of late modernist art which suppressed the possibility of a critical distance, the strategy miscalculated the imperialistic impact accompanying the export of such art: the mass-consumerist and industrial-technological modes and materials, conceived as a Trojan horse against the institutions, are too readily identified as visual surfaces of (especially US) corporate capitalism's global reach. This realisation, when it came, was too much for some to live with, as artists: at no other moment has there been such a mass defection by artists from their careers.

Nonetheless, for subsequent generations, this rupture was a fact of artistic life: an avant-garde romanticism had bound the artist and the object in a different and new set of relations. The object was no longer the focus of contemplation and the viewer was constituted within a conscious act of 'self-contemplation'. The art had shifted away from a contemplative and towards a reflexive (though not necessarily critical) mode. This displacement provokes parallels with the French Impressionists' turning away from an order of the world in which the human figure held a hierarchical and privileged place, a shift which made many subsequent experiments possible. The ontological break within modernist practices in the 1960s implied, on a number of levels, the re-invention of a hierarchical status, but with the viewer now as privileged subject.

In Australia, the ontology of modern art has always been confused with geography. A fundamental problem for artists has been how to invent a relation to European modernist practices which makes sense in the Australian context. In Nolan's art in the 1940s, this took on the character of a highly self-conscious and sometimes ironical project, with contradictions becoming something not to be glossed over or suppressed but rather to be exploited, played off against each other. Different intentions, needs and artistic conventions co-exist, enriching each other in the same critical space. It is a particular relation to European modernism which doesn't devalue its subject as part of a local tradition, and establishes a claim as a culturally specific modernist vernacular. The artist utilises a vocabulary of European modernism, at the same time calculatingly mocking the idea of dependence. The logic of such an approach resides not in the picture but in the viewer— the now privileged, culturally specific subject.

But the break with late modernism also fractured the logic of other 'fixed' relations— importantly, those between the artistic centres and peripheries. At the outposts of empire where late modernism had taken firm hold, artists intuited a (partial) release from cultural bondage to a 'mainstream' (in reality, perhaps only a shift in the nature of that bondage). From the early seventies, the cultural unity imposed by the centre began to disintegrate within acknowledgements of Other-ness. This engendered a feeling that the inequality of different (national, cultural) art histories could be ignored, passed over, which encouraged a radical decentring of avant-garde energies during the seventies. Once more, art's history and practice regained a potential to become historically specific to particular cultures.

From the early seventies, a tendency of critical practice at the centre has been to recast its cultural identity in terms against its own centricity. Examples of art based on critiques of institutional power and, more generally, of the aesthetic modes of imperialism are familiar and well documented in the publications emanating from the centre. Yet the critique from the periphery, implied and articulated by processes of mediation and distancing, holds little sway in those redefined relations of the centre. There has been scarcely any integration of the peripheries into the theoretical debates at the centre of contemporary art, either as participants or as topic. While the 'post-historical' art of today publicly rejects the historicism linked to late modernism, centrist practices maintain their centricity by a nostalgia for their own artistic heritage; the practices presuppose a privileged relation to an exaggeratedly historicist consciousness. In other words, centrist practice remains largely unreconstructed in terms of its own critique and history.

MARGARET PRESTON
Still Life, 1927
Reproduced in *Art in Australia*,
December 1927

FERNAND LÉGER
Nature Morte, 1923
Reproduced in *L'esprit Nouveau*, no 20,
1924

The blind-spot in histories of modern art is the failure to acknowledge the uneven development of modernism. A precondition of a centrist reading of modernism has generally been the assumption of the universal reference of its conclusions, which constructs an illusory sense of unity and coherence of history at the centre. Also overlooked is the fact that the autonomy of the work of art is less so as it travels away from the centre; nonetheless, it is this assumption of autonomy which encourages a sweeping disregard for reception and impact in artistic cultures elsewhere. This has been an issue, though differently so, for artists of both 'first' and 'third world' peripheries. In these marginal contexts, the significance of other 'meanings' in relation to particular styles is revealed, meanings which themselves have been previously designated as marginal, if recognised at all. This corresponded to the case of much art of the sixties emanating from New York.

Nolan's *Railway Guard* has a number of correspondences, besides compositional, with Léger's *The Mechanic* (1921). These may be speculated on, regardless of whether a direct or conscious relationship existed. Léger held a life-long identification with working-class people and ideas, as well as an enthusiasm for modernisation and an industrialised, streamlined future. Léger's *Mechanic* shows a worker, with tattooed arm and cigarette in hand, as the proletarian hero in the modern (machine) age. In comparison, Nolan's worker stands as the guardian of a modern rural industry in Australia, dispatching the myth of the rural worker as drover, stockman or swaggie. Given the under-industrialisation and continuing economic dependence on primary industries, a modern Australia could not be popularly conveyed by a machine aesthetic or industrial symbolism; Preston experimented with a machine aesthetic briefly, in the late twenties, but her modernity appears fixated on objects rather than an overall aesthetic. The guard's face sits large in the frame, without turning monumental, and the viewer is forced into a feeling of engagement, even identification, with the worker, thus becoming involved with the environs through the guard. The interaction between the guard and his environment becomes a complex expression of the social individual in the modern world, with the picture locked in a struggle (as it were) to establish itself as a paradigmatic materialist portrait.

If the art of the sixties is seen as a historical rupture within (late) modernism, how does it relate to the paradigmatic shift then occurring within art in Australia? The bitter conflict between Greenbergian modernism, with its claim to quality and the refined essence of modern art, and the iconoclastic and avant-garde styles of Pop and Minimalism had few resonances here; both were seen as reductive approaches and aspects of each were (and still are) happily and 'harmoniously' combined. Hence the reception of late modernism and Minimalism was in terms of a style, an object or sculpture with a particular 'look' which seemed to fetishise new materials. Minimalism's confrontational posture towards the institutionality of modern art was too specific to its source, especially to the museological New York with its public spaces privileging the private corporate world. Thus, in export, Minimalism appeared as another permutation 'within' the object and was not perceived in any critical relation to a system.

The dissemination of that critical function—the subversiveness towards institutional forms, intervention in the market and contestation of intellectual spaces—occurred to a greater extent through the modes of Conceptualism. It is no accident that the styles which have offered the greatest freedom and independence to peripheral cultures have been those with a marked bias towards a radical subjectivity, which promotes a demand that difference be recognised and not subsumed. Besides Conceptualism (referred to here in its broadest sense and including, in particular, various Art Povera styles), both Expressionism and Surrealism were crucial in this country in forming the basis of a culturally specific modernist vernacular. (Arguably, these two styles also provided the springboard by which means the locus of modern art was shifted from Europe to North America.)

The 'style-lessness' (more generally, the adoption of mass media 'styles') of Conceptual Art contributed to an international growth of Conceptual practices, part of whose critical intention was to undermine the monopolistic hold of a centrist 'mainstream'. During the sixties, the US had both exported the idea of a mainstream and encouraged the adoption of its institutional organisation and practices, including models of professionalism and success. This was the very institutionality of modern art against which Minimalism reacted. In the late sixties, that institutionality was only gaining a hold in Australia, and its exemplification is found in the re-alignment (reinterpretation) of Australian art to conform with the 'Americanised' histories of modernism, and its endorsement within exhibitions like *The Field* (1968). While the integration of the peripheries into the vision of the American mainstream was comparatively successful, Conceptualism encouraged the setting of private meanings against those institutionally-determined public meanings. Ironically, the implantation of these conditions provided artists with a platform from which to exploit, for different ends, the break with the conventionality of the object.

How do we account for Drysdale's exploitation of a Tanguy-like surrealist plain as a means of expressing the vastness of the outback landscape? Drysdale's image of this different kind of Australia doesn't spring fully-fledged out of Surrealism. Those plains are not just of a primordial unconscious but also convey the dense emptiness of a real landscape. The context for that imagery was precedented, a public awareness slowly achieved through anthropological studies and popular writers on the outback, through pictorial magazines (like *Walkabout*, published from 1934). It was also part of a growing public acceptance of mining (i.e. non-farming rural industries) as part of the popular concept of a modern Australia. The exaggerated recessions of Drysdale's imagery were enhanced through borrowings from Surrealism and gained a symbolic power, that is, a power to symbolise specific cultural forms and experiences. This also indicates the significance of

RUSSELL DRYSDALE
Man Reading a Newspaper, 1941
Oil on canvas
61 × 76
University of Sydney Collection
Gift of Lucy Swanton 1953

46

a style like Surrealism in peripheral cultures. Drysdale's lovingly painted, heavily glazed pictures of isolated rural life, which we are at once made to feel part of and estranged from, become a counterpoint to the artist's relation to a history of European modernism. It is a self-image as the Other, in which isolation becomes a token of rapprochement with marginality.

An underlying factor of Conceptualism's international appeal was its reassessment of traditional tokens of style. Style became a quality separated from the object, functioning at a level of conception and pre-planning. Thus the specificity of the art resided not within the institutionality of the style (as was the case with Minimalism) but within the terms of particular conceptual strategies.

At the periphery, style has been and remains a highly problematic concept, and hence this aspect was of perhaps greater significance than any challenge to the object's conventionality. Within the process of transmission from centre to periphery, style takes on a reified form, and hence has been perceived as a major conduit for diffusion of influences from overseas. Artists have frequently used a commitment in terms of style as a means of declaring an allegiance or affiliation to an 'international' movement, and of disenfranchising themselves from specific local practices. Alternatively, amalgamations of received styles can serve to obscure, even deliberately distance, a dependence on sources. In other words, artists have used this as a way of mediating influence. Within such mixes, the strategies of overlapping, of slippages and gaps can be exploited for different ends and contradictions played off against each other. Thus, complex hybrids and transgressions of 'pure' styles have been self-consciously developed, an approach which has given rise to a lot of the more distinctive art produced in this country.

Since the 1940s, however, there has been a marked tendency to interpret Australian art in terms confirming the pantheon of European styles, which has resulted in undervaluing the instability of stylistic categories within Australian art. This has produced the now-familiar dislocation between artistic solutions in Australian art and the rhetoric of theoretical-historical interpretation. Bernard Smith, for example, in *Place, Taste and Tradition* (1945) wrote about such stylistic mixes as mutations, impurities and compromises, but not as a legitimate basis of a specific culture. Others wrote with a similar conviction and, in particular, the late sixties and early seventies emerged as a period of considerable pressure for a stylistic purity from adherents to American modernism.

Significantly, an instability of stylistic categories is also accepted as characteristic of much of the art described today under the rubric of post-modernism. Or, more exactly, style is accepted as a function of the various conceptual strategies involved in representations. In other words, style today is a function of the critical or conceptual mediation of style in its former sense. But, arguably, even with this formulation, there remains a structural equivalence with that referred to above as the instability of stylistic categories at the periphery. The significant difference is that what was formerly perceived negatively (not of the centre) has now been transformed into a much-sought-after quality (by the centre).

Through his art, Nolan reveals an indifference to the authority of his influences, to their history, which effectively becomes the means of declaration of *difference* within modernist culture. It is an evasive strategy, of participation and demurring at the same time, without the fetishisation of stylistic sources which has characterised other periods of Australian art. Nolan's art rejects any sense of subjection to sources, and approaches influence more as the terms of a collaboration. Certainly this is the effect of Léger's participation in creating Nolan's *Guard* and, notwithstanding all the myths of individuality and originality, emphasises the extent to which the character of art unfolds as a collective enterprise. Yet it also makes us aware of the contradiction between influence as it is received and its influence in mediated form. But how should that contradiction be posed? Suppressed, or glossed over? By a fetishisation of one or other of its terms? Exploited by an ironical play between the terms? Such divergent approaches construct very different notions of value within Australian art.

Artists survive beyond their art through art history, so histories still have to be written as if they mattered, a matter of life and death. Consequently, cases have been made about the inherent post-modernism of Australian culture, proposing us all (as it were) as progeny of Ern Malley. In much the same way that it is arguable the characteristics of a post-industrial society emerged in Australia preceding its development as an industrial society, it is also possible to argue that conditions of post-modernity preceded (and now preclude) a 'proper' development of modernism in Australia. Indeed, a credible 'post-

ROBERT MORRIS
Untitled, 1967
Steel, 9 units, 91.4 × 91.4 × 91.4
Collection, Solomon R. Guggenheim
Museum, New York

Photographer Ian Burn

modernist' history of Australian art can be written since many of the popular definitions fit remarkably well. The contradictions of practice, the disunity and discontinuity, the stylistic instability and facsimile imagery, the inversions of values . . . are all too familiar.

But this half-truth obscures the fundamental issue. The issue for peripheral cultures is not about precedence, rather it is about the appropriation by the centre of qualities which have been characteristic of peripheral cultures. These appropriations are then re-presented in forms integrated into the practice and critical vocabulary of the centre. In other words, they are quoted back to us as 'news', as the latest advancement of the centre. By such means, the illusion is retained intact: the art of peripheral cultures reappears as a mirror held up to theories 'specific' to the centre.

Why has Léger's art been a specific subject of Australian art? Has it to do with the way Léger's cubism builds up dialectically, through contrasts of pictorial means: of colours, of scale, of curved and straight forms, of abstract and naturalistic forms, of different modes of representation and spatial logics? Has it to do with the way these are held together in tension, as unresolved contradictions in his pictures? We also experience our culture through a range of particular contradictions, unresolvable. The (uneven) development of modernism, together with resistance to particular aspects of the modernist project and the impossibly incomplete rapprochement with the environment, have become fundamental to our creativity. Haven't these contradictory forces underpinned the distinctiveness and vitality of much Australian art? This structural symbiosis with Léger's dialectic affirms a potential of collaboration and of exchange between cultures.

BIBLIOGRAPHICAL NOTE

An essay of this nature works off many sources, but can acknowledge only a few. The discussion of Nolan's work and its relation to that of Léger draws on previously published writings by the author, especially 'Landscape and Life: Nolan and the Australian tradition' in the *Age Monthly Review*, August 1984. My attention was drawn to the Léger source for Margaret Preston's painting (and illustrations provided) by Terry Smith.

The discussion of Minimalism is dependent for some of its terms on Hal Foster's 'The Crux of Minimalism', published in *Individuals: A Selected History of Contemporary Art 1945–1986* (Museum of Contemporary Art, Los Angeles, 1986); however, the comments made here critically engage that essay and what it leaves undeveloped. The references to Conceptual Art draw partly on the author's 'The Sixties: Crisis and Aftermath' in *Art & Text*, no 1, 1981.

Certain ideas were reinforced by the writings of Nelly Richard, especially her essay 'Latin America: Cultures of Repetition or Cultures of Difference?' (published in the 1984 Sydney Biennale catalogue), an essay which might well have been written within an Australian context.

IDOLS AND ICONS

DIANE WALDMAN

At first glance, the American artists in the 1988 Australian Biennale would appear to have very little in common. At the very least, they are divided by generation and by their individual responses to the issues of their time. Nevertheless, these artists share a single culture, a sense of time and place which sets their work apart from that produced anywhere else in the world.

The generation of artists—Willem de Kooning, Mark Rothko and David Smith—who spearheaded the movement now known as the New York School did so during one of the bleakest and most dramatic phases of American history. Their art was formed and framed by the cataclysmic events that occurred during the economic and social debacle of the Great Depression and the economic and political recovery that followed in the aftermath of World War II. Although the artists of the New York School were keenly aware of the current social and political issues, and were themselves among the poorest of the social classes, few were politically active. Some, like Rothko, joined the Artist's Union, which was formed in 1934 and did not confine itself solely to artists' problems but became engaged in other labour issues as well. The majority of the artists sought relief in the Works Progress Administration, a federal project initiated to support artists during the Depression. The WPA engendered a sense of community new to many artists and brought together people of very different backgrounds who might otherwise never have become friends. Their limited resources, their need for community, their desire for change, led to friendship. They exhibited together, drank together, fought with each other, picketed, protested and struggled for greatness. They admired the work of Miró and Klee well before these artists were accepted in Paris. They went to see Kandinsky's paintings at the Museum of Non-Objective Painting and were especially impressed with the Picassos reproduced in the French journal *Cahiers d'Art*. None of the social or political forces in play at the time proved to be deterrents to their ambition—to rival the great art of the European modernists. The presence in New York of many of Europe's leading painters and poets only reinforced their desire to achieve in their art the level of quality that they admired in the work of the Europeans.

Despite the diversity of these artist's approaches, it is possible to discern two major tendencies that emerged within the movement after a period of protracted experimentation and change. Rothko, Still and Newman, among others, explored the area of large-scale colour-field painting. The other direction, exemplified by de Kooning, Pollock and Kline, favoured the gesture, the mark, the drip and the brush stroke as vital evidence of the artist's activity, as documents of the path of the artist's process. While de Kooning, like his colleague Jackson Pollock, pioneered in the area of gesture, he remained committed to easel scale, the figure and the traditional figure-ground relationship, and these elements culminate in monumental pictorial tensions when paired with his dynamic, expressive brush work and his broad, sweeping gestures. In the epic paintings of women, de Kooning achieved a radical synthesis of figuration and abstraction and created some of the greatest icons of our age. Yet, at roughly the same time, he also executed some of the finest so-called abstractions of any member of the New York School. For although de Kooning, like his colleagues, argued over the meaning of abstraction, he never completely embraced it and preferred instead to alternate over the years between a form of figuration and a form of abstraction. With the 'Women', he produced one of his most potent symbols. Painted some thirty-five years ago, they still seem 'vociferous and ferocious', to use the artist's own words. They are breathless and chatty, like the funny and vulnerable sex symbol Marilyn Monroe portrayed so successfully in *Some Like It Hot*, they are operatic, like Wagner's Brünnhilde, and as resplendent as any Venus that has come down to us through the ages. De Kooning has said, 'The "Women" had to do with the female painted through all the ages, all those idols, and maybe I was stuck to a certain extent; I couldn't go on.' He added, 'It did one thing for me: it eliminated composition, arrangement, relationships, light—all this silly talk about line, colour and form— because that was the thing I wanted to get hold of. I put it in the centre of the canvas because there was no reason to put it a bit on the side . . .'[1] Idol and icon notwithstanding, there is also an element of parody in many of the artist's figures that predicts certain Pop attitudes in drawing upon aspects of popular culture and aggrandising the notoriety of certain celebrities and movie stars. Idols and icons, popular imagery, the juxtaposition of 'high' and 'low' art, the ambiguous roles of figure and abstraction are but some of the many issues that de Kooning has touched upon in his painting. It is not surprising, then, that he is as pivotal to today's art as he was to the painting of the 1940s and 1950s.

In vastly different ways, both Rothko and David Smith have also produced icons. In Rothko's mythic period of the 1940s, he drew upon Surrealist prototypes which he combined with the zones or registers of colours that had appeared in his work as early as the mid-1930s. By the late 1940s, however, he had eliminated all but the most vestigial semblance of an image in favour of large, floating colour-shapes anchored by one or two bands of colour. The soft pastel palette of his 1950s painting, influenced by Matisse and by Rothko's friend and mentor Milton Avery, was replaced in the 1960s by a light-suffused palette that recalls Rembrandt and by a superb command of form inspired by the powerful figures of Michelangelo. Rothko's mature paintings of the 1950s and 1960s share with the work of Barnett Newman and Clyfford Still a commitment to large scale, vast expanses of space and intense colour sequences. Rothko purified his art by rejecting the decorative surface qualities of paint and ridding his canvases of complex relationships of form, colour and structure. Having emptied his paintings of what appeared to him to be superfluous elements, he was able to express the material reality of the sublime. For Rothko, colour was form, nature, the human figure, area and volume, moods and emotions. Through his colour and the way in which he applied paint to canvas, Rothko has created a new and mythic imagery, one that combines the world of actuality and the world of the imagination. In his evocative and emotionally resonant painting, colour becomes the vehicle for exalted, transcendental experience.

The muscular, heroic and highly inflected work of David Smith, the pre-eminent sculptor of the Abstract Expressionist movement, achieves in the realm of sculpture the epic vision of New York School painting. Like many Abstract Expressionist painters, Smith was initially influenced by Surrealism; however, he soon renounced Surrealist allegory and allusion in favour of the more formalist aesthetic exemplified by Picasso's welded steel sculpture and the forged iron pieces of Julio Gonzalez. During the 1950s and 1960s, Smith worked on the floor, cutting out shapes or painting them in a manner reminiscent of Jackson Pollock. He then assembled the elements vertically, welded them together and refined and finished them. In extraordinary works like *Australia* of 1951, Smith's consummate ability to draw in space enabled him to delineate form, frame space and make it a dynamic and integral part of his sculpture. The works in the 'Cubi' series, begun in the early 1960s, are among the finest pieces Smith produced. He assembled and welded them in a manner similar to that which he had employed earlier. Preparatory drawings and collages preceded the final assembly and welding. Once welded, the constructions were roughly buffed to produce variegated surfaces and an iridescent sheen. These sculptures represent the first time Smith was able to incorporate light into his work, as Rothko had done. And like Rothko, he both emphasised the material aspect of his surface and dematerialised it, although his method was different from the painter's: whereas Rothko eliminated all vestiges of reality from the imagery in his painting, Smith incorporated the colour of nature into his sculpture. Like de Kooning, Smith relied to a large extent on anthropomorphic forms for his configurations. In his 'Cubi' series he arrived at idealised form.

By the early 1960s, the economic, political and social milieu of the art world had changed considerably. Some artists, such as Andy Warhol, were quick to pick up on the rampant consumerism in American society. Warhol not only saw the humour and irony in using Campbell's Soup cans and Brillo boxes as his subjects, but, in his portrayal of such dramatic and tragic figures as Marilyn, Liz and Elvis, he also observed the darker, seamier side of American success. Warhol's choice of notorious subjects, his matter-of-fact documentation of our society's symbols of fame, his use of mass-produced methods to reproduce art and his statement 'In the future everybody will be world famous for fifteen minutes',[2] which borders on the prophetic, reflects a Duchampian attitude carried to its

DAVID SMITH
Australia, 1951
Painted steel, 202 × 274 ×41
Collection, The Museum of Modern Art,
New York
Gift of William Rubin

This sculpture was named by Smith after
prehistoric Australian cave drawings,
photographs of which were sent to the
artist by his close friend, the critic
Clement Greenberg. (Edward F. Fry,
David Smith (catalogue), The Solomon R.
Guggenheim Foundation, New York,
1969.) Smith met Australian artist Robert
Klippel at the Parma Gallery in New York
City in 1958 and said he titled the work
'because to me it felt like Australia'.

farthest limits. While Warhol made some of the most telling and moving paintings of his time, among them a series on *The Last Supper*, his views about art and about art as a career could not have been more removed from the equally ambitious but far more innocent attitudes that prevailed among the Abstract Expressionists. Idols and icons were indeed the subjects of his paintings; they signified and continue to signify the extreme position in which Western society currently finds itself.

Edward and Nancy Reddin Kienholz and Richard Artschwager address society in vastly different ways from Warhol and from each other. They share with Warhol an awareness of American society at a particular crossroads in its history. Artschwager's work generally falls within the Pop idiom. He, like many of his colleagues who first came to prominence in the 1960s, chose to comment on the more mundane aspects of Pop culture and helped re-introduce into art a form of representation that the Abstract Expressionists had largely banned. The use of the single object with its deadpan anonymity, imagery culled from the media and mechanical methods of mass production are among the most salient features of Artschwager's work. In his recent paintings he has used impasto and pieces of wood, which can be read as near abstractions and thus enhance their iconic, object-like quality. Unlike Warhol, Artschwager avoids the lurid and the sensational; his art is laconic, cool, understated and conceptual.

Edward and Nancy Reddin Kienholzes' work reflects their own very particular social attitudes. They, like Warhol, will often portray the seamier side of our society, but their work contains the element of pathos that is lacking in Warhol's paintings. Both the Kienholzes and Warhol mirror aspects of society, both can sensationalise their subject matter, yet the Kienholzes depict social types and attitudes that Warhol disdained—the faceless 'everyman' was of no interest to Warhol. The Kienholzes' work admits sentiment, nostalgia, sensuality, tawdriness, pain and suffering. Warhol's paintings are masks, the Kienholzes' blood and guts.

The recent, grand rhetorical tableaux of Robert Morris share with the Kienholzes' art an indictment of society. While the Kienholzes' works have long been characterised by their political and social commentary, they often take the form of life-sized environments. Morris's tableaux, for all their three-dimensionality, resemble altarpieces. They share with the art of German painter Anselm Kiefer a sense of the apocalyptic. These new pieces, dark and brooding in mood and vast in size, include altered images of the Holocaust and developed from the 'Firestorm' series, executed in 1982–83. Morris's newest works seem light years away from the Minimalist sculpture that first brought him to public attention. Just as his early pieces of the 1960s were the very essence of understatement, so these newest wall reliefs are almost baroque in their density and complexity. Their wasted landscapes are composed of figures seeking refuge from Dante's inferno. Shown recently at Documenta in Kassel, West Germany, they are a horrific reminder of that nation's recent infamous past and of man's inhumanity to man since the beginning of time.

Unlike Morris, Richard Serra remains firmly rooted in the Minimalist aesthetic. While Morris's early work was impassive and uninflected, Serra's contained a very real element of danger. In his metal prop-pieces of the late 1960s, two or more units, usually geometric in shape, were balanced against one another in a rather tenuous equilibrium. Initially, Serra used lead antimony which, because of its malleability, allowed him to roll the plates, lean them against one another like a house of cards or, in its most molten state, to create a lead splash. His involvement with materials, gesture and process acknowledged the inspiration of the Abstract Expressionists.

But despite his use of gesture and process, his work has tended towards a greater formality in which highly resolved, closed and ordered forms create statements of compelling authority. More recently, his use of geometric units and such materials as Cor-Ten and hot-rolled steel has endowed his art with a new intensity. Despite this substantial change, however, his sculpture continues to engender a sense of imminent danger, made all the more potent by its increased scale. In the new work, the lyricism and poetry of Serra's earlier pieces has given way to a dynamic monumentality which, for all its simplicity and directness, evokes the dramatic presence of the awesome sculpture of Michelangelo and Rodin.

Martin Puryear is one of a number of artists who first came to public attention in the late 1970s, a decade after Minimalism was introduced. Unlike the Minimalists, for whom industrial materials were fundamental to their concept of producing neutral form, Puryear has a feeling for process and natural materials that is evident in his respect for craft and craftsmanship, in his frequent use of wood, and in the way in which he shapes it into evocative and poetic form. Puryear has created a vocabulary in which the single object regains the autonomy, mystery and presence that were often lacking in the work of the Minimalists. Organic in shape, his sculptures combine elements that are open and closed in structure, but although they are often bold in size they speak of a lyric rather than an epic art. Like other artists in this exhibition, Puryear creates icons of an intensely private nature, symbols of the self that echo forms from other times, other civilisations.

During the last decade Ross Bleckner's paintings have remained abstract; they are large in scale and intended to operate on a blatantly optical level. In them, patterned fields are interrupted by small images, often of birds, which the eye registers but can only focus on at close range, at which point the viewer loses awareness of the striped canvas. The artist also works on a smaller scale, and these canvases feature more perceptible images, but they, too, are lost in shadow, so that one is never completely cognisant of their totality. Bleckner's large-scale and small-scale paintings recall Joseph Cornell's diminutive constructions, for both contain a world full of light and shadow, nostalgia and loss, fantasy, poetry and the surreal.

Barbara Kruger, Jenny Holzer and Peter Halley are products of the TV age and the world of advertising and billboards. Their art reflects an era in which everything is called into question, particularly the notion of originality. Like Duchamp and Warhol before them, they are appropriators of their culture, freely borrowing from the mass media, from other artists, from anything available to them. Yet, ironically, they have quickly established their own identity, their own style and content, in an age in which both style and content are thought to be of little value. Theirs is an art that is cool and detached; it is possibly the least emotional art we have seen since that of the Minimalists. Halley has commented that 'perhaps the most far-reaching emotional experiment in the visual arts took place in the 1960s, when at a certain moment a few artists—Warhol, Stella, and Judd among them—dared to propose as a new emotional state the absence of any emotion at all'.[3] Like Warhol, Kruger, Holzer and Halley have chosen loaded subject matter that has given their work sensational, if not lurid, overtones; but at the same time, the very medium they have selected adds an element of detachment to the art.

Sarah Charlesworth's 'Objects of Desire' also address questions of originality. In this series of photographs, Charlesworth has drawn images from our common consumer culture and heightened their immediacy by isolating them against fields of vivid colour. Her work, like that of other artists active today, is a curious mixture of conceptual premise, Pop imagery and ironic interchange between object and void, presence and absence, desire and loss.

Artists working today face an art world completely different from the one first encountered by the Abstract Expressionists. Artists of de Kooning's generation became active at a time when there were few collectors, virtually no sales and little chance that their work would be exhibited. Theirs was a world of poverty, ours one of affluence. Despite the dramatic changes in our society in general and in the art world in particular, artists have continued to respond to the events they deem most pressing in contemporary life. To the extent to which they succeed, our culture and heritage are enriched by their reactions to the world around them.

1. 'Content Is a Glimpse', excerpts from an interview with David Sylvester for the BBC in *Location*, vol. 1, Spring 1963.
2. Quoted in *Andy Warhol*, catalogue, Neue National Galerie Berlin, Berlin, Gerd Fleischmann, 1969.
3. Peter Halley, 'A Note on the "New Expressionism" Phenomenon', *Arts Magazine*, vol. 57, March 1983.

ON THE DANGERS OF TRAVELLING

BERNARD BLISTÈNE

As I have been given the means to accomplish a journey many only dream of, it seemed fair to ask myself what reasons inspire such a journey, and what relationships this end of the ends of the earth maintains with us.

Lothar Baumgarten, in reply to Nick Waterlow's invitation to him to participate in the present Biennale, answered: 'Sure, but I'll have to be sent there by boat . . .' This jest, for all that, did appear significant to me. It is not so much that the artist seeks to re-live the adventures of Captain Cook—it is rather that the artist wants to investigate the reasons why everyone wants to go there. It is not so much the taste for travelling that Baumgarten wants to analyse—it is the situation with which every artist today finds himself confronted, a real commercial traveller carrying his work like a soliloquy.

Because he is above all clear-minded and lucid and aware, having 'navigated' the dangers of travel, Lothar Baumgarten gives us a warning. It isn't important to him to dream, as Joseph Beuys dreamed, of a disunited world at last reconciled. He understands the error of a utopia and knows that, in the etymological sense, the word means 'the other country'. In two words: he is wary of exoticism.

The Australian trip inspires me, when all is said and done, with similar reflections, and it is not so much me as that which was given to me to peddle that has made me think.

One has known for a long time about the dangers of tourism. A vehement Victor Segalen criticises the 'exotics' more than once and denounces with irony the dreamers of his century. He knows, having travelled and found himself in China at a time when going to Collioure was an adventure, that there is a geography in our heads before it exists as a country. He knows that exoticism and the exotic are not the same thing and that the journey conceals itself in the innermost recesses of our being before it can take form in a part of our world.

Segalen strongly advises all those tempted by wanderlust to watch out. He wants to make them reflect on the finality of the romanticism of travel, on the attraction of 'over there', on the derisory craving for another world. He knows that *the aesthetics of the diverse*, the subtitle of his essay on exoticism, values neither change of scenery nor vagrancy. In addition to this, he wants to understand our reasons for travelling and then denounce through them the temptation to take over or assimilate, which exists at the basis of all colonialism. Every one of his lines is a warning. Victor Segalen demands that we take precautions.

On the 'savage' that Gauguin wanted to become, he says that this desire would have died on the Marquesas Islands while he was painting a Breton landscape under snow. He reminds us that 'the other' is already within us, and that visas don't change anything. Rimbaud left not so much to discover the Negus and Ethiopia as to discover over there the self he had not yet found at home.

Do our contemporaries allow themselves to be tempted by the taste for travel? Certainly, Suez or Panama are now far behind us, and it would require little intelligence to believe the still thoughtlessly designated 'Third World' can be found on our soil. The scale is different. The stakes are elsewhere, and faraway lands, in this era of acceleration, certainly have little to do with the surveying of our own world. Could it be that Rimbaud's or Gauguin's lesson, as opposed to the derisory misadventures of Gleyre, a painter disappointed by his travels in Africa, still evades us? Could it be that we are, as ever, still shamelessly playing at explorers?

Since the aeroplane defeated distance, since images have been assailing us to the point of confusion, we see the singer, the artist or the curator going from north to south, from east to west. Each travels, in his own way. Each has an answer to everyone, and affirms: one is Carmen in Tokyo, Scheherazade in Berlin and Mimi in Rio. People are nowhere forced to be everywhere.

Such and such an artist exhibits his work at such and such a place and values his production like the couturier does a collection. Where are the precautions? Where are the instructions? Can it be that, to the very end, the pursuit of the wind transforms us into weather-vanes? Can it be that 'travelling without a compass' makes the majority of us forget the teaching of the philosopher who remained in his room, already knowing that one does not need to travel everywhere to see the world?

'To know the world,' said Kant, 'it is not enough simply to look at it. Whoever wants to benefit from his travel must have already formulated a plan in advance and must not regard the world only as an object of the external senses.'

The man meditating here knows very well what he is talking about. 'The object-world is within. What an absurdity to go looking for it beyond the self.'

'Let us prepare ourselves,' he also said. One cannot handle time or space roughly—it is imperative to employ a method to draw a lesson from it. Be careful of the denial of reality, the fear that over there one will only know how to find the bazaar and the palm tree. Or that one will disguise oneself to play at being a local. What is the use of this? Why do it? 'The detour to remote lands,' wrote the French critic Daniel Soutif, 'once again does nothing more than re-direct the self to the self; the careless traveller is hurled into the search for an imaginary other.'

One would like the artist today to know the stakes. One would like him to understand why he travels. Some who can know, do know, while others refuse. I am not saying they must always know, but they must be able to say why they are going there. We who know how a large proportion of contemporary works escape taxonomy while refuting all classification; we who know just how numerous the projects are that eventually take their style from objects, while the day before they were denying the foundations; we cannot help but say how perplexed we are in the face of a number of artists who—is this an inevitable compromise?—seem to yield to the necessity of finding themselves everywhere. We would like them to be a rare breed, yet they are omnipresent. We would like them to be masters of their game, yet they are mere puppets. There are only a few who still know how to leave and who don't confuse journey and destination. There are only a few who keep in reserve the folkloric readings and exhibitions suggested to them.

Because it is not about being at any old place, the work must once again have an effect in its own place. Isn't the work there to name the dangers that are threatening it? Exerting a lasting influence on a culture is knowing at the time how to reject contradictions and temptations, how to remove oneself from a game when it can no longer be played or when the rules can no longer be mastered.

I pay tribute to the artists who are today aware in what era they are navigating and who, free to act as they choose, refute or contradict the worlds and models presented to them. I pay tribute to all those who resist compromise and who *explore within* their work, and not *against* it, the limits of a world they would like to be otherwise, and of a universe whose parameters do not satisfy them. At least *these* exotics know how to navigate and invent other horizons where the journey will not be confused with the destination.

Translated by Gretchen Cook

RENATE ANGER
TOM ARTHUR
RICHARD ARTSCHWAGER
GIANNI ASDRUBALI

FRANCIS BACON
RALPH BALSON
BALTHUS
MAX BECKMANN
MICHAEL BIBERSTEIN
ROSS BLECKNER
CHRISTIAN BOLTANSKI
PIERRE BONNARD
PETER BOOTH
MARIE BOURGET
ARTHUR BOYD
GEORGES BRAQUE
JULIE BROWN-RRAP
GÜNTER BRUS
MICHAEL BUTHE

GENEVIÈVE CADIEUX
SARAH CHARLESWORTH
HANNAH COLLINS
ROBERT COMBAS

NEIL DAWSON
WILLEM DE KOONING
RICHARD DEACON
MARCEL DUCHAMP
LILI DUJOURIE
LESLEY DUMBRELL
RICHARD DUNN

BRIAN ENO

LUCIANO FABRO
IAN FAIRWEATHER
HELMUT FEDERLE
BILL FONTANA
KATHARINA FRITSCH

GÉRARD GAROUSTE

ROSALIE GASCOIGNE
ISA GENZKEN
GODBOLD & WOOD
FRANZ GRAF

PETER HALLEY
EITETSU HAYASHI
JOY HESTER
ROGER HILTON
TAISHI HIROKAWA
JENNY HOLZER
REBECCA HORN
ROBERT HUNTER

TOSHIMITSU IMAÏ
IRWIN

MICHAEL JOHNSON

ANSELM KIEFER
EDWARD & NANCY REDDIN KIENHOLZ
YVES KLEIN
ROBERT KLIPPEL
JANNIS KOUNELLIS
BARBARA KRUGER

NIKOLAUS LANG
MARIA LASSNIG
FERNAND LÉGER
INGEBORG LÜSCHER
LEN LYE

HILARIE MAIS
HENRI MATISSE
COLIN McCAHON
VICTOR MEERTENS
GERHARD MERZ
FRANÇOIS MORELLET
ROBERT MORRIS
OLIVIER MOSSET

NATSU NAKAJIMA

HERMANN NITSCH
JOHN NIXON
SIDNEY NOLAN
GIANFRANCO NOTARGIACOMO

MARIA OLSEN
TATSUMI ORIMOTO
SONJA OUDENDIJK

GIULIO PAOLINI
MIKE PARR
GIUSEPPE PENONE
PABLO PICASSO
MARGARET PRESTON
MARTIN PURYEAR

ARNULF RAINER
RAMINGINING ARTISTS COMMUNITY
JACKY REDGATE
GERHARD RICHTER
MARK ROTHKO

GARETH SANSOM
ANNA MARIA SANTOLINI
EVA SCHLEGEL
RICHARD SERRA
SEVERED HEADS
VIVIENNE SHARK LeWITT
DAVID SMITH
HENRYK STAŻEWSKI
GARY STEVENS & CAROLINE WILKINSON
ANDRZEJ SZEWCZYK

IMANTS TILLERS
WILLIAM TUCKER
TONY TUCKSON

BILL VIOLA

JEFF WALL
ANDY WARHOL
CAROLINE WILLIAMS
FRED WILLIAMS

PARTICIPATING COUNTRIES

AUSTRALIA
AUSTRIA
BELGIUM
BRITAIN
CANADA
FEDERAL REPUBLIC OF GERMANY
FRANCE
ITALY
JAPAN
NETHERLANDS
NEW ZEALAND
POLAND
SWITZERLAND
UNITED STATES OF AMERICA
YUGOSLAVIA

RENATE ANGER

Born Danzig, German Democratic Republic, 1943

Lives and works in Berlin

Space, the aura of a specific place and her personal psychogram entwine themselves into a new experience of space, which makes it possible to experience the always daring boundaries of inner and outer, experience and actuality, the expressible and that which cannot be put into words.

Excerpt from Dorothée Bauerle, *Renate Anger: Antworten* (catalogue), Künstlerhaus Bethanien, Berlin, 1987

UNTITLED, 1986
Egg tempera on cotton
Two pieces, 350 × 155

The work of Tom Arthur triggers the opening of instinct experiences, remembrances of those cleavages in mentation which tear open for one startling moment of disingenuous clarity. His installations and other sculptured work assert the possibility of transposing memory into new constructs in order to gain many different options of personal being and doing. Yet, such proposals are grounded in the pragmatic, earth-founded human body and in its intense, yet low-keyed histories.

His installation for the Sydney Biennale is a continuation in a more minimalist mode of previous works, in particular of *The Entire Contents of a Gentleman's Room*, Melbourne, 1987. He was pursuing the same intuition earlier in drawings (*Nocturnal Emmissions*, 1974–76), encased reliefs (*Love Letter . . . Let's Build a House*, 1986) and in earlier room constructions, such as *Goodbye Carpet, Goodbye Small Door*, 1983. These revealed the nature of a 'cut' across reality made by a peripheral subject on transversing the hierarchies of the 'interior'.

Critics have made heavy weather of Tom Arthur's Art, because they seem to get bogged down in an analysis of the details of the works. These details form carefully selected intensities that punctuate a vivified, living terrain, yet it is the *act* of the works, their kinetic quality, which is their essential experience—the quivering vibration which registers a 'passing-through'. Although the work is intense, loaded to strike at a specific experience, it is also highly detached, de-centred off the artist in a cool analysis, leaving open a personal space for the reflections of the viewer by the removal of the emotive overloading more commonly associated with work debating passion and death.

The work does not follow the geometry of rectilinearity already inscribed on the earth, but instead pursues the ellipses. It is no surrealist juxtaposition of forms, symbols and meanings, but a random cut through the whole: a sheering-away of the strata of the entire cultural presence—an unprivileged moment, all the more poignant and intense for its elision, composed of the familiar and the remembered.

At the circumference of the rounded, domestic forms of the central structure are the jagged planes and slivers of non-continuous spaces, parallel layers of erotic life and the dried bones of the dead, of the impassioned and the desolate, of meeting-points and recent absences, of the loss of something else which still waits on, urging after itself from the memory of the past to the long ellipses of a moment extended. Tom Arthur's work demystifies the Other of desire and of fear by following through the imperatives set by desire itself. At the end of the process, the Other is found to be neither illusion, nor alien, nor mystic, but oneself is displaced in the reflections of opaque and translucent mirrors, re-echoed in light-wells, or disjointed across the walls and ceilings of half-lit rooms whose customary cuboids are neutralised by parallels of light from a slowly-opened door. All such recurring motifs in his work indicate a quicksilver surface of entry to yet another track, another possibility for change and for unending movement from oneself to oneself.

The room-installations are spaces and surfaces of desire: webs, nets, intersecting metallic lines, arrows—reflecting, displacing, throwing-out and absorbing light. No single image metaphorises desire in the manner of traditional symbols, not even the arrows, whose extended length and attenuated fragility suggest as much the nervous, delicate stringing of highly-tuned mental processes as of physical sexuality. The rooms express the tearing-apart of reality which is the act of desire and, also, its own yearning.

The central concept is the sudden surprise of the breaking-into of the fabric of entirety. Everything that was 'stuck' has been scattered. Traces of the passing have left webs sown over the surfaces—as arrows, as light—but these are its marks only and no further interpretation is possible. However, the action that wreaked the disorder was a detached one, whose primary concern was not with the rooms themselves, but was mercurially intent on transit, devoid of polemic with the space of the motion. The disorder was not malicious and was *almost* made without deliberation. And, yet, it pulled the very sense out of the interiors, leaving them still quivering at its departure. These are scenes of irrevocable transformation, of the moments of de-centring and of obsession.

What complicates the reading of the installations is that they are not only witnesses to a tearing-apart, a dislocation, but are also the spaces of a fulfilment, that promise associated with the peripheral, of completion, of integration, of passion, and, therefore, of some sort of death. But, in that case, the nature of death, as Tom Arthur understands it, must be redefined. This involves the redefinition of memory. Instead of the opposition of passion and death, of life and death, there is a continuum so normal, so unremarkable, that it becomes a matter of some indifference. Death may still be melancholic, pitiful, curious, the trigger of a sense of loss, or a cause of bemusement, but, as in the many death-referents in his works, the macabre, the fearful impurities, the incompletion of the state of death, are absent. Instead, there is a certain dry pragmatism.

In death is a movement, an extension of passion, a natural unwinding of life, then memory, in turn, ceases to be passive, but takes on an active creative function. It becomes a-temporal and acts equally in the future, spinning the moment forward. Hence, the death-images in Tom Arthur's installations present an actuality, self-presence and integrity. There is a certain benevolence in their aspect. The dead enter our lives, but they do so because we freely invite them, and, indeed, go forward to meet them. This realisation of the continuing ability to choose changes one's understanding of the nature of the cut by the peripheral across the centre. Though it is still oddly angled and tilted, curiously dimensioned, it is seen to be the rediscovery of what is totally familiar. What remains is poignancy, but with a certain sense of celebration.

In Tom Arthur's use of death-symbology there is no sense that it is an agency outside oneself which is enforcing the extinction. The viewer is anchored in the familiar registrations of his own body, in those indices that register the process of dying and are always known subliminally by the psyche and the intellect. They monitor the transitioning of the body as both a living act and as an act of death. The works awaken the tactile sense so that the mind is not left disembodied, floating helplessly in the psyche.

From this point of view it is interesting to note the importance of the skeletal figures throughout Tom Arthur's oeuvre. They contribute towards a more vital understanding of human sexuality than that offered by the cultural stereotypes of genital eroticism. It was the feminist writers of the early seventies who observed that the body surface was an interactive erotic membrane, highly activated in women, according to their analysis, due to the socio-political suppression of the female. Denied access by the patriarchy to the polarities of reason and of genital sexuality, women had been forced to activate their tactile sense over the whole body surface and to locate their experiences of eroticism within their torsos as passion and nurturing. This provides a model of eroticism of wider application.

The conceptualist and minimalist element in Tom Arthur's installations and other sculpture removes all the indulgent superfluities that might produce murky effects in the dominant themes. The controlled selectivity means that the elements are effective triggers of networks of connections, memories and intuitions which may not be commonly verbalised, but which are not hidden in the unconscious. His signs are hyper-conscious and the act of exploration is, in the end, an act of reclamation.

Urszula Szulakowska, University of Queensland, October, 1987

THE ENTIRE CONTENTS OF A GENTLEMAN'S ROOM, 1987
Mixed media installation
300 × 860 × 720
Collection: The University of Melbourne

(Photo) Terence Bogue/Tom Arthur

RICHARD ARTSCHWAGER

Born Washington DC, USA, 1923

Lives and works in New York City

Richard Artschwager's work has gone in and out of public focus since its appearance in the early 1960s. Maker of dimensional painting-surrogates and pictorial, furniture-like sculpture, Artschwager has consistently sought to use art to alter the context of viewing. His attack on the conventions of art—how it should look, what its subjects should be, and its physical place in life—has been both radical and ingratiating. In this pursuit he has employed two principal tools: seemingly functional, body-scale objects and framed grisaille paintings that refer, literally and metaphorically, to the space inside and outside of themselves. His chosen media, formica and celotex, are unlikely carriers of meaning. But in his hands they are ennobled as art, which he defines as 'thought experiencing itself'.[1] For although his work is uniformly well made and physically appealing, its potency is as cerebral as it is sensual. Tactile and admirably crafted, it is intended above all else as a visual catalyst for thinking.

Artschwager was nearly forty before he was able to articulate his own aesthetic. An aversion to the Abstract Expressionist climate of New York in the 1950s and the need to earn a steady living (which he chose to do as a craftsman) delayed his artistic maturation. When he finally began to work seriously as a sculptor, he knew what he expected of his efforts; as he explained it some fifteen years later: 'It has been known since the Renaissance that art is produced by artists, and the notion has been available for more than a century that art is internal to the recipient; in a sense, "made" by the recipient. The first notion has tended to block off the availability of the second, and I think my contribution has been to make it not only available but Necessary, i.e. to force the issue of context, or to put it in more old-fashioned terms, to make art that has no boundaries.'[2]

As Artschwager worked with his chosen Photo-Realist, grisaille painting method, he realised the pictorial equivalence of celotex to the pre-patterned formica. When painted, the embossed, repeated patterns of celotex, either wavy explosions of concentric circular marks or interwoven cross-hatchings, were as visually loaded as formica. Both materials, with their inherent visual activity, simultaneously offer more than enough for the insatiable eye to read and prevent any attempt at holistic, instantaneous comprehension. Artschwager's work operates as a conceptual provocation rather than as an aesthetic manifestation. The sculptures exist as room-size monuments to furniture and the ghost-like celotex pieces as memorials to painting . . .

For twenty-five years, Richard Artschwager has sought to alter the context of viewing by making pictorial sculpture and dimensional, space-occupying paintings. Equally conceptual and physical, his work is not intended as a simple demonstration of thought or as a purely aesthetic experience. He engages mind and body by situating us in front of a thing, often familiar-looking and always convincingly well made. What he said of the early *Handle* could apply to all that followed: 'A grasp of the work is provided by the left and right sides of the work. This establishes the proper viewing distance for the work and locates the soles of the feet, also leaving a clear track between the work and one's shoulder and beyond.'[3] For Artschwager, that 'beyond' is a context without physical or theoretical boundaries, which he constantly invites us to enter. It is the vast intersection of thought and action, of looking and doing, of seeming and being; a place where enigma supersedes truth. And vice versa.

Excerpts from Richard Armstrong, 'Art Without Boundaries', *Richard Artschwager* (catalogue), Whitney Museum of American Art, New York, 1988

1. Richard Artschwager, unpublished lecture notes, California Institute of the Arts, Valencia, 1975.
2. Colin Naylor & Genesis P-Orridge (eds) *Contemporary Artists*, St Martin's Press, New York, 1977.
3. Richard Artschwager & Catherine Kord, *Richard Artschwager* (catalogue), Museum of Contemporary Art, Chicago, 1973.

The timelessness of Richard Artschwager's work is remarkable. Looking back at his production over the past twenty years, one can observe that it has always been at odds with the art around this production. His work has never lent itself to meaningful comparison, which may go a certain way to explaining why it has not aged—although this is not a criterion of quality. Cubist paintings by Braque or Picasso are clearly of their time, and so are, for example, Jackson Pollock's works. However, Artschwager's works, especially those after 1964, could have been made yesterday or today. At least that is the way I see it—and enjoy it.

Jean-Christophe Ammann, *Richard Artschwager* (catalogue), Kunsthalle Basel, Basle, 1985. Translated by Catherine Schelbert

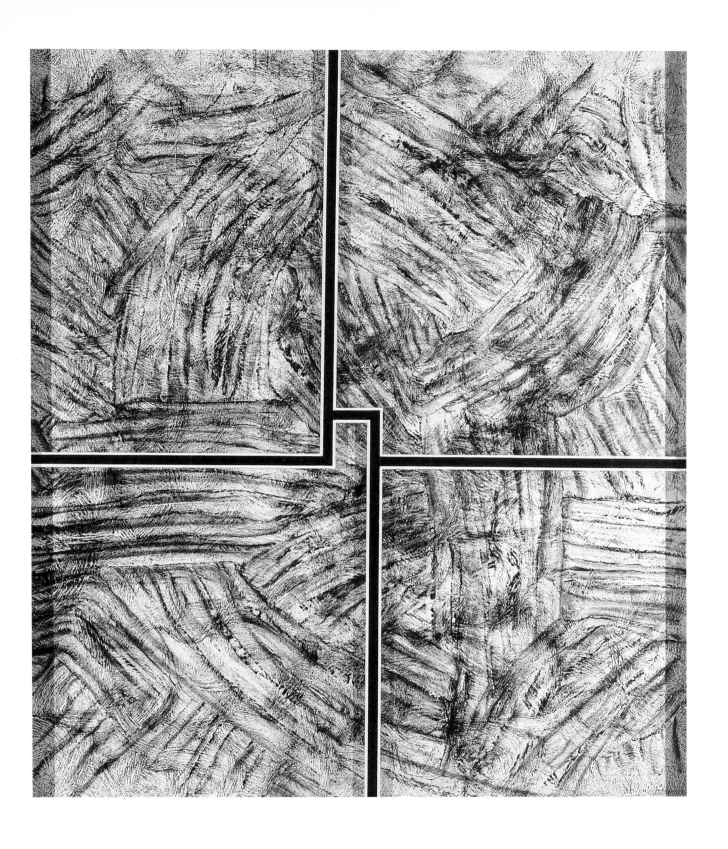

WEAVING, 1987
Acrylic on celotex and wood
157.5 × 136 × 10

GIANNI ASDRUBALI

Born Tuscany, Italy, 1955

Lives and works in Tuscany, Rome and Milan

DIALOGUE ABOUT

AN ABSTRACT FIGURE

GIOVANNI M. ACCAME: Rash and impervious but at the same time severe, your canvases appear like a space where signs, if certainly not born, meet up and find the best conditions for their actions. To me that much happens in your paintings. In the terminology of Gestalt Psychology you could say that your canvases constitute a 'field of strength'. This strength, concretised in a sign that passes, passes across and constitutes structure, seems to me to suggest the problem of an abstraction that does not abstract, or abstract itself, that doesn't seek to subtract but rather to shoulder the burden of its own presence until it makes out of itself an alluring and at the same time fleeting figure.

GIANNI ASDRUBALI: My signs are not motivated signs. They are born of an existential conflict that devolves on two constants: on the awareness of the alternative impressibility of the gesture and on the determination of a dead zone, pre-existent to action and that I call the zone of sense. In this conflict I am the super conscience that checks and blocks those signs in the magic instant of their appearance and of their denial of themselves. The sign gives itself and negates itself, and in this impossibility takes shape in a full structure that becomes the structure of your image. The image is yours because in the moment of its appearance it detaches itself from me and becomes everyone's. Abstraction is not the problem; the problem is the organisation of an image of sense that is strong and newly complex. A different image that constitutes itself in emptiness, an image without a father, because it is the offspring of itself.

GMA: Your painting has always had the need to express an experience that is born from antithetical forces. Some years ago the gesture would subdue its own violence and it would fold itself back in a deduced and shrinking form, while today the structure defines itself via a movement whose centre is the incessant losing of itself and confirming itself in the same flux. What made you seek to obtain a coincidence between the rapidity of the action with the stability of the image?

GA: What matters is not so much the rapidity of the action as the psychic motive that frees the movement of the action. The action is rapid because it has to block itself, its own motive that allows it to exist. The scream of the action must allow silence to emerge, the silence that looks over its shoulder, and then it must organise silence in a full image (a full void). In its turn the image becomes communicative via the action that blocks sense and its incessant movement.

The rapidity of the action and the stability of the image are therefore for me a single thing. Because the new image, which is the image of nothingness in movement, presumes them to be one and the same.

GMA: We know that today a vast and differently articulated area of work is being outlined, an area that for the most part revolves around an idea of abstraction where the border between reason and transgression, between rationality and risk has not so much to do with having a function which exists to separate as actually putting in communication.

Following on from your work, the two components already present themselves as being strictly complicit; or would you put them in a more dichotomous frame?

GA: In my opinion he who is only rational is mad, and he who is only irrational is mad just the same. You can't see things separately, there is always an organic and psychological relationship that cannot be ignored, otherwise you lose the sense of everything.

The problem is therefore not one of rationality and risk, the problem is both, because both exist, therefore you need to find the difference, to make a synthesis.

Maximum concentration and maximum constriction of all the forces at stake. This is what you have to do.

When I work I control and wreck everything, reason and madness converge and the work comes out of it whole and is therefore minimal and indivisible.

GMA: The strength, the compactness of your paintings is born, paradoxically, from a continual laceration. The huge gashes that you paint rarely converge, they are nearly always divergent. The centre of your paintings is not the centre of your gestures. Perhaps it is for this reason that you have spoken of a 'void' and of 'marble' as reconcilable values. In the sense of a gesture that crosses the canvas and creates a void, but leaves a resisting and persistent trail.

GA: The centre of my painting is the centre of my motivation and in this centre everything exists.

When I speak of a void, I speak of a dead zone which is however and above all a zone of life, because it is the generator of sense.

The void gives birth and thrusts forward the action in a full and affirmative gesture, and this movement in its turn folds back on itself. Incessantly until it makes of itself a structure, until it constitutes itself as an image of the void. The void becomes full, it takes shape and assumes the appearance of marble, and marble is as light as air.

GMA: This winter, shortly after a visit of mine to your studio in Rome, you wrote to me: 'The important thing is to construct an image of sense, complex, strong and new. Something that is inside and outside time in spite of time.' It is a phrase that appealed to me immediately because it is so contrary to the way in which art and artists couch their rationale today. Of course I record this phrase because I share its motivations and it interests me that it belongs to a young artist. The need to go beyond the climate that gratifies temporariness and nostalgia is not fortunately only yours. You, in your words and in your works, indicate it probably with more evidence, and also perhaps *because* you do so there emerges from your canvases more than a generic abstract picture, rather *an abstract figure*, a deep figure raised from the deep, and, as you say, that endures in time in spite of time.

GA: For an artist, as also for a scientist or a writer or a musician or whomever, who works at something that lasts for ever and who sees via the discovery of the new, the only real and vague problem is time. Time is ambiguous and ambivalent giving as it does the possibility of discovery which in its turn can then cancel such a discovery for a new one.

But it seems stunning to me that today many artists, those who emerged after the Transavantgarde, have forgotten the truth of this axiom (a mobile truth because ideas dictated by time are incessantly different in time).

By way of 'abstract figure' I would speak more of an 'organic/abstract' figure. My painting is not abstract, much less geometric, but substantially organic.

Excerpt from Giovanni M. Accame, *Gianni Asdrubali*,
Nuova Prearo Editore, Milan, February 1987.
Translated by Angela Kerley

NEMICO, 1987
Acrylic on canvas
230 × 165

(Photo) Carlo Cassani

FRANCIS BACON: I think that, when images drop in to me, although the paintings don't end up in the way the images drop in, the images themselves are suggestive of the way I can hope that chance and accident will work for me. I always think of myself not so much as a painter but as a medium for accident and chance.

DAVID SYLVESTER: Why do you say that?

FB: Because I think perhaps I am unique in that way; and perhaps it's a vanity to say such a thing. But I don't think I'm gifted. I just think I'm receptive.

DS: To some energy in the ether, so to speak?

FB: I think I'm energetic in myself and I think I'm very receptive to energy. By all this I hope you won't get the idea that I think I'm inspired—I just think that I receive.

DS: Do you feel that you might have worked in another medium— that you might have been a poet, that you might have been a film-maker?

FB: No, no. I think I even might make a film; I might make a film of all the images which have crowded into my brain, which I remember and haven't used. After all, most of my paintings are to do with images. I never look at a painting, hardly. If I go to the National Gallery and I look at one of the great paintings that excite me there, it's not so much the painting that excites me as that the painting unlocks all kinds of valves of sensation within me which return me to life more violently. I might make a film, but that would be even more complicated because I wouldn't be able ever to find the image which I can make with my painting. I don't know if in another medium things would come to me as easily as they are thrown down to me in my painting.

DS: Going back over those long discussions about chance or accident, I've been especially struck by two of the thoughts that recur. One is your dislike of paintings looking what you call 'chancy'. And the other is your belief that things which come about by chance are more likely to seem to have a certain inevitability than things which come about by will. Can you say why you feel that an image will tend to look more inevitable the more it comes about by accident?

FB: It hasn't been interfered with. And it seems to be fresher. The hinges of form come about by chance seem to be more organic and to work more inevitably.

DS: Lack of interference—is that the clue?

FB: Yes. The will has been subdued by the instinct.

DS: You're saying that, in allowing chance to work, one allows the deeper levels of the personality to come across?

FB: I certainly am trying to say that. But I'm also trying to say that they come over inevitably—they come over without the brain interfering with the inevitability of an image. It seems to come straight out of what we choose to call the unconscious with the foam of the unconscious locked around it—which is its freshness.

DS: Now, you often say that the accidents which are most fruitful tend to happen at the time of greatest despair about how to go on with a painting. On the other hand, when I once asked you whether, on days when conscious operations were going well, chance operations would also be likely to be going well, you said they would. Of course that statement isn't incompatible with the others, but could you enlarge?

FB: Well, there are certain days when you start working and the work seems to flow out of you quite easily, but that doesn't often happen and doesn't last for long. And I don't know that it's necessarily any better than when something happens out of your frustration and despair. I think that, quite possibly, when things are going badly you will be freer with the way you mess up by just putting paint through the images that you've been making, and you do it with a greater abandon than if things have been working for you. And therefore I think, perhaps, that despair is more helpful, because out of despair you may find yourself making the image in a more radical way by taking greater risks.

DS: You've told me that half of your painting activity is disrupting what you can do easily. What is it you can do easily and want to disrupt?

FB: I can quite easily sit down and make what is called a literal portrait of you. So what I'm disrupting all the time is this literalness, because I find it uninteresting.

DS: And I take it that marks made with the brush can be just as disruptive as operations like throwing paint or applying a rag.

FB: Oh certainly. With oil paint being so fluid, the image is changing all the time while you're working. One thing either builds on another or destroys the other. You see, I don't think that generally people really understand how mysterious, in a way, the actual manipulation of oil paint is. Because moving—even unconsciously moving—the brush one way rather than the other will completely alter the implications of the image. But you could only see it if it happened before you. I mean, it's in the way that one end of the brush may be filled with another colour and the pressing of the brush, by accident, makes a mark which gives a resonance to the other marks; and this leads on to a further development of the image. It's really a continuous question of the fight between accident and criticism. Because what I call accident may give you some mark that seems to be more real, truer to the image than another one, but it's only your critical sense that can select it. So that your critical faculty is going on at the same time as the sort of half-unconscious manipulation—or very unconscious, generally, if it works at all.

DS: Of course, trusting to chance seems to be something that pervades the whole way you live your life. For one thing, it's very obvious in your attitude to money. At the time I first knew you, you didn't get a lot of money for a painting but, even then, the moment you sold one you'd be buying champagne and caviar for everyone in sight. You never held back. You've always seemed free of prudence.

FB: Well, that's because of my greed. I'm greedy for life; and I'm greedy as an artist. I'm greedy for what I hope chance can give me far beyond anything that I can calculate logically. And it's partly my greed that has made me what's called live by chance—greed for food, for drink, for being with the people one likes, for the excitement of things happening. So the same thing applies to one's work. I nevertheless, when I cross the road, do look both ways. Because, with the greed for life, I don't play it in the way that I also want to be killed, as some people do. Because life is so short and, while I can move and see and feel, I want life to go on existing.

Excerpts from David Sylvester, *Interviews with Francis Bacon 1962–1979*, Thames & Hudson, 1975 and 1980

STUDY FOR THE HUMAN BODY, 1949
Oil on canvas
147 × 134.2
Collection: National Gallery of Victoria

RALPH BALSON

Born England, 1890

Died Sydney, Australia, 1964

Balson aligned painting to a model of science that was grand and romantic. Science encompassed experiment and analysis, but above all it was seen as the affirmative investigation of universal and timeless values. To Balson, painting too was an affirmative activity, and like science it was 'pure' in the sense that it pertained to absolute and benign laws of nature.

In explanation of the *Constructive Paintings*, a long series of geometric, non-figurative paintings which Balson first exhibited in 1941, Herbert Badham in 1949 restated the belief held by Balson that 'the source of true design is to be found in cosmic laws and that this truth offers a better basis for progress than any other'.[1] The language of this remark supports Balson's later admission that, especially in his geometric series, his 'greatest single influence' was Mondrian.[2] As early as the 1930s he had access to Mondrian's writings, notably the essay *Plastic Art and Pure Plastic Art*.[3] Mondrian urged a movement towards a spiritual though scientifically based art which embraced the universe and negated the individual ego, 'an evolution from the individual towards the universal, of the subjective towards the objective; towards the essence of things and of ourselves'.[4]

Science and art were seen as mutual concepts based upon inherent laws of nature. In practice what Mondrian called 'the true way of art'[5] became for painting a self-sufficient exercise concerning the formal relations of plastic elements on a picture plane. When Balson adopted purely geometric motifs in his 'Constructive Paintings', he was also adopting all the constraints of this shared, presumably objective style of painting.

Allusions to science continued through the non-figurative phases of Balson's work. Einstein especially fired his imagination, and during the 1950s changed his conception of the physical world and, correspondingly, his art. His acquaintance with Einstein's theory of relativity exposed the shortcomings of his more fundamental, mechanistic view of order and regularity. Balson began to appreciate a more complex and plausible model of science, as static unity gave way to the continuous flux and variability of an entropic, unbounded universe. It was a conceptual break which facilitated a stylistic shift, from the finite geometry of the 'Constructive Paintings' towards more exploratory, painterly procedures.

The 'Non-Objective Paintings', the series which flourished in 1956, after his retirement from housepainting, perhaps represented his maturity as an artist. They coincided with a number of statements in which Balson posited a visionary, allegorical role for his art, the first being in a letter to Michel Seuphor in 1955: 'It seems to me that today painting must dig deeper into the mystery and rhythm of the spectrum and that means existence of life itself. Not the age old form but the forces beyond the structure. Abstract, yes. Abstract from the surface, but more truly real with life.'[6]

The 'Non-Objective Paintings' consisted of an all-over, finely modulated field of dappled colour, which spread without major interval across the surface of each composition. In format and mood the paintings echoed the expansive fields of gesture and colour employed by the Abstract Expressionists in New York, whom Balson also acknowledged in his letter to Seuphor. There were affinities too with earlier painterly movements, to Seurat or Monet, but Balson looked outside the history of painting for his own explanations, as his note in the catalogue of the 1956 Pacific Loan Exhibition made clear: 'As one grows older one contemplates more and more, and maybe the ultimate goal of all the arts is the ineffable. With words James Joyce surely reached that condition in *Finnegan's Wake*, while in painting the Chinese came closest to it. I want my forms and colours to have the density and at the same time the fluidity of Joyce's words.'[7]

Balson may have responded too naively to science, making a fetish of its mystique, as some of his later critics have suggested,[8] but the allegory of science was a vital bridge for Balson, taking him out of his own individual circumstances into a wider community of thought. And then, despite the affirmation and idealism with which he had always embraced scientific theory, by 1962 he had come to recognise the human difficulties implied by his theoretical stance. There is an uncharacteristic and somewhat existential nihilism suggested in his last recorded statement, which he made that year. He described a 'world of ceaseless movement where reality is nothingness and nothingness reality',[9] a state of indeterminacy where man is no more than a 'lonely creature on his speck of matter'.[10]

After his exposure to European Tachism and Art Informel, during a trip to England and France in 1960, Balson commenced his last major series, the 'Matter Paintings'. Negating the meditative, formal procedures of his earlier work, Balson indulged in very fluid, automatic techniques, pouring his paint and allowing it to slip and bleed across the board and coagulate in heavy layers which cracked or rippled as they dried.

In the 'Matter Paintings' Balson took risks with his medium, and compared to the contemplative ease, the painterly refinement and subtlety of his previous series, they appeared to be difficult and restless works. But his current principle of indeterminacy stressed an infrastructure of variation, accident and growth, and it was as if Balson was putting this into effect. The 'Matter Paintings' were not to be seen merely as symbols, reflecting some notion of growth or change, but by their very form they demonstrated a truism, that as fully physical objects they were subject, like all physical objects, to natural, entropic processes. They seem to evoke Balson's earlier remark to Seuphor that he wished for an art 'more truly real with life', an art that was at one with the physical world.

The 'Matter Paintings' did mark a conclusive point in Balson's thinking. Paint was presented for what it was, a physical substance on a surface, obeying physical laws. It was not a vehicle for transcendence into some other realm. It was as if the scientific idealism of Balson's whole metaphorical quest for some universal 'essence' was finally resolved by a more earth-bound affirmation of physical fact. As Balson put it, rather rhetorically, in 1962: 'A rose is a rose because it's a rose. We don't try to make it a daffodil or a cabbage. Or do we?'[11]

Excerpts from Bruce Adams, 'Metaphors of Scientific Idealism: The Theoretical Background to the Painting of Ralph Balson', Anthony Bradley and Terry Smith (eds), *Australian Art and Architecture: Essays presented to Bernard Smith*, Melbourne, Oxford University Press, 1980

1. Herbert Badham, *A Study of Australian Art*, Sydney, 1949.
2. Ralph Balson, letter to Michel Seuphor, April 1955.
3. An English translation of Mondrian's 'Plastic Art and Pure Plastic Art' was available to Balson in the anthology *Circle*, edited by Ben Nicholson and Naum Gabo, London, 1937.
4. *Circle.*
5. *Ibid..*
6. Balson, letter to Seuphor, April 1955.
7. Balson, catalogue note, *Pacific Loan Exhibition*, S.S. Orcades, October 1956.
8. For example, Robert Hughes, *The Art of Australia*, Melbourne, 1970.
9. Balson, statement published in John Reed, *New Painting 1952–1962*, Melbourne, 1963.
10. *Ibid.*
11. Balson, letter to the Art Gallery of New South Wales, 1962.

NON-OBJECTIVE ABSTRACT, 1958
Oil on composition board
137.2 × 152.4
Collection: National Gallery of Victoria

Born into a cultured and cosmopolitan family that moved in high society in the 1900s, Balthus Klossowski de Rola was noticed at an early age by the German poet Rainer Maria Rilke. He soon became fascinated by the Far East, and also immersed himself in German and English literature—Hoffmann, Lewis Carroll and Emily Bronte. His series of illustrations for *Wuthering Heights* in 1933 was a glimpse into a timeless world steeped in the secret and fantastic moods of childhood, which Balthus would continue to explore. His first works appeared just when the critic Waldemar George was advocating a return to a neo-humanistic tradition, but they were nearer in some ways to the fringe of the Surrealist movement, as Balthus was very closely associated with such modern writers as Antonin Artaud and Pierre-Jean Jouve. It was Wilhelm Uhde, the champion of contemporary naive painters, who put on Balthus's first exhibition at the Galerie Pierre Loeb in 1934. Balthus, who at this time was associating with Derain, Gruber and Giacometti, now turned to the art of the past, to Piero della Francesca, Courbet and Cézanne, and tried to employ the lessons of these masters whom he so greatly admired in his own work, seeking to restore the quality of an interior vision which transcended the real. So Balthus cultivated an isolation which left him unknown to all but a small group of connoisseurs. After the war, two exhibitions at the Galerie des Arts in 1946 and 1956 revealed his work in all its silence and strangeness—an initiation that marked a significant rupture with the iconoclastic march of the avant-garde.

> Germain Viatte, 'Balthus', *Aftermath: France 1945–54*
> (catalogue), Barbican Art Gallery, London, 1982
> Translated by Sarah Wilson

It seems that painting, weary with describing wild beasts and extracting embryonic forms, wishes to return to a sort of organic realism, which far from fleeing the poetic, the marvellous, the fable, tends more towards it, but with certain means. For playing with the unfinished and embryonic aspect of forms to create the unexpected, the extraordinary, the marvellous, seems all the same, a bit too easy. One doesn't paint schemas, but the things that exist; one doesn't stop to study the work of the inarticulate with a microscope; but the painter, fully conscious of his means and his strengths, deliberately ventures into external space, and thence brings back objects, bodies, forms with which he plays in a more or less inspired manner. Balthus paints first of all lights and forms. It's with the light of a wall, a floor, a chair, or the surface of someone's skin that he invites us to enter into the mystery of a body with a sex that becomes distinct with all its harsh implications. A technique of David's time serves the violent, modern inspiration which is indeed the inspiration of a sick epoch, where the conspiratorial artist only makes use of the real for more effective crucifixions.

> Antonin Artaud, 'Exposition Balthus à la Galerie Pierre',
> *Nouvelle Revue Française*, no 248, May 1934

Balthus is haunted by the world of adolescence, by those troubled, hesitant, delirious moments which every adolescent has known, in the face of a world to conquer, a world where adults have decreed the laws which must be broken if life is to be breathed and lived as an adventure . . . Balthus is not only attracted by the 'Justines', as was Sade himself, he tries to evoke a picture of the world which surrounds these 'Justines'. He paints a universe in monochrome, filled with a majestic boredom. His windows look out onto princely courtyards, dusty, forsaken, where one contemplates the austere emptiness of a whole world in itself. It is here that Balthus represents better than any other the ambiguity of the actual world, where perverse reveries and the artist's own anxiety infuse the sinister and banal resignation of the bourgeoisie!

> Alain Jouffroy, *Arts-Spectacles*, no 557, 1956

NUDE WITH CAT, 1949
Oil on canvas
65 × 80.5
Collection: National Gallery of Victoria
Felton Bequest

What I want to show in my work is the idea which hides itself behind so-called reality. I am seeking the bridge which leads from the visible to the invisible, like the famous cabalist who once said: 'If you wish to get hold of the invisible you must penetrate as deeply as possible into the visible.' My aim is always to get hold of the magic of reality and to transfer this *reality* into painting—to make the invisible visible through reality. It may sound paradoxical, but it is, in fact, reality which forms the mystery of our existence. What helps me most in this task is the penetration of space. Height, width, and depth are the three phenomena which I must transfer into one plane to form the abstract surface of the picture, and thus to protect myself from the *infinity* of space. My figures come and go, suggested by fortune or misfortune. I try to fix them divested of their apparent accidental quality. One of my problems is to find the self, which has only one form and is immortal—to find it in animals and men, in the heaven and in the hell which together form the world in which we live. Space, and *space* again, is the infinite deity which surrounds us and in which we are ourselves contained. That is what I try to express through painting, a function different from poetry and music but, for me, predestined necessity . . .

Excerpt from 'Ueber meine Malerei', lecture given in London on 21 July 1938, in Mathilde Q Beckmann, *Mein Leben mit Max Beckmann*, Piper & Co., Munich, 1938

Max Beckmann regularly appears in three connections during discourses on German art: his vital early work in the Post-Impressionist style, then in the context of Expressionism and later in that of 'Neue Sachlichkeit'. His later work marks him as the great loner, creating extensive mythological portrayals of the time which fall into no category.

All three classifications have their justifications, but their definition of his work is too constricting. Max Beckmann did not grow out of Post-Impressionism, Expressionism and 'Neue Sachlichkeit' to become a unique figure in German twentieth-century art. He was not wholly part of the movements mentioned, even in the periods when he was closely associated with them or generally accepted to belong to them.

It is almost impossible to associate his early work with any contemporary movement in art, and his paintings were steeped in the traditions of the old masters. They essentially tended towards Realism and repeatedly depicted contemporary events. During a six-month stay in Paris in 1903 he was far more impressed by Delacroix than by Cézanne.

Beckmann's painting underwent a profound change as a result of his experiences in the First World War, and he adopted contemporary forms. Although his pictures now display aspects of Expressionist style, he is not motivated by the Expressionist vision of a uniform world which is found in Kirchner and the 'Brücke' painters. Beckmann's art is equally remote from 'Der blaue Reiter', from Franz Marc's crystalline forms and from the enthusiastic colour of August Macke.

By virtue of his pictures of the immediate post-war period and the early 1920s Beckmann has also been ascribed to 'Neue Sachlichkeit' . . .

Although Max Beckmann did not consider himself to be a member of any group or movement, the formula 'Sachlichkeit' (objectivity) appealed to him. He saw it as combining the two concepts 'Gegenständlichkeit' (figurative art) with 'Genauigkeit' (accuracy) . . .

The problem of the reason for our existence, the demand for knowledge of its metaphysical basis and the search for mythical order in the randomness of everyday life made Max Beckmann grow out of the bonds of 'Neue Sachlichkeit' despite his affinity with the way in which the movement regarded detail. This is shown most clearly in the different roles that objects were assigned by Beckmann and by the artists of 'Neue Sachlichkeit'. Objects had become so important to the painters of Objectivity because they appeared to be the last fixed entity one could grasp amidst the downfall of the old orders in religion, philosophy and politics. In Beckmann's work objects are loaded with meaning and full of hidden allusions. They never appear isolated and unrelated.

To Beckmann, objects are always both things and images. They exist within the context of a stage and play their part in the great world theatre, even though we may not immediately apprehend their role. At first, the artist is only a witness to this theatre but as time passes he learns to approach the figures with more confidence and finally becomes involved in the action and the creation of the universe. He is both king and jester, plays the part of martyr and clown and acts the criminal and victim.

The demand for Objectivity was applied more and more exclusively to the depiction of individual objects and not to the context they appeared in. The 'objectivity' of detail is replaced by the power of the 'inner visions' and subordinated to visions of space.

Space meant to Beckmann what colour did to Nolde. It was the great theme which dominated his life.

Excerpt from Wieland Schmied, 'Points of Departure and Transformations in German Art 1905–1985' in *German Art in the 20th Century, Painting and Sculpture 1905–1985* (catalogue), Royal Academy of Arts, London, 1985

AFTERNOON, 1946
Oil on canvas on plywood
89.5 × 133.5

Born Solothurn, Switzerland, 1948

Lives and works in Sintra, Portugal

SOME PREPOSITIONS

AND ASSUMPTIONS

UNDERLYING MY WORK

One thing that all utopias and visions of the ideal have in common is the assumption that it is possible to grasp, in its very essence, the world as we experience it: that there is some sentient or mental place from which all is surveyable and, therefore, at least indirectly controllable.

The inescapable conclusion that such an ideal state can never be attained seems in no way to lessen the need for (and usefulness of) reaching out for it. We derive satisfaction from moving towards the ideal, however fleetingly, by sensing the direction in which it lies, even when we know that what is gained today will be the starting-point of tomorrow. As in the race between the tortoise and Achilles, we can always cut in half the distance between us and our goal, keeping up the illusion of progress, only to be inexorably overtaken by the tortoise of entropy.

Landscape-painting is a subject-oriented utopia[1]: it does not want to teach, criticise, proclaim or convert; in fact, it is only truly seen by people who already practise some sort of landscape-gazing. It is this gaze that is both the means and the message: when, for example, we stand on a mountain-top, our eye wanders through the view with complete relaxation, not fixing on anything; the periphery of sight becomes as present as the centre and a certain timelessness sets in.

By landscape-painting I include the work of Rothko, Newman and Still, but also the monochrome work of people like Ryman, Klein and Mosset, the criteria being not the denotative elements of landscape, but the way the works make us look at them. In this sense monochrome painting becomes an axiom of landscape-painting, as we are given the choice of seeing it either object-related, by looking on the surface, or subject-related, by letting the eye transcend the surface into a vanishing-point perspective whose focal point lies at infinity. (This is stated very eloquently in a work by Anselmo, where he enlarged the dot of the 'i' in 'infinito' to a monochrome square of circa 40 by 40 centimetres.) In this way monochrome painting becomes a kind of litmus-test for our propensities, depending on whether we tend to look at, say, a two by four metre red painting by Mosset in the way we do a Monet waterlily painting or as a red object.

Statement by the artist, 1987 (adapted from text in catalogue, *Utopie in der Kunst*, Kunstmuseum Bochum, 1984

1. I divide the search for utopia by method into object-related and subject-related: the former aims at pacification and control of the actual world by conceiving of structural plans for an ideal society, presupposing the co-operation of everyone for their realisation. (Most political and religious systems fall into this category.) The latter, subject-related utopias, seek the ideal state on a personal level, with the idea that if we just learn to be, with and within ourselves, everything else will fall into place, making utopia available to everyone at any time.

UNTITLED (DIPTYCH), 1987
Oil on canvas and acrylic on wood
34 × 55 × 3

(Photo) Michael Biberstein

When an artist who has followed a personal course for many years is at a certain point 'discovered', the recognition often comes first from younger artists and critics who are attracted to and identify with the individualist or 'eccentric' quality of the work. Such is the case with Ross Bleckner, whose art is magnificently eccentric and individual. His paintings may be 'in style' right now, but they are not stylish, and never have been. Actually, Bleckner deals with such primary questions of painting as seeing and not seeing, and the classic physical and metaphysical subjects of birth (the realisation of being alive), love and death.

First and foremost, Bleckner's paintings are about light—about paint as light, object as light, light as symbol. Confronting their light, one discovers the space and the form of the works. Both in the early eighties and more recently, Bleckner has made 'stripe' paintings, canvases of long, narrow, usually vertical alternating bars. He calls the dark stripes 'gates'—they seem to stand between the viewer and the light evoked by the brighter stripes. He has also compared them to thin tall trees growing close together in a forest, and to telephone poles obstructing the view. All Bleckner's paintings are tightly structured and carefully blended, but it's most obvious in these stripe works. The edges of the stripes are blurred and soft, in an even, considered kind of way. They give the light a fuzziness, as if it were constantly contracting and expanding. The early images of this kind have a thick skin of glaze that stops you from seeing the light directly; in the recent ones the stripes themselves are the skin, as if they were protecting something inside the painting. In *Cage*, 1986, the light seems to flutter like the wings of some of the precisely rendered birds who fly or perch in this precisely unreal space, or like these small fragile creatures' racing hearts. All of the birds face in the same direction, perhaps the direction of hope—perhaps they hope to fly around the interior of the picture and behind the gates or bars into the open space, the light. One bird is caught within a dark stripe, in both a joke about painterly space and a metaphor for entrapment.

Light is not a light subject in Bleckner's art—it is the very atmosphere of his work, its material and immaterial substance. It creates both objects and spaces, symbolic chalices and chandeliers and airy corridors; sometimes it appears as just itself, in a scattering of spots, or in carefully controlled paths. Several paintings from around 1983 have the light we associate with Northern European art, here reimagined by an American artist (one work is entitled *Delaware*) and passing through like a breeze. Some of these paintings have the feeling of black and white, though actually other colours tinge or permeate them. The northern light sits on the surface of the image—it *is* the image, in landscapes and seascapes that look like religious paintings or romantic paintings, or like Turner's Venetian paintings. These are studies of seeing and of not seeing, as when one looks into a brilliant reflection or glare.

Historically, the word 'sublime' has connoted a range of ideas from awe through solemnity and immanence to their underside, terror; Bleckner's paintings are representations of those ideas in our time. His recent chandelier and light-spot works, with their overwhelmingly artificial quality of light, reflect the strange yet familiar feelings of deathliness we have right now, the awareness of death that touches so much of contemporary life. These paintings are pictures of the other side of the sublime, of the potential nothingness on the other side of the hypnotic image. But they are also about the joy of pulling an image of light out of darkness. Symbolic, surreal, and abstract all at once, their mysticism and poetry recalls William Blake and Odilon Redon.

Excerpt from Pat Steir, 'Where the Birds Fly, What the Lines Whisper', *Artforum*, vol. XXV, no 9, May 1987

HOSPITAL ROOM, 1985
Oil on linen
122 × 101.6

CHRISTIAN BOLTANSKI

Born Paris, France, 1944

Lives and works in Malakoff

DETECTIVE

These photographs appeared during 1972 in a magazine specialising in various subjects. The boxes of biscuits contain articles which relate to them; looking at these images, no one can say who was victim or criminal, the only thing that we know is that they are all linked to a drama.

Christian Boltanski, 1987

ARCHIVES: DETECTIVE, 1987
Installation on S.M. Amsterdam, 1987
Photographs, metal biscuit boxes, electric lights
400 × 1000

PIERRE BONNARD

Born Fontenay-les-Roses, France, 1867

Died Le Cannet, 1947

The presence of the object, the motif, is very restricting to the painter at the point when he is painting. Since a painting is based on an idea, if the object is there when he is working, there is always a danger of the artist letting himself be caught by the incidentals of what he sees immediately in front of him and losing his initial idea en route, so that after having worked for a while, he will no longer be able to recover that original idea again and will have recourse to the accidental. He will paint the shadows that he sees. He will try to describe such shadows as he perceives, such details as did not strike him in the beginning.

Excerpt from André Lhote, 'Le Bouquet de Roses', *Pierre Bonnard*, ed. du Chêne, Paris, 1944

Bonnard makes his own everything that nature can offer to his pictorial genius . . . He understands, loves and expresses everything he sees. Paul Signac

Bonnard's eyes, intent and patient, watchful, slightly slanted, and short-sighted behind his metal-rimmed spectacles, peer out at us from the self-portraits of his last years. But it could not be said of Bonnard, as it was of Monet, that he was 'only an eye'; Bonnard's form of realism is in no way a development of the naturalism of the Impressionists. Their serene objectivity is absent from his vision. The Impressionists started from an assured conviction about the actuality of nature, of light or atmosphere, whereas for Bonnard it was the subjective element, the play of sentiment and reason round what he had actually seen, the harmony between the scene before him and his own psychological and spiritual awareness, that determined his choice of subject, the form of a composition, the use of a particular light effect or a particular range of colours. He used his eyes as the means to research, in a basically poetic and symbolist way, into his whole experience of existence. Behind every formal invention, every compositional novelty, every figurative symbol of feeling and idea in his art, was his spontaneous response to the actual visible world. He worked by simultaneously extracting the rhythms of line and colour from nature and immersing all his senses and feelings in nature in order to set down images of a transient truth in all its aspects. From what he actually saw he extracted those elements that were most characteristic and most expressive of its real appearance, divorcing them from any possible literary and mythological overtones. Yet if Bonnard's vision of the world did not follow the Impressionists' account of external reality, it did not follow the Romantic illumination of a correspondence between sense and feeling either. His work, like the writings of Proust, gives us the very much more complex combi-nation of an image recorded at a certain time in a certain place with a sensation of the duration of time. His figures, caught in their momentary appearance, manage at the same time to live on memories and to evoke dreams; they function as both object and symbol, like the swan described by Mallarmé in his sonnet, 'Le vierge, le vivace et le bel aujourd'hui' ('The virginal, vigorous and beautiful today') . . .

There follows the marvellous series of nudes, of interiors, of meals on the terrace, of landscape vistas—intensely experienced pages from a diary of life, an existence continually investigated and analysed with the calm and tragic objectivity of true wisdom and with smiling comprehension. Nature and the atmosphere, the calm hours of the day are rendered in their joyous fascination as in their passive sweetness. Everything is dissolved in light and the stillness of time. The serenity of sheer description conceals the subtle torment of discernment. Fantasy and evasion are present but transformed among the various aspects of normal appearance. Even in the ever adolescent body of Marthe, the cool Eve of some already corrupt Eden, there are overtones of pain and mourning . . .

In all these pictures—views, still-lifes, nudes—the light gains resonance from the terracotta tonality, ebbs and flows in the handling, sizzles and showers like a hailstorm of pomegranate seeds. It is an eruption of burning matter, or a sheet of trembling transparency. The surface of the painting is as warm and thick as bread just out of the oven, as fragile and crumbling as an antique tapestry. The vision, the enchanted eye of this ever-young old man plucks elements from the spectacle of everyday life; a circus horse, domestic animals, a figure moving through the rooms of a house, the tiles of a bathroom, a bowl of fruit. Everything is both here and elsewhere, exists in both memory and fantasy. The miracle is born from analysis and the mirror records it. Bonnard sees all and tells all from his hidden position; he does not seem to intervene, but, with the genius born of the meeting between knowledge and recognition, is always there to give it form. He fills a corner of the canvas in such a way that the improvised scale creates an ecstatic space, giving us a glimpse of the actual process of creation in all its aspects.

For Bonnard, everything was contained in the tangible reality of life and everything could be said through the language of paint, very different from the language of theories and formulae. He said that it was easy to be an artist but difficult to be a painter. He did not think he had succeeded, but knew that he had tried with absolute dedication . . .

Excerpts from Franco Russoli, *Pierre Bonnard*, Purnell & Sons Limited, 1967

LA SIESTE, 1900
Oil on canvas
110 × 131
Collection: National Gallery of Victoria
Felton Bequest

Born Sheffield, England, 1940

Lives and works in Melbourne

Since 1970 Peter Booth has steadily emerged as one of Australia's finest painters. His work 'has a combination of bleakness and lushness that is a defining characteristic of ambitious contemporary figure painting in which drawing and composition remain essential', *New York Times* critic Michael Brenson wrote in 1986.

His early paintings, influenced by the American hard-edge style of the 1960s, are large in scale, abstract, and composed of flat areas of colour.

From 1970–74 Booth produced a deceptively simple series of black pictures, often edged thinly in colour. The character and surface texture of each work, done with quick drying acrylic, was changed by the manner in which the paint was applied. At times, pieces of paper, matches, grit, etc. were embedded into the face of the canvas.

While each painting has an elemental impact, its mysterious spatial aura is capable of provoking an intense emotional response in the onlooker.

In 1977 Booth's art became dramatically figurative. Private tensions, personal trauma and an eccentric imagination were the source for strange underworlds depicting the most aberrant human behaviour. With a dreadful immediacy and a palette of violent reds and blacks, these works tell of private nightmares. Unlike his earlier paintings they are executed in oil. With its in-built sensual and expressive qualities, it is a medium which Booth continues to use—with bare hands, palette knife or brush—to build up thick and textured surfaces recording his compulsive approach.

The overwhelming presence of paint adds to the dynamism of Booth's visionary art.

Jan Minchin, 'Peter Booth', *The ANZ Bicentennial Art Commissions*, ANZ Banking Group Ltd, Melbourne, 1987

BANSHEE, 1986
Oil on canvas
152 × 127
Collection: The University of Melbourne

(Photo) Terence Bogue

MARIE BOURGET

Born Bourgoin, Isère, France, 1952

Lives and works in Paris

'MY GOD, THE PAINTING IS FALLING!'

The pictorial modernity inaugurated by Cézanne can be seen as an exercise in deconstruction which 'gradually confines the subject and object of the painting to the signifying surface of the canvas'.[1] From this viewpoint, Toroni's painting is an example of the modernist pictorial practice maintaining just enough frivolity to avoid complete paralysis, whilst Ryman's painting, 'in its excess of reflexiveness'[2] merely delays the moment when the painted canvas becomes a solipsistic tautology. From the same angle Carl André brought the history of modernist sculpture to an end by adding volume and mass to the square. While the 'so-called naturalness of the old perspectivist order' lost all credibility and destroyed the classical notion of a subject 'in control of its perceptive field and its identity', the *signifying surface* ends up eventually referring only to itself.

The strategies implemented by post-minimalist artists sought to substitute language for the lost referent. Thus art, wrongly labelled as conceptual, is a statement where a variety of material procedures leads to an inscription of geometric figures onto surfaces or constructions in three dimensions. The visible object, however, originates in a code, while modernist painting refers to a non-coded reality beyond the painting (an exterior object, an 'interior' vision or an ideal space). In doing without a translation into images, the sculptural propositions of Lawrence Weiner address themselves directly to a viewer who is no more than a reader of a code.

When Marie Bourget presents us with something a little strange where disproportionately elongated stilt-like feet support a sloping plateau on which is placed a block of wood painted blue—and which she entitles *Tempête* (Storm)—one could see this as involving fairly traditional thought processes (halfway between representation and abstraction) coupled with timidity of approach in the choice of a simple noun as title. Or one could ally the *object* with an ideography: that is, with a system of signs representing Egyptian hieroglyphics or ancient Chinese characters, in which the meaning of the sign is closely related to the sensory experience. Yet what especially evokes the 'sculpture' of Marie Bourget is the mechanism of dreams, the structure of rebus in her phrasing, and her primordial ideographic characteristic where mental images and verbal formations are continually interconnected. It is the relationship between the word and the visible object that releases a stream of associations; the word substituting for the lost referent and the object for representation in a new relationship where the terms exchange priorities.

Sometimes it appears that we must interpret this world of symbols literally. It is like an exercise of language which occurs somewhere between sensory intuition and the word. A star is projected on the wall—a disc of light inside which the contours of a five-pointed star are haphazardly traced to create different arrangements . . . *disastrous*. A pentagon suspended by two black threads and three red from another star sketches the volume of a house. The eye here passes metonymically from contents—the star—to container—the pentagon (*Silence*). A horizontal line traced on the wall becomes a perspective point when projected from the ground—and creates a gabled facade. *Lac* (Lake) designates a sheet of paper painted blue supported by four hat-pins piercing it at each corner. Through a usage of the most common emblematic figures such as house, sky, stars, water, horizon, mountains . . . a play of figures operates which is not, however, figuration.

Here we are not dealing with the designation of a physical object or its negation, nor are we dealing with the manifestation of a real-life psychological experience—expressionism—or a symbolic demonstration. The sensory intuition *presented* to us—a sheet of paper painted blue—while associated with the word 'lake' in its lack of a functioning signifier, does give rise to an 'ideal objective unity which correlates with the act of perception'. Thus the flatness attributed to this object called 'Lake' is nothing more than sheer 'appearance', a surface effect without real depth! By arranging ten identical ideographic structures laterally from squares probably derived from Carl André, Marie Bourget has a quick look at the cubist problematic—trying to depict the object as perceived from all possible angles of vision on the flat surface of a canvas—an impossible compromise between surface and depth. Yet the main effect of these *unities* is that the spectator can lend his sensory intuition to an understanding of the natural landscape—mountains—and the constructed landscape—church tower. The reading of the works can thus proceed in the two senses—as if the notions themselves of natural and cultural landscapes were interchangeable stereotypes.

In the objects of Marie Bourget the loss of identity in favour of a stereotype intensifies in the presence of another object affected by the same phenomenon. Thus the mini-painting *Où* (Where?), as an empty frame, exchanges its quality of pseudo-painting for an appearance of depth with the addition of a column of wood as an extension. As well as this the image symbolically expelled beyond the painting traces its contours on the white page of the wall in a signifying ideographic 'progression' which simulates a *painting of a high mountain*.

The 'fabrications' of Marie Bourget are not pictorial, but they use the wall as a surface of inscription—a projection screen. Possessing neither volume nor mass, they cannot be seen as non-sculptural when they are inscribed three-dimensionally in the depth of space. In spite of their apparent fragility, the structures maintain a close relationship with volume. In classical representation, the point of view of the spectator is echoed at the vanishing point of perspective in a symbolic solidarity of subject and world. The spectator keeps distance from Marie Bourget's fabrications, but when they allude explicitly to a perspectivist projection, their orientation disallows any other manner of projection. This can be seen in *Point de Vue* (Point of View) and *Dessin* (Drawing) where a beam of light is projected along wall and floor, perpendicular to the field of vision. And if the traditional mechanism of a rectangular painting is seen as an open window to the world, it is to make it function as a mirror stereotype of cartoons, lit in such a way as to reveal no reflected image of depth.

'Depth spread out thinly has become breadth'[3] in a space of vast dimensions and shallow depth, the 'fabrications' avoid being locked up in a modernist tautology and become 'incorporeal'. Like Alice who grows and then gradually shrinks, Marie Bourget's propositions are often delivered in two senses, for example, from an *ideal unity* in the natural landscape to the constructed landscape, from mountains to house and vice versa. The spectator is not merely a subject opposite a model or a reader of a book, but is here invited to assist in an elegant and unusual translation into graphic form where artistic conventions and stereotypes, manipulated like signifiers, convey something that 'demands to be put into a phrase' and 'suffered wrongly' from this not happening before.

Excerpt from Claude Gintz, 'Mon dieu, le Tableau Tombe! . . .', *Marie Bourget*, ARC, Musée d'Art Moderne de la Ville de Paris, 1985/86.
Translated by Gretchen Cook

1. Thierry de Duve, *Nominalisme Pictural*, Les Editions de Minuit, 1984
2. Yves-Alain Bois, *Robert Ryman* (catalogue), Musee National d'Art Moderne, Paris, 1981
3. Gilles Deleuze, *Logique du sens*, Les Editions de Minuit, 1969

PEINTURE DE HAUTE MONTAGNE, 1985

(Photo) Galerie Claire Burrus, Paris

ARTHUR BOYD

Born Murrumbeena, Victoria, Australia, 1920

Lives and works near Nowra, New South Wales,

and in Suffolk, England

An outstanding feature of Arthur Boyd's *oeuvre* is its great variety. Landscapes, impressionist or expressionist, alternate with or combine with figure scenes; erotic or fantastic subjects occur alongside biblical or mythological scenes. Many of the latter are set into a bush wilderness; figures turn into animals; themes which occupied him in his youth reappear over the years in drawings, etchings, ceramic paintings; they undergo variations and sometimes reappear forty years later in a painting. He can work simultaneously in different pictorial modes, from lyrical landscapes to allegory, or both combined. The secret of Boyd's fecundity of invention is his sense of kinship with the whole world of art; past and present merge in his imagination. More than most Australian painters he is constantly aware of the Old Masters. Yet his work retains the unmistakable imprint of his own hand—set down, as it is, *alla prima*, swiftly with seemingly little premeditation. He often makes version after version, until the original impulse is exhausted. An unceasing flow of rapid drawings forms a *continuo* accompaniment to the painted *oeuvre.*

The most unusual element in Boyd's performance is the persistence with which he returns to his origins; the way in which both the art of his father and his own youthful work became a reserve from which he draws new ideas and to which he returns in between explorations of new ground. In the middle sixties he repeated a large number of drawings from his South Melbourne period, the imagery of which is again transfigured in even later works. The bush, conceived as primeval wilderness in the war years, provides the background for many of the Bride paintings of the fifties as well as for the *Nude with Beast* and Nebuchadnezzar series in the sixties. His tree forms were often related to the swaying lines of his father's pottery designs. His father's drawings of clumps of tree trunks as well as the Sherbroke Forest interior by Tom Roberts in the Art Gallery of New South Wales were points of departure for the vertical forest scenes of the seventies.

The roots of Boyd's figure compositions also reach back to family tradition, though not to paintings. Biblical stories read to him by his maternal grandmother filled his imagination with parables which have continued in his memory throughout his life . . .

When Boyd became acquainted with the theories and practices of Modernism he was made aware of methods of working radically different from those pursued by his family or prescribed by the National Gallery Art School. His early years coincided with the influx into Australia of Surrealism and Expressionism.

Boyd shared the Expressionists' conviction that the purpose of art lies in the combination of significant content with a form that immortalises it.

One may ask to what extent such a belief finds expression in landscape painting. It would be misleading to describe Boyd's work as alternating between modes of working; to divide it into realistic renderings of nature and imaginative compositions, or to oppose *plein air* and studio painting. Even his landscapes go beyond mere resemblance to reality. In many of the early figureless scenes, obtrusively handled dead trees, skeletal forms and black crows evoke intimations of death. The arid open air settings of the painter *in extremis* have symbolic significance . . . Bush scenes painted in the Shoalhaven region seem meticulously 'real' compared with earlier bush scenes in Boyd's *oeuvre*; it was the relatively untouched nature of the area that had attracted the artist to it. The portrayal of its riverbanks no longer romanticises the bush, but neither are the paintings literal transcripts of a given spot.

He gives a diagrammatic account of its formation and a graphic image of the precarious hold in the ground of the fragile eucalyptus of that region. The element of destruction in nature itself, the struggle of each live organism against chaos as well as the threat posed to nature by man's activities are present in the Shoalhaven landscapes, just as they had been present in a different form in earlier landscapes. Boyd now looks at the scenery with the objective eye of the naturalist as well as with the anxious care of the conservationist. The subjectivity of the expressionist trend has given way to a new classicism.

Boyd is the only Australian painter I know of who has explicitly used his art to justify or question the artist's calling. The distracted scenes of the early seventies are unprecedented even in his own *oeuvre*. One is reminded of Picasso's illustrations to Balzac's *Chef d'oeuvre inconnu*, which deal with the painter's increasing estrangement from reason and reality, and of Picasso's drawings of the painter and his model. Both series arose from the Spanish artist's fear of aging and of losing his inspiration. They are personal and humorously resigned. Boyd's thoughts tend towards a trans-cendental despair inspired by the times in which we live.

Throughout its varied and manifold imagery Arthur Boyd's art remains fundamentally consistent and coherent in its aim. The spirit of Art Nouveau which inspired Merric Boyd's decorations and drawings and the *fin de siècle* mood inherent in the novels of Martin Boyd have sustained Boyd's art in all its phases.

Excerpts from Ursula Hoff, *The Art of Arthur Boyd*,
Andre Deutsch, London, 1986

BATHERS AND PULPIT ROCK, 1984/85
Oil on canvas
244 × 457
Collection: Queensland Art Gallery

GEORGES BRAQUE

Born Argenteuil, France, 1882

Died Paris, 1963

Braque always claimed that the paintings of his Fauve period were his first truly creative works. Of Fauvism he later said, 'that very physical painting delighted me'. Towards the end of his life, however, Braque was unable to recapture his enthusiasm for a style which he had come to find contrived and artificial. Yet this was understandable in an artist, who, at the end of his career, was able to discuss his own work in these terms: 'You see, I have made a great discovery: I no longer believe in anything, Objects don't exist for me except in so far as a *rapport* exists between them, or between them and myself. When one attains this harmony, one reaches a sort of intellectual non-existence—what I can only describe as a state of peace—which makes everything possible and right. Life then becomes a perpetual revelation. That is true poetry.' And indeed Braque's artistic evolution can be seen as the gradual transformation of the physical into the metaphysical, a movement from the world of clearly defined ideas and intentions to the world of abstract speculation which at times borders on mysticism.

Excerpt from John Golding, *Georges Braque*,
Purnell & Sons Limited, 1966

The colour came later. A space must be created before it can be furnished. But once created, it must be furnished. And that was another key moment for Cubism: it was the reaction against local colour that produced both the palette that was used and, later, the paper collage. But it's very difficult to explain all that . . . It's also very difficult to understand how that progression was made in my case ... As to local colour, first you draw the object, don't you, and implicitly it has its colour? So, you've noticed that colour operates independently of form. Look, you put a touch of yellow there and another on the other side of the canvas and there immediately arises a relationship between them. Colour works like music, if you like. I'm not saying that this is a discovery. On the contrary, this independent action of colours has long been sensed by painters, but we concentrated all our attention on it. That was what we started from, but as soon as you start doing it, you must stop calculating— that's the only reason why it lives: it has stopped being speculative in order to become real—I've thought a lot about all these things and it's very difficult to account for them.

Excerpt from Dora Vallier, *Braque, La Peinture et Nous*,
Cahiers d'Art, XXXIX, 1953

Art is made to disturb. Science reassures.
I do not do what I want, I do what I can.
You must not imitate that which you wish to create.
There is only one thing of value in art: that which cannot be explained.
I like the rule that corrects emotion.
Every situation is always complementary to the one that has preceded it.
The painter thinks in forms and colours, the poetry is in the object.

Excerpt from Maurice Gieure, 'Réflexions', *Georges Braque*, ed.
Pierre Tisne, Paris, 1956

LES CHAMPS (CIEL BAS), 1956
Oil on canvas
27 × 45

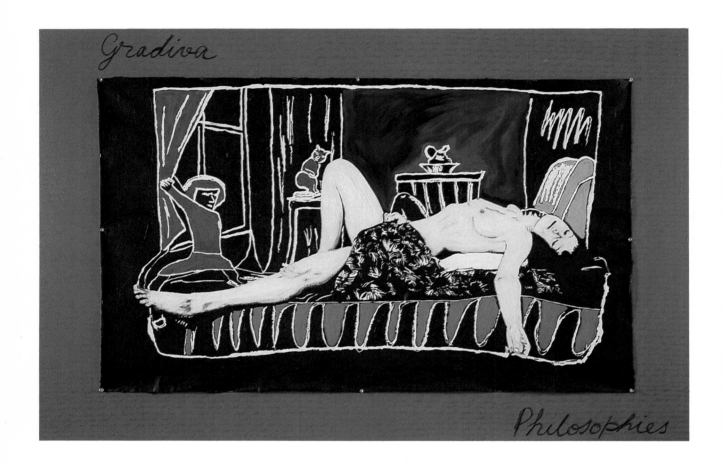

TRANSPOSITIONS

Text 1

Woman's special form of neurosis would be to 'mimic' a work of art, to be *a bad (copy of a) work of art*. Her neurosis would be recognised as a counterfeit or parody of an artistic process. It is transformed into an aesthetic object, but one without value, which has to be condemned because it is a *forgery*. It is neither 'nature' nor an appropriate technique for reproducing nature. Artifice, lie, deception, snare—these are the kinds of judgements society confers upon the tableaux, the scenes, the dramas, the pantomimes produced by the hysteric. And if woman's instincts try to command public recognition in this way, their demand and de-monstration will be met with derision, anathema and punishment. Or at least by belittling interpretations, appeals to common sense or to reason. A society has the duty to ban forgeries. And the hysterical woman who flaunts an appearance exceeding and defying the natural, the legally sanctioned mean, must be chastised. She must be curbed, humiliated, brought back to chastity, whether she likes it or not. Asceticism, decency, shame, are the forms of 'sublimation' required of woman.

Luce Irigaray, *Speculum of the Other Woman*

THE INVISIBLE BODY

Text 2

It is this other space of the studio, of the body of labour, which western painting negates; we are *given* the body with an intensity of disclosure and publicity without counterpart outside Europe, but it is the body in a different guise, as picture, to be apprehended simultaneously by the Gaze: the Gaze takes the body and returns it in altered form, as product but never as production of work; it posits the body only as content, never as source. Compensating this impoverishment of the body, the tradition rewards it with all the pleasures of seduction, for the body of the Gaze is nothing other than a sexual mask: the galleries of the West constantly display the Gaze of pleasure, as an archive that is there to be cruised.

The body of labour, in its studio space, is hidden by the brilliance of the posture, the facial or bodily feature, in which the viewer discovers his or her sexual interest: it is through the mask of seduction that the *scaena* becomes most coherent and most opaque—through local and libidinal fusions that the image solidifies around the 'this', this moment and this body of pleasure, in the here and now of its sexual engagement; the *durée* of labour gives way to the immediacy of appetitive time.

Norman Bryson, *Vision and Painting*

GRADIVA/GRAVIDA—PHILOSOPHIES OF THE BOUDOIR, 1985/86
Photo-emulsion, acrylic, oil on canvas on three-ply
Two panels, each 122 × 183

THE INDEPENDENT

An artist has no profession.

Nor has an artist a calling.

An artist only banishes from time to time a fixation of being able to evade death.

Death has no profession.

Death only banishes the fixation of some beings who are able to fathom it.

Were God a merciful natural scientist, then he would have enlightened the world—that place where beings shiver, with only occasional relief.

He, however, a harsh captain in the gods' war of succession, declares himself from the beginning to be a magician's assistant when it comes to the BIG MACHINE.

The Independent understands that the BIG MACHINE is eternal. However, this eternity is determined only by the individual's GRAND DEATH or by the MINISCULE LIFE OF ETERNAL variety.

The GREAT VARIETY ultimately solves the question of death. Namely, when WE, GOD and the BIG MACHINE have become one, then the question of where We, God and the Big Machine come from is no longer posed.

The degodified God machine WE will continue questioning—continue driving, and it will be allowed to enjoy a different kind of happiness in life: relaxed, free of religion, refreshed by a primeval sleep.

Only out of the subsistence minimum of the INTENSIVE CARE UNIT can the sought-after goal of UN-COLOUR be achieved—and only out of the subsistence maximum SELF IMMOLATION.

Art (in the meantime off taking the cure) only promotes clique wars because it only fathoms itself as a salon religion for the initiated.

Long live the artless joy of the MUNDANE!

Statement by the artist, 1987

DER SELBSTMENSCH, 1987
Crayon on paper
No 1 in a series of five, each 106.5 × 80.5

Born Sonthofen, Allgäu, Federal Republic of Germany, 1944

Lives and works in Cologne and Marrakesh, Morocco

THE LAST SECRET OF FATIMA

In 1917 in the Portuguese province of Estremadura, three shepherd's children from the village of Fatima experienced a vision of Mary as 'Mother of God of the Rosary' walking along and prophesying. In the same year the vision repeated itself continually and the predictions were fulfilled. Fatima became a place of pilgrimage.

One of the sisters is still alive today and, according to the legend, the last secret of the Fatima revelations cannot be disclosed until the death of this last sister.

———————————

Michael Buthe entitled his 1986 installation 'The last secret of Fatima'. It is comprised of four multi-sectional panels and several sculptures. In four stages he outlines a process of clarification in terms of content and form, which begins with the first tableau, an assemblage of painting, collage and gold and velvet panels. By orientating these panels around an almost magnetic centre, their highly conflicting powers are unleashed to build up two antagonistically opposing cycles of energy: the one where the quietly pulsating warmth of the gold is prevented from flowing naturally into the heat-accumulating velvet, and the circulation is again allowed; the other in the thick density of colours thrust against each other in the painting and collage zone and the devastating collection of human images as objects. The energy developing here is simultaneously disintegrating, expending itself the moment it emerges. Both cycles of energy stand face to face in hostile polarity, representing the principles of construction and destruction fighting for priority.

In the next phase Buthe filters into both triptyches the dynamic primal power of his painting, preserving two qualities of this energy: gold and silver with their respective colour equivalents red and blue as an antagonistic concentrate. The sources are respectively the middle gold and silver panels, which transmit their heat and cold potential to the red and blue side panels. Their vigorous application of colour is reduced to a uniform surface under the network of stars drawn on top, even to the tiniest ornamental element. While gold and silver became the light of colour, thus equally composed of wave and warmth, they pit their strength against the sunlight and become autonomous. And because the physical energy of the colour corresponds to its psychic energy, it becomes clear why Michael Buthe conceives gold and silver as states rather than non-material elements.

In the last process of clarification, colour is completely filtered out—what remains is the primal energy behind it: gold as the symbol of the most intensely energetic supercharge, over which stretches the red membrane of stars, as sculptural rudiment as it were.

Thus Buthe has extracted from his images via an almost chemical process their biggest abstract concentrate. He then confronts this distillate with sculptures in the same space, figures of animals, masks and idols, which in all cultures are the symbolic bearers of natural energies. They come about when those primal energies are conjured up; energies civilised man can no longer utilise, of which he is no longer even aware. When Buthe creates these sculptures, the same natural energies which he previously extracted as essences from his images are again conjured up. Abstraction and figure are concentrated in the elementary sculptural desire of man.

With this work Buthe achieves an essential narrowing of his image language, those dynamic basic elements made up of his images and sculptures, as he replaces the sign with the direct energy symbol. Naturally his signs refer to everyday objects and idols of foreign cultures, their market scenes as rituals. The energy forming them, however, springs from a higher individual experience, which does not recognise the heterogeneity of another civilisation. For in this recognition, the 'otherness' becomes a component of our own personality; the collective primary substance is integrated. Buthe is not concerned with the translation of a cultural phenomenon in his image world or with a so-called illustrative process—rather, he is concerned with tapping into the energies stored there and conveying these through his artistic work.

In this liberation from all sculptural burdens, in this filtering and concentration process, Buthe's hopes of the contents of the last prophecy from Fatima are formulated: to strengthen the extremely fine umbilical cord that connects mankind to the natural primal energies, and once again to build up that cycle of energy, whose qualities preserve contemplation.

Juliane Schulze
Translated by Gretchen Cook

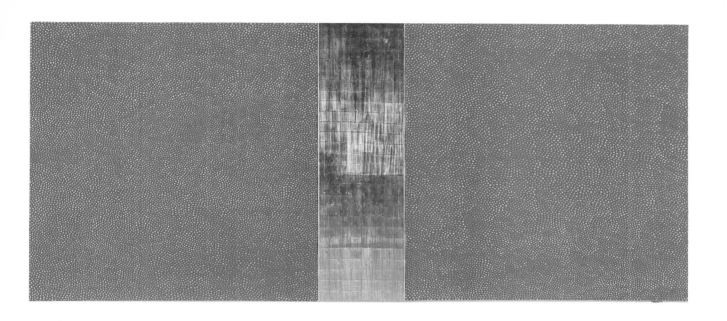

LE DERNIER SECRET DE FATIMA, 1986
Oil and gold on canvas
200 × 460
(Photo) Friedrich Rosenstiel

LE DERNIER SECRET DE FATIMA, 1986
Oil and silver on canvas
200 × 460

(Photo) Friedrich Rosenstiel

Voilà le meilleur portrait que, plus tard, j'ai réussi à faire de lui.

Geneviève Cadieux elaborates on the condition of the gaze where image, system of representation and spectator are closely interwoven. Her installations summon multiple references to the histories of painting, photography and film, and in their representation of women, evoke notions of sexuality, voyeurism and power. Whether the images are archaic and charged with historical connotations, or portraits of anonymous, contemporary subjects, or even a juxtaposition of the two, women are subjected to a mechanical representational apparatus, alternately revealing consent to being objectified and resistance to the authority of the photographic system. The artist's attitude oscillates between modesty and respect for the subject on the one hand, and exposing the inherent violence and voyeurism of the photographic image on the other. A similar ambiguity governs her relationship to the photographic system; often working with equipment that predates modern apparatus, the artist pays homage to the history of photography, while at the same time inferring a subjectivity by deploying various strategies to subvert its function.

Serge Bérard, *Lumières/Perception-Projection*,
C.I.A.C., Montreal, 1986

LA BLESSURE D'UNE CICATRICE OU LES ANGES, 1987
Photo enlargement, gouache, paper and wood frame
Two elements, 297 × 231 × 17 and 300 × 300 × 9

(Photo) Louis Lussier, courtesy Galerie René Blouin

SARAH CHARLESWORTH

Born East Orange, New Jersey, USA, 1947

Lives and works in New York

Sarah Charlesworth is an artist who, while engaging questions of photographic representation, has developed a genre of images that refuses to submit to the dominance of the word. They are images that, by her own account, position themselves specifically in a visual language: 'the problem of unwriting is for me a far more interesting challenge than the problem of writing'.

In a deliberate attempt to define how a photographic image communicates to us, that first generation weaned entirely on photography and TV, Charlesworth hands us the image framed, hermetically sealed from all encroaching images, demanding to be processed in its own proprietary vacuum. A Charlesworth is both concrete object/real image and, at the same time, pure ephemera— asserting simultaneously an aggressive/alluring physical presence as object and a denial of tangibility as image. The object, laminated with matching lacquered frame, presents itself as Fact. But the image itself resides in that purgatory that is the first home of photographs, the neither here nor there of ontological identity.

As an image it is 'objective', yet our cognitive perception does not remain static; we weave back and forth in our seduction/repulsion. It is the viewer's subjectivity which is always brought into question. Do we like David Bowie's cool or do we find the narcissism repulsive? Do we find reassurance in the sense of eternity with which the status is imbued, or do we find the religious classicism too historically remote and alienating?

There is a parallel dialectic in the relationship between the apparently 'positive' presence of the primary, central image and the apparently 'negative' background. But the background is not neutral: it is an active and significant element in the whole . . .

The background's absence of tangible facts also serves as a visual reminder of absence in general; i.e. what has been edited? . . . What is missing sets in relief that which is present. Photography gives us a glimpse into the kind of ontological absence which the speed of real-life activity obscures. It is a glimpse into what Buddhists called 'Sunyata', or the doctrine of emptiness. But this notion of absence is far from nihilistic: 'being "serenely vibrant" it has both negative and positive facets'. Whereas definition is the marking of boundaries or limits, the insistence on the notion of absence in Charlesworth's work reveals a visual, as opposed to verbal, point of view. It is thus that the entire image, as object, speaks of the dialectical presence and absence that is at the very heart of the photographic experience. And, by definition, that absence is non-verbal . . .

Each isolated image is completely and bluntly a categorical self-definition; i.e. It is a Bride, It is a Statue, etc. It is the embarrassing Achilles' heel of Idealism. No one can really believe in this. But no one can really disbelieve or ridicule this. The strict theology of the didactic stereotype cannot keep itself afloat in the age of deflated belief-systems, but nor can it be completely discarded. The repulsion/attraction toward the meaning of an image is as rapid and as integral a part of the pieces as is the viewer's response to the background/frame. These images elicit a kind of ambivalence, a love/hate response to a cultural given. Both end in an extreme confrontation with visual language, that purgatory of recognition.

Not everyone has always believed in the problematic and eternally fluid nature of definitional language. Structuralism assumes (or desires) the revelatory powers of language. It assumes (or desires) a language model with which life could be informed. Saussure, by accelerating the shift away from the study of discrete objects (such as were the subject-matter of biology and pre-Einsteinian physics), to the study of methods, secured a direction that was followed by other linguists and structuralists; namely, the programmatic use of the model.

This notion of language, wherein the linguistic signs perform a reactive function revealing deep social connections and psychological meanings, is at basis a synthetic one. Language and symbols are not in themselves natural responses to the world. They are constructed out of our social connections and our individual responses, making the privileged object of structuralism the unconscious value system on which we base our existence.

What Charlesworth has done is to completely and radically challenge some of the static assumptions of structuralism, while still retaining an interest in the political and deconstructive aspects. She, like many other people whose trade is not in the word-business, rejects the verbal language model as a definitive organising function. If our generation is about anything, it is about growing up with the photograph, knowing how to read a photograph, knowing how to decipher the world through its represented forms.

But the effects of this are much more than 'just looking at the pictures'. Some of the very serious pitfalls in structuralism have been successfully addressed by Charlesworth. In its original intent, structuralism was an attempt to escape from the rigid idealism of the continental thinkers, particularly German Idealism. Language was not 'natural', ideal and unchanging, but was rather a result of societal connections. But, with its emphasis on the signifier, structuralism placed us several steps away from the word's referent in the real world. It was the sign that was under discussion. And, with the increasing tendency to locate meaning in the connections between different signifiers, the effect was to exclude any investigation into the thing itself. This isolated the mental framework, 'thereby reinforcing the very same idealist tendencies that it intended to overcome'.

What Charlesworth has done is to extract the image from any associated dialogue, to let the image breathe, to let it generate the visual dialectic between its inherent oppositions. Meanings in a Charlesworth are not didactic and the oppositions are not static, binary oppositions. The unconscious, to Charlesworth, is not a static given but a responsive function continually informing and informed by the world . . .

Visual perception is more like ad hoc rapid computerisation than it is an adherence to a pre-defined and idealistic model based on static, binary oppositions. The presence of information is constantly being negated by its contradiction (or its absence), thereby resolving into a new edition or vision. Perception is a resolvent; it is as informed by an absence as it is by a presence.

Charlesworth's work is an aesthetic slo-mo examination of what happens every time we look at a photograph. We think we instantly understand, there's a tiny fraction of a second where we see that an element slips between the fingers of the symbolic coherence, and then the (usually) ignored conclusion that an image has instantaneously transcended itself from the everyday familiar to the realm of the-thing-not-in-itself. It is that which mutely speaks of the visual.

Excerpts from Dena Shottenkirk, 'Sarah Charlesworth, Imaging the Other', *C Magazine*, Spring 1987

BUDDHA OF IMMEASURABLE LIGHT (DIPTYCH), 1987
Laminated Cibachrome prints with lacquer frame
Two interlocking panels, each 101.6 × 76.2

(Photo) International With Monument Gallery, New York

Born London, England, 1956

Lives and works in London

CITIES ECLIPSED,

SPACES REINVENTED

Cities also believe they are the work of the mind or of chance, but neither the one nor the other suffices to hold up their walls.
You take delight not in a city's seven or seventy wonders, but in the answer it gives to a question of yours.
Or the question it asks you, forcing you to answer, like Thebes through the mouth of the Sphinx.

Italo Calvino

If the city becomes the sum of its fragments, how can it pose and answer questions in its constellation of spaces and arrangements of interiors demarcated by the outside? In Hannah Collins' images of isolated, 'emptied' interiors and barren desert views, connections are mapped and responses triggered against the imaginary backdrop of urban activity. In its difference or absence (deserted, the desert), the city nonetheless makes an entry in an edited and distanced form, not to reveal some neglected aspect in need of documentation—a truth to be recognised and understood—but to propose 'ways of seeing' which can draw on and bring into play different registers of knowledge and experience. The photo pieces attempt to articulate an edge where the desire for interpretation meets with the refusal of the image to announce its *raison d'être*. It is perhaps worth remembering that the Sphinx, too, marked an edge, a divide. Half-woman half-beast, occupying the borderline between city and desert, her riddles threatened the logic of civilisation and its economy of identification.

In *Things Covered and Emptied*, the bareness of walls and floor hidden behind plastic and cardboard covers can be imagined, but no indication is given as to the purpose and function of the space. Neither do the traces of human occupation/activity point to a reality outside the picture. There seems to be no obvious reason for the space to exist, and to exist in its particular form. The text fragments add to rather than diminish the conceptual distance between spectator and image. What might be called the 'resistant' quality of the work is further stressed through the emphasis on surface by means of balanced lighting and a low camera angle, which combine to flatten the pictorial space. As a consequence, the identity of what is seen oscillates between a large interior and enclosing surfaces that act as barriers to 'vision', restricting the movement of the I/eye across the image that is placed in uncertain co-ordinates of time and place. Like a film still separated from its narrative structure, the image is 'frozen' in the vacuum created by an apparent absence of context and history.

Possibilities of articulating the subjective in terms other than 'individual experience' have for some time been a central concern of critical post-modern theory and art practice alike. The issues surrounding considerations of subjectivity and representation have most consistently been explored in relation to film and, since the 1970s, a number of artists have drawn on the insights of film theory both to question and subvert what could be called the 'ideology of the look'. Hannah Collins' work cannot be separated from this critical tradition, but it also marks a shift of emphasis, discernible in other recent photographic work as well, from deconstruction to an aesthetic that tries to move beyond the dichotomies of Subject/Object and Same/Other. Again, film provides an important point of reference for this 'logic of the image'.

Collins' photographs relate to film in a number of ways, most obviously in their size analogous to the cinema screen and in their 'frozen' quality reminiscent of film stills. But a third, less readily discernible, connection can be established which, I believe, relies on the first two and combines them to elicit a response to the work in terms of effect. Not the result of interpretative function (the symbolic level), which may produce feelings of awe, fear, uneasiness, etc., the effect seems to be generated by the uncertainty, the not knowing of the boundaries within which the encounter between image and subject takes place.

In his discussion of stills from Eisenstein's films, Roland Barthes distinguishes between the obvious and the obtuse meaning of the film still and insists that the latter is carried not by knowledge but by emotion. Both meanings co-exist, but unlike the obvious, the obtuse meaning resides outside the language system; it is a signifier without the signified, which interferes with metalanguage (of interpretation and criticism): it can be recognised but it cannot be named.

However, the image effect can also be considered as having a twofold and contradictory function specifically in relation to (film) narrative. On the one hand it acts as a catalyst inducing and propelling the narrative, on the other hand it remains outside the story as a kind of passive expenditure, persistent and tenacious. Acting as the *mise en scène* of narrative, it simultaneously disrupts the signifying chain. In this capacity it has been used as a deliberate device to dislocate and problematise the patterns of identification that classical narrative cinema holds out. One might think of recurrent images in films by Tarkowsky—a large wooden gate, for instance, opening onto a brick wall and thereby erasing the difference between open and closed. Whatever symbolic significance might be attributed to this image, the absence of narrative links to the preceding and subsequent frames prevents the picture from definitely falling into place. Less symbolically loaded, the opening sequence of *Down by Law* (1986), a film by Jim Jarmusch, presents the rapid succession of facades of houses lining a street. Appearing wholly two-dimensional, the representations of these buildings contradict the very concept of a house. Like in dream images or those impressions on the verge of sleep, distinctions between the 'real' and the 'fantasised' break down as the ego loses its grip on what is seen. A different kind of structure begins to unfold around the hidden or eclipsed. This structure is not centred in the individual conscious or unconscious and productive of unmediated personal expression as most surrealists believed. Rather it is a socio-psychological process that is constituted through the (largely unconscious) discriminatory mechanisms of recognition and identification. Closer perhaps to Kristeva's notion of *significance* than simply a matter of repression or alienation, the eclipsed resurfaces at the moment when the image loses and re-invents itself in the reality of artifice.

Desa Philippi, October 1987

Everything was covered in it and everyone was coated in it and people couldn't find one another.

Amounts gathered

THIN PROTECTIVE COVERINGS, 1986
Gelatin silver print mounted on canvas
670 × 366

ROBERT COMBAS

Born Lyons, France, 1957

Lives and works in Paris

THE WORK OF ART
AS A CRITIQUE

There is no denying that Art, over these past decades, and in particular that of the sixties, has devoted all its energy to imitate science and extol the notion of materiality, while asserting a determined dedication to literature, thereby requiring the work of art to prove its 'moral' (and artistic) legitimacy through the endorsement of theoretical speech. But it is nonetheless quite obvious that a number of artists have, over these past few years, sought to play down this dedication to theory and stress the value of action. Actually, they have chosen to focus again on the work of art itself as the key element which gives rise to both theory and action, energy and meditation. In this perspective, the work of art is seen as a constantly active organism. This is precisely the case with the work of young French artist Robert Combas. Indeed, his works make up a perpetually open structure, and this is the reason why they are in constant need of new fuel in order to stay alive. Needless to say, such nourishment implies the presence of the 'Other', namely, the spectator. The latter finds himself connected, through a complementary relationship of mutual dependence, with the works of the artist. The artist needs the spectator, because he rejects any elitist artistic isolation; as for the spectator, he needs the artist to celebrate his existence, to inspire him with visions, to make him dream and, last but not least, to give shape to his innermost longings, his most secret desires.

Now, this intimate process of interaction, which might be compared with a ritual, indefatigable dance (the few moments when the dancers stop are none but those during which the work of art is born), is being helped by a mediating instrument, endowed with a double power, able to simultaneously 'provoke' and 'invite'. The Image is this instrument, and Robert Combas wields it to 'provoke', that is, to trigger a reaction in the spectator only to 'invite' him, beckoning him in and whispering in his ear, 'Come over and talk to me, I want to tell you about the stupidity, violence, beauty, love, hatred, seriousness and fun, the logic and senselessness that pervade our day-to-day lives'. The Image, in Robert Combas' works, cannot, therefore, remain motionless; as a matter of fact, it could quite accurately be likened to a labyrinth, as the spectator's eye, starting from a particular element in the pictorial space—that which appears most obviously, is then led on to meet successively all the microcosmic elements which make up the macrocosm of the painting, this boundless, constantly open space created by the artist.

For the artistic language does not stop at the borders of the inner self. Quite the opposite, in fact, it only surges from the inner self to expand that self and reach out towards the social world. That language is a positive attitude, insofar as, beyond the crude scenes of violence or sexuality on the rampage, beyond the blending of words—or sentences—with images, Robert Combas' work is first and foremost an attitude. Not a didactic one, since it does not have the 'I' as its epicentre, but, rather, a resolute attempt to expand its very field of action, far beyond the limits of the self-contained, circular rhetoric of art history, striving to include elements thus far held in contempt by the elite who had ruled the art world during the seventies, elements such as drawings made by children or madmen, comics, rock music, etc. The 'childish' element in it is only the result of a strategy, that of a painter who decided to push back the limits of this capacity for action together with those of his image world.

This is what Robert Combas' work is all about: turning an artist's behaviour, involved in a process of constant metamorphosis, into an attitude which involves not only an artistic stand, but a social one as well. In other words, a critical stand.

Excerpt from Démosthènes Davvetas, 'Conversation with Robert Combas', *Robert Combas, Peintures 1985–87* (catalogue), capc Musée d'Art Contemporain de Bordeaux, Bordeaux, 1987

LE BEAUJOLAIS NOUVEAU EST ARRIVÉ, 1986
Acrylic on canvas
235 × 302

(Photo) Jacques Hoereemer

'Not at all the same thing, [said Gladia]. You're viewing me right now. You can't touch me, can you, or smell me, or anything like that. You could if you were seeing me. Right now I'm two hundred miles away at least. So how can it be the same thing?'

Bayley grew interested. 'But I can see you with my eyes.'

'No, you don't see me. You see my image. You're viewing me.'

'And that makes a difference?'

'All the difference there is.'[1]

No you don't see me. You see my image. You're viewing me. In New Zealand our art is pretty much an art born of reproduction. We are good at analysing and leaching out ideas from the images we see in magazines, photographs, books and catalogues. Much of our art experience is viewing as opposed to seeing, as it were. These skills, the skills of gleaning through reproduction, are, of course, particularly valuable with sculptural installations as many of them are dismantled when exhibitions close.

And that makes a difference? In the case of Neil Dawson there is more to view at the moment than there is to see. Many of his installations (*Echo, Paper/scissors/rock, Reflections, Seascape, Vanishing points* etc) have been cleared away and only a couple (*The rock* and *Light well*) are in place in Wellington where we live. Although we have seen most of them, at one time or another, as we write we must refer to them in photographs.

To view Dawson's work then becomes a necessary part of any involvement with it. (Of course we might also say the same thing of Stella, Giotto and Krazner). With Dawson, though, the inevitability of viewing as opposed to seeing has been catered for—knowingly. This is, after all, sculpture produced in the age of mechanical reproduction. Sculpture that is able to play with the fact that a photograph is stable and to allow that photographs can often present illusion most convincingly. Sculpture that recognises that ideas removed from their physical context can still speak clearly even if in a different language.

Sure, in the cramped quarters of a colour picture we might not feel the space between us and *Paper/scissors/rock* positioned high in the ceiling of the Robert McDougall Art Gallery. But its illusion is still complete and its neat idea isn't cluttered up by the junk on the walls around it. We don't have to crane our necks to look at a photograph of a work as so many of Dawson's sculptures wilfully demand. And we can spread the pictures out on the table and connect ideas, see repetitions of elements and conjunctions. We can shuffle, say, the suspended works into one pile and the taped and painted ones into another. The almost monocular view of photographs can suggest access points to a concept which Dawson has worked with in very different installations. In the kingdom of the point of view the camera is king.

Dawson knows all this and is an addicted recorder of his own work. He prepared a recent exhibition of his installations filling it with images and relics to stand in for the works that could not be there. A room for a view. This playing with the idea of viewing as the only way most people will know his work bounces off the fact that for those who could be there Dawson had literally turned the National Art Gallery on its head with *Reflections* or that he was about to sign himself in at New Plymouth with the sculptured mountain Taranaki.

All the difference in the world. For to see Dawson's work is to share with him the site. For an example we might as well go straight to the centre of the country and look at his most successful large scale work to date—*The rock* outside the BNZ Centre in Wellington, New Zealand. *The rock* is a skeletal structure that spends most of its time trying to kid the mirror glass building opposite that it, too, is a member of the grid family. There's lots of room in all those gaps for ideas to get through. In fact it is a sculpture more about gaps than substance. And this on a site that is so self-consciously solemn. But there in front of the money market's black box, suspended by an act of confidence, *The rock* remains steady while currencies rise and fall. Solid as a bank in fact.

Or stick yourself in front of *Ripple*, another of Dawson's high flyers, outside the Waikato Art Museum in Hamilton. To see this work is also to feel the presence of the Waikato River, to connect its powerful flow with the agitated movements of the clouds behind the image stamped in the sky. It is to take part in the work's suggestion by its scale of the disparity between this place and *pakeha* culture.

OK, so to view Dawson's work is not to see it, but then to see it is not to view it either. We're not talking about losses here, but differences.

Jim and Mary Barr

1. Isaac Asimov, *The Naked Sun*, Panther, London, 1960.

RIPPLES, 1987
PVC, rigid foam, carbon fibre, epoxy resin, stainless steel wire
450 × 600 × 0.3
Collection: Waikato Museum of Art and History, Hamilton. Funded by McCaw, Lewis, Chapman

Born Rotterdam, Netherlands, 1904

Lives and works in The Springs, Long Island, New York

From the time of his first inclusion in exhibitions, de Kooning has been recognised and, increasingly, his work has helped focus international attention on American art. It is rarely noted that on his arrival in New York he was already thoroughly grounded in the Dutch avant-garde movement of his own day, de Stijl, the reductionist painting and design of Mondrian, van Doesberg and the others. He was also familiar at first hand with Dutch Art Nouveau, the dominant style of his own childhood. But, as de Kooning has said, 'Style is a fraud. I always felt that the Greeks were hiding behind their columns.'

It is possible, now that his great work is done, to look back at fifty years of painting by Willem de Kooning, and to discern clearly the shape of his achievement and the progress of his formal concerns. As ever, much that seems perfectly logical and explicable after the fact was invisible at the time of its creation.

In order to describe his painting and its shifts in style, we must first consider his series *Women*, which so obsessed him after 1950, the year in which he invented the radical format that expresses so well his amazement and trepidation at the fact and the idea of Woman.

Up to the mid-1950s virtually all of de Kooning's work was figural. This bewitchment can be traced back to his academic training in Holland and to his natural fascination with the human form as portrait and self-portrait, the classic concern of Western art from the time of the Greeks. The human body as a ruling passion would be hardly worth mentioning were it not so rare among postwar artists of the avant-garde. Francis Bacon in the late forties, his first paintings we know anything about, was poised on a similar knife-edge between the figure and its deliquescence into paint. But, grand as he is, Bacon never carried his search any further than its first adumbration, whereas de Kooning would constantly alter the balance between figure and ground, between his concern for the female figure and his growing passion for landscape—on the same canvas.

On the subject of his Women, Clement Greenberg once told de Kooning, 'It's impossible today to paint a face', to which de Kooning replied 'That's right and it's impossible not to.'

His canvases have always had joy, playfulness and ribaldry among their attributes; packed with shapes, allusions, actions and counteractions, they pile ambiguity on ambiguity; sometimes, it would seem, they are painted at lightning speed, at others in a more relaxed contour-loving gesture. De Kooning's work sustains a fusion of perceptions, feelings and ideas which—as his great friend Thomas Hess wrote—'succeed by banishing nothing'.

'In art,' de Kooning has said, 'one idea is as good as another.' The extent to which Willem de Kooning pulls his images and his energy from within is clear in what is perhaps his most famous statement: 'The argument often used that science is really abstract, and that painting could be like music and, for this reason, that you cannot paint a man leaning against a lamp-post, is utterly ridiculous. That space of science—the space of the physicists—I am truly bored with by now. Their lenses are so thick that seen through them, the space gets more and more melancholy. There seems to be no end to the misery of the scientist's space. All that it contains is billions and billions of hunks of matter, hot or cold, floating around in darkness according to a great design of aimlessness. The stars I think about, if I could fly, I could reach in a few old-fashioned days. But physicists' stars I use as buttons, buttoning up curtains of emptiness. If I stretch my arms next to the rest of myself and wonder where my fingers are—that is all the space I need as a painter.'[1]

Excerpt from Henry Geldzahler, Introduction to *Willem de Kooning: Abstract Landscapes 1955–63* (catalogue), Larry Gagosian Gallery, New York, 1987

1. 'What Abstract Art Means to Me', written for a Museum of Modern Art symposium, reprinted from the *Museum of Modern Art Bulletin*, vol. XVIII, no 3, Spring 1951.

In painting his urban landscapes de Kooning continued to rely on methods that had proven so successful in the *Women*. This involved the collaging of disparate and discrete shapes and a montage-like technique of overlays that resulted in abrupt shifts in scale and a perceptible, if shallow, illusion of space . . .

Unlike the works of the late 1960s, which seem to bulge and strain the two-dimensional integrity of the picture plane, those of the mid-to-late 1970s are a marvel of innovation. They achieve a new reconciliation of three-dimensional form with the canvas surface and an even further integration of figure with landscape. The 'no-environment' of the earlier work, the subsequent emphasis upon the figure, upon landscape, and finally the integration of Woman and landscape into Woman as landscape have given way to a new synthesis that is as close to abstraction as the efforts of the late 1940s.

Excerpts from Diane Waldman, 'De Kooning's Work of the 1970s', *De Kooning*, Harry N. Abrams, New York, 1988

WOMAN, 1950
Oil on canvas
163 × 117.5

(Photo) David Roselle

RICHARD DEACON

Born Bangor, Wales, 1949

Lives and works in London

JON THOMPSON: I would pick up on three things that you've said which seem to me worth expanding in terms of your own work. One, you seem to emphasise the notion of contour a great deal and that's worth talking about. You used the term eroticism and, when we were coming down on the train, you used the term desire, both of which seem to me to be worth expanding. The other thing is that it seems that you use the term material as though that was very important too. So you've got a kind of triumvirate of elements. You've got eroticism and desire, you've got materiality and you've got contour and I notice that in your works often you employ a very bizarre form of geometry in order to achieve the final forms that you get, so there's something of that in the middle of that triangle.

RICHARD DEACON: It seems to me that when you look at something, when you see something, what you see is the skin, the outside surface and that's the only part you have any information about at all. If you attempt to discover what lies underneath the skin, you find another surface; so, although one on the one hand proposes that a body for example is built up through skeleton, musculature, organs etc., what constitutes the body for you, for me, is an appearance, a skin and there is nothing else. When I'm making sculpture, I have a resistance to making things which are built up from the inside out.

JT: Well, that's the point I was trying to make.

RD: Because somehow if I do that, then I hide the bit that I've just been working on. Whereas if I try and make it as if it were a skin all the time, then I have a continuous acquaintance with what constitutes the work, the surface.

JT: The second point was eroticism and desire, but you can leave that 'til last if you like.

RD: Well, looking and listening as ways of interacting with the world and in relation to my own work are two primary modes of experience which I use. I would differentiate looking from listening on the level of eroticism. Listening seems to me to belong to authenticity. Looking seems to me to be an activity that is absolutely permeated with sexuality. The eye is a kind of avaricious instrument that grasps the world and wants the world and the way that it wants the world seems to be very closely analogous to sexual desire. The eroticism that I think a lot of my work relates to has to do with a kind of voyeurism and the resistance to that voyeurism. The third thing you mentioned was what?

JT: Materiality, I know that you're very, very particular about the way that you choose the material for any piece.

RD: Yes.

JT: And it has a lot to do with both form and content, I think.

RD: I am very particular. I don't know if it has to do with form and content. I've noticed that I tend to use materials which come in sheet form. The materials that interest me are materials which are not like pieces of stone and not like clay. Clay has no form and a piece of stone has a very strong form. Whereas a sheet of steel, a sheet of fairly thin steel has a bit of both and the same for a thin strip of wood or a sheet of lino, I think that's what attracts me. A lot of what I do is involved in giving structure to those materials. It's a kind of act of will that's involved and I suppose why those sorts of materials interest me is because they seem to be matter in a way that the clay or the stone aren't matter. The one is too unformed, too amorphous and the other is too . . . solid.

JT: It seems to me to be a feature of a great deal of the construction that you do that one's very aware of the fact that it's made from a skin and that the skin is pieced together.

RD: Yes. What seems interesting is the whole work. Working in a repetitive way allows you to slowly make the whole work without there ever coming a point where you are up against a kind of focus. I spend, I don't know if I spend an equal amount of time, but I do spend a lot of time deciding whether I should put rivets at two-inch or three-inch intervals as much as I spend time sort of thinking about sexuality or the associations or whatever. When I'm making work, I'm very close to it. You know it's only afterwards or when I'm not really there that I begin to see it in other ways; but whilst I'm making it, my attention is actually very, very close. I enjoy putting screws in and putting rivets in and I think you can talk about those things. I enjoy putting screws in and I enjoy the fact that they have a pattern in relationship to the work. I also think that putting one thing on top of another and joining it together by a piece that goes through it has connotations, as does laying one thing on top of another and glueing it together repeatedly. Those activities of construction have connotations with the ways in which things in the world take on references or meanings, either by having them applied to them or by building up or by having a meaning hidden. I think all those things are a part of those constructive processes. I also think that making things is an activity which, in that it forms the world, has some relationship to language. One of the prime functions of language is to describe the world or to re-form the world. Language is something that is neither yours nor mine, but is ours and lies between us and all this stuff out there. Making is a not dissimilar process.

Richard Deacon in conversation with Jon Thompson,
Southampton Art Gallery, June 18 1985

LISTENING TO REASON, 1986
Laminated timber
226 × 609 × 579

(Photo) Marian Goodman Gallery, New York

His sequence of moves toward a unique position in the history of modern art was breathtakingly swift, compressed into the space of four crucial years. At the start of 1910 he was producing Fauve-influenced paintings with an eye to Cézanne and Matisse; by the end of 1912 he had passed through experiments with Cubist fragmentation of space and studies of figures in motion to achieve a unique mechanomorphic style in the *Bride*. By 1914, he had executed a quantity of notes and studies for his great project, *The Bride Stripped Bare by Her Bachelors, Even* (the *Large Glass*), he had ceased to paint, in any conventional sense, and he had purchased an ordinary household object from a Paris department store and signed it as if it were a sculpture by his own hand.

From this point on, the development of his work seems less a matter of linear chronological advance than of the gradual filling-in of a total picture, rather like the progress of a jigsaw puzzle. Viewed as a whole, the complex array of paintings and drawings, notes and puns, rotating machines and a movie, Readymades and elaborate constructions offers a bewildering diversity of media and methods. Gertrude Stein put her finger squarely upon the problem that Duchamp was determined to confront in his own career:

'It is awfully hard to go on painting. I often think about this thing. It is awfully hard for anyone to go on doing anything because everybody is troubled by everything. Having done anything you naturally want to do it again and if you do it again then you know you are doing it again and it is not interesting . . .'[1]

Duchamp's response to this basic dilemma was a resolution 'to put painting once again at the service of the mind'.[2] He often expressed his disgust with 'retinal' painters, concerned purely with sense impressions, who in his opinion continued to paint the same picture over and over again. Eschewing the painting of the recent past as an influence, Duchamp rapidly arrived at the point (around 1912) where he deliberately chose his own sources. Not Courbet (the father of 'retinal' painting) but Mallarmé, not the sensuous, architectonic paint structure of Cézanne but the enigmatic imagery of Odilon Redon[3], not Picasso and Braque but Alfred Jarry and Raymond Roussel served as *agents provocateurs*. Not painting but language, sometimes literary but often colloquial, not colour theory but chronophotography and the concept of a fourth dimension caught his imagination. Despite a small group of major paintings, Duchamp was not a painter but a jack-of-all-trades, and perhaps a poet as well. His contribution was to the broad field of art itself, a field that under his intelligent scrutiny and subversive methods expanded, distorted itself, and occasionally exploded in all directions.

The reverse of the proverbial philosopher who loved humanity and hated men, Duchamp remarked, 'Art doesn't interest me. Artists interest me.'[4] He could wage brilliant war on the pretensions and commercialism of the art world while warmly encouraging individual artists and gauging the quality of individual works with a keen and sensitive eye. His repeated attacks on 'retinal' painting did not conflict with a profound admiration for Matisse, nor did his disgust with inflated prices and the art market prevent him from assisting Brancusi by purchasing a large group of his sculptures from the Quinn collection in 1926 when a public auction threatened the sculptor's reputation and livelihood. His conviction that the work of art had a 'life' of only about fifty years, and that that life and its possible revival at a later date depended heavily upon the spectator, did not discourage him from efforts to preserve his own work in the *Box in a Valise* or in the collections of his friends.

Anne d'Harnoncourt, Introduction to *Marcel Duchamp* (catalogue), Museum of Modern Art, New York, and Philadelphia Museum of Art, Pennsylvania, 1973

1. Gertrude Stein, *Everybody's Autobiography*, 1937, Vintage Books, Random House, New York, 1973
2. See Walter Pach, *Queer Thing, Painting*, Harper & Brothers, New York, 1938
3. See 'Eleven Europeans in America', ed. James Johnson Sweeney, *The Museum of Modern Art Bulletin*, vol. XIII, nos 4–5, New York, 1946
4. Interview by William C. Seitz, 'What's Happened to Art?', *Vogue*, New York, 15 February 1963

LA BOÎTE EN VALISE

Duchamp slowly and painstakingly assembled the material for the box, frequently experimenting with new methods of reproduction. There were seventy-one items in the original set of boxes, and the twenty *de luxe* copies contained an original work . . . The total number of boxes in existence was not, Duchamp said, to exceed 300 and on his death in 1968 this number had been completed. He started work on it in Paris in 1935 or 1936; after the occupation of France by Germany in 1940, Duchamp patiently transported the material down to Marseilles, in the unoccupied zone, thence to be shipped across to New York. Armed with a cheese merchant's identity card, he carried his 'merchandise' safely over the frontier. Perhaps the very idea of the portable museum was in anticipation of the necessity for sudden flight should the threat of war which hung over Europe during the thirties be realised. Robert Lebel remembered that 'characteristically, one year before the war Duchamp foresaw that he must pack his bags in as small a space as possible'. In this way he could carry all the works he liked, in reality scattered in collections all over the world, with him . . .

Dawn Ades, 'Marcel Duchamp's Portable Museum', *Marcel Duchamp's Travelling Box*, Centre Georges Pompidou, Paris, and Arts Council of Great Britain, London, 1982

WHY NOT SNEEZE ROSE SÉLAVY?

Duchamp commented on the title of this work during an interview on French television: 'The cage filled with sugar cubes is called *Why not sneeze . . . ?* and, of course, the title seems weird to you since there's really no connection between the sugar cubes and a sneeze . . . First of all there's the dissociational gap between the idea of sneezing and the idea of 'Why not sneeze?' because, after all, you don't sneeze at will; you usually sneeze in spite of your will. So the answer to the question 'Why not sneeze?' is simply that you can't sneeze *at will*! And then there's the literary side if I may call it that—but 'literary' is such a stupid word—it doesn't mean anything—but at any rate there's the marble with its coldness, and this meant that you can even say you're cold, because of the marble, and all of the associations are permissible.'

The 'Rose Sélavy' of the title was a pseudonym Duchamp adopted in 1920. He had first considered using a Jewish name, as he was Catholic, but eventually decided that female identity would be more extreme. 'Rose' was chosen as the most common of feminine names of the period—'an awful name in 1920'—and 'Sélavy' (*c'est la vie*) as a typical Duchampian pun. Soon after this work was completed 'Rose' gained a double 'r' becoming 'Rrose'.

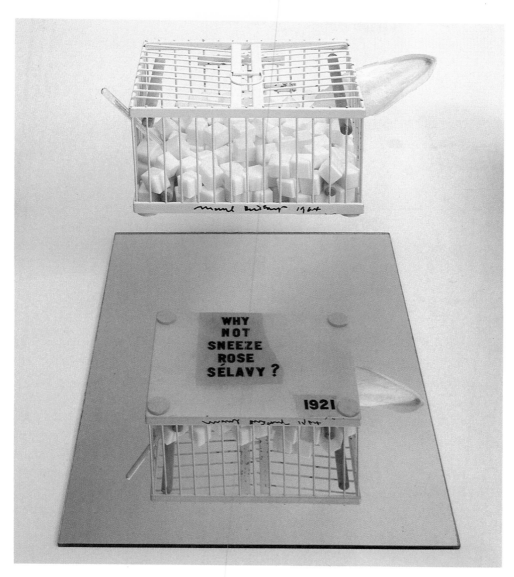

WHY NOT SNEEZE ROSE SÉLAVY?, 1921/1964
Painted metal birdcage, marble cubes, thermometer and cuttlebone
12.4 × 22.2 × 16.2
Collection: Australian National Gallery

LA BOÎTE EN VALISE,
Mixed media
174 × 142 × 74

Born Roeselare, Belgium, 1941

Lives and works in Lovendegem, Ghent

LILI DUJOURIE:

ENCOUNTERS WITH ABSENCE

In 1972 Lili Dujourie made a sculpture by resting an iron sheet against a wall, every inch of which was painted except for the space below the metal. From the front nothing seemed amiss, but from the side a sliver of white came into view as if something had been left undone. Any superficial resemblances to transatlantic minimalism were dispelled by the title: *American Imperialism*. Adjusting an aesthetic which seemed to replace scale with size, emotion with repression, subtlety with obviousness and richness of effect with sheer forthrightness, she had begun working in human dimensions, with human feelings and subtleties. It was a calculated decision. Under the circumstances, opting for intimacy was the most aggressive choice she could make.

American Imperialism explained a lot about Dujourie's art. It proved that it has often been conceived as a deliberate reaction against prevailing trends. At least twice in her career, for example, she has made a conscious decision to use native Belgian materials. It demonstrates that the prevailing metaphor of the seventies, 'the disappearance of the art object' was never far from her mind. And it showed that she has always been intent on confronting the nothingness that resulted. Her artworks have become the site of dramatised social encounters, each with its private tensions and pleasures and its own internal system of balances.

The higher the increment of exclusion the occasion demanded, for instance, the greater the quotient of fantasy. Returning to traditional modes, Dujourie made life studies. But characteristically, her videos of an unclothed female model, rolling to and fro on a bed, shot in real time with a single camera, were of the artist herself, conscious of her own posing because of a monitor out of sight of the viewer, but feigning unselfconsciousness nevertheless. In subsequent male nude photographs, eye-contact with the model resulted in deadlock. Neither subservience nor mastery, engagement nor disengagement, ensued. Rather, the potential for each was gauged and the process of perception was turned in on itself. As in a later work, where the observer was invited to gaze into a cracked mirror, the outcome was self-referential in every sense. Most disconcerting of all, perhaps, was an installation consisting of two life-size slides of a female nude facing sideways and forwards: the image of a woman to be switched on and off at will. Such immateriality signifies a refusal, an enforced awareness that defiance of anthropomorphism leads to an examination of states of mind that result from absence.

When a sudden glimpse of empty space appeared, it could be wall-sized, as in Dujourie's three-metre long collages with a few small additions: pictures culled from women's magazines. Or as big as the palm of a hand, like those booklets in which other such images were arranged in a pseudo-narrative. ('My novels', Dujourie called them.) And in the reaction to each, awareness or oblivion, enforced or voluntary, operated according to an economy of its own. Gradually the tone would darken, self-absorption would suffer an apparent reversal into loss of selfhood, and the imaginative collaboration any artwork entails would be presented in terms of death itself. That chink of colour from *American Imperialism* appeared in different guises. *Paris* featured a mirror wedged between two blocks of granite, with an artificial hand and apple transforming single onlookers into the hapless shepherd of Greek mythology, while *The Kiss*, with its triangular black guillotine motif, lured visitors into a space where a poised chalice awaited.

That gradual emotional intensification, which culminated in a death sentence for the unfortunate viewer, began in 1982. Dismayed by the vogue for 'internationalism', Dujourie celebrated her Flemish background by using fabrics. 'The history of Flemish painting is in velvet,' she has claimed, thinking of the folds of cloth in paintings by Jan van Eyck or Rogier van der Weyden. Her new works evoked a particular range of emotions: sumptuousness and languor, excess and the vacuity it brings about. Actual hollowness served as a metaphor for Dujourie's plan to persuade others to confront a lack, a vacancy, a refusal. And a further dimension was added to this exposure: self-regard, ripe-rottenness, self-fuelling fiction. A certain perverse relish is involved in the life-style of professional modernists, paid to commit hara-kiri in front of eager audiences. Refusal to align this with myths of female masochism was demonstrated by Dujourie's paradoxical construction method. Those fluttering draperies seemed as free as air. In fact, they were attached to a metal substructure which was mounted on wood. Perhaps there had always been an iron fist beneath the velvet glove; the more flagrantly feminine it became in traditional terms, the more powerfully her work battled to establish a position of resistance.

In time, the conception became overtly dramatic. Works hung vertically like curtains, with independent elements in front of them, like surrogate viewers observing their real-life counterparts. A rotating motif emerged, most obviously in the centre panel of the triptych *Places Devoted to the Night, Remote from Tumults and Noise*, a shape which embraced vacancy as if caressing it and cherishing the melancholy it signified. The need to perform grief while perceiving that very performance might find perfect fulfilment in dance. Indeed, the stasis of Dujourie's draperies invokes absent, living bodies, rolling back and forth, as free as in this variation on the metaphor as her models had been unfree in the videos, slides and photographs.

Dujourie's most recent experiments suggest that the visual may indeed be such a metaphor: that precise measurement, however crucial, proves ultimately unattainable, that visual evidence is summoned solely by desire and that the truth of such evidence must necessarily prove deceptive, at best. Problems abound. While a design for a fountain would involve sheer walls of light and water, impossible to look through but so insubstantial that touch could penetrate them, a marble and plaster corner-piece is titled *Aurore*, simultaneously a girl's name and the word for 'dawn'. Only by failure in traditional terms, it seems, is it possible to succeed in that theatrical realm which Dujourie identifies with willing torment, the self-deception which sight entails. Whether we collaborate willingly or the play is forced upon us, vision is presented as a function of desire and death. Looking is identified with need, wanting to be needed with wanting to be looked at, being looked at with a kind of perilous mastery in which the gaze becomes a rebuff, and the centrality that attention assumes with self-absorption and annihilation. In Dujourie's thinking art becomes an elaborate play of conventions in which attainment and annihilation run parallel. Only a certain prevention, a sense that both the viewer and the art must be held in check, prolongs the ordeal. In this strange hiatus the distinction between love-song and threnody is blurred and the very concept of identity becomes frighteningly precious. Need struggles with reality as questions of permanence, longing and loneliness are posed in a way that is almost cruel. Questions? Facts, rather, and hard facts at that. The way she presents it, anything is easier to endure than an emptiness where something has been.

Stuart Morgan

UNTITLED, 1987
Water sculpture/fountain installation
360 × 160 ×210

(Photo) Jannes Linders

LESLEY DUMBRELL

Born Melbourne, Australia, 1941

Lives and works in Melbourne

Lesley Dumbrell perceives *Foxglove* as central to her current concerns and to her continuing absorption with the properties of light, an absorption which amplifies as her work advances. While it is true to say that all painting uses light in one way or another to cast an exact mood or atmosphere, Lesley Dumbrell uses the change of light, either throughout the year, or throughout the day, to make explicit the context of colour and pictorial space.

The artist explains *Foxglove* as being about the magic hour when day turns into night, 'when colours glow vividly and momentarily before being lost to darkness'.

The painting alludes to flowers, but not in a literal sense. A small garden adjacent to the artist's studio is a constant reminder of the audacity of colour in nature—'the intensity of red set against green foliage'. The title *Foxglove* is not specific—it is the name of a flower, but it also refers to something else, and so sets the imagination on a lateral course.

To the artist, the most important aspect is that, after working for two years with memories of the light and colour of Italy, *Foxglove* is firmly located in Australia and is therefore specifically about the light of Melbourne. 'Maybe', she says, 'one needs to have a time for looking at other places, to understand better what is so familiar in the environment you have always known. I am glad I am no longer looking over my shoulder at a foreign culture.'

Excerpt from Elizabeth Churcher, 'A New Acquisition, Lesley Dumbrell's *Foxglove*' 1986, *Australian and International ART Monthly*, September 1987

FOXGLOVE (TRIPTYCH), 1986/87
Acrylic on canvas
Three panels, each 213.3 × 152.4
Collection: Art Gallery of Western Australia

They passed down the busy street that led to the yards. It was still early morning, and everything was at its high tide of activity. A steady stream of employees was pouring through the gate—employees of the higher sort, at this hour, clerks and stenographers and such. For the women there were waiting big two-horse wagons, which set off at a gallop as fast as they were filled. In the distance there was heard again the lowing of the cattle, a sound as of a far-off ocean calling. They followed it, this time, as eager as children in sight of a circus menagerie—which, indeed, the scene a good deal resembled. They crossed the railroad tracks, and then on each side of the street were the pens full of cattle; they would have stopped to look, but Jokubas hurried them on, to where there was a stairway and a raised gallery, from which everything could be seen. Here they stood, staring, breathless with wonder.

There is over a square mile of space in the yards, and more than half of it is occupied by cattle-pens; north and south as far as the eye can reach there stretches a sea of pens. And they were all filled—so many cattle no one had ever dreamed existed in the world. Red cattle, black, white, and yellow cattle; old cattle and young cattle; great bellowing bulls and little calves not an hour born; meek-eyed milch cows and fierce, long-horned Texas steers. The sound of them here was as of all the barnyards of the universe; and as for counting them—it would have taken all day simply to count the pens. Here and there ran long alleys, blocked at intervals by gates; and Jokubas told them that the number of these gates was twenty-five thousand. Jokubas had recently been reading a newspaper article which was full of statistics such as that, and he was very proud as he repeated them and made his guests cry out with wonder. Jurgis, too, had a little of this sense of pride. Had he not just gotten a job, and become a sharer in all this activity, a cog in this marvellous machine?

Here and there about the alleys galloped men upon horseback, booted and carrying long whips; they were very busy, calling to each other, and to those who were driving the cattle. They were drovers and stock-raisers, who had come from far States, and brokers and commission-merchants, and buyers for all the big packing-houses. Here and there they would stop to inspect a bunch of cattle, and there would be a parley, brief and businesslike. The buyer would nod or drop his whip, and that would mean a bargain; and he would note it in his little book, along with hundreds of others he had made that morning. Then Jokubas pointed out the place where the cattle were driven to be weighed, upon a great scale that would weigh a hundred thousand pounds at once and record it automatically. It was near to the east entrance that they stood, and all along this east side of the yards ran the railroad tracks, into which the cars were run, loaded with cattle. All night long this had been going on, and now the pens were full; by tonight they would all be empty, and the same thing would be done again.

'And what will become of all these creatures?' cried Teta Elzbieta.

'By tonight,' Jokubas answered, 'they will all be killed and cut up; and over there on the other side of the packing-houses are more railroad tracks, where the cars come to take them away.'

There were two hundred and fifty miles of track within the yards, their guide went on to tell them. They brought about ten thousand head of cattle every day, and as many hogs, and half as many sheep—which meant some eight or ten million live creatures turned into food every year. One stood and watched, and little by little caught the drift of the tide, as it set in the direction of the packing-houses. There were groups of cattle being driven to the chutes, which were roadways about fifteen feet wide, raised high above the pens. In these chutes the stream of animals was continuous; it was quite uncanny to watch them, pressing on to their fate, all unsuspicious—a very river of death. Our friends were not poetical, and the sight suggested to them no metaphors of human destiny; they thought only of the wonderful efficiency of it all. The chutes into which the hogs went climbed high up—to the very top of the distant buildings; and Jokubas explained that the hogs went up by the power of their own legs, and then their weight carried them back through all the processes necessary to make them into pork.

'They don't waste anything here,' said the guide, and then he laughed and added a witticism, which he was pleased that his unsophisticated friends should take to be his own: 'They use everything about the hog except the squeal.' In front of Brown's General Office building there grows a tiny plot of grass, and this, you may learn, is the only bit of green thing in Packingtown; likewise this jest about the hog and his squeal, the stock in trade of all the guides, is the one gleam of humour that you will find there.

After they had seen enough of the pens, the party went up the street, to the mass of buildings which occupy the centre of the yards. These buildings, made of brick and stained with innumerable layers of Packingtown smoke, were painted all over with advertising signs, from which the visitor realized suddenly that he had come to the home of many of the torments of his life. It was here that they made those products with the wonders of which they pestered him so—by placards that defaced the landscape when he travelled, and by staring advertisements in the newspapers and magazines—by silly little jingles that he could not get out of his mind, and gaudy pictures that lurked for him around every street corner. Here was where they made Brown's Imperial Hams and Bacon, Brown's Dressed Beef, Brown's Excelsior Sausages! Here was the headquarters of Durham's Pure Leaf Lard, of Durham's Breakfast Bacon, Durham's Canned Beef, Potted Ham, Devilled Chicken, Peerless Fertilizer!

Excerpt from Upton Sinclair, *The Jungle*, 1906

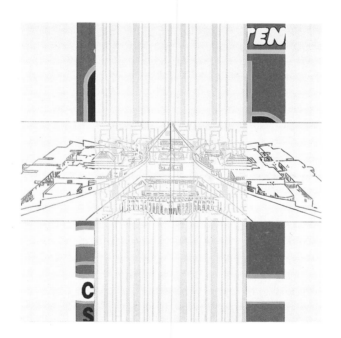

SURVEILLANCE AND PUNISHMENT (OLIMPICO), 1987
Acrylic on canvas
228 × 224

(Photo) Fenn Hinchcliffe

SURVEILLANCE AND PUNISHMENT (PARLIAMENT), 1987
Acrylic on canvas
228 × 224

(Photo) Fenn Hinchcliffe

At art school in the sixties, Brian Eno studied to be a painter and, by a series of oblique strategies worthy of his own oracle cards, this is what he has finally become: a painter of sound and of light.

Many of those who discover Eno through his Ambient records and video installations of the eighties are surprised to learn of his career as Roxy Music's androgynous synthesiser star in the early seventies. The flamboyance was short-lived, but Eno's commitment to rock music—as creator, collaborator and producer—lasted the decade and has continued, intermittently, into the eighties.

His early solo albums, *Here Come the Warm Jets* and *Taking Tiger Mountain (by Strategy)*, are marked by wild invention, a ready embrace of 'chance' procedures and a non-musician's glee at the possibilities of the tape-recorder and the recording studio. But in many ways (*No Pussyfooting*) (1973), the album of synthesised guitar loops that he recorded with Robert Fripp, now sounds like a more characteristic project.

It wasn't until 1975, though, with the release of *Another Green World*, his album of brilliant song and instrumental miniatures, and *Discreet Music*, on his own Obscure record label, that Eno really found his form. On *Another Green World*, the recording studio itself became an essential tool in the compositional process; while *Discreet Music* set a 'self-regulating' musical system in motion and let it run its course with surprisingly attractive results. Eno continued his dub-influenced studio experiments with *Before and After Science* (1977) but felt increasingly constrained by the rock song format. This was his last solo album as singer/ songwriter. Subsequent forays into rock have been confined to collaborations with, among others, David Bowie, David Byrne, Talking Heads and, most recently, U2.

In 1978 Eno released *Music for Films*, his album of soundtracks for real and imaginary movies, and the fragile, contemplative *Music for Airports*, a development of the idea of musical 'ambience' that he had begun to explore on *Discreet Music*. In a now famous definition accompanying *Airports* he writes: 'Ambient Music must be able to accommodate many levels of listening attention without enforcing one in particular; it must be as ignorable as it is interesting.' The style has been widely misrepresented as 'Muzak' ever since.

Three further Ambient records followed, including *The Plateaux of Mirror* (with Harold Budd) and *On Land*, Eno's 1982 master-piece, which attempts to situate the listener *inside* a musical landscape, rather than placing him in front of a bas-relief screen of stereo sound, as with conventional productions. The record also demonstrates Eno's increasing interest, first heard on *Another Green World*, in the background texture of his music. In a very different vein, the following year's *Apollo: Atmospheres and Soundtracks* showed that the style could bear more conventional country-and-western inflections.

In 1985, Eno released his first compact disc-only recording, the sixty-one minute *Thursday Afternoon*, a soundtrack to his video of the same name. Fascinated by the medium's potential as a way of painting with light, he first turned to video in 1979, and in the last seven years he has staged more than fifty installations in public spaces around the world—in the USA, Canada, France, Italy, Sweden, Germany, Japan and the UK. Early works such as *Two Fifth Avenue* (1979), and *Mistaken Memories of Mediaeval Manhattan* (1981)—slow-moving, intensely coloured shots of the New York skyline—are like gently animated paintings. Invariably accompanied by Eno's own music, these works are intended to be the very opposite of conventional television and music video. To accommodate the vertical image, the TV set must be turned on its side and there is no narrative development: it is quite possible to leave the video and come back again without 'missing' anything.

In 1983, Eno began to conceal his monitors inside three-dimensional 'crystal' sculptures and paintings constructed out of perspex and card, using the video as a way of illuminating the pieces from within. Visitors to the darkened interior spaces in which these prismatic pieces are shown find themselves slowing down, almost involuntarily, to the rhythms of a womb-like world. These environments are the ultimate expression of Eno's desire 'to induce calm and a space to think'. Sound and image fuse inextricably.

Opal Ltd, London, 1986

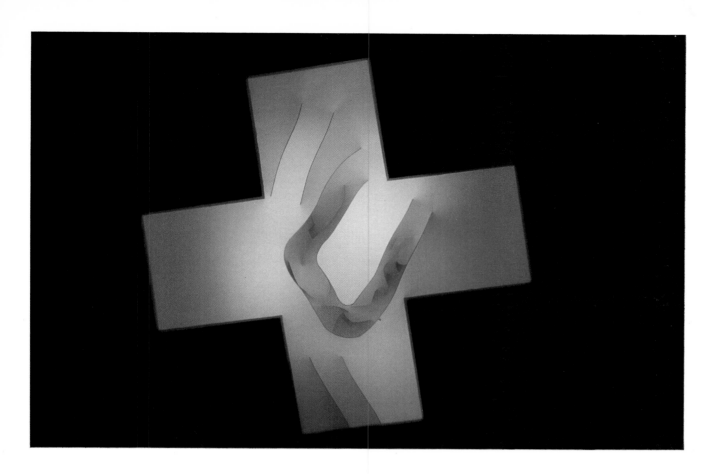

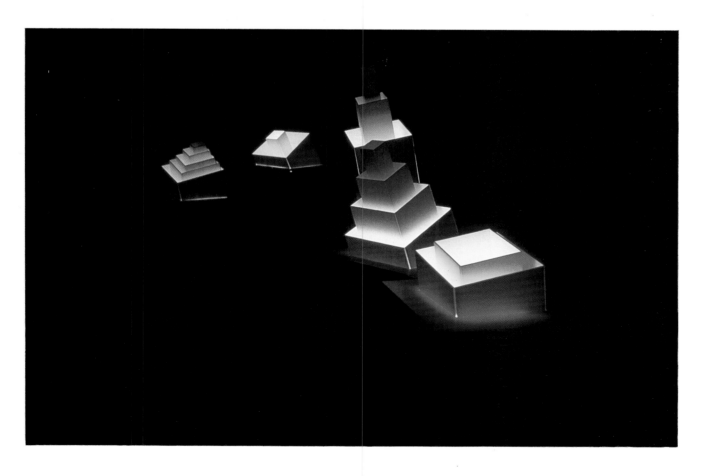

WORKS CONSTRUCTED WITH SOUND AND LIGHT

Born Turin, Italy, 1936

Lives and works in Milan

Languages are like wave lengths or frequency graphs. People, places and situations make it preferable to tune into one frequency as opposed to another. And if the frequency chosen happens to be obstructed then it's just as well to find another without worrying about ethereal fidelity.[1]

Luciano Fabro occupies an elusive place within the art of the past twenty years. Best known as a central figure in the Arte Povera group, which emerged in Italy in the mid-sixties and which sought to fuse a political with an aesthetic stance, in recent years his work has been relatively little seen compared with that of others from this circle, such as Jannis Kounellis and Mario Merz: substantial critical studies of his work have also been remarkably scarce. Responsibility partly resides with the artist himself: Fabro's oeuvre is relatively small (some two hundred works over a twenty-year period) and extraordinarily heterogeneous in form, material and character. Like other Arte Povera artists he has been concerned to eschew any trace of a signature style in order to maintain what he considers a radical stance: the ability to make work which is freshly interventionist and critical. Through the sixties and early seventies this approach led to incorporating provocatively non-art materials and strategies, as seen in Kounellis' exhibition of twelve live horses in Rome in 1960, and the plethora of unusual materials from neon (Merz) through cactus (Kounellis) to fur (Fabro) that initially typified Arte Povera.

More recently, however, permutations of an identifiable lexicon have gradually replaced that insistently chameleon-like activity which marked the early years. They manifest themselves both in a preference for particular materials—gas-jets amongst others in the case of Kounellis—as well as for a preoccupation with certain identifiable forms—his stacked and blocked apertures. In most respects Fabro has remained aloof from this tendency, although one constant can be traced in his oeuvre: the use of the silhouette of his native land . . . Running concurrently with this strand is a second and more diverse one, one that tends to focus on a vocabulary derived from either architecture or nature. In the works of the mid-sixties especially, Fabro's sculpture mapped out, almost literally, certain sites, providing an awareness of space through an understanding of place, as in *In Cubo* (1966), a rectilinear volume whose size was determined by a man's reach. Subsequently, more sumptuous stuffs, from silk to murano glass and gorgeously veined marbles have been incorporated into works which increasingly engage with the details and emblems of classical architecture as metaphors through which to examine our method of at once glorifying and rendering ineffectual all understanding of the past. Throughout, Fabro's is a critical rather than a transcendental modernism, one which is resolutely materialist in character.

While Kounellis seeks to challenge history, to remind us of our quintessentially contemporary plight—of our cultural fragmentation, our loss of wholeness, our dislocation—Fabro by contrast focuses on the way current cultural modes and artefacts shape and define our sense of the world as well as of history . . .

For Fabro art is not an instrument of knowledge (and therefore cannot be didactic), it presents a state of consciousness: thus, 'the artist of today must re-educate the senses for the good of the intellect'.[1] Neither subjective nor expressionist, his sculpture shuns the personal for the collective statement. The value of art, for him, lies in providing an imaginary site of passage, it offers less an analytical critique than an emotional destabilising. In undermining unitary praxis and univocal definition, in exorcising programmatic platforms so that, as Germano Celant states (approvingly), 'every work presents itself as a baffling fragment',[2] Fabro's oeuvre runs the risk of becoming too fractured, too oblique, too elliptical. His work needs, as this exhibition confirms, to control and order its context into a unified entity for significant meaning to accrue.

It is not therefore by way of his guise as a chameleon that Fabro is best able to decentre and question, and to explore those tropes and modes by which we construct reality for ourselves, but through taking on the role of a calculated strategist. It is in substantial solo shows like this that he succeeds most fully in realising his aesthetic.

Excerpts from Lynne Cooke, 'Luciano Fabro', review of 'Fabro: Works 1963–1986', *Artscribe International*, London, Summer 1987

1. Luciano Fabro, 1977, statement reprinted in *Fabro: Works 1963–1986*, The Fruitmarket Gallery, Edinburgh, 1987.
2. Germano Celant, unpublished lecture 'The Italian Complexity—Aspects of Recent Italian Art', The Fruitmarket Gallery, Edinburgh, 30 January 1987.

NUDE DESCENDING A STAIRCASE, 1987
Marble
6 × 45 × 180

IAN FAIRWEATHER

Born Stirling, Scotland, 1891

Died Brisbane, Australia, 1974

Ian Fairweather was an erratic artist. The long course of his art can be seen as a jagged path of advances and hasty retreats, hopeful side-tracks, as he searched for and eventually found and mastered his own originality. He was never satisfied, never confident. At the peak of his powers towards the end of his life, Fairweather, like Cézanne, realised he was only just beginning.

His career was a lifelong attempt to overthrow his Englishness: the deep-seated sensible empiricism, and the academicism of the Slade School which demanded a recoiling from abstraction, and even—as late as the 1920s—an ingrained hostility to the sacrilegious tenets of Post-Impressionism. Inherent and sometimes spoiling Fairweather's art was the contradiction between his drummed-in reliance on English empiricism, the figure, and his great transcending gifts of intuitive line and abstraction.

He came late to art. Perhaps that was fortuitous. Fairweather was aged forty-five before his first, reluctant, one-man exhibition. He came late also to the central concerns of Modernism; time or careerism were never priorities. He investigated Post-Impressionism roughly half a century after its 'invention', and like any gifted painter produced a reasonable quota of exquisite oils; but Post-Impressionism, that most pleasant of art styles, soon failed to contain him. Out of necessity he entered the spacious realms of Cubism and, to a lesser extent, Futurism. Again, forty years after the event. But the discipline proved crucial. Cubism allowed Fairweather to rely on line without ending up with decorative flatness. From 1954 his work displays a mounting influence of Aboriginal painting, and of Chinese calligraphy—the calligraphy especially of the language. His finest work was invariably a merging of all three: Cubism, trace elements of Aboriginal art, the expressive force of the Chinese line. Among Australian painters Fairweather was a pioneer in mixing with the cultures of the region—while maintaining his European origins. But because his experiences of the East were both physical and spiritually deep his influence could, at best, only be by remote, exalted example. He avoided the art world like the plague.

In Australian art he was exceptionally diversified. Yet through each stage his individuality is immediately apparent and dominant with its surprises.

The large compositions of 1933, in particular the Tate Gallery's *Bathing Scene, Bali*, are powerful though conventionally academic for the period. Fairweather's experiences entered his work with greater force between 1933–39, spreading through the intensely felt gouaches of the 1940s and mid-1950s. Results as distinctive as *Chinese Mountain*, 1933, *Marca*, c. 1934, *Bridge in Peking* and *Voyage to the Philippines*, 1935, *Temple, West Lake, Hangchow*, 1936, *Beach at Manicahan*, 1938, *Canal Scene, China*, 1954, to suggest but a few, establish Fairweather among Australia's finest Post-Impressionists. The exotic subject matter, and their general unavailability in public collections or in reproductions, has obscured his achievement here.

A similar judgement applies to those more emotional compositions which seem to spill over into Expressionism. (The writer accepts that some readers may still classify them under Post-Impressionism.) The effective distortions in colour and composition of *Tea House Peking* (Ulster Museum), *Head* and *Near Hangchow*, all painted in the 1930s; *Foochow Canal* and *Corn-sifting*,

Soochow, 1945–47, *Landscape*, 1948 and *The Hill*, 1954, were in advance of their day. Along with his Post-Impressionism, they make most other Australian painting of the period seem heavy-handed, deadly earnest.

Fairweather's restraint in colour, composition and forms remains rare in Australian art. Naturally sophisticated, it sometimes verged on the aristocratic. He was a master colourist. The only skill Fairweather *acquired* was drawing.

Fairweather's Cubism of the mid-1950s was not the classical, analytical model like Eric Wilson's. It was not concerned with still life surfaces so much as line; twisting and stretching it to introduce space and 'content', side-stepping the decorative flatness. Fairweather's Cubism was always individual, characteristic of the artist, and not the long-conquered esperanto investigation of surfaces.

Cubism provided the modernist framework for his great period 1957–63. The paintings grew both in size and in their ambitions. He trusted his arm. He moved from gouache to plastic paint (Dulux Nu-Plastic). These were the years of sustained brilliance: *Last Supper*, *Kite Flying*, *Flight into Egypt*, *Monastery*, *Shalimar*, *Marriage at Cana*, *Mangrove*, *Monsoon*; and sandwiched among them the serene group of pure abstract paintings, mostly 1960, which look so impressive today. Later came *Turtle and Temple Gong*, 1965 and *House by the Sea*, 1967.

In these, his finest paintings, Fairweather has overcome the halting contradictions of his Englishness. The influence of European Cubism and the line taken from China are combined with consummate ease, establishing a convincing personal imagery. At the same time, these are paintings very much encouraged by the aura of his adopted landscape, northern Australia: not only in the clear references to Aboriginal art, which seem entirely natural here and not superimposed; but also in the strong yet contemplative earth colours, their casual almost careless spaciousness. Perhaps above all it is declared in their raucousness, a revealing untidiness like the dry-tangled Australian landscape—in *Mangrove* of course, and developed to an inspired degree in *Shalimar*, *Monsoon* and *House by the Sea*.

All this is impressive enough. But the sign of Fairweather's greatness is the amount of himself which enters the work. For all their successful references to Europe, the East and Australia, his paintings are essentially 'written' by his own experiences. Much then depends on the quality of the experiences. Fairweather has conceded he was a religious artist—and not merely in occasional religious subject matter. Through his art he attempted to reach and understand some deep equilibrium of the senses, based upon his experiences. It is this which was withheld from Fairweather until very late in his life, and which gives the paintings their enduring interest. It becomes unnatural to localise them: emotions, worth repeating, are always more general than circumstances.

Fairweather is the least parochial of Australian painters, an artist of exceptional force and originality. Due to the nature of things, reticence and distance on Fairweather's part, the rest of the world scarcely knew, or even knows now, of his existence.

Excerpt from Murray Bail, *Ian Fairweather*, Bay Books, Sydney, 1981

MONSOON, 1961/62
Synthetic polymer paint and gouache on cardboard
98 × 188.5
Collection: Art Gallery of Western Australia

HELMUT FEDERLE

Born Uznach, Switzerland, 1944

Lives and works in Vienna, Austria

BERNHARD BÜRGI: In Vienna I experienced these two contrapuntal ways of working. I'm thinking of the works of the studio, for instance *Great Wall* (1986, oil on canvas). The contours of the figural signs are clearly defined and interwoven with the background; to put it more simply, in the New York picture the forms are floating on the background, whereas now an equivalence of form and background has become apparent. The work follows the principle of rarified monumentality, it exudes serenity. The pictorial structure shows a signal-like character that is, however, atmospherically tempered by its subtle, painterly concentration.

HELMUT FEDERLE: After years of working on formal aspects of this kind, a certain quality of control has emerged, along with a more even psychic component that underlies my work today. Thus, personal emotions have yielded to a more contemplative, harmonising form. I don't want it to be determined by the state of my emotions but by the compelling logic of the picture itself.

BB: The symbolic references you used to make, at least on an associative level, such as allusions to figuration or your own initials as elements of your composition, have almost completely disappeared. Today the quality of the picture is more purely the outcome of the interplay between colour and form. Could one say that you are coming closer to an absolute approach to the picture as propagated by Ad Reinhardt?

HF: I can certainly identify with the issues raised by Reinhardt. Only I must say that the quest for absolute truths is no longer feasible or, rather, you can still look for absolute values and ideals but you will have to face up to the fact that they can no longer be found in our materialistic, jaded world. This does not, however, diminish the value of ideals.

BB: Emotional sources used to be apparent in the work process but today—how shall I put it—a more objective structural order prevails. How do you see the psychic component of your imagery today?

HF: I'm sure it still plays a role but it's not as decisive any more; my new pictures no longer expose the state of my soul as they once did. I think this is a positive development; in fact I am consciously working on it. To repeat, I no longer want my pictures to depend so heavily on personal parameters. In the course of my confrontation with painting, I have come to the realisation that there are immanent artistic criteria that override individual motives. It took me a long time to realise this since I have no intellectual background.

BB: You have always stressed a compositional principle that Barnett Newman has gone so far as to call the basic failing of European art. We were talking before about working towards the absolute picture, which brings us face to face with monochrome painting. What does structure, sign and order mean to you, what prevents you from doing monochrome work?

HF: Composition is certainly my main concern. It enables me to take determining steps, i.e. composition includes the possibility of setting accents, of conveying an intention by defining one form in relation to another or by defining the temperature and weight of another colour—in other words, the classical issue of colour and form used to convey spiritual concerns. However, if I were to get involved with monochromy, I would have to deal with a theoretical totality of thought, which I accept intellectually and sense very strongly, but I have the feeling this intellectual-conceptual totality would impose greater constraints on me than composition does. I

think the fragility of composition is terribly important and it is lost in monochrome work. It's like a mathematical approach to composition ($2+2=4$), which is something I could not subject myself to. Some compositional criteria can be legitimised neither mathematically nor arbitrarily. They are determined by concentration and experience on the intellectual as well as emotional level, but also on a fragile, relative level. They mature gradually.

BB: Does the expression 'pictorial ritual' mean anything to you? Your experience has equipped you with criteria regarding basic elements like colour and sign, which are your artistic building blocks and which you have to employ new in every pictorial process.

HF: The aspect of controlling a composition is central, in other words, ritualised. Suppose the sketch of a composition looks the same as the final product. Then why not stop at the sketch and leave it at that? This illustrates the necessity of allotting weight to colour, for instance. The picture may already have unmistakable form but cannot acquire a compelling dimension in itself if the weight of the colours isn't right. Otherwise the form has to be changed. This mutual adjustment reflects the concept of classical modernism that posits measurable criteria for a colour, a form or an intuition, which means that a valid picture is not the product of chance. The preliminary sketch is a skeleton that is readable without investing much time. This is followed by a period of ritualised study, control, doubt. The final ritual breathes life into the picture.

BB: But in the beginnings of abstract painting the attempt was made to demonstrate cosmic laws through pictorial qualities, to establish a kind of correspondence between cosmic order and pictorial order. There was great utopian potential and even faith in the capacity of art to change the world. Today we find ourselves facing much greater relativity regarding pictorial possibilities since the great designs for the world did not come true and bourgeois-capitalist society has laid claim to ideal values. How can you have emotional, uncynical strength in such a disillusioning context, in this broken situation?

HF: I don't hold much with the idea that art can change society anyway. Art always refers back to art and I think we simply have to face up to the limitations of art, which is, incidentally, also the means of reaching heights that only art can give us. Ultimately art stands for nothing but itself; it is a fallacy to make it stand in for day-to-day politics.

A spiritual quality—that's where I see the greatest potential. Through pictorial invention, the vital questions of life and death are simulated, not illustratively but through the potential of art itself.

BB: The aura of the picture refers beyond its purely material substance to a spiritual level which is unnamed and somewhat numinous in character.

HF: The greatest impact of art lies in the fact that it is ultimately not a particular person's material. A superior work acquires such inner impetus, such a life of its own, that the creator of the work fades into the background; the work defines a space, an environment, or takes root as a felt value in the soul of the beholder.

Excerpt from Bernhard Bürgi, 'Conversation with Helmut Federle in Zürich, December 1986', *Abstrakte Kunst aus Europa und Amerika*, Galerie nächst St Stephan, Vienna, & Ritter Verlag, Klagenfurt

NAME WITHOUT M, 1980
Acrylic on canvas
204 × 304

(Photo) Galerie nächst St Stephan, Vienna

Born Cleveland, Ohio, USA, 1947

Lives and works in Berkeley, California

THE RELOCATION OF AMBIENT SOUND: URBAN SOUND SCULPTURE

lasting
Sounds leaving from
different places and forming
Sounding
a sculpture which lasts[1]

I have been working in the genre of sound sculpture since 1974. My explorations of the compositional aspects of ambient sound, however, date back to the mid-1960s. Relying primarily on the use of field recording, I have investigated a wide range of normal experiences of ambient sound to learn and document how various instances of sound possess musical form—musical form in this case being the broadest possible definition of interesting compositional relationships. The purchase, in 1972, of a tape recorder that was small enough to take with me wherever I went enabled me to investigate many different types of ambient sound situations. After six years of serious field recording, I began to realise how full of aesthetic possibilities these ambient sound situations were, and how unexplored or even lost such an aesthetic sensibility of them was in our Western culture.

My transition from working with field recording to sound sculpture occurred as a solution to an unsolved question that became increasingly urgent as my experience with field recording grew: How can I make art out of ambient sounds?

Influenced by Duchamp's strategy of the found object, I began to realise that the relocation of an ambient sound source within a new context would alter radically the acoustic meaning of the ambient sound source. I conceived such relocations in sculptural terms because ambient sounds are sculptural in the way they belong to a particular place. To make art out of an ambient sound, the act of placing this sound would have considerable aesthetic importance.

In both my field recording and sound sculpture, sounds are not isolated from their contexts; in relocating sounds, I have been concerned with the contexts in which the sounds are placed and with the sculptural/spatial qualities of the sound source. For me, the richness and beauty of ambient sounds come from their interaction with a living situation. For this reason, I have installed most of my recent sound sculptures outdoors, in juxtaposition with actual contexts of ambient sound. In addition to the sound content, the acoustic conditions and architectural qualities of such contexts have played important roles in my selection of sculpture sites. The medium of radio has also proven an effective context in which to present ambient sounds. When played on radio, a given sound is juxtaposed instantaneously with thousands of different ambient sound contexts. I have thus included live radio components in several recent sound sculptures that were site-specific, which has had the effect of extending them in new and surprising ways.

In addition to their sculptural ability to belong to a particular space, ambient sounds are sculptural as volumes of space in terms of how a given sound source occupies its own sound field. Through multiple-perspective field recordings and live relocations of environmental sound processes, I have investigated this sculptural property of sound in many different circumstances. Real-time multiple-acoustic perspectives reveal qualities in sound sources that are not explicit in our typical perception of them. Such factors as acoustic delays, the Doppler effect and phasing reveal elegant musical structures in even the most simple of environmental sound sources. When a multiple-perspective rendering of the sounds of one place (either live or recorded) is installed in another space and played from a number of carefully positioned loudspeakers, dynamic and vivid relocations of the sound sources can be realised. When thinking about the transformed acoustic meaning that a familiar sound acquires when its whole sound field is considered, I

ask myself, 'What is this sound that I am now hearing?' The answer I give is that this sound is all the possible ways there are to hear it.

During the past few years I have had the opportunity to realise sound projects in New York, San Francisco, Hawaii, Alaska, West Berlin, Cologne, Paris, Amsterdam, Stockholm, Thailand, Australia and Japan. Three of these projects, described below, illustrated different ways of relocating an ambient sound source within a new environmental context.

OSCILLATING STEEL GRIDS ALONG THE BROOKLYN BRIDGE

The road surface of the Brooklyn Bridge is a studded steel grid. A car driving over this surface produces an oscillating tone, the exact frequency of which is determined by the speed of the car. The pervasive droning quality of this sound makes it musical (in the language of contemporary music). Many people in the immediate environment of the Brooklyn Bridge, such as pedestrians on the bridge's walkway or passengers in a car, respond negatively to the humming of the bridge, perhaps because the sound is so loud when heard close up.

For the centenary of the Brooklyn Bridge in 1983, I wanted to take this humming sound and put it somewhere else in New York City where it would be out of context and a surprise to hear. I selected a large open plaza below the World Trade Center towers. Acoustically, this large open space has a low ambient sound level, as it is far from traffic sounds and is surrounded by high buildings. The World Trade Center is also a contemporary New York landmark, while the Brooklyn Bridge is a much older one. Additionally, I find that the towers of the World Trade Center have a science-fiction quality that works well with and is shared by the humming of the Brooklyn Bridge. Loudspeakers were hidden in the facade of Tower One so that the humming sound of the bridge would become the sound of the World Trade Center towers. These humming sounds were transmitted live from the Brooklyn Bridge to the World Trade Center by means of equalised broadcast-quality telephone lines. This meant that the normal changes of the day, such as traffic (less traffic meant faster cars producing higher-pitched tones) and weather (thunderstorms occurring simultaneously at the bridge and the plaza created an interesting acoustical delay) could be heard, as well as the special sounds of the Brooklyn Bridge centenary (the parade, boat whistles and fireworks).

ENTFERNTE ZÜGE (DISTANT TRAINS)

In the fall of 1983, while living in West Berlin as a composer, I was invited to design a temporary site-specific work for one of several possible locations in the city as part of a city-wide architectural exhibition scheduled for the fall of 1984.[2]

I selected the former Anhalter Bahnhof as the site for *Entfernte Züge* because the ruins of this former train station were suggestive of sound to me. The first time I visited the Anhalter Bahnhof, the empty field behind the shattered facade seemed strangely quiet, as if haunted by the sounds of trains and people. This 'acoustical haunting' was so vivid that I decided to design a sound sculpture that would suggest the same experience to anyone passing through the site.

I wanted to take the sound of the busiest contemporary German train station and relocate it in Berlin at the Anhalter Bahnhof. After some research, I selected the Köln Hauptbahnhof, the busiest train station in Europe. There the sounds of the train announcements are nearly constant. Often several simultaneous

announcements create a spontaneous kind of sound poetry. The sounds of the trains themselves, the signals at both ends of the station and the voices and footsteps of people are also ever-present.

My original design called for the live sound from the Köln Hauptbahnhof to be played at Anhalter Bahnhof. As a live relocation of sound, the times of the train announcements coming from Köln would also be actual in Berlin. However, because of its political and geographic isolation within East Germany, West Berlin had only limited broadcast facilities, which made a live eight-channel audio transmission to the city impossible. The alternative was to make an eight-channel tape version in which the feeling of real time was preserved.

METROPOLIS KÖLN

An invitation to make a live acoustic portrait of the city of Köln for a symposium to be held in September 1985 provided me with the opportunity to combine my interests in many different types of sounds into one large project[3]. In all of my previous sound sculptures, I had concentrated on relocating one type of sound source to a new context. In making these relocations, I had been concerned with the perceived scale of the sound source. I had manipulated this sense of acoustic scale by juxtaposing sound with the physical/architectural elements of the sculpture site. I had learned that this use of acoustic relocation and acoustic scale was a powerful method for altering the perceived acoustical meaning of ordinary and familiar sounds. For *Metropolis Köln* I would need to relocate simultaneously many different types of sounds to a suitable sculpture site and also to realise a live radio concert of the city's sounds.

The sculpture site of this work was Roncalliplatz, the large square plaza adjacent to the south facade of the Kölner Dom (cathedral). With its towering Gothic spires and overwhelming presence, the Dom is the dominant architectural element of this plaza. Because it has the feeling of being the center and heart of Köln, the plaza seemed suitable as the site for this live acoustic portrait. A total of 18 loudspeakers were hidden on the four sides of the plaza, each one corresponding to live sound coming from 18 microphones placed around the city. Six loudspeakers were hidden along a balcony of the Dom located about 80 feet above the plaza. Twelve more loudspeakers were placed on the roofs of buildings bordering the other three sides of Roncalliplatz.

Live microphones were positioned at various acoustic landmarks around Köln; these included the Hauptbahnhof, four different bridges over the Rhine River, the clock and bell towers of six Romanesque churches, a pedestrian street, three locations in the Kölner Zoo and two locations along the Rhine River. These river locations created the constant sound of waves and water, each one having a different timbre: one came from a microphone that transmitted the sound of waves at the water's edge, the other came from a hydrophone in the Rhine. The live sound from the hydrophone was broadcast to a loudspeaker on the edge of Roncalliplatz in the Old Roman Harbor Street.

During the day and early evening, the city was alive with many sounds and activities, with these river sounds providing a constant texture among many other sounds. In the evening as the city became quieter, the sound of the river would take over, apparently becoming the sound of the Dom. In the early morning and at twilight, the live microphones broadcasting from the Zoo became very active, as if sea lions, birds and apes were suddenly calling from the balcony of the Dom. On the hour, the Romanesque bell towers told the time from positions all around Roncalliplatz; the time they told was not entirely correct since they were all off slightly from each other. Ships passing under bridges, trams and trains making the bridges resonate could be heard from the Dom and the roof of the Römanisch/Germanisch Museum. A microphone placed under a manhole cover on a pedestrian street would broadcast the resonant and percussive sounds of footsteps and the sounds of muted voices. Microphones in the Hauptbahnhof would broadcast train announcements, the whistles from the Wagenmeister and the loud signals at the end of a platform. The changing combinations of these sounds heard from different positions around the large open space of Roncalliplatz created the compositional and spatial form of this sound sculpture.

For the fiftieth anniversary of the San Francisco Golden Gate Bridge in May 1987, I realised *Sound Sculptures through the Golden Gate*. This work was a trilogy of adjacent sound sculptures corresponding to three adjacent acoustic zones found in the Gulf of the Farallones at the entrance to San Francisco Bay: the sounds of thousands of birds and marine mammals on SE Farallon, the underwater sounds of whales and dolphins between the Farallones and the entrance to San Francisco Bay, and the sounds of the Golden Gate Bridge with its foghorns and expansion joints. Microphones and hydrophones transmitted the sounds simultaneously to the San Francisco Museum of Modern Art and the Museum Ludwig in Köln. This work was also a live radio event broadcast simultaneously throughout the USA and Europe.[4]

Statement by the artist in *Leonardo*, vol. 20, no 1, 1987.

1. Marcel Duchamp, *The Bride Stripped Bare by her Bachelors Even*, Richard Hamilton version, and G.H. Hamilton, trans. 3rd ed., Jaap Reitman, New York, 1976.
2. This temporary site-specific work was commissioned by West Berlin's redevelopment agency (International Building Exhibitions). At the time, I was a guest composer of the Berliner Künstlerprogramm des DAAD (Berlin Artists Program of the German Academic Exchange Service).
3. This invitation was proffered by the Hörspiele (sound play or drama) department of West German Radio (WDR) in Köln. The symposium was called *Acustica International*.
4. In the USA, it was broadcast by American Public Radio; in Europe, by WDR Köln.

In the end the artworks could become so similar, so similar to the everyday, that they disappear as it were. That would be a version of the dream of the blending of art and life. But, although Katharina Fritsch seems to pursue this path to some extent, the similarity of her objects is certainly of another kind. It is similarity with a difference. In these small deviations, immediately tangible but at the same time traceless and difficult to pin down, which lie between the alike and the similar, is concentrated the meaning of these works. Katharina Fritsch employs no ready-mades; each object is expressly constructed, or at least so treated, that one is no longer sure of its origin. There are not just those 'usual things, which each man can take for granted' (Rilke). This difference, however, is always only minimal; also if she distinguishes the art object from the usual object, she doesn't carry it off into the complete other, into a silent mystery of art. There remains a prosaic object-world that possesses just enough poetry and aura to produce a game with them all which makes the objects interesting to us: the amazement and questions, the recollections and comparisons, the meaning of it, that has for one moment concentrated a complex slice of life at one point and made it quite clear. For one moment then the object disappears, submerges the sculpture in the uniformity of the remaining objects, in order to step to another place as a pictorial metaphor in the consciousness again. In the works of Katharina Fritsch there is no dark and profoundly secret proceeding, nor the conclusion of a theoretical strategy, but a prosaic and lovely movement, which results from an intuitive and calculated association with the objects and their similarities. That the similarity in her works is at the same time completely evident and concealed goes without saying.

Excerpt from Julian Heynen, *Katharina Fritsch: Elefant*
(catalogue), Kaiser Wilhelm Museum, Krefeld, 1987
Translated by Josephine Heitter

GRÜNER SEIDENSCHAL   M : 1 : 4

ENTWURF FÜR EINEN SEIDENSCHAL
Print

Born Paris, France, 1946

Lives and works in Marcilly-sur-Eure

Man does not find the truth.
He makes it up, as he makes up his history,
and both get even with him.
Paul Veyne

The critics, in another period, led people to believe just how 'unqualifiable' Garouste's art was.

The formal description broke its back thereupon. The iconography was as if taken off its guard. As for the style, it navigated amongst as many referents as the amateur could decipher by doing his utmost.

In short, Gérard Garouste refuted all the categories enumerated up till then, and said above all it was impossible to think all that.

But Garouste was a painter resorting to conventions to the point where it was accepted from the word go that this type of painting was all the more *present* in order for standard values to be liquidated and liquefied by it and through it. So: Garouste was a painter at a time (not so long ago) when others were saying it was no good painting any more, and others again—such as art still harbours today as naive—were wont to confess, 'I'm a painter, but that's not what you'd call painting.'

Now, let's get this straight. Garouste is a painter and has always wished to remain so. He knows all the tricks of the trade, and the conventions, too. He knows the effect produced by a glaze, by a 'flochetage', a grisaille or a chiaroscuro. He has *savoir faire*.

And beyond that, he knew, and still knows—in an age that decries the virtues of myths and their origins—what a subject and the choice of a story imply: Garouste knows his History and the manners it has.

And it is not so much the specificity of a genre as the reasons why we recognise it that he wished to interrogate. Now, the very same people who, ten years ago, proudly said that Garouste did not know how to paint, are nonplussed, exclaiming, 'What a lot of progress he has made—what a master of *his* style he has turned out to be!'

Others, who had sworn by God Almighty that painting was out for good, and who had, despite themselves, become the chlorotic surgeons of what Picabia called 'already old-time movements', glibly talked about *return*.

And what of Garouste, floundering all of a sudden beneath yet another history of vicissitudes—comparable for many to that *end*, that disillusion of the avant-garde who established themselves during the inter-war years.

The eternal rebirth of history.

But there we are: Garouste is not La Patellière, nor is he the herald of some form of nostalgia or another. He is not one of those actors at grips with the negative, a figure of Melancholy or of Nostos. We are definitely not back in 1930. The stakes and regulations cannot be, and are no longer, the same. Garouste is fully aware that the artist's gestures have to be valid.

On his own, and in a context still nourished by abstinence, he has dedicated his work to abundance. Versus the poverty of art become supreme luxury these past years versus all the *ad minima* practices to which the sole beauty of a welcoming spot still grants them credit, Garouste has designedly (and I do mean, by design) displaced all that, in the course of time, had become the current stake of that time.

I say *stake*, as one says in card games, to make it quite clear that the oeuvre and the devices it constructs—the scaffolding—are based on conventions. In every oeuvre as in everything, 'whether it be art or not, in accordance with the famous formula', there are blows, rules and tricks of the trade. Garouste named this principle 'la règle du je'—just another of his untranslatable plays upon words in a work wherein the sleights of hand, the substitutions and conjuring tricks come close to astronomy and the language of the stars, together with the fables, and with all those who are aware that it is by way of fiction that the verity is expressed . . .

Bernard Blistène, 'Gérard Garouste: Hors du Calme', *Galeries Magazine*, no 21, October/November 1987

UNTITLED, 1987
Oil on canvas
200 × 235

(Photo) Adam Rzepka

Born Auckland, New Zealand, 1917

Lives and works in Canberra, Australia

Streeton's colours for the Australian landscape were yellow and blue; and in the last few years yellow and black have become Rosalie Gascoigne's colours. Her 'panels' are made of the wood of old packing cases stencilled with brand names—'Schweppes', etc—and from the staring retro-reflective material of old road signs. Bold and ungentle material to work with, those road signs.

First she finds the material. Gascoigne's forays are as crucial, and sometimes as anxious, as a landscape painter's search for a subject. Streeton climbed the 120-metre high 'Gib' near Mittagong to find the subject of his 1892 water colour '*Vale of Mittagong*'. In a similar hot and sweaty state of physical exertion, Gascoigne scans the countryside within an eighty-kilometre radius of Canberra. Distinctly different from work in the studio, the day-length journeys in her station wagon are voyages of liberation and possible discovery, on which the artist may find a few scarred road signs or a vista of low yellow hills stencilled with roads. Journeys the world over have the same meaning and the same hazards, though Gascoigne is by way of being a professional voyager travelling the roads she knows and 'moving in the landscape as if she were part of it'. The real journey is internal. The spoils come back to the studio.

The journeys are mentioned because they are profoundly important, providing not only the materials but the experiences of which art is made. Gascoigne has always said that her work is about the landscape and the feelings it arouses in her. The sorts of things she notices, threading her way up the country and back, year after year, are the teeming grasses in a good year, and the brown, heavier look of their prosperity, the black shadows of clouds fleeing with the wind over pastureland, and the sheen and pallor of grass when its season is over and it is thin in the paddocks, bleached of colour and stripped of seedheads. Because she *knows* the shape of this landscape, and the roads that map it, she notices more (or at least speaks about) the mutable aspects of colour, light, texture and movement.

Landscape and art are not connected in a direct way. Very rarely Gascoigne splits the wood and assembles the pieces with a particular idea in mind. The title comes after a work has been made, lived with and accepted by the artist as complete: very much after the event. Gascoigne's titles are mnemonic, associative, precise and personal, whereas the feelings or moods expressed by the art are generalised. The artist named *Tiger Tiger* after William Blake's poem—and liking its double word formation because the title matches the work's powerful yellow and black colours, the two equal panels, the strength of a square grid and the wide, squat lettering. Another retro-reflective panel, *Plain Song*, is named for its straight lines, its dignity, cool colour, the singing letter 'O', and the reedy quality of its scratched surface. Thus the title of a work by Gascoigne is a pointer to formal qualities even though the associations between work and title may not be as well aligned for others as they are for the artist.

Landscape is evoked in Gascoigne's art by formal analogy and metaphor. By the work's *presence*. She has written about other artists' work in ways that are appropriate to her own: 'Ken Whisson's paintings are full of the look and feel of nature. He is good at clouds. He can paint the quality of air. He knows about the sea. He is a passionate student of the human condition. He paints like a man who needs space both to move in and to think in.' In 1973 she wrote about John Armstrong: 'The one I liked has a quality some of the others haven't. Definite presence. Nothing to be added and nothing to be taken away. Also neatness and lasting qualities. Disciplined. Not full of romping fun. Strangely spiritual—

ecclesiastical, classical . . .' Of Colin McCahon's *Victory over Death, 2* she wrote in 1984, 'a banner of great presence . . . monumental and absolute'.

'Classical' is a word she constantly uses, so is 'presence'. Their significance for the artist was clarified by a unique training.

Gascoigne matured as a woman and artist before she entered the art community—'Art confirmed me' she has said. 'Her work is unlike anybody else's in Australia', wrote Daniel Thomas in 1975. And since first exhibiting in 1974 her art hasn't altered all that much, not in the way it would have had she been discovering everything since then. So where did Rosalie Gascoigne begin, if not in 1970s so-called informal sculpture? My guess is that the decisive moment was in 1963 or 1964 on the steps of Mark Foy's, Sydney, drinking coffee and reading a big new book about *Ikebana* by Norman Sparnon, whose classes she had joined. 'I read, feeling that I knew for myself everything he was saying.'

'I was already bringing back the hill-tops and rivers in the form of dried native flowers, river stones and grasses. I was all wild surmise. *Ikebana* gave an absolute. It gave form. To do things exactly steadied you down. From practising *Ikebana* I got the vision of how to use the things I liked.'

It sounds like neoplatonism, this vision or precious intimation of a perfect form or absolute, towards which the artist drives. Rosalie Gascoigne doesn't know the term. The vital step for her between a wild surmise and knowing how to realise a work of art was the *Ikebana* exercises. Like practising scales in music, one year was spent following a few rigid rules. Gascoigne abandoned *Ikebana* classes when she wanted more freedom, but not before *Ikebana*, like Plato's abstract form, had provided her with an internalised sense of perfect order. She now had her original, passionate acquisitiveness plus that rare sculptural sense which the art community noticed.

That feeling for form has been the ruler against which some constructions pass as art and the occasional one is recognised as still-born. Likewise, as a sense of balance and of space, it informs the artist's feeling for landscape.

There is one particular cultural expression of the Australian landscape, recurring in Australian art and literature which quite a few of her works come up with. This landscape of our culture is edgeless, going on beyond the reach of imagination, various without repetition, quiet, austere. Aboriginal songs and paintings are like this, analogous to maps. Tom Collins wrote in the 1890s: 'Mile after mile we go at a good walk, till the dark boundary of the scrub country disappears northward in the glassy haze, and in front, southward, the level black-soil plains of Riverina Proper mark a straight skyline, broken here and there by a monumental clump of pine-ridge. And away beyond the horizon, southward still, the geodesic curve carries that monotony across the zone of saltbush, myall, and swamp box . . .'. Gerald Murnane wrote in the early 1980s: 'The plains that I crossed in those days were not endlessly alike. Sometimes I looked over a great shallow valley with scattered trees and idle cattle and perhaps a meagre stream at its centre. Sometimes, at the end of a tract of utterly unpromising country, the road rose towards what was unquestionably a hill before I saw ahead only another plain, level and bare and daunting.' Many of Gascoigne's works, through repetition that is never actual repetition, and minimal variations, memorise a journey, many journeys, across a landscape without edges.

Mary Eagle

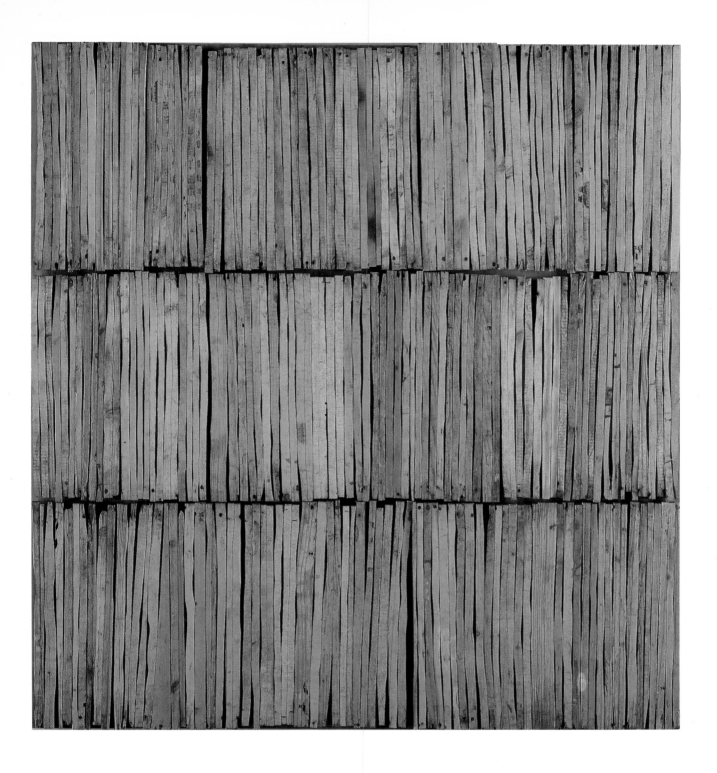

ROADSIDE, 1988
Wood and aluminium strip
125 × 122

(Photo) Matt Kelso

Born Bad Oldeslohe, Federal Republic of Germany, 1948

Lives and works in Cologne

Isa Genzken is concerned with the idiomatic and totemic characteristics of early and high-modernist architectural forms. Distantly related to Hilla and Bernd Becher's photographs of nineteenth-century German architectural structures, her objects are instances of specific social/cultural frameworks. Genzken articulates the inherent systemisation of an archive of modernist architectural forms. She celebrates, and is critical of, certain design conventions dominant in architectural ideology and practice.

Her recent sculptures, some based loosely on buildings designed by the architects Eliel Saarinen, Walter Gropius, Adolf Meyer and Adolf Loos, are intended to be viewed as autonomous objects as well as units in a sequence of subtly altered structural episodes. Radical 'undifferentiation' becomes a principle of sculptural invention. Her objects are reductive yet elegant, perched atop specially designed pedestals that reinforce the unique sculptural variation and architectonic nuance of each piece. On one level, Genzken implies a correspondence between the ubiquitous presence of high modernist architecture and the structural conjugation of such objects as anti-functional 'models'. She seems to suggest that the architectural idiom of the 1940s and 1950s may correspond to a more general cultural paradigm of aesthetic production, such as seriality in certain conceptual art practices.

Genzken's recent concrete sculptures, *Quelle* (1986) and *Tor* (1986), explore notions of infrastructure, essence and decay. These objects connote some of the essential, distilled formal strategies of modernist form and design. Similarly, they are somewhere between a literal architectonic structure and metaphoric reference, becoming surrogates or 'models' of potentially existing edifices.

Genzken uses concrete and paint subtly applied to create surfaces and textures that suggest an ambiguity between structural decay and integral progression. Her forms are purposefully unresolved and incomplete, suggesting fragments excerpted from existing buildings. At once elegant and rudely, brutally tactile, Genzken's recent work is an index of material immediacy, metaphorical architectural reference, social/cultural convention and sculptural beauty.

Excerpt from Joshua Decter, 'Sculptural Transgressions: Observing Paradigms of Cultural Experience', *Juxtapositions: Recent Sculpture from England and Germany* (catalogue), P.S.1, The Institute for Art and Urban Resources, Inc., New York, 1987

(Left) GUARDINI, 1987
Concrete and steel
226 × 81 × 46

(Right) KUSS, 1987
Concrete and steel
228 × 98 × 61

John Wood, born Bath, England, 1945

Lives and works in London

David Godbold, born Norfolk, England, 1961

Lives and works in London

John Wood and David Godbold first began collaborating in November 1984, having given performances and made installation-works as individual artists.

John Wood and David Godbold's *Captive*, the latest in a series of six works made since their decision to collaborate three years ago, began with a sentence from Kant's *The Fundamental Principles of Metaphysics and Ethics*: 'If appearances are things-in-themselves,' he wrote, 'then freedom cannot be saved.' With the rise of the new physics and the (not unrelated) sense of imminent religiosity which marks the last years of the twentieth century, things and appearances have become indistinguishable. Indeed, the very basis for their initial separation has been abandoned. Kant's question remains. It needs an extreme case of belief or disbelief, a miracle or an almost impossible event like the appearance of an extraterrestrial, to put matters to the test.

In a dimly-lit room the visitor finds a lamp and three mirrors. A figure appears, or seems to appear. Ageless, sexless, weightless, it hovers like a moth around the lamp. Has the figure escaped from its confines or has the viewer entered them? Questioning our own perceptions, we are forced to consider the limits of the self. 'The self can never reach the other and can never do without it,' Thomas McEvilley has written. 'The self's love of and need for the other is matched only by its hatred of and repulsion from it. The other is the eternally elusive beloved and the eternally pursuing enemy.' Revealing the fictionality of fiction and therefore refuting a world of facts and figures, the orbiting apparition stresses that appearances are what we must confront, that they should never be confused with fact, and that they are as satisfactory an approach to reality as we are ever likely to achieve. Is the little captive a mystic vision, like Thomas Southwell's Burning Babe? Or a piece of cheap and nasty trickery, with its sci-fi starbursts? Whether we shrug it off or accept it as a miracle, it has everything to do with our picture of ourselves, our margins and the doomed project of their overthrow.

Stuart Morgan, London, July 1987

Now where determination according to laws of nature ceases, there all explanation ceases also, and nothing remains but defence, i.e. the removal of the objections of those who pretend to have seen deeper into the nature of things, and thereupon boldly declare freedom impossible. We can only point out to them that the supposed contradiction that they have discovered in it arises only from this; that in order to be able to apply the law of nature to human actions, they must necessarily consider man as an appearance: then when we demand of them that they should also think of him *qua* intelligence as a thing-in-itself, they still persist in considering him in this respect also as an appearance. In this view it would no doubt be a contradiction to suppose the causality of the same subject (that is, his will) to be withdrawn from the natural laws of the sensible world. But this contradiction disappears, if they would only bethink themselves and admit, as is reasonable, that behind the appearances there must also lie at their root (although hidden) the things-in-themselves, and that we cannot expect the laws of these to be the same as those that govern their appearances.

Excerpt from Immanuel Kant, *The Fundamental Principles of the Metaphysics of Ethics*

Detail from CAPTIVE, 1987
Mixed media installation
112 × 104 × 68.5

FRANZ GRAF

Born Tülln, Vienna, Austria, 1954

Lives and works in Vienna

UNTITLED, 1987
Pencil on transparent paper
Series of six pieces, each 46 × 34

PETER HALLEY

Born New York City, USA, 1953

Lives and works in New York

THE DEPLOYMENT

OF THE GEOMETRIC

The deployment of the geometric dominates the landscape. Space is divided into discrete, isolated cells, explicitly determined as to extent and function. Cells are reached through complex networks of corridors and roadways that must be travelled at prescribed speeds and at prescribed times. The constant increase of the complexity and scale of these geometries continuously transforms the landscape.

Conduits supply various resources to the cells. Electricity, water, gas, communication lines, and, in some cases, even air are piped in. The conduits are almost always buried underground, away from sight. The great networks of transportation give the illusion of tremendous movement and interaction. But the networks of conduits minimalise the need to leave the cells.

The regimentation of human movement, activity and perception accompanies the geometric division of space. It is governed by the use of time-keeping devices, the application of standards of normalcy, and the police apparatus. In the factory, human movement is made to conform to rigorous spatial and temporal geometries. At the office, the endless recording of figures and statistics is presided over by clerical workers.

Along with the geometrisation of the landscape, there occurs the geometrisation of thought. Specific reality is displaced by the primacy of the model. And the model is in turn imposed on the landscape, further displacing reality in a process of ever more complete circularity.

Art, or what remains of art, has also been geometrised. But in art the geometric has been curiously associated with the transcendental. In Mondrian, Newman, even in Noland, the geometric is heralded as the timeless, the heroic, and the religious. Geometry, ironically, is deemed the privileged link to the nature it displaces.

In this way, geometric art has been made to justify the deployment of the geometric. It has linked the modern deployment of geometry to the wisdom of the ancients, to the tradition of religious truth, and to the esoteric meditative practices of non-Western cultures. Geometric art has served to hide the fact that the modern deployment of geometry is stranger than the strange myths of traditional societies. Geometric art has sought to convince us, despite all the evidence to the contrary, that the progress of geometry is humanistic, that it is part of the 'march of civilisation', that it embodies continuity with the past. In this, geometric art has succeeded completely. In so doing, it has helped make possible the second phase of geometrisation (that coincides with the post-war period) in which coercion is replaced by fascination.

We are convinced. We volunteer. Today Foucauldian confinement is replaced by Baudrillardian deterrence. The worker need no longer be coerced into the factory. We sign up for body-building at the health club. The prisoner need no longer be confined in the jail. We invest in condominiums. The madman need no longer wander the corridors of the asylum. We cruise the interstates.

We are today enraptured by the very geometries that once represented coercive discipline. Today children sit for hours fascinated by the day-glo geometric displays of video games. Adolescents are enchanted by the arithmetic mysteries of their computers. As adults, we finally gain 'access' to participation in our cybernetic hyperreal, with its charge cards, telephone answering machines, and professional hierarchies. Today we can live in 'spectral suburbs' or simulated cities. We can play the corporate game, the entrepreneurial game, the investment game, or even the art game.

Now that we are enraptured by geometry, geometric art has disappeared. There is no need for any more Mardens or Rymans to convince us of the essential beauty of the geometric field embodied in the television set's glowing image. Today we have instead 'figurative art' to convince us that the old humanist body hasn't disappeared (though it has). It is only now that geometric art has been discarded that it can begin to describe the deployment of the geometric.

Statement by the artist, 1984

TWO CELLS WITH CIRCULATING CONDUIT, 1987
Day-Glo acrylic, Roll-A-Tex on canvas
197 × 350.5

EITETSU HAYASHI

Born Hiroshima, Japan, 1952

Lives and works in Tokyo

RHYTHM OF A DIFFERENT

DRUMMER

To preserve tradition is easy enough, and to turn your back on it is even easier. But to work within the framework of tradition, and at the same time add something new to it, is an achievement that few musicians in any country, let alone Japan, can claim.

According to Eitetsu Hayashi, *wadaiko* (Japanese drum) music has no set tradition; having played them for fifteen years, he should know. His performances over the last year—on his own, with a *taiko*-based quartet, with the more rock-oriented Ryudogumi, and in duet (occasionally battle) with jazz pianist Yosuke Yamashita—have consistently been the most stimulating musical entertainment Tokyo offers. He takes a purely Japanese instrument and sound and makes music that transcends all boundaries.

The year was 1971: hippy ideals had yet to give way to seventies cynicism. Hayashi had just moved to Tokyo from Hiroshima when he met the members of what would become Ondekoza. The drum group came together with the goal of eventually founding a school for artists on Sado island. To accomplish this they set up a seven-year program to raise funds: two years of training followed by five years of international tours. Each of them signed a contract for that period, during which all living expenses would be loaned by sponsors.

Although none of the members had any *taiko* experience, their actual training concentrated on running full-length marathons day after day, rather than on drumming technique. The objective was development of a oneness between the runner and the environment, above building stamina. However, because of the inexperience of the group (only Hayashi had played the trap drums previously), the initial two years set aside for training were doubled. When they finally began performing, their showmanship and sheer energy were given rave reviews, especially in Europe. Eventually the original school building dream faded to the glamour of greasepaint and the mundane obligation to pay off debts.

Belonging to Ondekoza did have its share of drawbacks. The extremely arduous training and daily life under a dictatorial leader persuaded some to return to the society from which they had deviated. Somehow they managed to maintain a membership of about fifteen, but there was never sufficient time for training. Hayashi claims, 'The performances gradually became a pale imitation of what we originally set out to achieve.' Feeling that to quit before the contract was up would be a personal failure, Hayashi stifled his dissatisfaction for eleven years until the project came to a halt.

For six months after that Hayashi worked as a consultant with Kodo, a splinter group of Ondekoza. Then he went out on his own as a solo performer.

PETER BARAKAN: Your improvised performance with Yosuke Yamashita was quite remarkable. As a drummer do you find it easier to improvise on stage or do you prefer to play structured rehearsed material?

EITETSU HAYASHI: The two are quite similar but perhaps there is less tension on stage with rehearsed material—you are confident that you can play it unless you make a mistake. With improvisation the excitement is fantastic when it works, but on a bad night it is awful. Often I work improvised parts into a structured piece anyway, or sometimes I work out my own start and finish. With improvisation it's a question of finding the right balance.

Of course, the easiest style of performing is to play a composition written by someone else—you just have to learn the score. The only trouble is I very rarely like the music that has been written. No matter how well structured a piece is, it rarely equals the tension achievable in improvisation.

PB: Though Hayashi stopped playing western drums when he joined Ondekoza, his music still reveals the presence of non-Japanese rhythms. He is interested in the polyrhythms of salsa and Cuban music and admits to a penchant for African music but adds, 'It's so far away from my own experiences that I can't feel a true involvement with it.' He considers his own rhythms to be more Korean than anything else, although his first exposure to Korean music came only a few years ago.

EH: I feel a proximity to the Korean people and the music stirs a kind of nostalgia in me that I can't really explain. Its rhythms are quite different from both Japanese and Chinese, based almost exclusively on three-quarters time. I remember when I was running marathons in Sado—your breathing is supposed to go in-in out-out—but mine lapsed into a kind of syncopated three-quarters pattern. The coach corrected it and that improved my stamina, but I still feel more natural with three-quarters rhythm in my drumming.

PB: Do foreign audiences react to your music differently from the Japanese?

EH: Essentially they're the same. Japanese living in Tokyo get little exposure to traditional music. Foreign audiences, I think, still tend to have certain illusions of the 'mysterious East' and Japan is very much in fashion now, so they are perhaps more predisposed to listen to the music than the Japanese from the start. The Japanese see *taiko* as being much more commonplace but, once you actually get them to listen, their energy level is just as high.

PB: To what extent is your music traditional?

EH: There isn't really a strong tradition in *taiko* like there is with most Japanese music. When I first joined Ondekoza we had to study the *shakuhachi*, *fue*, *koto*, *samisen* and both Japanese dance and ballet. I learned a lot about the basics of Japanese music. although I never developed a real proficiency on any of the instruments in just two years. Occassionally we came into contact with traditional arts preservation societies, which I found interesting, though that approach didn't really appeal to me—we wanted music that would turn us on. I suppose that was the rock fan in me. I used to think that our music was just as progressive as Pink Floyd.

I don't try to refute tradition and I'm aware that what I am now depends on the entire body of history that has gone before me. I am attracted by certain aspects of that whole traditional world too—the concept of manners and all that—but on the other hand I was brought up and educated in the post-war American system and there are times when I can't help feeling a conflict betwen the two. I don't really think that what I'm doing is traditional. Perhaps it has the potential to become a kind of new tradition, but only if it can be kept free from institutionalisation that would stifle its growth. What it really needs is a whole batch of oddballs like me.

Peter Barakan, 'Rhythm of a Different Drummer:
Eitetsu Hayashi', *Rag*, 1986

This special event is presented as part of 'Close-up of Japan, Sydney 1988' sponsored by THE MITSUI PUBLIC RELATIONS COMMITTEE.

THE MITSUI
PUBLIC RELATIONS
COMMITTEE

EITETSU HAYASHI

JOY HESTER

Born Melbourne, Australia, 1920

Died Melbourne, 1960

Recently the art of the 1940s has enjoyed a revival that is most favourable to a fuller understanding of our past—as long as it does not slide into an infatuation with nostalgia. Nostalgia is history degutted of politics.

Joy Hester has benefited from this renewal of interest. She had no luck with the imprimatur of success during her life—good reviews, acquisition by public or private collections, financial reward. She had a small audience of faithful supporters but this did not relieve some of the bitterness she felt towards the end of her life. She died unrecognised. She knew this and encouraged her friend the poet Barrie Reid to write a book on her. Neglect is a commonplace of any account of an artist's early life, except for the most fortunate, but the reasons for Joy's neglect are relevant because of what they reveal about the time in which she lived and the limitations that operated—on the art and the woman.

First she chose to draw and not to paint. This suited her temperament, her work method and what she wanted to convey. Within the hierarchy of media, drawing has often been seen as a less complete means of artistic expression. Thus Hester has been relegated to the position as a less serious artist. She did, however, accurately and sensitively define the medium and the language that would best convey her expression. If some of her early watercolours, like *Two Girls in the Street* (c. 1941), suggest by their 'finished' quality that they may have been studies for and would certainly have made good paintings, then her later mature series like *Faces* and *Love* would have lost a great deal of their immediacy if they were elaborately described in oils. It was the right choice for her and she knew it. She was the only artist of her generation to make such a choice.

The two periods to which Joy Hester contributed as an artist were the 1940s (the 'Angry Decade') and the 1950s. As a poet her voice was less articulate though the sensibility of her poems corresponds to the 'mood' of Melbourne art in the 50s. She was part of a 'school' of image-making that straddles these decades; in fact, she was one of its originators. In the 1940s many of the images of Melbourne painting presented, with great fervour, a society torn by social conflict. For Joy psychological conflict, personality, the search for identity were the true aims of her art. She became less overtly interested in the social or narrative functions of art but the 'real' world, questions posed by living in post-war Australia occupied her and directed the source of some of her imagery. She embarked on a series of brutal and agonised images of human beings only after seeing the newsfilms of the Nazi concentration camps. In the 1950s she was increasingly preoccupied with issues of Australian identity that emerged equally from her own fervent nationalism as it did from her 'spiritual' home in the Australian bush. The milieu she was attracted to prized inner representations and it was there the ideas that shaped her art were formed, but Joy remained consistently engaged in a dialogue that encompassed the 'inner' world of the feelings and the 'outer' world where experience gave rise to them.

Excerpts from Janine Burke, *Joy Hester*, Greenhouse Publications, Melbourne, 1983

John Reed, Joy Hester, Sunday Reed with Sweeney Tucker (later Reed), and Sidney Nolan on the beach at Point Lonsdale, c. 1946. Photograph by Albert Tucker.

LOVE II, 1949
Charcoal, brush and ink, blue pastel, gouache
31.4 × 25.3
Courtesy Greenhouse Publications, Melbourne, (printed in Janine Burke *Joy Hester*, 1983)

ROGER HILTON

Born Northwood, Middlesex, England, 1911

Died Cornwall, 1975

Hilton came to maturity as a painter after the age of forty; he was one of the small band of artists in Britain who turned to abstraction around 1950. His paintings of 1950–52, in which forms are located in shallow pictorial space, reflect Paris abstraction of the time. In 1953 after meeting the Dutch artist Constant, later described by Hilton as being 'a humanised Mondrian', and visiting Holland with him and seeing paintings by Mondrian, Hilton simplified his painting, limiting his palette to the primaries, black, white and a few earth colours, applying them in a few ragged shaped areas; forms appear to move out into the real space in front of the picture plane. Some of the paintings of 1953–54 are among the most uncompromisingly abstract of their time produced in Britain while others suggest landscape or the human, female, body.

From 1955 shallow pictorial space and more allusions to the visible world appear in Hilton's painting. Visits to St Ives in Cornwall from 1956 onwards were reflected in the work by suggestions of rocks, the sea, boats and figures floating in water; a shape like a boat or shield seems to be a surrogate for a female body.

As an artist Hilton alternated periods of intense activity with quiet periods of several weeks when he painted little. However he drew almost every day, abstracts as well as many female nudes, done from memory extended by the imagination. In 1961 he painted the first of a small number of oils of overtly female figures, which at a time when abstract art had become a powerful force among artists in Britain, surprised and perhaps dismayed some of his friends and admirers. From then on he was able to move completely freely between abstraction and figuration.

Hilton expressed something of his attitude in a catalogue introduction published in 1961: 'All art is an attempt to exteriorise one's sensations and feelings, to give them a form.

'It may be thought that technique which has been built up for the purposes of figurative art ceases to apply where non-figuration is concerned. But I think that the figurative parts of pictures are not, in a final analysis, what the picture is really concerned with. It follows that the technique has been built up not so much for the purposes of representing the visible world as for being an instrument capable of embodying men's inner truths. Abstraction has been due not so much to a positive thing but to the absence of a valid image.

'Abstraction in itself is nothing. It is only a step towards a new sort of figuration, that is one which is more true . . .

'Now that we have conquered new plastic ground during the last fifty years, there is no reason why images should not return to painting without fear of repeating what has already been done.'

Much of Hilton's work has an edgy eroticism and humour. There are shapes evoking sexual hollows and protuberances, breasts and bottoms. Throughout there are hints of the experience of occupying a body which is ever changing day by day, subject to the effects of feelings and passions as well as the regular physiological processes, tempered by the action of chance . . .

Hilton drew animals, both real and imaginary, all his life; best known perhaps are those painted in gouache during the last two and a half years of his life when confined to bed through ill-health.

Making art involves taking risks and that is something Hilton was always doing. He was a courageous painter and his work was frequently well ahead of the taste of even the informed public, so that his achievement was often not fully recognised at the time.

Excerpts from David Brown, Introduction to *Roger Hilton* (catalogue), Waddington Galleries, London, 1983

UNTITLED, 1974
Graphite, pastel, gouache on paper
25.5 × 40
Collection: Ray Hughes

The first exhibition of Roger Hilton's work in Australia took place at the Ray Hughes Gallery in Brisbane in 1975.

The theme of this painting originated during a holiday in France in 1962 when Hilton and his wife were quarrelling and she was dancing up and down naked on a balcony shouting 'Oi Yoi Yoi', (and, incidentally, distracting the attention of a crowd of watching firemen fighting a blaze in a house opposite).

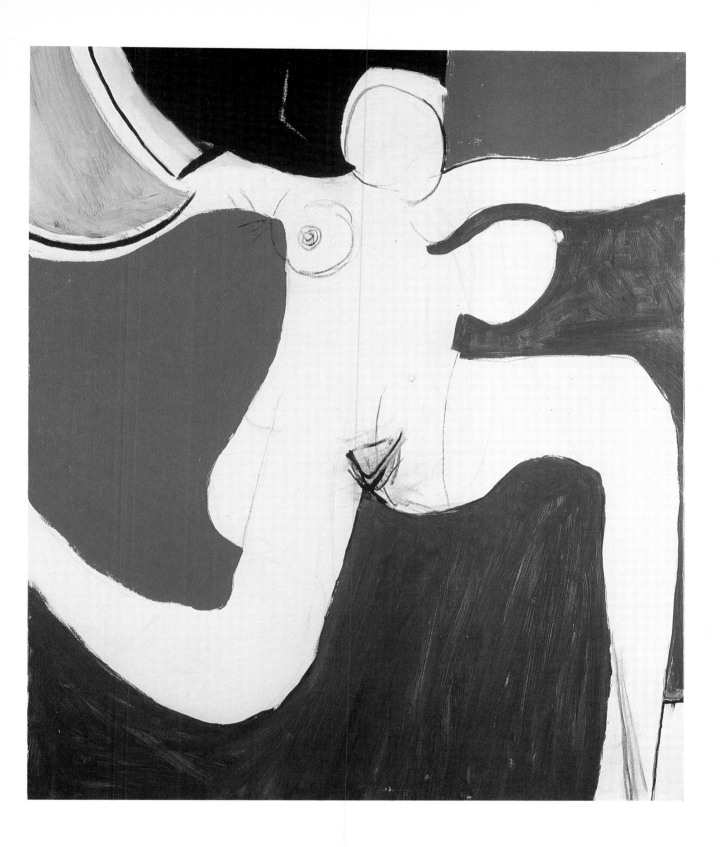

OI YOI YOI, 1963
Oil on canvas
152.4 × 127

TAISHI HIROKAWA

Born Zushi, Kanagawa, Japan, 1950

Lives and works in Tokyo

THE CUCUMBER THEORY

TAISHI HIROKAWA: You know how most vegetables and fruit these days are artificially 'enhanced', so that they look perfect, but don't have any smell or taste? It struck me that people are a bit like that too. Sort of innocuous but insubstantial, boring. They look like human beings but there's nothing inside. Then you go to the country, and discover there are still real people full of human content . . .

KIMIE HATA: People with their own character, right?

TH: I felt instantly at home with them, it was like suddenly coming across something you'd forgotten, I don't think the blame lies exclusively with designers, but they make their clothes according to a certain aesthetic, with certain proportions . . . It's like cultivating cucumbers to grow absolutely straight. I mean people get that way too. In the country you still find people who are, in cucumber terms, crooked and a bit smelly but taste great. If a designer has real understanding their clothes will look just as good on those people as on fashion models. Looking at the pictures in this book you get the feeling that these people have always worn these clothes, they look so natural in them. Without the credits it could just be a book of rural snapshots.

I wanted to shoot just in black and white, because some of the designer's clothes are in very strong colours. I'm sure those colours would look remarkable on someone standing in a field, but I thought that by holding the colours in check by shooting in black and white I might be able to achieve a better balance between the people and the clothes, with the people coming out slightly on top. The great thing with black and white is that you can retain what is essential to you and cut out everything else. Also it doesn't get to look dated. New things can look old if seen in a certain way, and vice versa.

KH: Our 'models' for this project have no awareness of fashion, and designers names mean nothing to them, but they knew when a fabric was something special, when it felt nice to wear.

TH: They didn't really care about design as much as whether the clothes were comfortable and fitted them. When we have our pictures taken we check in the mirror to make sure we look all right, don't we? Especially if the person taking the picture is someone we have never laid eyes on before who has suddenly appeared from nowhere and asked us to wear some strange clothes. But not them, they weren't bothered in the least, they didn't give a damn what anyone thought. Not one person asked for a mirror.

For the people who took part I think it was almost like one of those amateur talent shows—'why not, it's a bit of a lark', you know? It's not so much me taking the pictures as them supplying this incredible action, each of them wearing the clothes in their own individual way.

So much for my preconceptions! People living close to the earth are very sensitive. Their life is not in opposition to nature. Which should be a normal thing, of course. Their perceptions are more instinctive than logical, and I feel I was able to communicate with them on that level. That was why the photographs worked out as they did.

Each of them has their own place. They live there, have their roots there, drink the water, eat crops grown in that soil, they absorb the sunshine that falls on their own special place.

People who always need a mirror—including ourselves—are forever concerned about comparing themselves with others. To these people being different is something you take for granted, they have this amazing confidence in themselves. To come back to the vegetable metaphor once again, who can define the crookedness of a cucumber?

Excerpt from a discussion between Taishi Hirokawa and Kimie Hata, *Sonomama sonomama*, Ryuko Tsushin Co. Ltd, Tokyo, 1987
Translated by Peter Barakan

FARMER AND WIFE, FUKUSHIMA PREFECTURE, 1982
Gelatin silver print
50.8 × 40.6
Costumes: Men's Bigi (man), Half Moon (woman)

FARMER AND WIFE WITH THEIR SCARECROW, KAGAWA PREFECTURE, 1986
Gelatin silver print
50.8 × 40.6
Costumes: Arrston Volaju

POULTRY FARM WIVES, KAGAWA PREFECTURE, 1986
Gelatin silver print
50.8 × 40.6
Costumes: Obscure Desire of Bourgeoisie

RETIRED FISHERMAN, KOCHI PREFECTURE, 1986
Gelatin silver print
50.8 × 40.6
Costume: Ozone Community

JENNY HOLZER

Born Gallipolis, Ohio, USA, 1950

Lives and works in New York City

What most attracts the eye is the chemist's shop of Mr Homais opposite the Golden Lion inn. And especially the sign, as wide as the shop itself, proclaiming in golden letters: 'Homais, chemist'.

Gustave Flaubert, *Madame Bovary*

The work of Jenny Holzer, in its various forms, deals with communication and spectacular demonstration. As far back as 1980 her very strong desire for expression was evident when she put up a massive panel in the centre of Times Square in full view of pedestrians and motorists, with the unexpected inscription: PRIVATE PROPERTY CREATED CRIME. Since 1977, the series of inscriptions titled TRUISMS—of which there are more than 300 different kinds—has given her a public which goes well beyond the world of art and encompasses people from all walks of life.

The TRUISMS have been extended in her subsequent series: INFLAMMATORY ESSAYS (1979), LIVING (1981)—undertaken in collaboration with the New York artist Peter Nadin—SURVIVAL SERIES (1983), and most recently UNDER A ROCK.

The TRUISMS consist of texts of one line or more which, despite the obviously simple nature of their content, have a double meaning. Sometimes their very banality makes them ambiguous and difficult to grasp. Other times they propose several possible meanings within a single mode of appearance. They lead the reader to doubt because they seem much truer than reality itself and excessively objective. Over and above their content they seem to confirm the old saying about using deceit to reach the truth.

Confronted with these truisms, the spectator once again feels isolated, although the texts refer to some everyday event or commonplace situation. The Truisms, as the term itself suggests, do not follow the rules of Cartesian logic. They are statements of the obvious, tautological arguments, closed propositions, communicated by hollow-sounding words which state aphorisms.

In this way perception becomes a delayed process: the message does not appear all at once; we need several long seconds to read and grasp its full meaning. 'All truths are arbitrary,' says Jenny Holzer. If a spectator finds his own meaning in any given truism, this is not the only possible or 'correct' one. This is the paradox of the Truisms: a message which is difficult to decode gives rise to a plurality of possible meanings. It is as if the content of the message lies outside the words and sentences which make it up. In the 1960s Marshall McLuhan explained the phenomenon of the appearance of messages by saying that the message exists only in itself and that its appearance was the meaning. In 'Gutenberg galaxy: the making of typographic man' (1962), he turns, like Jenny Holzer in her work, to the reader. He describes this decoder of messages as a typographic man who has a new sense of time which is cinematic, sequential and pictorial.

The 'Truisms' of Jenny Holzer, because they are written, imply an impersonal form of writing, such as that achieved by the typewriter. McLuhan points out that this technique is a means of transcribing a thought or concept rather than expressing it. Jenny Holzer transmits messages, creates events but she herself does not appear. It is as if she wants to remain in the background and maintain a certain distance from the spectator.

From the beginning it is impossible to determine who will arbitrate between an 'invisible' artist and the spectator who is well and truly present. However the messages of Jenny Holzer imply the establishment of contact with the public. Hence the need to address a very large audience and achieve maximum participation.

Thus the 'Truisms' and the other categories of messages refer to the life of people and those anodyne remarks which are heard in public or private places. In the same way, the events which the artist relates are inspired by personal feelings which everyone has experienced: the evocation of pain, anguish, death, religion, etc. Sometimes they refer to the problems of 'heartland' America: in 1984, SIGN OF A TRUCK, a collection of videos and interviews with artists (Keith Haring, Leon Golub etc.) and people encountered on the street, the content is announced clearly and unambiguously on a huge panel hanging from a truck parked near the Hotel Plaza: WE ARE GOING TO DISCREDIT (CANDIDATE REAGAN) BECAUSE HE HAS MONEY AND GOD IN HIS POCKET.

Jenny Holzer, like many other artists of the 1980s (Richard Prince, Barbara Kruger, etc.) is interested in the power of the media and advertising on the environment. In terms of the history of the art she does not claim any direct descendants but refers constantly to a 'culture of images'. Her work may be the source of a slow and patient observation of all the information channels of the major American metropoli: newspaper headlines, television spots, street ads, posters, etc.

Jenny Holzer looks at all the activities of a city as if she were synchronising a film. Impressed by the lights of that most artificial of American cities, Las Vegas, she did not hesitate to inscribe on the walls of Caesar's Palace the apposite words: MONEY CREATED CRIME (1986).

All the features of the urban landscape, such as parking meters, doorstops, telephone booths, are used as props for the truisms. In various contexts, the inscriptions sometimes express a sense of revolt or subversion: in 1983 the words ABUSE OF POWER COMES AS NO SURPRISE appeared on a Lady Pink T shirt, using the absurd as a proof of male chauvinism and the rejection of feminism.

Other inscriptions appear in minority neighbourhoods—FASHION MODA IN THE SOUTH BRONX (1979).

The spectacle of communication is based on the collective memory and the different stages in the lives of people. As Guy Debord has written (*La societé du spectacle*, Paris 1971), spectacle is not a collection of images but a relationship between people, mediatised by images. The streets of modern cities witness the same events as the cities of old: the steel plaques which the artist places on doorsteps are to some extent like ex votos, whilst the granite benches (UNDER A ROCK, 1986) with their block letter inscriptions, are as imposing as funeral steles . . .

By giving an almost symphonic resonance to the spectacle of communication, Jenny Holzer indirectly reworks the remark by Flaubert that 'the surface is but a pretext for calculating what lies beneath'.

Jean-Pierre Bordaz, 'Jenny Holzer and the Spectacle of Communication', *Parkett*, no 13, 1987. Translation by Brian Mallet

PROTECT ME FROM WHAT I WANT, 1986
Signboard at Caesar's Palace, Las Vegas, Nevada

(Photo) Thomas Holder

Born Michelstadt, Federal Republic of Germany, 1944

Lives and works in Bad König-Zell

Since 1968, Rebecca Horn has been working with mythic images and memories which she translates into objects and films that communicate marvellous equivalents of her experience. Her works move in a kind of *temps perdu*, as if reality were caught in a continuous extension between mythology and history. Some of her works take the form of archaic, magical machines; obsessively and energetically repeating themselves, their cycles have no end. A needle-like pendulum perilously grazes the surface of a frail egg or a sheet of calm blue water, suggesting erotic and symbolic passages from object to object, situation to situation, male to female. Yet no transformation occurs; it remains only a possibility, a threat. Sometimes the machines are camouflaged zoologically, imitating a peacock or some other animal; sometimes they remain blades, needles, wheels. They become terrible wonders at the extreme limit of human relations. They invade one another psychologically and visually, but never touch, evoking cold, lucid paradises of mating, a metallic love affair.

Excerpt from Germano Celant, 'Isolation Cells', *Individuals* (catalogue), Abbeville Press and The Museum of Contemporary Art, Los Angeles, 1986

At the core of Rebecca Horn's art one finds the notable absence of a fused set of ideas that might conveniently be referred to as an *aesthetic*. Intensely personal and intensively speculative, her art practically refutes the possibility that abstract ideas have any validity beyond their temporary ascription of value and/or meaning to human experience. Concepts seem to become as restrictive as canons in Horn's work, as remote from perceived truths as the earth is from the sun. This hardly makes her work anti-intellectual; on the contrary, it reveals a critical self-consciousness that chooses to locate pure thought within, rather than outside, the body. The dilemmas Horn constructs are shot through with tensions that are inseparable from the qualified role played by visual perception in her work. The visible properties of her objects are often overwhelmed by their adamant tactility, an aspect that the viewer can only passively witness. Frequently repeated actions draw us into a circle of ritual outside of which we are forced to stand, excluded.

Opposing pairs of dichotomies help to compromise the essential poetry within all of Rebecca Horn's output. Her frequent use of feathers, to take an example, explores both the decorative and the defensive (or otherwise mechanical) uses that we ascribe to these ornithological necessities—not excluding an awareness that only humans perceive vanity as a characteristic of plumage. This double identity, as armour and costume, creates a metaphor of the self, revealed and concealed by the same device. As with other motifs in Horn's work, feathers signify an extension of the body's chemistry into space, a point where inner and outer realities fuse within the fleeting dynamic of touch itself. Although each of our senses acts as an emissary, seeking contact between the internal and external, touch is the only means of perception that links us to the subject in a manner that suggests the possibility of integration, the collapse of subject/object dichotomies, even of the danger of self-dissolution. For Horn, touch is also inextricably bound with the idea of healing.

The existence of a traumatic rupture seems to mark the artistic growth of both Joseph Beuys and Rebecca Horn at an early stage, just as such an event gave birth to modern-day Germany. For Beuys it was his million-to-one survival from the crash of a plane he was piloting. With Horn, the passage occurred in the form of near-death by asphyxiation from the materials she was using as a young sculptor fresh out of art school. These parallel events created in both artists a shock of such magnitude that every waking hour afterwards seems to have become a heightened event, punctuated by an astonishing sensitivity to all perceptions, meanings, and feelings that might indicate how, and in what way, the organism, the self, is truly alive. Whereas the precise human dimension of these experiences parallels that of the numerous people who have had brushes with death, one can postulate that in the cases of both Beuys and Horn, it was the long recovery process—nearly a year for Horn—that defined some crucial aspects of the artistic life to follow.

Horn's first post-recovery work sets the tone for much of her later work, albeit in an elemental state. The most radical aspect of this initial sculpture was Horn's treatment of the barrier between machine and organism. Since the Industrial Revolution we have tended to rely on machines as surrogates, separate 'selves' that function apart from the body in order to do man's work with greater expediency and/or efficiency. In Horn's work, put simply, the machine is no longer perceived as an Other, but rather as an extension of the body's reality, integrated in such a way as to bring the external world that much closer to the subject's felt experience.

Excerpt from Dan Cameron, 'Horn's Dilemma: The Art of Rebecca Horn', *Arts Magazine*, November 1987

BLINDFOLDED BINOCULARS, 1986
Metal motor binoculars
400

Since his participation in *The Field* exhibition in 1968, Robert Hunter has gradually acquired a reputation as Australia's most significant minimalist painter.

Unlike many of the artists who participated in *The Field*, Hunter did not shift into figuration in the late seventies and early eighties. Rather he chose to explore rigorously the subtle variations drawn from white, abstract grids.

Eschewing aleatory sources, Hunter has opted for a coolly mechanical technique and a systematic approach to pushing against the limits of painting. In this sense, his work over the past twenty years may be seen as a series: from the slightly textured, basic geometry of the early pictures to the smooth acrylic surfaces and crystalline structures of his current work. This is not to suggest a model of progressive succession, but rather to emphasise Hunter's sustained examination of process, and particularly the processes of perception.

At first glance, it is not apparent that the severe simplicity of these works differs significantly from the white walls on which they are hung. On closer inspection, however, the delicate under-painting of some sections in the grid emerge as softly luminous areas of blue/grey, rose and yellow. Hunter rotates three primary colours in combination with four-sided geometrical figures, syncopating tonal shifts and variations which imbue the work with a subtle sense of movement.

A minimal sense of movement is also apparent in the way the large-scale white paintings seem to expand beyond their edges, and (especially in groups) appear to hover, shifting slightly on the wall.

The fine structural balancing of incised line, tone and colour is as ordered as the parts of a machine, yet such formal 'equivalences' require active viewer participation. The passive gaze is tricked by the barely perceptible transitions in the work, so that the eye, in re-negotiating these minimal shifts, is drawn into a more contemplative visual process.

Through the quiet elegance of his work, Hunter surpasses the purely retinal aspects of painting by concentrating on the conceptual processes of viewer reception. He explores the criteria of identity that we employ for distinguishing all painting. And his sustained concentration on perceptual limits is in many ways cognate with the scrupulous analyses of perception in phenomenological method.

Linda Hicks-Williams, Melbourne, 1987

PAINTING NO 3, 1984
Acrylic on board
122 × 244

(Photo) Yuill/Crowley Gallery

Toshimitsu Imaï has ceased to be a painter as so many others still are: the light is born in him, as it were. I seek to capture the specific quality of a vision which owes nothing to technical mastery and owes all to the radiant power of that inner order which it organically reflects.

A prophet speaks in metaphors. Fundamental truths come with pretexts. Imaï's truth assumes the shape of landscapes blurred in the distance, of streams strewn with rocks, of ornamental stretches of grass, of galactic nebulae dotted with wings of birds. So much wind. And yet this very wind which we are given to see by the painter through its manifestations, as compelling as they are subtle, this wind, which generates the spell of the picture, is the indelible mark of an essential quality of life, the sensory materialisation of great emotional power, of love for beauty.

One could wax eloquent on the theme of love for beauty. Suffice it to say that it need not so much be defined, as felt from within through the tell-tale surge of emotion that proclaims its presence in a work of art.

I experienced this irrevocable sense of self-evidence in March 1983 at Imaï's Paris studio as I was introduced to his new 'Imaï-grams': designs from printed cloth for kimonos are stencilled over gold or silver backgrounds. The pattern of motifs is determined by automatism in gesture: this is what disseminates the image, which is interchangeable with respect to the horizon, and wholly fluid in its perspective.

This automatic writing is hardly a technical innovation, since it belongs by its form to the tradition of stamping, as widespread in the East as it is in the West. It is broadly acknowledged as a point where two skills and two cultures meet. Furthermore this method relates in spirit to the spontaneous gestural approach which for thirty years characterised Imaï's *informel* calligraphy.

But when systematic reliance on random gestures brings a feeling of profound beauty, nothing will ever be the same. Indeed this sense of beauty conveys with immediate clarity a human miracle: getting back in touch with nature. One's relationship to nature is fundamental to the Japanese sense of self, whose every existential manifestation it determines, explains, or colours. My pen falters as I write these words: I reluctantly resort to such a cliché, yet how can one otherwise speak of a self-evident truth, of an ability to become one with the immediacy of nature, with the climate and with the change of the seasons? Clothing, food, the human habitat, the metaphors of language—these speak of themselves.

Of nature, however, I do feel entitled to speak. This notion of nature as the underlying drive of sensibility would surely have been lost for me, were it not for Yves Klein's constant example and memory which compelled me to seek, live, and feel this impression of total nature in the remotest depths of Brazil's Amazonas in August 1978. Imaï's painting made me feel from the outset this harmony with deep nature, and I thought of Yves Klein. As a monochrome painter he would initially have felt irritated at the configuration of motifs which disrupt the purity of the gold background. Eventually I believe he would have understood the message of the new Imaï, painter of the wind, architect of the air in the nature of things.

I must therefore assume that this organic link with nature is what the Japanese painter currently refers to when alluding to his tradition, the spirit of *Ka-cho-fu-getsu* (flower-bird-wind-moon). I will use a quotation that Imai borrowed from the poet Kenko Yoshida in his 1330 collection of essays entitled *Tsurezuregusa*: 'It goes without saying that the moon and the flowers touch the human heart. But the wind touches it most.'

The operational metaphor of the wind thus warrants this call to the tradition of *Ka-cho-fu-getsu*. In his intuitive call to tradition, on the wing of the wind of sensibility, Imai is by no means alone, Technology in modern Japan anticipates with lightning speed the post-modern world of the 21st century. But what will technological culture be without the spirit of *Ka-cho-fu-getsu*? And what would computers and biogenetics be without the poetry of *kokinshu* and *haiku*, the artful arrangement of flowers and gardens in *ikebana* and *sakutei*, the *bonsai* or miniature tree and *nodate* or outdoor tea ceremony? And what would Tsukuba be without Kyoto or Nara?

Forty years have elapsed since 1945, and the Western eye, despite all the shortcomings of its insight, can detect within the realm of appearances of contemporary Japanese art the subtle emergence of a form of cultural nationalism which increasingly proclaims its preference for the spirit of tradition.

During the seventies, Japan saw the rise of *Monoha*; this movement, which seeks to establish an intimate and basic relationship between man and environment is a minimal-conceptual version of *Ka-cho-fu-getsu*. Meanwhile, traditional Japanese painting thrives and bravely depicts the round of seasons.

It might occur to a Japanese fellow critic to place the wind-painting of the new Imai midwqay between *Monoha* and *Nihon-ga*, between Lee-U-Fan's gouache dot serial compositions and Yoson Ikeda's rice paddies after harvest.

There might be some truth in such a parallel, precarious as it seems. During a festival of Japanese art in Genoa last May, I experienced a similar flavour of integral naturalism in the photographs of the 'acquademician' Yoshiaki Tono. Before leaving for Japan at the end of April, Imai had given me a copy of William Porter's translation of *Hyaku-nin-isshyu*. I asked my students at Milan's Domus Academy, a postgraduate research centre in architecture and design, to illustrate one of the poems of the collection. It was a poem by First Councillor of State Kinto, who died in 1041. It recalled the music of a waterfall which had been famous before it stopped running. One of my Italian students thought of setting on a metal panel a cotton rope, whose twists recalled the meandering waterfall; after soaking it in alcohol, he proceeded to set it on fire—we all felt this magical moment as a reminder of the poetic order of nature.

Such is the admirable object lesson I was given by Imai, painter of the wind and prophet of *Ka-cho-fu-getsu*. Beauty, more than ever, is a matter of nature, and the best way to reach it is undoubtedly on the wing of the wind of sensibility.

Pierre Restany, Milan, 1985

This special event is presented as part of 'Close-up of Japan, Sydney 1988' sponsored by THE MITSUI PUBLIC RELATIONS COMMITTEE.

THE MITSUI
PUBLIC RELATIONS
COMMITTEE

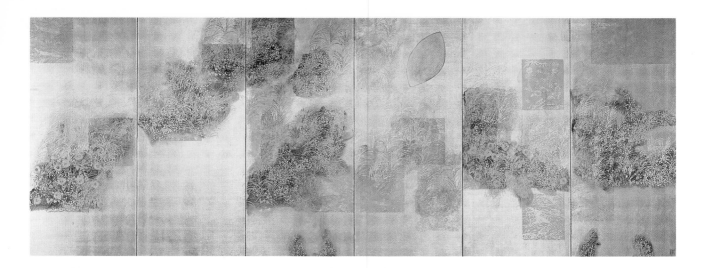

MUSASHINO, 1986
Acrylic and mixed media
210 × 540

I R W I N

DUŠAN MANDIČ, born Ljubljana, Yugoslavia, 1954

BORUT VOGELNIK, born Kranj, Yugoslavia, 1959

ANDREJ SAVSKI, born Ljubljana, Yugoslavia, 1961

ROMAN URANJEK, born Trbovlje, Yugoslavia, 1961

MIRAN MOHAR, born Novo mesto, Yugoslavia, 1958

The IRWIN group lives and works in Ljubljana

Irwin is a dialectic development of the historical experience of modernism in so much as it has brought the national culture into value, made the collective spirit triumph and praised those characteristics of plastic art which the eclectic culture assimilates. Irwin shows the continuity of the Slovene past and its traumatic experiences as the unique horizon of the future. Art represents a retro ritual in affirming the eclecticism as a dynamic element within a nation's culture. The final aim of the activity of the group Irwin is to reaffirm the Slovene culture in a monumental-spectacular way.

Statement by IRWIN, April 1984

The Irwin painting group consists of five painters who live and work in Ljubljana, Slovenia. The group works together collectively on each Irwin project, both in its conception and its execution.

Two main principles govern its work: the Retro Principle and the Principle of Potentialised Eclecticism, both of which are used to affirm Slovenian culture. The works use formal methods to form a discourse about formal aesthetic problems. The main elements in Irwin's pictures consist of the following:

characteristics which reveal a socio-realistic origin;
modernist forms, languages and ideologies;
the combination of different painting techniques and motifs;
a Slovene iconography with a constant reference to 'Neue
    Slowenische Kunst'.

These elements are combined using oil paint, tempera, gold leaf, silk screen, wax, bitumen and coal. The result is a formal, conceptual discourse executed in an immediately accessible, tactile, aesthetic technique which allows access to the works on many different levels, from the purely intellectual to the aesthetic and emotional. It is the synthesis of these two poles which gives the work its strength and impact.

Irwin is organically bound to its native soil; it jealously guards its instinctive ties with the nation and its history, and is conscious of its role within the Slovenian cultural-political polygon: the organic 'retro principle' expresses the embodiment of a belonging to the Slovenian spiritual legacy, a belonging determined by birth.

Irwin respects tradition and remakes it by means of the device: TO PAINT ONE TO REPRESENT THE OTHER. It is extremely critical of the fashionable eclecticism in the art of the last few years. Sheer repetition of the past as a form of the present is just a mask concealing an absence of creativity. 'We know very well the delusions and contradictions of disillusioned post-modernist thinking. We do not intend either to reproduce or reinterpret art. The ideology of "surpassing" has been surpassed. Never again should it be possible for an observer-consumer to take a product's plastic wrapping for a piece of art and a copy for an original.'

In this period of absolute dissolution, in a period of accentuated personal mythology and of New German expressionism, Irwin, through collective labour (within 'Neue Slowenische Kunst') appears with the will to establish order. Art should paint and shape permanent values, in permanent techniques and in substances that radiate a maximum of power and efficiency. Substances like stone, wheat, steel, honey, granite, blood, tar, gold, oil on canvas.

Irwin rejects individuality as meaningless when considering art. Irwin is devoted to the work of art itself and constructs it from the point of view of the laws from which it is built.

The work of Irwin is without an author. One member may change or re-do the work of another or submit it to a third. Irwin understands the author's signature as an elementary feature of the art from the Renaissance to the present and holds the authorial question worth answering.

THE FUTURE IS THE SEED OF THE PAST

The artist has always been a chronicler, called to speak about the things he knew best.

One painter's canvas alone is never more persuasive than five. A collective has the possibility of expressing the difference by repeating the same motif.

History has forgotten an enormous number of excellent paintings from which it was possible to grasp the difference as compared to the general run of painters; precision expressed within the painting should reward quality. Precision in painting results in quality.

To influence the understanding of the works of dead painters is the highest responsibility an artist can assume.

Every painter can be at the service of another—the Retro Principle—and every painting can be changed and redone.

Choice of motif is a personal decision. The method of painting is the responsibility of the time. Only superficial lovers of art judge a work by its motif; only superficial painters judge a work by its form.

When thought and form are combined a painting may be given any motif.

WAS IST KUNST, 1987
Mixed media
Twenty works, each 53 × 56 to 110 × 70
Installation for 'Trigon 87', Neue Galerie, Graz

Members of IRWIN group

159

The man who transforms himself a great deal needs many prejudices. They should not bother us in a very lively man; we should measure him by his vibrations and not what holds him down.

Elias Canetti

When Michael Johnson speaks of a desire to create in painting 'a place that doesn't exist', he touches on the idea of *utopia*, which in ancient Greek literally meant 'no place'. We usually think of utopias as realms of wishful thinking, avenues of imaginary escape, but the first impression we receive of Johnson's paintings is usually of an impassable barrier. This applies to the solid colours and bevelled relief of *Frontal 2* (1986) as well as to the densely interwoven screen of *Buji* (1986).

Frontal 2 developed from a series of modular, shaped canvases Johnson began in 1965. In many respects it is a characteristic example of avant-garde painting in the 1960s—self-conscious about its status as an object and intent upon maintaining a taut relationship with the wall. As a true product of its time, the painting strives to impress upon viewers that its literalness (its flatness, frontality and emblematic clarity) is climactic, 'tough', irreducible and is much a moral as an aesthetic virtue.

Frontal 2 eschews virtually all of the illusionistic tricks that might establish it as a *picture*. At the time it was painted Johnson was interested in developing effects which weren't necessarily derived from the history of painting but had been specified by psychologists of perception: R.L. Gregory's book *The Eye and the Brain* alerted him to the way peripheral vision could create encompassing illusions—illusions that seemed to spring off the picture-plane, reaching around and behind the viewer, resulting in a sort of 'wrapping of the environment'. Colour was isolated as one of the principal agents of illusion: in *Frontal 2* the ultramarine pigment has been mixed with very little medium. The velvety surface is at once alluringly tactile and ferociously 'optical' due to its chromatic saturation. The resulting perceptual ambiguity secures the artist's purpose, which was 'to make the eye unreliable, to put the eye to work'.

Frontal 2 poses questions typical of avant-garde art in the 1960s: What is the zero degree of painting? What are the minimal requirements for a painted surface to function pictorially? At what point does an object exceed or transcend its objecthood and assume the status of an image?

No doubt it is significant that the format of *Frontal 2* suggests a door or window: the work is conceived as a threshold communicating between antithetical extremes. At one extreme, painting is stripped to its basics of pigment, surface and frame. At the other, the work remains obsessed with an idea of pictoriality—pictoriality as an abstract condition, as a charismatic essence.

Pictoriality need not rely on figuration or spatial illusion, as this work demonstrates. However, its prerequisite is a kind of enchantment—Johnson calls it intoxication—which he believes is fundamental to any experience of art. 'Paintings present an experience which is accessible to everyone,' he says. 'Everyone brings their own ideas to bear on the work, but there's an intoxication before the ideas come, before you can look critically at the painting and accept or reject it. This happens with bad paintings as well as good ones.'

When Johnson was a teenager he saw a reproduction of a painting by the American artist Albert Pinkham Ryder, which exemplified for him the way a painting could fluctuate between a matter-of-fact surface and a fictitious dimension without ever resolving into one or the other. Ryder's composition was centred upon three bands of colour flanked by two treetrunks. The three bands dilated into zones of a landscape, yet there was no apparent intention of illustrating the landscape. Ryder 'found the theme in the painting,' Johnson realised. His vivid recollection of the image decades afterwards testifies to its special relationship to one of his own persistent themes—the three colour-zones recurring in so many of his paintings, including *Buji*.

Frontal 2 and *Buji* both confront the viewer with physically dense surfaces teetering on the verge of a phantom dimension, 'a place that doesn't exist'. The relation of this dimension to the 'no place' contained in the idea of *utopia* becomes more explicit in his recent work, which evokes visions of beneficent Nature as well as suggesting paradigms of physical and spiritual wholeness.

However, Johnson greets anyone's guesses about his paintings' content and intentions with acute discomfort, and he is equally uneasy about attributions of artistic influence. His evasiveness does not amount to a denial that his works refer to particular places or experiences, that they were influenced by other artists, or that they hold especial significance for him. On the contrary—he realises that speculations on these lines tend to stick and limit a viewer's latitude of interpretation. Because of their inevitable oversimplification, they tend to overshadow the fact that a multiplicity of allusions and a dense residue of experience are silted into each canvas. Johnson has the ironic predicament of needing on the one hand to defend the complex determinations and ideas informing his work while on the other safeguarding the work's romantic, utopian features of indeterminacy and incommensurability.

The painting's surface becomes a place where a vision is both articulated and disarticulated. The 'no place' is glimpsed through the veil of an obtrusive material code. It can be intimated as a possibility, a promise beyond the tangle of the here-and-now, but it is inaccessible to vicarious experience, off-limits to tourists, perhaps invisible to unbelievers.

The three zones of *Buji* suggest water, forest and sky, yet the painting's amphibious space cannot be unified into a naturalistic image—the view underwater cannot be reconciled with the view over the water. Furthermore, it is undecidable whether the landscape is stationary or is flashing past, as if seen through the window of a speeding vehicle. The work encourages or tolerates comparison with the diagrams of medieval cosmologies, dividing space into celestial and terrestrial strata, and also with the wave/particle/field theories of modern physics.

Johnson says he wants to 'recreate the feeling rather than represent the experience' in his paintings. Re-creation of feeling results in a generalisation, in an abstraction, yet Johnson's recent work distils many qualities characteristic of Australia, qualities that are human and cultural as well as natural: largeness and openness, ruggedness, bracing air, forthrightness, balmy nights, sensuality, mystery, speed, courage. The glimpses of earthly paradise and the hard core of optimism are no doubt part of it too.

Terence Maloon, Sydney, 1988

BUJI, 1986
Oil on linen
198 × 426.7

(Photo) Henry Jolles

ANSELM KIEFER

Born Donaueschingen,
Federal Republic of Germany, 1945

Lives and works in Hornbach/Odenwald

Anselm Kiefer is one of the leading students of Joseph Beuys. Although he makes paintings, he is as much a sculptor in the tradition of Arte Povera and of Fluxus. He uses materials in a literal sense as well as metaphorically and alchemically. In this work, *Glaube, Hoffnung, Liebe,* he has practically recreated the rocky surface of a Baltic seashore. Yet the propeller that is attached simultaneously lies upon this surface and stands far in front of it, as if driving through the air high above the sea.

The propeller in *Glaube, Hoffnung, Liebe* is unique in having three blades, allowing for an additional symbolic layer. Beuys, Kiefer's teacher, was a World War II pilot and often made works involving texts on blackboards. Hence the words drawn on this propeller remind us of him. The more esoteric symbolism of the piece may require more study. The propeller creates a helix with its implied forward motion. The helix is a Dionysian symbol of transcendence but it is constructed out of lead, a saturnine and earthbound material which contradicts the first reading. This interpretation overlays the more prosaic contradiction of an instrument of flight made from the heaviest of materials. The three blades are multiplied by the three rocks which are applied to the surface. This is an even more esoteric reference to the order of the seraphim in the celestial hierarchies of Mediaeval Gnosticism.

The experience of the work is extraordinary because, at the one level, it has a literal presence: scorched surfaces are produced by fire, the rock surface is made of rocky matter, and these things exist in the viewer's real time; yet the fire is simultaneously a reference to the traces of historic conflicts and a symbol of transformative power and creativity. These observations by no means complete the inventory of complex intentions nor the formal layering of the work, which stands as a metaphor for the layering of European history itself.

Some commentators have identified Kiefer as a heavy Neo-Expressionist, reviving dangerous elements of romanticism in the Germanic soul. On the contrary, he carefully confronts the past tragedy of such unbridled expressionism and yet seeks to recoup what is important for the soul while recognising the past and its horror. His use of Jewish traditions within essentially Germanic landscape scarred by time, the plough and the grenade, is calculated to bring these issues into sharp relief.

Tony Bond, 1987

Most of what is commonly stated about the theme of history and mythology in the work of Anselm Kiefer seems to miss the realisation that it deals with the loss of both of these categories endowing human existence with a purpose and consequently culminating in the term *eschaton,* the idea of salvation. With astonishing pertinacity, the popular flat interpretations of Kiefer's art as a subjective effort to surmount the Nazi past—and the natural inverse of this reading, a glorification of Fascism—overlook the pictures themselves. The circumstantial evidence that Kiefer's metaphors are derived mainly from Nordic instead of Greco-Roman mythology (thereby insincerely paying homage to a hollow ideal of bourgeois-humanistic education) speaks for itself, especially when related to the way German interpreters see themselves. As for the small percentage of outspoken Nazi themes in Kiefer's work, they are integrated in the context extrapolated above, just as much as the far greater number of other historical subjects. National Socialism hypostatises history—namely that which it produced—into mythology. In a fatal manner, history and mythology coincide in this construction. It postulates a cosmic awareness of history which in its outward appearance comes close to that of Judaism. At its core, however, it is a gruesome distorting-mirror. In an act of destruction, the Nazi ideology fuses that above and that below to an idol of the Golden Calf and results in the monster of mythologised violence. History *as* mythology is never the same as history *and* mythology. As a last monstrosity of modern enlightenment, the misinterpretation aims at the philosophy itself by denying the great idea of a free, individualistic postulate in an awareness of historical and moral responsibility.

The disaster at the end of the enlightenment, the devastated feeling for mythology and history, necessarily takes its place in an oeuvre which is concerned with understanding and reconstructive in interpretation. The sense-destroying annexation of mythology to history has credibility only in terms of a polar opposite to the purposeful dialogue between mythology and history. *Without mythology every culture loses its healthy, creative, natural strength: only a horizon surrounded by myths seals an entire cultural movement into unity.* What Friedrich Nietzsche anticipated for a world without mythology bears an emphatic relevance for an age in which historical memory is lost. In Kiefer's post-historical landscapes, corresponding to that which is beyond the horizon and reflecting it, the up-rooted mythology seeks that below in which its sense may again be made manifest.

Gudrun Inboden, *Exodus from Historical Time*

In both material and technique, Kiefer well evokes the leaden skies and barren fields of the German countryside in winter. The snow-topped furrows of his landscapes appear identical to his poppled oceans with their saline froth. Much of the impact of Kiefer's paintings lies in his intuitive conjunctions of material, myth and landscape, each with a unique symbolic charge. The effect is German in the extreme. Strangely, it is not in Germany that Kiefer's strongest supporters are found, but in those countries (Britain, Israel, Italy) that suffered most from the illogical consequences of German national myth. German critics have taken exception to Kiefer's work, not on aesthetic but on ideological grounds. Writes Heinz Liesbrock in the *Frankfurter Allgemeine Zeitung,* 'The particular combination of mythology, national history, and representation of nature gave the idea that through his paintings he shows the potential thought and feeling out of which grew German Fascism.' Kiefer himself claims the following: 'It is my art form to think about Fascism.'

The myth of the artist, supported by Kiefer's continual use of the palette and wings, is inevitably presented as a parable for all humanity, that of a tragic emptiness. Apparently, expressionism in Germany indicates political engagement. Kiefer's, however, is a purely symbolic form of commitment. He is, with his art, willing to incarnate the collective guilt of an entire nation, and succeeds in piquing the fascination of the West with evocations of technological evil. Guilt is a hot item; those without it are criminals, psychotics, children. That's precisely whom we see on TV.

Excerpt from Robert Kleyn, 'Anselm Kiefer', *Tema Celeste,*
April/June 1987

GLAUBE, HOFFNUNG, LIEBE, 1984/86
Emulsion, acrylic, shellac on photodocument paper on linen with lead
280 × 380
Collection: Art Gallery of New South Wales. Part of the Mervyn Horton Bequest Fund

EDWARD & NANCY REDDIN KIENHOLZ

Edward Kienholz, born Fairfield, Washington, USA, 1927

Nancy Reddin Kienholz, born Los Angeles, USA, 1943

Both live and work in Hope, Idaho and Berlin

In a passage from Walt Whitman's great long poem, *Song of Myself*, the poet conjures up a catalogue of those who have suffered at the hands of society: 'martyrs'; 'the mother of old, condemned for a witch'; 'the hounded slave that flags in the race'. And he utters one of the most powerful among his numerous powerful lines: 'I am the man, I suffer'd, I was there.' For the past three decades, Edward Kienholz—first on his own, and for the past fifteen years with Nancy Reddin Kienholz—has constructed assemblages, mixed media sculptures and human-scale tableaux informed by much the same principle. For the subjects of their work have often been societal victims or its marginal types, depicted as cast, life-size figures placed in everyday settings, or alluded to through objects. And when confronted with any number of their works, one consistently feels something equivalent to Whitman's eloquent expression of identification and compassion.

Informed by this approach to social themes, Kienholz and Reddin Kienholz have given us one of the powerful and enduring oeuvres of the post-war period. Born in 1927 in the small north-east Washington farming community of Fairfield, Kienholz is a self-taught artist. He arrived in Los Angeles, California, in 1952 or 1953 and during the 1950s he painted in an abstract expressionist style on wood relief surfaces. By 1959, the works protruded so far out from the wall that Kienholz decided they should be free-standing and thus his career as a sculptor began.

From 1959 until he left Los Angeles in 1974, Kienholz produced a remarkable number of major works. 1961 was pivotal, for he created the first of his human-scale environments, *Roxy's*, a meticulously detailed interpretation of a brothel. And during the decade which followed, he produced numerous large-scale works—tableaux, as he termed them. The best known are perhaps *The Illegal Operation* (1962), *The Birthday* (1964), *The Back Seat Dodge '38* (1964–65), *The Beanery* (1965) and *The State Hospital* (1966).

There were historical precedents for Kienholz's tableaux, though he was unaware of them when he made his first large-scale works; the most significant are the temporary environments created by Surrealists such as Salvador Dali, Wolfgang Paalen and André Masson for l'Exposition Internationale du Surréalisme of 1938 in Paris. Moreover, there were contemporaneous developments: the environments—some used to stage 'happenings'—created by Allan Kaprow, Claes Oldenburg, Robert Whitman and others in New York during the 1960s. Yet Kienholz's approach, with its direct treatment of social themes, had no close equivalents in the visual arts. Rather, one has to look to Beat literature—Allen Ginsberg's *Howl* (1956), Norman Mailer's *The White Negro* (1957) and William Burroughs' *Naked Lunch* (1959) among other texts—to find works of art as persuasively socially critical as Kienholz's sculptures.[1]

The theme of victimisation, which persists in *Holdin' the Dog* (1983–84) and *The Last Buffalo from Worley* (1986), has its origins in two thematically related assemblages which preceded the tableaux: *John Doe* (1959) and *Jane Doe* (1960). Kienholz's 'everyman' consists of a head and torso of a mannequin resting in a stroller. Red paint drips down his face and body like blood, projecting an aura of violence. Thus he becomes an archetypal aggressor figure. His counterpart is a metaphor for the woman as sexual object. She consists of a doll's head attached to a cabinet with drawers, covered up to her neck by a lace cloth which functions as a bridal gown. This costume conceals the trinkets concealed in her drawers—metaphors, of course, for her emotional and sexual secrets.

With the tableaux, Kienholz was to expand and refine the presentation of that theme in startling ways. In *Roxy's* (1961), a horrific recreation of a brothel, one is inside the scene of degradation, as it were. Its eight figures are grotesque versions of prostitutes: 'The Madame', for instance, consists of a wigged boar's skull atop a propped-up dress-form on a pedestal. All of the furnishings and props in his constructed room specifically date the room to 1943.

Much of Kienholz's work of the 1960s was brutally honest, shockingly direct in its presentation of victimisation. There is no precise moment at which we can locate a shift in tone. Yet clearly, the work he has created in collaboration with Reddin Kienholz takes a different approach to the same themes. It is more presentational in nature, often informed by sadness more than anger.

Born in 1943, Reddin Kienholz worked as a court reporter, medical assistant and emergency room attendant before becoming an artist. She and Kienholz met in 1972 and within months they were married. They left Los Angeles in 1974, at which time they began dividing their time between Berlin, Germany, and the small town of Hope, Idaho. In 1979, Kienholz declared all work would be co-signed by Reddin Kienholz and that she would also be credited with work made since 1972.

Holdin' the Dog and *The Last Buffalo from Worley*, both produced in their Idaho studio, testify to the continuing strength and vitality of their work. In each, the notion of victimisation is convincingly dramatised. The sight of a dead dog held aloft by two bulky men is a pathetic sight. The buffalo head juts aggressively into the viewer's space, forcing us to pay attention to the forlorn object it is.

The cast version of a dog in *Holdin' the Dog* would seem to be a surrogate for a human victim, since the human figures look remotely like Ku Klux Klansmen. They wear metal welding masks with white crosses painted on them and hold a little arch-shaped row of miniature American flags aloft, too. Indeed, as Kienholz explains, the genesis of the piece was a story about the brutal murder of a young black man by whites—an act inspired by their exposure to ideas of White Supremacism. Yet it is also about the hunting of animals for 'trophies', as he puts it—killing for sport rather than food.[2]

The Last Buffalo from Worley is an elegy of sorts—for an earlier America in which both buffalo and Indians flourished before the coming of white settlers in the eighteenth and nineteenth centuries. Worley, a small town not far from Hope, is still inhabited by Indians. And when the Kienholzes bought their buffalo head some ten to twelve years ago, they were told it was the last buffalo shot by an Indian with a bow and arrow.

It is not a sentimental or melodramatic work. Like *Holdin' the Dog*, it asserts that presentation is enough. The horror and sadness of the world can be communicated by the powerfully metaphorical three-dimensional image. Gazing upon their work, we do indeed make the suffering of the victims it depicts our own.

Robert L. Pincus, 1987

1. This argument concerning the context of Kienholz's development is presented in a detailed fashion in Robert L. Pincus, *On a Scale that Competes with the World: the Art of Edward Kienholz and Nancy Reddin Kienholz*, dissertation, University of Southern California, 1987.
2. Information on the two exhibited works is derived from Edward Kienholz, telephone interview, 24 November, 1987.

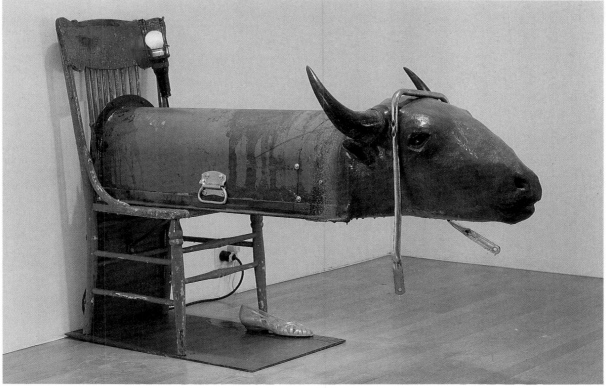

HOLDIN' THE DOG, 1983/84 (detail)
Mixed media
203.2 × 170.2 × 66

THE LAST BUFFALO FROM WORLEY, 1986
Mixed media
102.9 × 57.2 × 152.4

Born Nice, France, 1928

Died Paris, 1962

1947: It was in 1947 that the idea of a conscious monochrome vision came to me. I ought to say that at that time it was rather through my intellect that it came; it was the result of all the passionate researches I was then engaged in. Pure, existential space was regularly winking at me, each time in a more impressive manner, and this sensation of total freedom attracted me so powerfully that I painted some monochrome surfaces just to 'see', to 'see' with my own eyes what existential sensibility granted me: absolute freedom! But each time I could neither imagine nor think of the possibility of considering this as a painting, a picture, until the day when I said: Why not?

Around 1947–8 I created a 'monotone' symphony whose theme is what I want my life to be. This symphony lasts for forty minutes and consists of one single, continuous, long-drawn-out 'sound'; it has neither beginning nor end, which creates a dizzy feeling, a sense of aspiration, of a sensibility outside and beyond time.

1956: Dubbed a Knight of the Order of Saint Sebastian, I espoused the cause of pure colour, which had been invaded by guile, occupied and oppressed in cowardly fashion by line and its manifestation: drawing in Art. I aimed to defend and deliver it, and lead it to triumph and final glory.

At the Galerie Colette Allendy I exhibited some twenty monochrome surfaces, all in different colours: greens, reds, yellows, purples, blues, oranges . . . and so found myself at the start of my career in this style . . . I was trying to show colour, but I realised at the private view that the public were prisoners of a preconceived point of view and that, confronted with all these surfaces of different colours, they responded far more to the inter-relationship of the different propositions, they reconstituted the elements of a decorative polychromy.

1957: It was then that I remembered the colour blue, the blue of the sky in Nice that was at the origin of my career as a monochromist. I started work towards the end of 1956 and in 1957 I had an exhibition in Milan which consisted entirely of what I dared to call my 'Époque bleue'.

This period of blue monochromes was the product of my pursuit of the indefinable in painting which that master, Delacroix, was able to indicate even in his day.

The glaring obviousness of my paternity of monochromy in the twentieth century is such that even if I myself were to fight hard against that fact I should probably never manage to rid myself of it.

My monochrome pictures are not my definite works, but the preparation for my works. They are the left-overs from the creative processes, the ashes. My pictures, after all, are only the title-deeds to my property which I have to produce when I am asked to prove that I am a proprietor.

Yves Klein, quotations from *Yves Klein 1928–62: Selected writings*, ed. Jacques Caumont & Jennifer Gough-Cooper, The Tate Gallery, London, 1974

Lines, bars of the psychological prison in my view, certainly exist in us and in nature, but they are our chains. They are the concretisation of our mortal state, our sentimentality, our intellect and even our spiritual domain. They are our heritage, our education, our skeleton, our vices, our aspirations, our qualities, our cunning . . . In short, our psychological world whole and entire, right down to its most subtle hidden corners.

Colour, by contrast, on the level of nature and man, is that which is most deeply immersed in cosmic sensibility. Now, sensibility has no hidden corners. It is like the humidity in the air. Colour to me is 'materialised' sensibility.

Colour suffuses everything by the same quality as everything that is sensibility, indefinable, formless and limitless. It is material-space, abstract and real at the same time.

The line can be infinite, as the spiritual is, but it does not have the quality of filling the incommensurable whole. It does not have that faculty of suffusion that colour has.

Yves Klein, 'L'Aventure Monochrome', *Yves Klein* (catalogue), Centre Georges Pompidou, Paris, 1983

ARMAN, 1962
Portrait relief
175 × 95 × 26

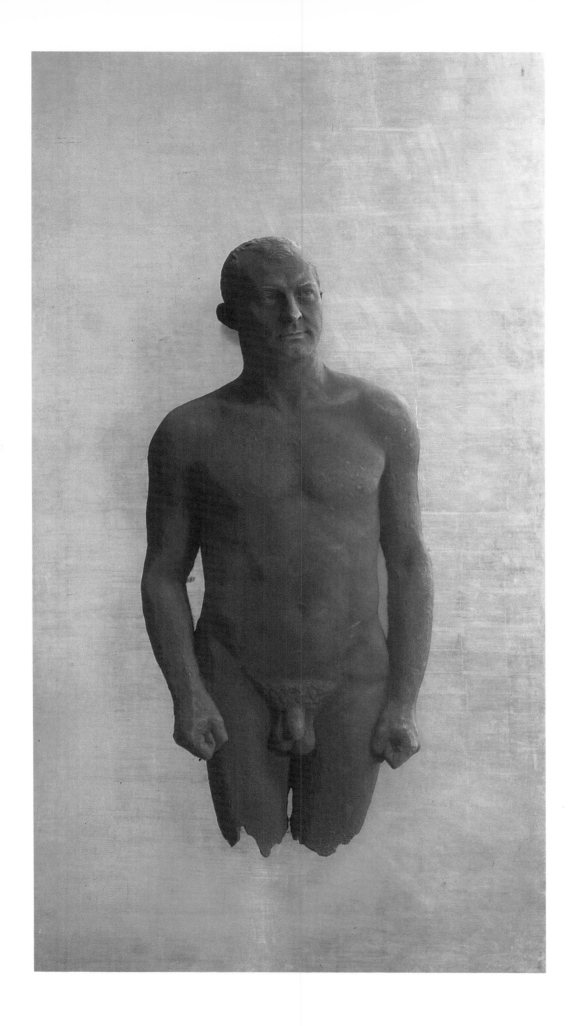

ROBERT KLIPPEL

Born Sydney, Australia, 1920

Lives and works in Sydney

The mathematician and philosopher Bertrand Russell once had occasion to draw a parallel between his own field of study and that of sculpture. According to Russell, both mathematics and sculpture were distinguished by a particular quality of truth, by a 'supreme beauty' at once 'sublimely pure and capable of a stern perfection'.

We cannot be certain of the actual sculpture underlying Russell's analogy. However, it is fair to assume that if the great Englishman had been pressed to amplify his claim, he may well have alluded to the example afforded by sculpture of an essentially constructivist ethic—thereby providing ample opportunity for the discussion of the shared attributes of exquisite logic and lucid, inviolable order. To continue in a speculative vein, we might say that Russell's analogy could hardly be demonstrated in a more convincing manner than by citing the example of Robert Klippel's recent wood assemblages and bronze casts. After all, Klippel's sculpture—as protean as it is—impresses for its fundamental veracity of structure and its resolute, formal authority. Klippel's sculpture engages the viewer's visual and cerebral faculties with a remarkably firm grasp.

Although individual sculptures can be schematically complex, comprising a dense field of autonomous incidents, they still communicate their message in a thoroughly spontaneous language unencumbered by rhetoric or embellishment.

Most of the elements in Klippel's latest large-scale sculptures are geometric solids. In these works, the sculptor adapts colourful eccentrically-shaped wood patterns salvaged from foundries where they were devised for the casting of machine parts. His fastidious selection, alteration and re-assembly of these disparate patterns is conducive to the frequent interpretation of his sculpture as a species of fantastic mechanism; a breathtakingly spare and superbly tailored assemblage comprising cogs, cones, columns, bosses and cusps of black, dull red and faded yellow hue—all of which appear poised to crank into action at the depression of a concealed lever. But it is not simply the geometricised foundation of Klippel's sculpture which recalls Russell's statement. More significantly, the interconnection revolves around an awareness of the sculptor's extraordinarily rigorous approach to composition. Even where his forms are massive, dense and enclosed—as opposed to the pieces which delight in slender, open or transparent spatial configurations—the assimilation of parts and the evolution of the composition are revealed in a plastic scheme which is utterly lucid, supremely intelligent and absolutely resolved with a rare economy of means and a masterly understatement of process.

It is no easy matter to bring to mind the work of another sculptor as prolific as Klippel who works in quite the same exhaustive, investigative manner. In his case, it appears that the unfolding pageant of an exceptionally eloquent language is a function of the sculptor's insistence on ranging freely across the dimensional spectrum from miniature bronzes capable of being held in the palm of a hand, to monumental compositions which tower above a person with the crisp, awesome demeanour of the mighty machines for which the foundry patterns were designed initially.

At the same time, Klippel's works on paper—the intricate collages, pastels and ink drawings—constitute a vital forum in which the sculptor examines the identical spatial conundrums that lie at the heart of the inspiration for his large sculptures. These collages and drawings are not working drawings, as such, for specific sculptures. Invariably, they elicit no obvious reference to a concurrent three-dimensional image. They must, however, serve to clarify and resolve certain compositional or notational issues embedded deep within the genesis and fabric of the diminutive bronzes (cast from assembled sections from plastic model kits or modelled waxes) and the larger wood and bronze constructions alike.

Until recently, most of Klippel's sculpture operated within the noble constraints of a fundamentally vertical format. The latest assemblages, by contrast, demonstrate a greater willingness by the sculptor to allow the forms to spread laterally in compositions that evoke something of the sensation of a jostling, urban landscape. These new assemblages represent a critical and dramatic juncture in Klippel's approach. Not only do they signal an awakened interest in tackling works of increasingly ambitious scale, but they also provide evidence of a more relaxed attitude to finish. Previously, the sculptor would automatically have handed over his completed assemblages of foundry patterns to the craftsmen at a specialist sculpture foundry for sand casting in bronze—albeit an ironical reincarnation for the original foundry prototypes. Now, more often than not, he prefers to leave the compositions in their 'raw' wood state, enjoying the chromatic vitality achieved within the delicate—if restricted—palette established by the gentle abrasion of the original black and primary-coloured surfaces of the patterns. In many instances, the sculptor will rub back the painted surfaces of the patterns so that no more than a gossamer veil of pigment shrouds the pale timber forms beneath. Where necessary, he fills interstices or fleshes out specific forms with a proprietary filler compound and the soft grey of this material will complement the fugitive polychrome scheme of adjoining sections.

The new works exhibit a fresh and provocative transparency of structure. Even so, it may be difficult to identify within these current works a single, predominant axis or focal component—such is their gestural and rhythmic complexity. In a certain recent sculpture, for example, a sweeping arm traces a wide arc around a soaring columnar unit while slanting, blocky sections serve as far-flung outposts on the periphery of a richly stratified, curiously joined composition. The weight of narrative borne by each member of this particular structure and the dialogue between them is sufficiently engrossing that the essential 'maypole' aspect of the work becomes a secondary consideration in the reading of the piece.

As always with Klippel's sculpture, the viewer's enjoyment is enriched by a keen appreciation of unflinching attention to detail and meticulous planning on the one hand and, on the other, the sharpness of wit which readily accommodates the totally unexpected, chance incident. In some respects, the sculpture is rather like a partially collapsed house of cards. Instantly, we recognise a distinct, static form at the core of a splendidly asymmetric and dynamic field. But we respond to this form in its dramatic state of flux. We perceive turbulent transformation at a point when it is arrested. A teeming, disintegrating mini-metropolis might have been brought to a standstill to permit our closer inspection of its densely interwoven carriageways, crossovers and confluences.

This is not to suggest that the latest sculpture reveals a quality of nascent literalness. In fact, this is far from the truth. Rather, the truth is that Klippel's new sculpture presents us with a remarkably bold development of his schematic assemblage idiom. The larger works, in particular, lay bare to our gaze a dazzling complexity of musculature and a phenomenal precision of balance between major components and the myriad of subtly realised, minor 'players'. Ultimately, however, these recent sculptures impress for their remarkable sense of self-containment and resolution; distinguished by what can be described as a Platonic rationality of concept. Once more, as Bertrand Russell would have it, theirs might well be a 'beauty cold and austere', but it is undeniably a beauty that is 'sublimely pure and capable of a stern perfection'.

Geoffrey Edwards, Melbourne, 1987

THE TRAIN, 1987
Painted wood sculpture
226 × 415 × 152

Born Piraeus, Greece, 1936

Lives and works in Rome

. . . the funeral as a starting point, as a facet of our cultural identity, as a means of discovery after a long period of oblivion fostered by decadence and submissions . . . faith in a civilised and cultured world.[1]

Kounellis' statement, from the libretto to his operatic performance *Funeral* first staged at Documenta 7 in Kassel in 1982, bears upon his work as a whole over the past few years in that it highlights certain paramount and abiding preoccupations: with ritual, death and regeneration, with cultural identity, historical accountability and relevance. His concern with great themes on an archetypal and symbolic level, is expressed not through didactic statements, but in poetic, metaphorical and ritualistic terms, terms which invoke, without directly addressing, the plight of the individual conceived as a social being at a particular historical juncture.

Kounellis sees the role of the artist as an unchanging one, though he acknowledges that the outward conditions or context inevitably alter. An identifiable repertoire of images, materials and forms has consequently been deployed in his work over the past three decades. The resulting sense of continuity can also be perceived at a deeper level where it stems from his preoccupation with certain recurrent themes, like the four elements, creation and death; from his incorporation of modes and allusions pertaining to alchemy, religion and classical culture; and from his preference for a mystical rather than a cerebral art. The ways in which these motifs and materials are utilised, the conjunctions in which they occur, depend on a confluence of circumstances that are particular as well as general, from the physical proportions of the gallery, and its geographical location, to its distinctive cultural nexus. For Kounellis, art in the twentieth century has become nomadic, divested of its former fixed social and religious roles. Thus every occasion for exhibition requires that the artist attempt to redefine and re-establish its function for himself. Since nothing is given or preordained, one means of re-establishing a coherent and communal character may lie in treating the gallery/museum space as a self-contained environment. Sometimes this is achieved by means of a site-specific installation, with temporary works or a performance; on other occasions it comes about through the particular conjunction of individual, autonomous works related in theme, material and form.

Common to this group of works is the fact that all are wall-pieces, and that almost all therefore partake of a format that is pictorial in both its orientation and mode of presentation. Flat rectangular sheets of steel provide a back plane against which the other components are deployed. Yet the massiveness of this pictorial ground—its weight, texture and palpability—is so insistent that the metal slabs assert themselves as *objects* in ways and to a degree that paintings rarely equal. Composed of a few spare monumental forms, these works refuse comfortably to occupy any category. If they propose questions fundamental to painting, it is a notion of painting that has been radically reinterpreted. Looking back on his work of the early sixties Kounellis stated, in 1972: 'The problem in those days was to establish a new kind of painting.'[2] In recent years he has returned to this question, albeit intermittently, and from a different perspective, seeking less to devise a novel mode of painting than to use its established conventions and identity as a point of departure for a new art, one which is divested of the illusory, self-contained and separate existence that easel painting traditionally postulated . . .

Germano Celant, the theorist of Arte Povera, under which Kounellis' works were often bracketed, argued:

The artist-alchemist organises living things in magical ways. He eagerly searches for essences, rediscovers them and brings them out. He is not interested, though, in using elementary materials and processes . . . to describe or represent nature. What interests him is instead the discovery, the presentation, the insurrection of the magical and astonishing value of natural elements . . . He broadens his threshold of perception, and he sets up a new relationship with the world of things. He does all this, however, without reworking that world. He does not pass judgement on it. He does not seek a moral or social value. He does not manipulate it. He simply discloses it . . . and thus begins again to experience the meaning of life and nature, a meaning that implies . . . the sensory, the sensational, the sensitive, the sensible, the sentimental, and the sensuous. He chooses direct experience over representation . . .[3]

These new works, which are more akin to paintings and icons than much else that Kounellis has recently made, reflect his belief that in collective memory, shared discourses, communal rites and social rituals lies the starting point for an art that bears witness to his 'faith in a civilised and cultured world': he has no allegiance to these art-forms on their own account. (It also indicates the sources of the shortcomings that he soon perceived in an art that was based exclusively in pure, organic matter in a natural or unmodified state.) In 1982 Kounellis wrote:

What disorder, the fragment of the eye of Athene's statue (on the stairs that lead to the garden), the flag, the battle, the gun, the iron bridge, the river, the orders, the shots, the pain, the loss, the march, the defeat, the head of the relief above the window near the corner, the hand of the bronze knight in the hall, the illegible signs of an inscription; iron; sewing-machine; cane; trumpet; umbrella; socks; painted goblets; shattered glass . . .

I remember Schwitters
I remember Picasso
I remember Cézanne
I remember Pollock[4]

In the face of chaos, the memory of four great artists instils a calming, ordering note, represented formally in the simple terse quatrain following the rapid breathless prose, and conceptually by counterpointing artistic achievement with disconnected concrete matter. The past subdues and contains the cacophonous sprawl of the present, physical confrontation gives way before introspection. Though the majority of these recent works, like this prose-poem, address the viewer singly, separately and in a meditative spirit, they do not permit any lapse into solipsism, for it is not the subjectivity of the individual that they confirm but a conception of the individual as a conscious participant in a collective culture.

Excerpts from Lynne Cooke, 'Luminous Penumbra', *Jannis Kounellis* (catalogue), Anthony d'Offay Gallery, London, 1986

1. Quoted in Bruno Cora, 'Burning Is the Image In the House Of the Eclipse', *Parkett*, no 6, 1985
2. Quoted in 'Structure and Sensibility: An Interview with Jannis Kounellis' (with Willoughby Sharp), *Avalanche*, no 5, Summer 1972.
3. Germano Celant, 'Arte Povera' (1969), republished in Germano Celant, *Arte Povera, Histories and Protagonists*, Milan, 1985
4. Quoted in 'Jannis Kounellis', *Zeitgeist*, Weidenfeld and Nicholson, London, 1983

UNTITLED, 1987
Steel, wood, stone, cloth, paint, gas burner and smoke
Twelve panels, each 201 × 91

JEANNE SIEGEL: Since the early '80s Barbara Kruger's work has provoked strong reactions. The reason lies in her unique combinations of texts with photographs. Compelling images, whether in seductive or threatening poses, are coupled with pungently confrontational assertions to expose stereotypes beneath. Kruger uses aphorisms that are lifted straight ('Divide and conquer') or, like some of Duchamp's Readymades, are aided to inflect their meanings. This lends a familiar ring to the work, which is part of its intention—in Kruger's words, 'part of its strategic innuendo'. Although many of Kruger's targeted 'myth explosions' appear to be universal, and some of them certainly are, she predominantly focuses on unmasking late capitalism's consumerism, the role of power in patriarchal societies, the power of the media, stereotypes of women, and occasionally art. Within these themes, she juggles the universal with pointed specificity—no small task.

Kruger makes a big point of stating that she comes out of advertising (she worked as a designer and picture editor for various Condé Nast publications for ten years). From the poster and magazine advertising, she has learned how crucial it is to convey the urgency and feeling of the moment: this occurs both in her choice of image and a style that suggests quick execution. Kruger has learned that in order to have force the message must be brief and declarative, the words (more often than not) monosyllabic. At the same time, applying her piercing intelligence and wit, she has constructed and fine-tuned her own rhetoric in an effort to avoid categorisation and to keep herself open—a traditional strategy of the fine artist. In this sense, her forthright manner and fluid speech are deceptive. Ambiguity is couched in a fresh role.

In the work itself, there are formal compositional devices that are used repeatedly, for example, broken glass or flowing hair, that effect an allover patterning which lifts it above the usual advertising display into the realm of aesthetic beauty. Kruger has been impressed by Walter Benjamin's discussions on semblance of beauty as well as Roland Barthes' conclusions that through that pleasure within a combination you are made to look at something and pay attention. At the same time, she acknowledges that the formal arrangement becomes pleasurable for her to construct. She sees pleasure as very much the motor of the production also . . .

BARBARA KRUGER: I think there are precedents for working with pictures excised from the media which go back a long way. But of course, I had friendships with many of the artists who were developing a vernacular sort of signage. However, the use of words lent my work a kind of uncool explicitness. I have to say that the biggest influence on my work, on a visual and formal level, was my experience as a graphic designer—the years spent performing serialised exercises with pictures and words. So, in a sort of circular fashion, my 'labor' as a designer became, with a few adjustments, my 'work' as an artist.

JS: Specifically, what do you think you held onto from that experience?

BK: Almost everything. I learned how to deal with an economy of image and text which beckoned and fixed the spectator. I learned how to think about a kind of quickened effectivity, an accelerated seeing and reading which reaches a near apotheosis in television.

JS: How do you think the image and the text work in advertising?

BK: It's difficult for me to engage in an analysis of advertising. Like TV, it promiscuously solicits me and every other viewer. In the face of these global come-ons I claim no expertise. I become as fascinated as the next person, but every now and then I feel the need to come up for air. In these forays above the watermark, I try to figure out certain procedures and manage some swift reversals. But there is no single methodology which can explain advertising. Its choreographics change from medium to medium: from print, to billboards, to radio, to TV. Each medium, according to its own technological capabilities, stages its own brand of exhortation and entrapment.

JS: Weren't you attracted to advertising because of the awareness that the image gets one's attention—it piques the viewer's curiosity or desire? Then you use its seductiveness to reveal some aggression.

BK: I have frequently said, and I will repeat again, in the manner of any well-meaning seriality, that I'm interested in mixing the ingratiation of wishful thinking with the criticality of knowing better. Or what I say is I'm interested in *coupling* the ingratiation of wishful thinking with the criticality of knowing better. To use the device to get people to look at the picture, and then to displace the conventional meaning that that image usually carries with perhaps a number of different readings.

Excerpt from Jeanne Siegel, 'Barbara Kruger: Pictures and Words', *Arts Magazine*, Summer 1987

UNTITLED (GOD SAID IT, I BELIEVE IT, AND THAT SETTLES IT), 1987
Plastic letters, felt on aluminium
150 × 51 × 35.6

NIKOLAUS LANG

Born Oberammergau, Germany, 1941

Lives and works in Bayersoien and Adelaide

Lang's work is an artist's homage to the opposite of art; it is a homage to nature.

However, he is not a nature-preservationist, not a protector of isolated sections of present-day nature from damage inflicted by humankind.

Just as every race—Jewish, German, Australian Aboriginal—is a part of humankind, so must humankind be accepted as inextricably interconnected with nature; we are all part of nature. And just as present-day conditions impose themselves on us, producing an unconscious impulse for us to preserve the present, so Lang draws attention to the inextricable interconnections between the present and the past, even to the prehistoric human past and to the pre-human past of plants and animals and, earlier still, of geology.

Thus his works are made on site, rather than in the studio. They modify or impose on nature as little as possible, although he accepts that he is a traditional artist and must do more than collect *objets trouvés*. His works are experienced by spectators as being the permanent traces of a gentle caress. A beautiful natural 'painting' found in 60-million-year-old earth deposits in a sand quarry is transferred, unmodified, onto canvas. A beautiful 'drawing' made by insects in the bark of a tree is transferred, by rubbing, onto a sheet of paper. Casts might be made of naturally occurring 'sculptures'.

Likewise a kind of caress are the coloured earth samples, collected, carried home, and set out in pairs; as found and as reduced by hand to fine powder. The coloured earths then imply potential artists' pigments, ready for marking a human body, or a cave at Lascaux or Altamira, or for being used in ancient Etruscan wall paintings, or Italian Renaissance frescoes. Deconstructed nature, in the form of powdered earth, is reconstructed by means of caressing handwork, on the walls of caves and other permanent surfaces.

Lang also caresses nature by walking through it, gazing at it, picking things up, understanding the proximity of a prehistoric midden to a 19th-century Australian landtaker's dump, using found flint tools to make his own wooden implements, or dead animals' skins and feathers to make his own cloaks or boots.

Why does he do these things? Well, he went to an art academy (in Munich), graduated in 1966, became an artist at a time when Minimalism had begun, when Land Art, Process Art, Ecology Art, Archaeology Art were soon to be named: the United Nations would proclaim 1970 International Ecology Year; the *Documenta 6* exhibition at Kassel in 1977 would include Lang with the Poiriers, Anna Oppermann, Charles Simonds and others in a group introduced as 'Schöne Wissenschaften oder die Archäologie des Humanen'. He is, inevitably, an artist of his own international artistic and political times.

But he is also an artist of his own individual circumstances. He was born and grew up in Catholic Bavaria, in Oberammergau, an alpine village where a medieval Passion Play is preserved in its late Victorian form as a highly commercial event, and where painted wooden toys have long been a handcraft industry. Lang reacted violently from the artificialities, the fixed attitudes, the preservationism of Oberammergau; instead he chose the flux of nature. On the other hand, Catholic Christianity does include the continuities, through infinite time, of death and resurrection, and Lang's first art action, aged twelve, in 1953, was probably his burial of a human jawbone (stolen from the school's drawing class) in order to dig it up.

Why did he work in Australia for several months in 1979 and again since late 1986? In 1967 in London, at the Museum of Mankind, he found a booklet on the Australian Aborigines. He had never hitherto heard of a society in which the material and the spiritual were so completely interwoven. He also learnt of the glistening 'Dingo's blood' ochre which occurs at Parachilna in the Flinders Ranges and was once a prized item of Aboriginal trade throughout Australia.

Lang is not the only visiting European artist to have admired Australian Aboriginal culture, but his own nature-based art and his determination to connect prehistory with the present are unusually close to the Aboriginal spirit. Lang says that natural materials '. . . help me slip into the past, but I'm not saying the past is a Golden Age; rather the past helps me understand today—and maybe a touch of the future'.

Daniel Thomas, Adelaide, October, 1987

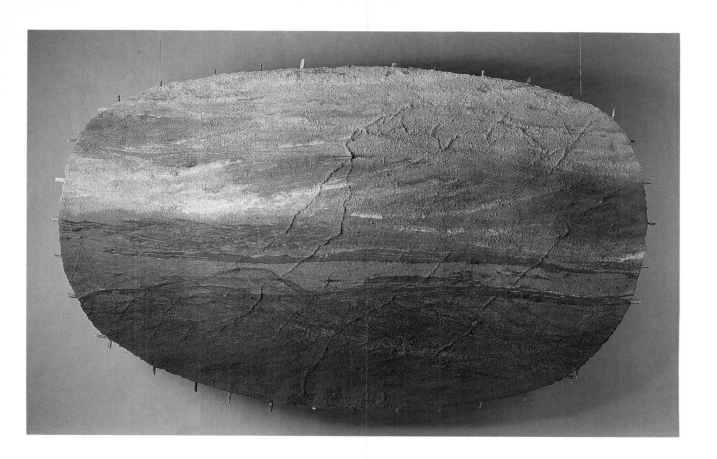

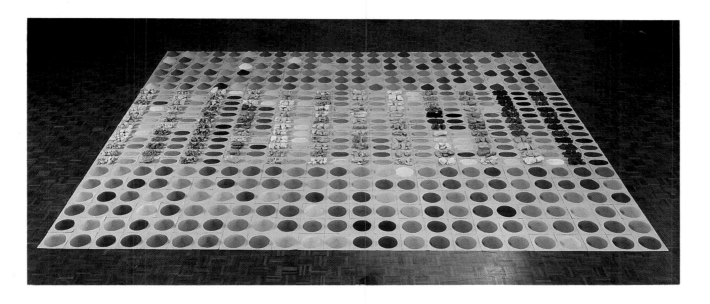

PETER IN THE SKY — DEDICATED TO PUTTAPA BOB,
UNCLE BERT AND GARY FOLEY — IMAGINARY FIGURATIONS NO 6, 1987
Cross-section of 'coloured sands' deposits (calico, glue on stick framework), Maslin Sand Quarry
210 × 340 × 28

OCHRE AND SAND: DEDICATED TO THE
VANISHED TRIBES OF THE FLINDERS RANGE AND ADELAIDE AREA, 1987
Ochre and sand displayed on paper
6 × 600 × 504

(Photo) Grant Hancock

Born Kappel, Carinthia, Austria, 1919

Lives and works in Vienna

THE ART OF GOOD

AND BAD FEELINGS

AN EXCURSION INTO THE

WORKSHOP OF A PAINTER

Maria Lassnig paints a world of niches, in which the subject is still allowed to be left to itself and achieves peace through an 'inner monologue'. The Ancient Greek expression 'know thyself' still applies to an art form which, while holding an inner discussion about self-image, doesn't seek flight from reality, but rather the basis for a confrontation with it. Against the merry-go-round style of things modern, the female artist's armour has been an aesthetic maxim, which in many respects is often richly informational for her own artistic path to independence as well as for the fragmented history of women artists in the last two hundred years: 'Reject style! Mankind will exploit itself soon enough.' It is a maxim which appeals to the female pastime of experimenting with the drug known as loneliness. 'Women have themselves been at the mercy of withdrawal—they still are, it has become their strength.' With the 'female inability to exploit others', the female artist takes cognisance of her shortcoming, which is not only a result and expression of female alienation in patriarchal society, but also opens a possibility of critical distancing and self-determination of an at least imaginary other self.

Maria Lassnig has entered into the realm of the heroic woman's artistic heritage and further cultivated it. Her titanic human pillars, the self-assurance she incorporates and the fact that she provides counterparts to dejected female torsos with broken-off extremities (both of which are a part of her world of form, existing next to and setting off each other), are all in contrast to a Baroque Atlas: hers are neither overstrained athletes nor fatigued gladiators; they are not without hope, but rather they bend and wind upward without visible effort, an expression as much of boundless burden as of a capacity for burden itself, of female impotence as well as the triumph of female strength and resilience.

As Atlas, the Titan of Greek mythology, was destined to support the vaults of Heaven, in her 1982 watercolour entitled *Alpen-karyatide*, Lassnig carries earth's mantle above her head and shoulders. Rural landscapes and body forms are vexingly intertwined. Her recent grand format painting is entitled *Atlas* and shows a travestied, i.e. female, Atlas who appears to rule playfully over an entire mountain range or, better still, seems to merge with it like an earthly spirit. As in a great cosmic exchange of energy, she presumes to be able to make her bodily contours disintegrate and flow away. In any event, a less rigid aggregate condition of the bodies predominates in her later rurally set (frequently water-coloured) self-portraits, imparting a cosmic feeling which would like to embody itself in great 'oceanic' pictorial expanses and assume the strength of a religious feeling of eternity.

Peter Gorsen

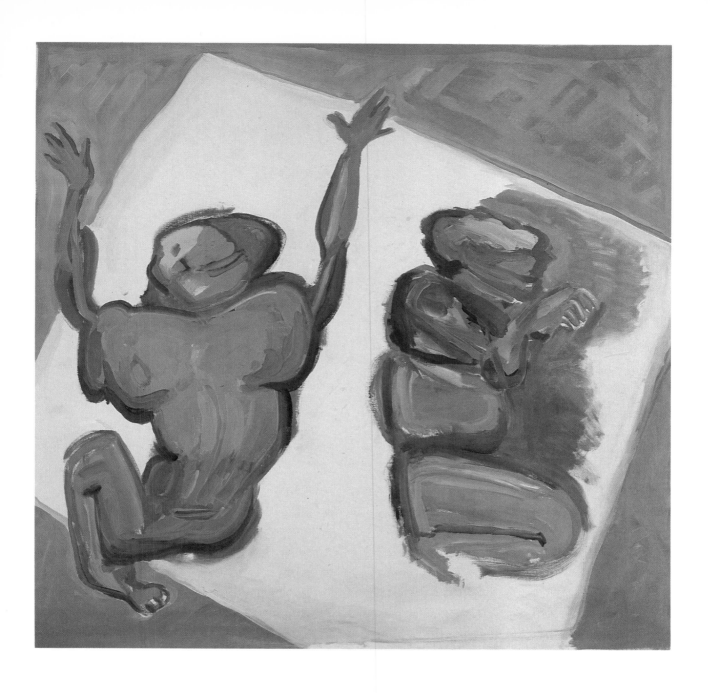

DUODRAMA, 1987
Oil on canvas
200 × 205

FERNAND LÉGER

Born Argentan, France, 1881

Died Gif-sur-Yvette, 1955

Just as no other artist of the heroic period of twentieth century European art better demonstrates the remarkable achievements of French Modernism than does Fernand Léger, so does the work of Léger in its totality reveal the dimensions of the pre-World War II School of Paris. Léger's career exemplifies the consequences of this tradition, the roots of which extend backward at least as far as Chardin and the brothers Le Nain. The locus of this tradition may best be situated in the consciousness of the intelligent peasant or petit-bourgeois artisan: honest craftsmanship; 'plastic values'; attentions to the surface manifestation of things and events rather than to their intangible significations; an honest, stubborn solidity; in all, the recording and reordering of the tangible appearances and objects of the world as ends in themselves, with less regard for the mental structures, inter-relationships and ultimate implications of such appearances and objects. Such an approach, with its implicit non-intellectualism, compounded in Léger's case by his enormous physical vitality, places a premium on the effects of experience on the observer, who reacts to, and reorders this world of experiences rather than interrogating it with a countervailing intellect. It is a stance of vigorous receptivity which accepts the world as it is, along with the experience it provides, be they traditional or 'modern', as givens—faits accomplis—to which the only imaginable response is a more or less active, more or less stylised reordering and rearranging. The achievement of Léger is thus the full and dynamic realisation of a pragmatic intelligence in which the inward and subjective being is not so much suppressed as simply merged with an external world of objects and events. That the ultimate political consequences of this viewpoint are populist, syndicalist and working-class communist, in contrast to the intellectual/technocratic operations of a ruling class, should come as no surprise, as they are evidenced by Léger's own political beliefs and lifelong identification with working-class attitudes, interests and activities.

Léger's direction of inward mind into external objecthood and the persistent focus of his consciousness upon the life-world of the artisan and petit-bourgeois are nevertheless only two of the underlying elements of his work, predominant and perhaps fundamental as they may be. A more complete inventory, leading to a more precise situating of his life and work, would necessarily include certain biographical and historical factors: his rural Norman background; his entry into the cultural life of Paris early in the twentieth century; and the essentially nineteenth century quality of Parisian life before 1914, with the still lingering traditions of an almost village existence in many neighbourhoods. This inventory would also have to include the ambiguous acceptance of an industrial society by a France that had remained until recently an essentially agrarian culture, as well as the curiously filtered and unbalanced acceptance of industrial life after World War I on the part of the cultural elite. Also of importance are the consequences, for French political rhetoric and practice, of that selectively accepted industrialism, in company with a nevertheless naive enthusiasm for the extreme exemplars of industrialism—above all, America and the spectacle of New York. To these, one must finally add the deep-seated French desire, persistent to this day, to absorb the modes and artefacts of industrial modernism into nostalgic traditions of craftsmanship . . .

The central issue presented by Léger's work as a whole is the adequacy of style and formal values as a basis for modern painting. It is an issue which emerges only gradually in his development, being partially obscured before 1914 by his exploration of Cubism, during the 1920s by his engagement with urban/proletarian iconography, and in the early 1930s by his version of surrealism. Léger's formal gifts were considerable, and they increased with the scale and simplicity of his later work. The subtlety and finesse of his 1910–14 accomplishments were tranformed into a schematic generalisation of the Cubist planar grid, of which the late 'Constructors' series is the final perfected version. It is ironic that Léger, who was never a truly Cubist artist, would later reach a large public with a nominally representational style based on Cubist-derived formal elements. The obvious parallel is with Picasso, but on a formal level only, for Picasso's later work, from the 1930s to the end, was not based on the artist's prior stylistic inventions alone. It was, rather, generated by his own intensely lived private experiences for the adequate rendition of which he was always reinterpreting not just his own Cubism but much of the history of art as well. Léger by contrast seems always to have been a public or at least anti-subjective personality in his art. Objects, artefacts, buildings, plants, the human figure as formal object—the familiar trappings of everyday life provided the major inspiration for Léger's art. Almost all of his extensive writings were concerned either with formal problems or with the physical experience of the modern world, the modern city and modern innovations—from the cinema to publicity to industrial design.

In many ways Léger became a French, Cubist-derived equivalent of the attitudes and ideals of the Bauhaus, including its neo-mediaeval collectivism in both its internal organisation and in its external political allegiances. The French equivalent of Bauhaus attitudes had its immediate locus in the milieu of *L'Esprit Nouveau*, and its emphasis on the impersonal, material and implicitly collective bases of modern life, as was subsequently demonstrated by the political ideals of its founders . .

It is, however, more important to realise that Léger was born before the Eiffel Tower was erected. His was the generation that witnessed a wholesale material transformation of everyday life, in which candle and gaslight gave way to electricity, the horse-cart to the automobile and airplane; and above all, in which a predominantly rural society was becoming increasingly and unremittingly urban. Such a transformation of social conditions also created a new cultural situation, exemplified by Léger, whereby the old simplicities and certainties of visible, tangible experience remained present in altered form within the rapidly expanding urban environment. There, in the quintessential transaction of twentieth-century life and art, the direct experience of the natural world was gradually supplanted by the rise of the new, artificial nature of man-made tools, machines and all the other appurtenances of the modern city. At first, this new world of human artifice would be seen with eyes and minds conditioned by nature. Later, long after Léger's generation had reached maturity, urban reality would be understood in its own terms. The overall direction of this change was from the dualist phenomenology of man and nature to the more internalised and abstracted mental phenomenology of man and culture.

There is a trajectory of gradual change in Léger's art over a period of fifty years, from his direct involvement with the visible world of nature before 1909, to an interaction between mind and the world from around 1910 through the 1920s, to a preoccupation with the purely abstract mental and cultural world of form, style and structure after 1930. Léger's work thus parallels the fundamental shift in human experience during the twentieth century. But even at the end, he never quite let go of those vestiges of direct experience which remained from his youth, just as he never left the visible world in order to explore the invisible subjective mind. For him the goal was always either the direct experience, the object, or the rearrangement of objects into a clear-cut external and physical order. Such are the limitations but also the enduring virtues of his art.

Excerpts from Edward F. Fry, 'Léger and the French Tradition', *Fernand Léger* (catalogue), Albright-Knox Art Gallery, Buffalo, New York, & Abbeville Press, New York, 1982

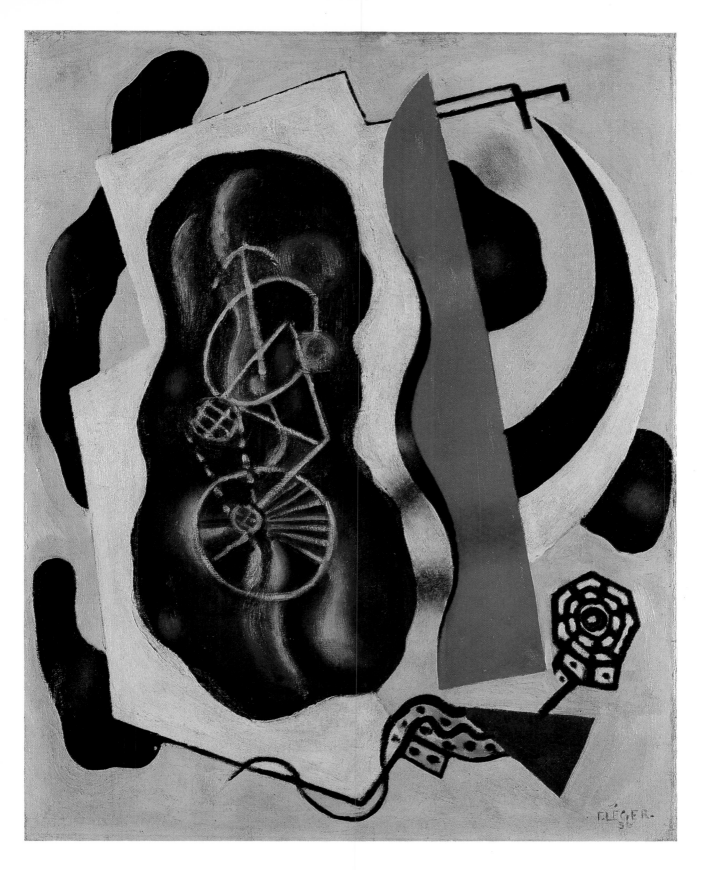

THE BICYCLE, 1930
Oil on canvas
64.8 × 50.8
Collection: Art Gallery of New South Wales
Gift of Mrs H. V. Evatt, March 1966, in memory of Dr H.V. Evatt

INGEBORG LÜSCHER

Born Freiberg, German Democratic Republic, 1936

Lives and works in Tegna, Switzerland

CONCERNING AN ELEMENT AND THE ELEMENTARY, SULPHUR, LIFE, ART AND THE THREE STEPS TOWARDS SCULPTURE

A first movement around and through the sculptures of Ingeborg Lüscher.

Ingeborg Lüscher has been called by André Kamber 'actress, film and television actress, painter, writer, actionist, object-maker, photographer, concept artist'. These designations refer to different spheres of skill and life. Faces appear and disappear. These appearances lead, after the widening of the art concept, to an abundance of intricately rich work in the plastic range. These 'small—often impudent—sample balloons', which distinguished Edvard Münch's work, are kept here in close focus. We are writing here about *one* of Lüscher's faces. We call this woman—modestly— a sculptor, as this text deals mainly with the sculptures created during recent months. Not only the many forms of her own work, but also the intercession between life and work of marginalised beings, other artists like Armand Schultheiss or Laurence Pfautz, and finally the revelation and treatment of her own life, have again and again motivated various interpreters to write texts about the 'connection between life and art' of Ingeborg Lüscher without achieving clarity about the content.

The following text, on the other hand, deals exclusively with the work, with the part of the work already mentioned, the sculptures. Only so can the effect of her work be thrown back harmlessly upon the artist and be examined for its particular fundamental and compulsory cultural context. Obviously no attempt will be spared to show how life and work are entwined. But this talk about the connection between life and art, which exhausts itself seeking for remote stages of life in the work, and which misunderstands the art also as an illustrative and elucidatory means of looking back at the artist's life in a favourable way, refutes in the end even the personal dimension which has entered into the work.

The fortunately utopic project of the connection between life and art, in making the artist free in the work, the hope, in markedly differentiated sorts of conditions in the artwork for seeing and looking, for paintings, connections, processes . . . life laid out in such a way that with the creations new regularities are able to be formed which render the artwork independent. Demand for the connection between life and art must not therefore be consumed in the outer compulsory congruence of artist and work, but can obtain an obligatory dimension, including artist, work and viewer likewise in the sense-foundation. Art is indeed capital!

After the choir of interpreting voices has faded, the steps break away towards the sculptures that stimulate me to write this text. The fundamental effect produced on the viewer by Ingeborg Lüscher's work is to inspire emotion. One must move around the apparently meaningless form several times. Slowly the essential nature of the work, the theme staged within it, is shown. This aspect of her art has been evident in her work so far and is always brought up in discussions of the connection between Ingeborg Lüscher's life and art. The motive of the encounter and the dialogue is not only that which occupies people who search for pictures but also that of the elementary adventures of each life—which includes sculpture. In each single sculpture the genealogical moment is depicted.

The artistic attitude towards sculpture is shown in the choice of materials. In a sociological context, used objects become the core of the sculptures, which, through the sulphur-patina and modest form—certainly not a highly finished, but an adequately worked object—are able to offer an idea of what is possible in bright stillness: *Fiat lux et lux fecit!* The betrayal of this sublimity in homage to the simple sufficient formation rescues the sculpture from slipping away into the impenetrable and from profane use. A sculpture is not only created from the three steps of core, coat (wood-dust, plaster, glue) and patina, but realises itself for art as the utopia of a cosmos without abrasion.

The existence of the sculptures lies in the relationship between at least two elements. Consequently they are never uniform bodies but plastic creations which represent organisms grown out of themselves. The sculptures appear through the almost completely enveloping sulphur as closed bodies of light. Because of their foundation of at least two complementary elements, the thematic and visibility of the poles, for example, in relation to the order of the materials used and the multiplication of similar elements within the created field of tension, point those works not only towards the condition of their own constitution, but carry as an example within themselves transition, birth and being of further body constel- lations and new organisms. Not only in the literal meaning has the beginning of each sculpture the suggestion of a core. An authentic form of contemporary sculpture is realised through several means: through the repeated use of a pure crystalline substance, produced plastically and won from the earth, pointing as a cover for the sculpture towards the potency of the surface area; associating waste created through technical production processes with classic sculpture materials; understanding sculpture as an independent body; and finally, in spite of the meaning which burdens the art, creations arise which do not disclose concern but deal with devotion.

Excerpt from Roman Kurzmeyer, *Von einem Element und Elementarem, von Schwefel, Leben, Kunst und dem Dreischritt zur Skulptur*, Basle, October 1987

UNTITLED, 1987
Wood, wood pulp, paste, plaster, sulphur
37.5 × 50 × 31.5

Born Christchurch, New Zealand, 1901

Died New York, USA, 1980

Len Lye, expatriate New Zealander, is best known for his achievements as a film-maker and kinetic sculptor, but he was also a painter, a genetic theorist, and an experimental prose writer.

Lye's life-time inspiration and motivation was to achieve what he described as a 'one-world'—a level at which a person achieves complete wholeness in his relationship with his own being, with others, and with his natural environment. The personal language Lye developed to implement such an achievement and translate it to his society is a complex but consistent one. A remarkable coherence of philosophy exists between Lye's diverse artistic endeavours, and this is based upon the artist's personal progression towards his ambition—a progression on both a subconscious and cognitive level.

During the years 1977–79 Lye produced a series of thirteen large unstretched canvases. Each of these works is the culmination of Lye's artistic and philosophical aim to understand completely man's position in the universe. In itself this is not an innovative or startling achievement. Many of the greatest artists of the twentieth century have followed the same path in their careers. Lye's achievement, as illustrated by these thirteen paintings is, however, significant because of his personal means of attaining such a complete level of understanding.

Lye believed that the basis of his 'one-world' was a deep knowledge of natural phenomena. Only in possession of such truths could man's survival and a harmonious relationship with his world be ensured. Lye equated this aim with that of the mythology of primitive cultures who developed such narratives to illustrate and attempt to elucidate popular perceptions of natural phenomena. Thus Lye developed what he termed the 'fine-art myth'—he used art to translate the myths about natural phenomena developed by primitive people, and to illustrate the shaping role on man's environment and evolutionary development played by such forces. *Raintree* and *Earth*, two images which are conceived as a pair, depict on an obvious level rain falling from a tree and sustaining and fertilizing the earth beneath. However, on a mythological level based on an Aztec poem and notes Lye discovered in *Antaeus* magazine, this painting refers to the Mexican concept of sustenance being dependent on sacrifice. This is symbolised by the blood-red arrow raindrops which sustain the sun, and are therefore a vital life giving force.

An important factor of Lye's 'fine-art myths' was his belief in the potential of these paintings to provoke intense personal feelings in both the artist and viewer. He also considered these works capable of helping the viewer to recognise his own intuitive ability to realise important truths about himself and his environment.

One of Lye's central beliefs was that the intuitive mind is genetically in possession of natural truths and therefore man has merely to learn to recognise and employ such revelations. This idea is proven by Lye's series of thirteen large paintings, the content of which was intuitively discovered and then sometimes thirty years later given a scientific context in the light of subsequent scientific discoveries. The subject of *Ancestor* (1978) is a coelacanth fish based on a doodle Lye created twenty years before it was possible for him to be aware of the existence of such a fish. To Lye, this supports his conviction that knowledge of phenomena important to our relationship with nature is encoded in our genes or 'old brain'.

Lye likens the intuitive knowledge possessed by primitive people, which he so admires, to the ability of all people's 'old-brain'. In biological terms the 'old-brain' was the first part of our brain to evolve. Lye believed that by concentrating on producing unconscious doodles our old-brain was able to release images, and he determined early in his career to produce artistic works based solely on such ideas. In his thirteen large paintings Lye presents a series of images that evolved in such a manner, which he subsequently subjected to the interpretative skills of the cognitive brain. Thus two stages are simultaneously represented providing a scientific, microscopic depiction of natural phenomena existent millions of years ago. *Raintree*, which illustrates a time when the earth was just cool enough for the atmosphere to condense and fall as rain, is an example of this juxtaposition of stages.

The mythological expression of Lye's philosophy means his paintings are primarily narrative in nature. His first aim is to express the potential of the progression toward the 'one-world' state. In this respect his paintings can be seen as diametrically opposed to the 'art-for-art's-sake' nature of much contemporary abstract art. The composition and colour arrived at are merely by-products of the process of artistic myth-telling. The same can be said for Lye's kinetic sculptures, which are not in the first instance conceived as aesthetic objects but as tools used to relate the experience of the progression towards understanding of the natural phenomenon illustrated.

Lye's emphasis on the importance of the 'old-brain' or primitive intuitive knowledge in the search for an understanding of natural forces and our relationship to them, means his artistic language is an intensely personal and individualistic one. While Lye reflects a variety of ethnographic and stylistic influences, based on both his position as a twentieth century artist and his fascination with primitive art forms, he has ultimately achieved and implemented his early art teacher H. Linley Richardson's recommendation 'that a person who had his own theory of art, right or wrong, was better than he who was sweating it out with somebody else's theory'.

Lye's personal philosophy and resulting artistic mythology, found consistently throughout his artistic achievements, is a deeply private language but one which is still accessible, and valuable to his public.

The Len Lye Foundation, New Plymouth, New Zealand, 1987

Len Lye (with hat, sitting on the right) at a film-making workshop in London in December 1929. Others present include Sergei Eisenstein (with policeman's helmet), Hans Richter (lower left), Mark Segal (playing the warming pan), Lionel Britton (with telephone), Jimmy Rogers (with camera), and—to the right of Rogers—Michael Hankinson, Basil Wright, and Towndrow.

BLADE, 1962/76
Stainless steel, motor, timing mechanism, formica, chipboard, cork
206 × 91

(Photo) Len Lye Foundation

The works in this Biennale occupy a provocative space between sculpture and painting. At first sight their geometry takes the form of minimal constructivist relief. Their actual presence, however, is far from formal. A blue grid made of square sectioned lengths of timber is as precise as graph paper when seen in the frontal plane but, with a shift of perspective by an inch or two, the second layer behind the frontal lattice comes into play. This layer creates the secondary image of a cross like that of the Vitruvian man in his circle and square, or the St Andrew's spider in its web. Subtle as this image is, it takes optical precedence over another layer which is only detected subliminally at first. The whole grid is leaning against the wall with the base about one foot out. The lighting is very carefully specified to produce just one shadow image; there is a blue cross which echoes the optical cross in the grid. The viewer infers that this image is the reflection of a cross painted on the reverse of the grid but its existence is like some supernatural effect of light so delicate as to seem incidental, yet it is an essential element in the work. The formal presence of the grid is in itself a satisfying visual experience but it is deceptively simple. The ephemeral use of optics and the play of light give this piece another life beyond its obvious aesthetic appeal. Because it comes off the wall the object has an anxious ambiguity. It occupies part of the viewer's real space as sculpture does but it works simultaneously in the ideal space of painting and illusion. We deal with sculpture and painting in very different ways perceptually. We expect to be able to realise the total reality of a sculpture by moving around it. It is in a sense actual and must compete in the world of real objects. Painting on the other hand is traditionally expected to convey an illusion or to exist in an imaginative space that is not experienced as actual. This separation has of course been the subject of much research and opposition by artists this century but the mode of reception remains different for wall and floor objects. This work manages to occupy a transitional space where the subjective responses of the viewer are heightened. The deep associations that are built into the structure are able to escape between conscious recognition and the subjective defence systems of the psyche. The human presence in the grid is itself disturbing. It is as if some entity is caught into the matrix itself, not caged but actually integrated into it. The shadow image however seems to have the possibility of an independent existence projected into an indeterminate space behind the wall.

A grid is a traditional and effective abstract device but it is also a powerful symbol of something quite explicit. In some of these works the lattice becomes a portcullis or a gateway. The door however is not open, nor does it invite entry. The grille keeps us at bay: it may even have a chain which proclaims our exclusion more explicitly. The gate, however, must always represent the option of passage even as it denies access. One form of passage that these works specifically invoke is between the conscious domain and the unconscious mind. Between the visible exterior and the internal continent of the interior. On the other hand it can be thought of as a screen between the viewer's normal world and the psyche of the artist. It could be possible to interpret the grid as self portraiture, so that the compelling human presence in the work becomes that of the artist herself.

Anthony Bond, 1987

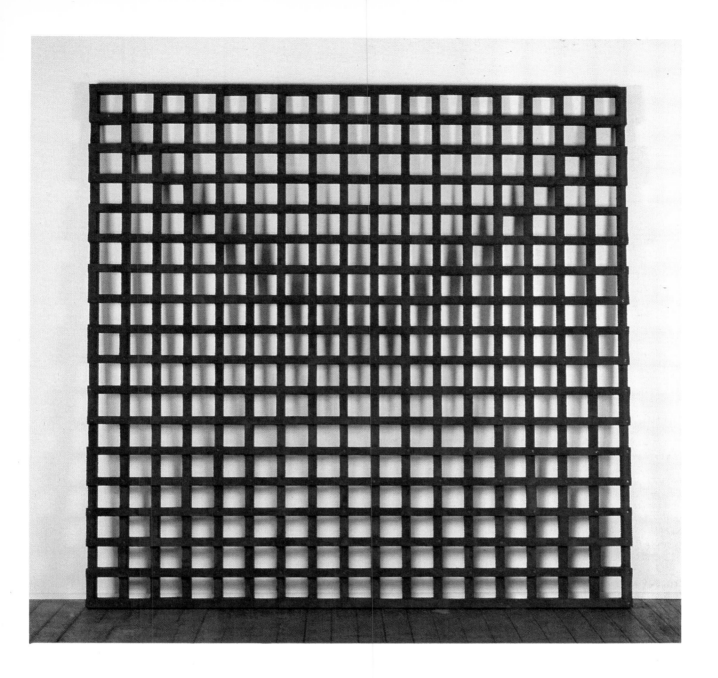

THE GRID, 1987
Oil paint on wood
190 × 190 × 6

HENRI MATISSE

Born Le Cateau-Cambrésis, France, 1869

Died Nice, 1954

What matters more to me than anything else is expression. Sometimes a kind of knowledge has been attributed to me, with the proviso that my ambition is limited and does not go beyond a merely visual satisfaction that looking at a painting can give. But a painter's philosophy must not be isolated by his means, which must be as complete (and by complete, I do not mean complicated) as his ideas are profound. I refuse to make distinctions between my feelings for life and the way in which I translate them into painting.

In my opinion expression does not lie in the passion that suddenly appears on a face or makes itself felt in a violent movement. It exists in the entire composition of my paintings: the positions in which the objects are placed, the spaces surrounding them, the proportions: everything carries out its own function. Composition is the art of arranging in a decorative manner the various elements available to the painter in order to express his emotions. In a painting, each single part must be visible, and must have its own particular function, whether it be an important or a secondary one. Anything that is not useful immediately becomes harmful to the painting. A completed work of art presupposes a total harmony: any superfluous detail would be interpreted as an essential element in the eyes of the observer . . .

In the past, I used not to leave my canvases hanging on the walls because they brought to mind certain moments of over-excitement which I did not want to relive when I was feeling calm and peaceful. Now I work at a painting calmly, and I continue working at it until this inner calm of mine has become part of the painting itself . . .

What really interests me most of all is neither still life nor landscape: it is the human body. This alone allows me to express fully my almost religious sentiment of life. I am not interested in lingering over the detailed features of a face, reproducing them each one in their anatomical exactness. I have an Italian model who at first sight gives one the impression only of animal existence; instead I have discovered his essential features, I penetrate the outlines of his face which communicate the depths to be found in every human being. A work of art must contain its whole significance, and force it on the spectator before he knows what the subject of the painting is. When I look at Giotto's frescoes in Padua, I do not want to know which episode of the life of Christ he is illustrating, but I immediately understand the sentiment he is expressing, because it shines through the lines, the composition and the colour: and the title merely confirms my impression.

My dream is of an art that is balanced, pure, serene, without worrying or disturbing subjects, so that it becomes a soothing influence for the intellectual, businessman or for the literary artist, something that calms the unquiet mind, something rather like a really comfortable armchair that gives him repose after his physical labours.

We often discuss the value of the various procedures, and their relations with the various characters. We make distinctions between painters who work directly from life and those who work from their imagination. In my opinion, it is not necessary to adopt one of these two methods to the exclusion of the other. It happens that the same artist uses sometimes one and sometimes the other. Either because he feels the need of the actual presence of the objects in order to receive sensations and thus stimulate his creative faculties, or because his sensations are already classified: in one case or the other he is able to reach that synthesis which constitutes the painting. However, I think that the vitality and the power of an artist can be judged inasmuch as he, under the direct impression of a natural spectacle, is able to organise his sensations and re-enter that spiritual mood more than once, even over a period of several days. This ability presupposes a man who is master of himself and able to discipline his character. The simplest means are those which enable the painter to express himself in the best way. If he fears banality, he will not avoid it by using eccentric elements, having recourse to bizarre colours and drawing techniques. His means must necessarily be derived from his temperament. He must have that simplicity of spirit which makes him think he has painted only what he sees.

Excerpt from *La Grande Revue*, 25 December, 1908

This new language you refer to doesn't in my view imply the condemnation of oil painting and consequently of easel painting. I myself have turned to more matt, more direct materials at the moment, which leads me to look for a new means of expression. Cut paper enables me to draw in colour. What I want is a simplification. Instead of drawing the outline and applying the colour inside it— the one modifying the other—I draw directly in colour, which is the more considered the more it is not transposed. This simplification guarantees a precision in the reunion of the two means which are no longer anything but one.

Excerpt from *Propos de Henri Matisse*, Amis de l'Art, October 1951

POLYNÉSIE LA MER, 1946
Collages on paper
197 × 310

COLIN McCAHON

Born Timaru, New Zealand, 1919

Died Auckland, 1987

6 DAYS IN NELSON AND CANTERBURY

This painting came at the end of a decade of landscapes and of landscapes filled with figures from the Gospels. It also comes at the beginning of a long line of paintings of journeys. Here there are six landscapes in one picture, each with its own frame. Each represents a remembered moment, an elementary outline of a place, and a time of day.

While looking to typify a landscape, it also sets it in a kind of narrative framework. McCahon travelled across the south island on his bicycle, from Christchurch to Nelson, to go fruit-picking in the summer. The 'bit of blood shed in the middle' was, as he told a friend, his own—when he fell off the bicycle. Anecdote aside, it is also typical of McCahon's notion of the land as something yet to be treated with love by its *pakeha* (white) inhabitants. The land is shown in its barest, most naked form, as if at the time of its original creation. For McCahon, searching for a Promised Land, this land is yet to be redeemed.

The format is something like that of a cartoon-strip, or perhaps a postcard with several views of a town. It is not unusual in McCahon's practice to find him trying to link his art with popular uses of imagery.

Later, in the 1950s, he treats landscape first as overlapping multiple views within the rectangular frame, then from 1958 on, as a series of loose hanging unframed paintings, in rows, edge to edge. You are invited to walk the length of the painting, rather than to stand in front of the single picture. In 1966, the journey through a landscape becomes associated with the Stations of the Cross, and the walk of Christ to Calvary. Over and over, McCahon repeats this theme in landscape series in the 1970s. At least one of these paintings is called *Walk*, and two others are called *Walk With Me*.

HERE I GIVE THANKS TO MONDRIAN

This is one of the first of an important series, the 'Gates', of 1961. After a year with almost no painting, here was a new beginning. Apparently abstract—a term McCahon disliked—they were based on a view through his bedroom window and also on recollections of landscape.

Notes made by Wystan Curnow at a lecture given by McCahon in May 1963 state the theme of the 'Gates': 'He says he is concerned with the sense of restriction the individual feels . . . but a "Gate" is postulated, a way out, an avenue to freedom.'

McCahon showed eighteen 'Gate' paintings at The Gallery, Symonds St, Auckland in August 1961. In the following year he painted a long series of panels called the 'Gate Series', which he showed at Gallery 91, Christchurch, in September 1962, together with some of the first 'Gates'.

By this time, the images of dark obstructions and passages between them had become linked with a broader theme: a protest against nuclear weapons. In addition to the apparently abstract forms, many of them contained written texts from the Old Testament prophets: 'Cry! You inhabitants of the plain' . . . 'The Hammer of the whole earth is split asunder', and so on.

As to Mondrian: 'The words "Here I Give Thanks to Mondrian" reflect my admiration for the gentleman. It was only at this stage did I realise his importance as a painter. I had seen some early works in San Francisco, and also saw some of his later works in other parts of the States. What really impressed me was that, although they were often very small, they had an openness and scale that extended beyond the actual edges of the painting—a thing I find only happens in front of the originals and which cannot be seen in a reproduction . . .'[1]

It is typical of McCahon to make use of household paints at this time, not only because of the cost of artist's colours, but also as a link with a painting vernacular. Of course enamel gloss does not work well with masking tape, as can be seen in this picture. 'As a painter, how do you get round either a Michelangelo or a Mondrian? It seems that the only way is not more "masking-tape" but more involvement in the human situation,' he said in 1972.[2]

THE LARK'S SONG

Frequently in his painting, McCahon turns to brush-written texts. Often, as here, the words overlap the merest suggestions of landscape or sky. Such paintings make something like the text, usually embroidered, which adorned the walls of some houses in the nineteenth century. Colin McCahon is like the great Romantic English poets, who, in Virginia Woolf's words, 'give us text after text to be hung upon the wall saying after saying to be laid upon the heart like an amulet against disaster'. But McCahon's writing is a kind of breathing painting, painting the rhythmic sound with the brush's phrasing: the loaded brush is exhausted and dipped in the paint over and over. He is content to lay one system of signs over another; here the images of clouds, the painted words and the dotted line that shows the movement of the lark ascending.

The texts are mixed, too. The main Maori text comes from Matire Kereama's *The Tail of the Fish*. But the 'Can you hear me, St Francis?' comes from a poem by Peter Hooper. McCahon painted at least six other works relating to *The Tail of the Fish*, but this one was his favourite. It is painted, as are many of his paintings, on materials immediately at hand, in this case, cupboard doors. In 1972, he remarked: 'From August to October I struggled with Mrs Kereama's *Lark's Song*. I loved it, I read the poem out loud while I painted and finally the little lark took off up the painting and out of sight. The words must be read for their sound, they are signs for the lark's song. This whole series of paintings gave me great joy. Please don't give yourself the pain of worrying out a translation of the words but try for the sound of the painting . . .'

In 1974, the lark's song gave way to that of another bird and another Maori poem, this time in acrylic on a smooth and fine canvas, *The Song of the Shining Cuckoo*. This, too, has a broken line for the bird's flight, from panel to panel of the work, which is simultaneously numbered from one to fourteen for the Stations of the Cross, accumulating a mass of reference typical of McCahon's later painting.

Tony Green, 1987

1. Colin McCahon, *Auckland City Art Gallery Quarterly*, no 44, 1969.
2. Survey Exhibition catalogue, Auckland City Art Gallery.

SIX DAYS IN NELSON AND CANTERBURY, 1950
Oil on board
87.5 × 112

Born Seymour, Victoria, Australia, 1955

Lives and works in Melbourne

ANY OF OUR STUFF?

I ventured into the junkyard for the first time in a couple of weeks. Geoff greeted me, 'Gidday Vic, after some new tin?' (I like the way he calls me Vic—so convincing . . . like a brother at arms.) 'Don't worry 'bout that, I'll have some soon.' 'O.K.,' I said, 'but this time can you scrunch it up for me? How's about using the caterpillar claw, or the front-end loader?' 'Don't worry, I'll take care of it.'

(It's hardly a case of making found-object-based work any more. This junkyard has turned into the best art shop I've ever known and frequented.)

I walked out with some tin a while ago and passed Geoff who was standing by the front gate. 'Top stuff that, Vic! Knock it on, just like it is!'

Gone are the days of dragging my feet in the gutter, looking for junk. Talk about civilised! I never thought once that I would have got in the habit of buying beer to exchange for art materials. And that's how it is. Since the summer of '85. Geoff has the last word—I handed him a catalogue of a Brisbane exhibition—his reply, 'Any of our stuff in this?'

Statement by the artist, 1987

LOCOMOTIF and A BUTTATA, 1987
Galvanised iron, galvanised iron primer, wood
344 × 94 × 144 and 386 × 97 × 148

(Photo) Alexis Ensor

Born Mammendorf, Federal Republic of Germany, 1947

Lives and works in Munich

When Gerhard Merz came to Kassel yet again, in the middle of April 1987, to determine finally his contribution to Documenta, he was carrying *H.D. (Hilda Doolittle) The End of Torment* with him as his travel reading. A passage in this slim book subtitled 'A memory of Ezra Pound' pleased him especially, and he gave it to me and to spectators as a motto for his new work in hand. It is a quotation by Ezra Pound from Canto 92:

Le Paradis n'est pas artificiel
          but is jagged,
For a flash,
          for an hour.
Then agony,
          then an hour,
             then agony,. . .

The work comes out of three-dimensional, plastic, painterly elements and text, which are linked variously with one another and produce the work together. According to Merz's wishes, a room was built for him which, unlike the normal interior of the Fridericianum, is right-angled, has a ceiling and leaves the window wall free. The spectator steps through a narrow entrance, which the hint of a portico makes narrower. He stands in the middle of a narrow, very long space in front of the window wall of the Fridericianum, which is made up of five floor-length windows and their deep plastically constructed bays. The view to the outside is prevented, however, as the window glass is blank. As he turns back to the entrance wall, he sees on his left seven very tall and narrow monochromatic red paintings (300 × 55 cm); on the right seven skulls in bronze (lifesize, i.e. surprisingly small); above the entrance and the skulls the lines MCMLXXXVII VITTORIA DEL SOLE. All this is found in front of the shiny bright orange surfaces of the wall.

Excerpt from Ludwig Rinn, *Documenta 1987* (catalogue),
Kassel, 1987

DIE GLORIE DESSEN, DER MIT SEINEM FINGER
BEWEGUNG SCHAFFT, DURCHDRINGT DAS ALL UND GLEISST
AN EINER STELLE MEHR UND SONST GERINGER.

DANTEUM III, 1987
Pigment on canvas
Three paintings, 90 × 350 × 10

(Photo) Franz Fischer

FRANCOIS MORELLET

Born Cholet, France, 1926

Lives and works in Cholet, Paris and New York

HELP, THE STRAIGHT
LINE'S COMING BACK[1]

Yes, it's on the way everywhere, from Vienna to New York, from Melbourne to Dijon!

The latest news is that young folk seem to be deserting en masse the dirty fight which placed art on its figurative base. The last word is that abstraction doesn't seem to be at death's door, and the last we heard geometry was doing fine, thanks.[2] And to think that they left us in such peace, those of us who stoked the fires of the straight line!

But it's all over. They're going to dig us up again, push us about, maybe like us (but certainly not the things we'd like them to like about us), or worse still, ignore us. What should we expect, we who are so pure, and so hard (well, those who have been unwise enough to stay that way), from this ambiguous geo-metry which has its authority Joseph Beuys, Walt Disney or Bridget Riley.*

And then after a few art fairs, Biennales or Documenta shows with their geometric orientation, the shame of being once more out of fashion and this time with no hope (given our age) of ever being rehabilitated a second time.

So, come what may, I must save my geometry, camouflage it (at least temporarily), and what better to disfigure it with than figuration. Ignoble figuration in the process of going out of fashion yet again.

In *Géométrie, figures hâtives*[3] figuration is there from the start in the figurative impressions (borrowed with a wink[4] from my own anatomy) painstakingly disfigured by the geometric figures which they create.

In *La géométrie dans les spasmes*[5] it is the geometric figures which are disfigured by pornographically oriented anthropomorphic figuration.**

Statement by the artist, Cholet, October 1986

---

* Between you and me I don't really have anything against these neo-geos (as they call them in New York) when they don't take themselves too seriously, and when they play the part of fourth generation, ironical, nihilistic atheists, ready to satisfy inspired picnickers.

** Any other picnic will be justified and welcome. In these two attempts, for example, we can spy two disasters. And as a result the proof that the very archaic means of a prehistoric and slightly lewd artist are as badly made for geometry as the very technical means of a slightly ascetic geometric artist for pornography.

1. *La droite* means both 'the straight line' and 'the right wing'.
2. The translator's nightmare! The sentences—*Ce SALLE COMBAS CHIA BASELITZ hoire de l'art sur la figuration. Le fin MOSSET que l'abstraction n'a PALERMO ribonde et qu'aux dernières nouvelles la géométrie HALLEY très bien, MERZi,*—are a reference to the eight artists whose names have been wittily used to construct the following 'real' sentence: *Ce sale combat qui a basé l'histoire de l'art sur la figuration. Le fin mot c'est que l'abstraction n'a pas l'air moribond et qu'aux dernières nouvelles la géométrie allait très bien, merci.*
3. *Figures hâtives*—figurative.
4. Wink in French is *clin d'oeil*. Morellet's text reads *KLEIN d'oeil*.
5. Literally translated: Geometry in spasms, witch misses the paw on *géométrie dans l'espace*, the French term for 'three-dimensional geometry'.

Translated by Simon Pleasance

PAR DERRIÈRE (A 2) (LA GÉOMÉTRIE DANS LES SPASMES), 1986
Acrylic on canvas
Two paintings 200 × 200 and 400 × 100

Robert Morris stands before us today as an undismissible presence that forces us to rethink the entire basis of modern American life, the entire history and ideology of American cultural and artistic modernism, and, not incidentally, his own role in that modernism . . . a role that now, suddenly, takes on a new meaning and coherence and which changes totally the way we understand both past and present.

Since the end of the 1970s Morris has made works that seem to reject every tenet that he supposedly espoused in, or contributed to, the situation of art from the early 1960s onward. His new works break with apparently every formal, aesthetic concern and display what seems to be the inexcusably bad taste of celebrating death and morbidity: cenotaphs, skeletal reliefs and, more recently, the firestorms of nuclear holocaust. In his brilliant monumental works in 1984 Morris went even further in the direction of an apparently renegade loss of aesthetic faith by combining sculpture—the medium by which he has always been known—with painting and architecture into a new kind of composite art, culminating in such extraordinary achievements as *Enterprise* and *The Astronomer*, which have no precedent in American modernism. Morris has thus apparently broken two taboos of the modernist faith at once: the integrity and purity of a given medium and the corruption of high art by literary and metaphorical intrusions from the outside worlds of politics, science and power.

But Morris is not offering a personal version of *Apocalypse Now*, nor a backsliding, Turneresque version of the neo-sublime. His ambition here is of a higher and more encompassing degree, which one may initially identify as a radical, neo-modern attempt to confront the tragic failure of the Protestant, American version of the Enlightenment. In doing so he addresses many levels simultaneously, ranging from the mental and technical domination of nature and the fatal role of rationality, to the inability of American artistic modernism either to remain modern or to escape its self-imposed and self-sterilising limits. His strategy is that of irony, raised to the intensity of the anti-sublime, an anti-sublimity that acknowledges the fatal seductiveness of apocalyptic sublimity, especially for the American mind, but which, somewhat like Terry Southern's *Dr Strangelove*, dissolves that false sublimity by revealing another, authentic, and more awesome sublimity both in the universe itself and in human consciousness and will as they interact with the cosmos . . .

The enormous, almost insuperable task Morris has set before himself in his works of the 1980s is to confront the tragedy of Enlightenment modernity in both autonomous art and science, to break down the barriers separating the two so that the parallels between their respective estrangements from self-aware modernism will become evident, and to do so in such a way that an exhausted artistic modernism will be transformed and re-emerge with a new emancipatory power. It is a measure of his ambition and achievement as an artist that he has come within reach of that goal in his recent works. In a long series of composite structures—part painting, part relief sculpture, part architectural frame/portal—he surrounds paintings derived from his *Firestorm* drawings with frames containing relief castings, in life-size, of skulls, bodies, foetuses, sexual organs, brains, eyes, entrails, thrusting fists and phalluses of aggressive male will, flotsam and jetsam from all of Western life and culture. These frames, which developed out of Morris's *Hypnerotomachia* plaster reliefs, bend and contort as if under the most extreme forces imaginable, the detritus of earthly human existence being melded into an unspeakable flux, each element in the reliefs tinted with the flowing colours of the central firestorm. Just as these frames, moulded by the artist's hands and body, are highlighted with the mental/visual attribute of colour, so the images of the central firestorms are painted with his fingers: an interlocking complementarity of mind and body, unequally accented, coming together in painting and in relief, the parts inextricably juxtaposed physically and mentally within the unifying theme of apocalypse.

In the greatest of these works thus far, the regeneration of aesthetic modernism by means of disruption and reformulation of the very foundations of Protestant modernity becomes so interlocked with the tragic hubris of Enlightenment science that the double nature of Morris's emancipatory neo-modernism merges into a virtually inseparable whole, a wholeness comparable to that of Pollock's earlier modernism but now far more difficult to attain in a world incomparably more dangerous than the 1940s and bereft of those last shreds of innocence which still lingered in that earlier age. In *The Astronomer* (1984), the human mind's eye, a barbed weapon like a feline phallus, thrusts with the speed of light into the cosmos to see and think its ultimate entropic secrets, consumed by the very firestorm it begets. In *Enterprise*, also of 1984 and, I believe, the greatest work until now in Morris's entire career, the firestorm spreads an ironic glow across the human detritus of its pulsating frame, watched by a Michelangelesque owl of death perched at the top; a structure of rods and spheres skirts the front of the work as a second ironic commentary on both applied physics and the vast folly of the organised enterprise of technology, the results of which it is now confronting.

Underlying all these unforgettable images and references is the brilliance of a second great dialectical act, comparable to Morris's original move in the early 1960s from the pictorial to the sculptural. In this second step Morris has synthesised the pictorialism of Pollock's achievement with the space-time phenomenalism of his own prior attempts to regain Pollock's original emancipatory modernism. The result is the fusion of painting and sculpture, of aesthetics and the most tragic issue in real, non-aesthetic life, and an almost coming together again of mind and body. The two touch, interlock, almost merge, as they would in the apocalyptic ecstasy of death, but the residual tension between them generates an all-important, neo-modern awareness of the enormity of the dangers of modernity. This is an art that struggles to regain the lost wholeness of free beingness; it is a struggle to become modern again in the face of the decline of full, emancipatory self-awareness, be that decline the result of fatigue alone or of a wilful embrace of new-old myths and their soothing amnesia. In the cultural history of the modern world, these works mark the emergence of a baroque Protestant modernism which subsumes all that preceded it into a new, fuller representation of a world torn by extreme opposing forces. Other, potentially even more catastrophic, consequences of human knowledge will undoubtedly follow our own, just as man will discover ever more violent forces in the cosmos itself. But works of art such as these stand alone in our present culture, unique in their embodiment of multiple levels of consciousness, knowledge, and meaning and in their presence as admonitory guardians of the idea of a possible free, fully human existence. For this philosophical and ultimately moral vision and for his ability to communicate that vision indelibly and unforgettably, Robert Morris deserves not only praise and gratitude but our most serious attention.

Excerpts from Edward F. Fry, 'Robert Morris in the 1980s',
Robert Morris: Works of the Eighties (catalogue), Museum
of Contemporary Art, Chicago, and Newport Harbor Art
Museum, 1986

UNTITLED, 1987
Encaustic and silkscreen on aluminium panel and painted cast fibreglass
256.5 × 315

OLIVIER MOSSET

Born Berne, Switzerland, 1944

Lives and works in New York

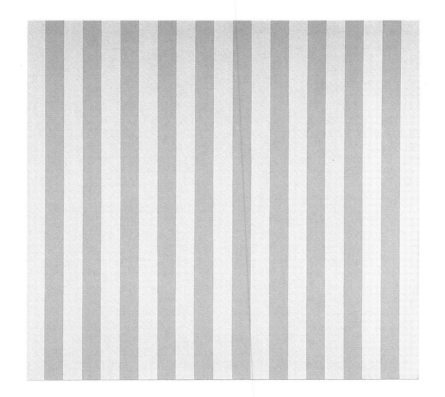

UNTITLED, 1975
Acrylic on canvas
203.2 × 213.3

SMACK, 1986
Oil on canvas
200 × 210

NATSU NAKAJIMA

Born Sakhalin, Japan, 1943

Lives and works in Tokyo

Natsu Nakajima, who founded Muteki-sha in 1969, was born in 1943 in Sakhalin. As a baby she was evacuated from the island as the Russians invaded. The sound of the fog horn of the departing ship—the *Muteki*—still resonates in her work. Nakijima's dance training began in 1955 when she studied Western classical and modern dance forms in Tokyo. In 1962 she saw a work performed by Hijikata and his newly formed *Ankoku Butoh* group (Dance of Total Darkness), and immediately moved away from established schools to study with Kazuo Ohno and then with Tatsumi Hijikata. Rejecting Japanese traditional dances—*Kabuki, Noh, Nihon Buyo*—and the Western forms, this new dance—*Butoh*—struggled to achieve a dance that could challenge historical restraints with a movement where a living face could replace the stillness of the mask.

Natsu Nakajima was one of the first female students of the two leaders of the *Butoh* movement (Hijikata and Kazuo Ohno). Throughout the sixties she danced in a number of Hijikata's pieces before forming her own company, Muteki-sha, in 1969 . . .

Nakajima holds a very important position within the *Butoh* world that has developed since the early sixties; she has also widened her influence by leading many workshop courses during her foreign tours over the past four years. Her most recent work, *Sleep and Reincarnation* from *Empty Land*, received its world premiere in Tokyo in July 1987.

SLEEP AND REINCARNATION

---

from EMPTY LAND

This piece is dedicated to my teacher, Tatsumi Hijikata, who died two years ago in 1986.

In this piece I am considering this land and another land. Hijikata once told me that 'We are made to live by the dead'. When I was younger I could not understand this, but now I realise that we are living together with the dead.

Two pilgrims travelling (they could be more, or only one); this journey has no time, no place and no aim. However, in the total darkness, they are searching for a light.

There are passing scenes; previous scenes reappear and disappear again; the wind blows; dead souls return; fleeting visions; flowers bloom.

Sleep . . .

Within the bosom of this shallow yet deep sleep,
What does this sleeper dream of?
Sleeper lying down, dream stands up.

Finally, just as tiny smiles invite other smiles,
Become a huge smile spreading into a ring,
So, fragmented life gathers itself, strings towards everlasting darkness.

Statement by the artist, Tokyo, January 1988

TO MY COMRADE

—For Natsu Nakajima

We modern people are not living as that skin that we have shed; we modern people are not pursued by the 'time of that cast-off skin'—we can extend and reduce this time, because it is full of much diverting and chatting dance. We are living surrounded by a mass of tricky symbols and systems and using pre-determined movements as our alibi.

This cast-off skin is our own land and home, which our body has forcibly ripped away. This cast-off skin is totally different from that other skin that our body has lost—divided in two—one skin which is the body approved by society, the other skin that has lost its identity. So they need to be sewn together, but this sewing together only forms a shadow.

I admire our ancestors who took good care of the feeling in their souls.

As modern people are aware of the dark uneasiness in front of their eyes, and fear running with wide open eyes, they would not try to escape from the advantages of this condition: 'I would rather go into the blinded body and be bewildered, I am afraid of being attacked by my own eyes, which have seen what I am . . . In fact, we do not feel comfortable with a dance which is danced with open eyes. I know that our ancestors could run with the soul blinded.

But we shake hands with the dead, who send us encouragement from beyond our body; this is the unlimited power of *Butoh*. In our body history, something is hiding in our subconscious, collected in our unconscious body, which will appear in each detail of our expression. Here we can rediscover time with an elasticity, sent by the dead. We can find *Butoh*, in the same way we can touch our hidden reality, something can be born, can appear, living and dying in the moment.

So the character of *Butoh* might just be shaped through these attitudes, which have already been rejected by the body's own thoughtful intuition, whose basis is a hidden violence. It is a filthy child who has a special ability in *Butoh*—because he knows how to create beautiful patterns.

The character of this child: he can walk under the obscure light, would like to play with this light, would try to punish this light, his eyes would fade away, his nose would sniff with tears, his cry would touch the reality of something. It could be very similar to an old man, sleeping with a paralysed body; he is bringing a strange language and whispering with his hidden tongue.

Butoh should be viewed as enigmatic as life itself. I am not sure whether, in the end, it is a trap or a secret correspondence with something, or even tracking down a criminal by illusion.

You know, you could see and hear the impression of life through your activity when you were a child—you could catch its pleasure, fear, mystery, a feeling for differences. Then, you used these feelings as your main guide in your *Butoh* expression. It should be natural. Because we have not become entirely human yet . . . these may be the tidings and basis of *Butoh*.

You glimpsed *Butoh*, and went into *Butoh*, then your life was danced by this *Butoh*. By realising life is mysterious, you were able to change your ideas and your life, so your *Butoh* appeared succinct, subtle, delicate, lyrical and innocent. You have touched your 'real fire in life' after your frustrating experiences. All things have a destiny to be shaped after imitating an earlier established life, after being prosecuted for discovering truth, new shapes will appear, beauty will go through the same. You are seeking your life—love and fire in life through *Butoh*—it is you.

Oh, I have not got the palms to pray for us who stand accused by a new-born *Butoh*. So I only stick out my tongue under the rain.

My lovely comrade, now I am a frog being far away from the shadow of an idea.

Tatsumi Hijikata, 1984.
Translated by Natsu Nakajima and Lizzie Slater.

This special event is presented as part of 'Close-up of Japan, Sydney 1988' sponsored by THE MITSUI PUBLIC RELATIONS COMMITTEE.

THE MITSUI
PUBLIC RELATIONS
COMMITTEE

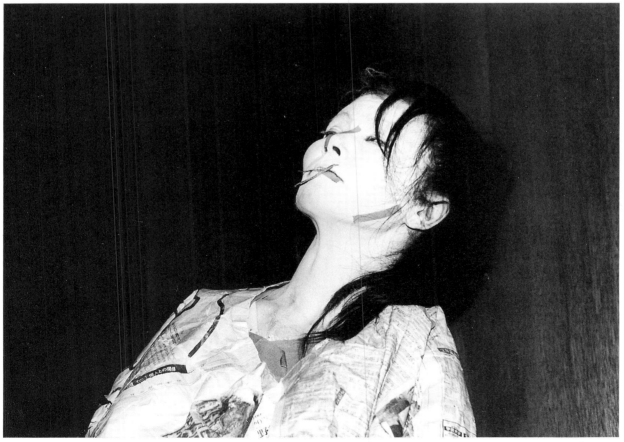

SLEEP AND REINCARNATION from EMPTY LAND
Performance work

HERMANN NITSCH

Born Vienna, Austria, 1938

Lives and works in Prinzendorf

At the time of my earliest discussions it was obvious to me that art was something similar to religion and the performance of art corresponded to a ritual, just as I wanted and still want to expand theatre into ritual. I saw similar thoughts realised by Stephan George and Gustav Klimt. They also understood their role as priesthood. Klimt painted in a ritual-robe. In this sense I was already dressed in a cowl-like shirt during my first painting-actions, without which my present painting-rituals are unimaginable. By the way, one met with fierce resistance having thoughts like these in 1960. The Conservatives didn't understand me anyway and the avant-garde was very much keyed to rationalism . . .

Very early on I played with the thought of keeping the colour-stained shirt as a relic. Three years after the first painting-action I took pains to preserve the action-relics. Used white cloths and even action-robes were displayed as relics at the actions. Around 1969 I started to hang the ritual-robes of the Christian church in front of my action-paintings. Later I did the same with my used painting-shirts. The robe as the bearer of marks of the bloodiest suffering corresponds to the earliest and direct development of the painting . . .

Again and again I try to work up my own action in a didactic way. Through my work I want to tell the history of the origin of the psyche and the consciousness. At the same time the logical development of my work is related. In this sense I repeatedly show my action-painting as the first element of my action. My theatre is an extremely visual theatre. The qualities of my painting declare themselves in an increased sense at every action. Nevertheless it makes me very happy to bring the actionistic happening back onto a perspective plane from which it can expand into the space up to the courses of the stars towards infinity. In my theatre my painting should always have a function like a litany, comparable to the Gregorian chorale. My painting ought to be an initiation formula, a meditation formula towards the orgiastic happening of dramatic excess. It would be my goal that the participants in the play in my theatre should take part in the painting-ritual and the liturgy.

They themselves would spill colour or blood upon white varnished surfaces. The painting should open our senses to a deeper and more intense sensual regimentation . . .

When I was young my environment educated me to be a Christian. Schopenhauer revealed to me an understanding of Asiatic philosophy. Overall a strict denial of the world in favour of a transcendant being resulted from this. The particular vitality, most intensive and overwhelming experiences with nature and the impression that Nietzsche's works left on me—and the studying of psychoanalysis—brought me to an unreserved affirmation of life and being. I love the event of creation and want to be completely at one with it, realising myself as well as the creation itself. I was deeply touched by the thought that the vitality repressed by Christianity and the suppressed orgiastic plot are resurrected in the fact of the Passion. The Passion is the reversal of the orgiastic plot. Suppressed life shows up at any price, it needs intensity even at the price of suffering. Intensive living is very close to suffering. Blood is the fluid of life and red surging blood signifies the wound, the pain, the danger and death. The Passion is life, uplifted to the Dionysian fact of the tragic suffering of being. In registering the great Passion presentations in painting and music, the power of life and the deep gruesome abysmality of life in its everlastingness and endlessness moved me again and again. This enormous nature emerging from its own abyss has deeply upset and scared me. I had to see in what dreadful masks life presents itself. Again and again the deep and enormous power of life in the pain-filled abysses of the Passion touched me. Red is the most intensive colour I know. Red is the colour that registers most intensely, for it is the colour of life and death at the same time.

Excerpts from Otmar Rychlik, 'Interview with Hermann Nitsch', *Hermann Nitsch: 20. Malaktion*, Wiener Secession, Vienna, 1987.
Translated by Tina Messer

PAINTING ACTION, 1987
Installation at Vienna Secession

(Photo) Liesl Biber

JOHN NIXON

Born Sydney, Australia, 1949

Lives and works in Melbourne and Brisbane

IT IS SIMPLE

From 1968 on, Nixon's art, which is strongly self-referential, 'abstract', oppositional and romantic points to an art which harks back ideologically to the spiritual, revolutionary and psychological fervour of another era—that of Constructivism as well as to Arte Povera, Minimalism and Conceptualism.

LIFE BLOOD

The drama, the catharsis is always present in Nixon's work—unrepenting thirst for freedom, autonomous expression and a longing for truth and purity expressed through the simplest emblem like forms—paintings, etchings, drawings, sculpture and monuments—using the cross, the rectangle, the circle, the square, the oval, the vertical and everyday objects from the world of culture, labour and nature.

THE LONG JOURNEY

These 'self portraits', these 'culture of materials'—they are simple and forthright works—a journey dealing with the 'Abstract' and the 'Real'.

John Barlycorn. 17.10.85. Melbourne.

LEGACY

The work (of J.N.) constitutes a Journey—
an Inventory, a Retrospective, a Voyage
and a Direction—
an Aktion of Discovery.
His concern is with the Poetry of Abstraction/
of Nature/ of the Readymade/ of Surface/ of Arte Povera/
of the Imagination/ of Self Expression/ of Purity/
of Colour/ of the Earth/ of the Spirit/ of the Monochrome.
As an Artist he is well aware of the Legacy of History—
something we must Love and Cherish and (like Nature itself)
work in Harmony with.
It is through such a Journey, through such Joy of Aktion and
Investigation
that he moves through the Kingdom of Art.
Give yourself over to this Enlightenment—
to this Didactic Demonstration of Experiment/ of Virtue/ of a
search
for Truth and Essence.

John Barlycorn. 15.7.86. Melbourne.

THE FRUITS OF LABOUR

Freedom is a positive condition—specifically freedom to create, freedom to become what one *is*. The work implies an obligation. Freedom is not a state of rest, of least resistance. It is a state of action, of projection, of self realization.

Herbert Read, 'Chains of Freedom' in *Anarchy and Order*,
Faber and Faber, London, 1954

Within the modernist project and with conceptual authority, Nixon's art is by its very nature an analysis—an analysis of painting, of sculpture etc—drawing strength from history to move into the present—both of what art can be and what it is—such is (like) the continuum of nature—such is an appreciation of the endeavour.

A synthesis of opposites—of art and life, rudimentary geometry with simple selections from the worlds of nature, labour and culture.

Nixon's art is also imbued with a striking life force—of spiritual and emotive significance (an art that is 'healing' and 'good') proposing hope in dark times.

From humble materials and artisan methods to studio 'rooms of the magnificent'—a laboratory of investigation. Collectively his house/store constitute a great *Gesamtkunstwerk*, a 'monument' to his action (labour) over twenty years.

This work was born in song—filled with the great spirit of experimentation.

THE TAPESTRY OF ART + LIFE John Barlycorn, May 1987, Melbourne.

SELF PORTRAIT (NON-OBJECTIVE COMPOSITION), 1983
Acrylic on hessian
60 × 60

(Photo) Roslyn Oxley9 Gallery, Sydney, and United Artists Gallery, Melbourne

Born Melbourne, Australia, 1917

Lives and works in Herefordshire, England

Sidney Nolan is known, I suppose, as 'the Australian painter', a description which needs considerably qualifying if it suggests that we should put him in a special niche as an astonishing phenomenon, one of the two or three extremely original painters who have come out of Australia in the past decades . . . By now he has made a great deal of the world his Australia . . . It is not just that he travels widely and has a seemingly inexhaustible visual appetite for many countries, but that he also has a world consciousness, and, at times . . . he expresses a world conscience.

Stephen Spender, London, 1960

The impact of the Second World War, and interest in painting as a means of elaborating and celebrating myths and a concern with the socially cohesive value of myths as opposed to ideologies, all had their effects upon Nolan, who, called up for army training in 1942, found himself in the flat, dry Wimmera, two hundred miles from Melbourne and centuries from Rimbaud and Klee. Abstraction may have appeared inadequate, somewhat dégagé to him, but for Nolan painting is the eventual crystallisation of his emotional, pictorial and intellectual environment and just as he was ready to utilise various media so was he open to new visual experiences . . .

In parts of the flat lands of Australia, the European compositional categories of foreground, middle distance and distance have little application; this has made the landscape awkward for many painters, but Nolan has used it in a way that gives a hillock or tree a mesmeric effect. In later paintings of 1964 to 1966 he has used the European categories so that the middle distance crops up like a pause before the uncanny suggestiveness of the fading horizon. But the early Wimmera works and the central Australian and explorer paintings make dramatically emphatic use of the hard, blue sky, cutting into the horizon like a broad blade. To emphasise the still solidity and suggestion of eternal sameness he avoided any hint of the atmospheric perspective that he was to adopt in his Antarctic series and the landscapes of the early sixties. There was no need to lift the horizon in order to give the landscape more frontality as in Cézanne's vistas, for the Wimmera landscape pushes itself hard up against the eye. Tom Roberts veiled the abruptness of hills and horizons with screens of trees and smoky, smudged haze; in order to stress the transition from foreground to distance, Arthur Streeton, in a painting such as *Still Glides the Stream and Shall Forever Glide* of 1889, depicted trees and a winding stream both diminishing with distance. Furthermore, Nolan, though appreciating the pastoral sweep, was by no means in search of comfortable versions of the plains and, in fact, there was an unequivocal rejection of a number of European attitudes to landscape: for Nolan landscape was not a repository of a variety of human feelings, of demoniacal powers, of metaphysical implications or of sublime cosmic forces, though the last begin to emerge in his Antarctic paintings. Nolan dotted the Dimboola paddocks with round trees that appeared again as the giant mushroom shape in the sets that he prepared for the 1962 performance of Igor Stravinsky's *Rite of Spring* and in landscapes of 1965 and 1966.

Abstract painting had conditioned him to treating landscape as an object, a formal presence with a self-sufficient individuality, and his Dimboola scenes, eschewing the landscape of continuous line, are squared up like his abstract collages, with a shed, a road, the sky and the land arranged with clear formality. In the Art Gallery of New South Wales is a small work, *Boy in a Township* of 1943, which is one of the Wimmera series modified by the St Kilda paintings that followed: the horizon has two round trees like those that pop up in the Wimmera with zany unpredictability. What is more important are the methods and iconography revealed, for the painting has been repainted and turned upside down, the former fawn sky with a wisp of smoke is now the foreground and indicates the inventive waywardness with which Nolan was later to invert birds and helicopters. The burnt house is like a helmet on its side, and one sees the dark, slotted square emerging again as a pictorial device, later to be used for a variety of purposes in the Kelly series of 1946 to 1947, those done in 1954 to 1956 and the more recent ones of the early sixties.

Nolan's presentation, without subterfuge, with luminous clarity, with an innocent immediacy and with little regard for orthodox techniques, originated a myth almost as prevalent as that of the Kellys: that Nolan was an unsophisticated bush-boy . . .

Excerpts from Elwyn Lynn, *Sidney Nolan: Myth and Imagery*, Macmillan, London, 1967

Far from reworking his own earlier successful modes, the Nolan of the 1970s and 1980s has become an increasingly bewildering figure to his audience as he pushes his art around, looking for the new way and the new range of motifs. The Nolan of the past is the wish of his audience. There is on Nolan's part a strenuous effort to bring the present back into his art, to move away from the images of memory. When he turns to long-cherished motifs—inland Australia, for example—the new way is frequently, even perversely at times, at odds with his own earlier, well-established manner. Such a path necessarily involves the artist in risks and in unevenness of success. The work of the last decade and more has gone without proper evaluation largely because of its strangeness and its abandonment of his earlier canons of narrative landscape painting. General taste wishes him to be as he once was.

What has persisted into the best of the recent works is the inferno vision of the landscape or the wider environment as the arena of punishment and travail. The catastrophic still haunts Nolan's imagination. And he does not flinch from the fact that hatred and lust may be the goads of human action and the motifs of art. He has for so long been regarded and accepted as lyricist or ironist that it has obscured the harsher, less accommodating side of his art. It was there at the beginning in those sharp focus images which allow no escape from the experience. In the long march of his art from the sun-filled landscapes and legends of the 1940s to the present cloudy and smoky apparitions, Nolan has never relinquished a sense of the human as victim, vulnerable to the world in which he lives.

Excerpt from Patrick McCaughey, 'Sidney Nolan: Experience, Memory and the Emphatic Present', *Sidney Nolan, Landscapes & Legends 1937–87* (catalogue), National Gallery of Victoria, Melbourne, and International Cultural Corporation of Australia Ltd, Sydney, 1987

RAILWAY GUARD, DIMBOOLA, 1943
Ripolin enamel on canvas
77 × 64
Collection: National Gallery of Victoria

GIANFRANCO NOTARGIACOMO

Born Rome, Italy, 1945

Lives and works in Rome and Florence

The allusion to *Sturm und Drang* unfolds naturally from the first semantic evocation. And it grows in the palpable reality of the painting; the eye loses itself in whirlpools of stormy leaden matter, the ashen greys warring with clotted atmospheric density in fast and threatening clouds streaked by flaming and bloody borders, whether from thunderclaps or torpedoes one knows not; the brush-strokes chase one another with impetuosity, with the anxiety of a deep cataclysm that tries to open up a small hole of itself to the light. Turner meets Boccioni who meets Pollock, who meets the impotent lucidity of our time. We are at war, a war of the eye and the heart, a war that has the courage to disavow every current, formal model, and to search for its own roots, its own chosen affinity there where in history it dwells, whether near or far. We can even say that we are facing a new species of 'action painting', more latently a renewal of that post-war culture that went under the name of 'informal'. The phenomenon is of great interest because it can be compared with other experiences in our time (even if not yet tangible and not yet at this level of expressive maturity) and above all because the comparison obtains today as then in a precarious ideological situation and a climate of deep existential unease. Since I would discard the hypothesis of a simple 'citative' phenomenon (in the sense that art is always born in some way or another from other art) that would flatten the emotive richness of such consistent artists like Notargiacomo, it is necessary to seek out a rationale for a diversity that goes far past actual assonances.

The post-war 'informal' school was born out of a rupture, and as a school it represents this rupture, that of a break in traditional European culture, the abyss caused by the war, the biological insecurity—visceral, contemporary—the lacerating absence of a past on which to build a new system of values. The 'informal' school of the eighties is born out of a lack, an ideological lack that cannot speak to the future. Protected by its own values, the depth warns of a fracture not already in the past, but at some imprecise point in the future, a chilly but creatively fecund sensibility.

It is 'primary' to a black wall, to a 'cork at the bottom'. From this comes the sense of dizziness, but a lucid dizziness, mindful, mortal and cultural, not least that it is existential. Who knows: the torpedoes of Notargiacomo are really shot across a leaden sky that occludes the sight of tomorrow across the black wall that 'from such a great part of the last horizon our gaze is excluded'.

Excerpt from Flavio Caroli, 'Torna l'informale', *Corriere della Sera*, 1 February 1981. Translated by Angela Kerley

---

I have already said that Gianfranco Notargiacomo has a history that goes back to the seventies. For this reason his painting is more characteristically gestural than that of others. But take a look at his latest paintings—the racing and hysterical image of five years ago is sort of frozen, taking on a shiny and icy varnish, a kind of unnatural facial film superimposed on the streaked skin of the world, the glove, which is implicitly the theme of his paintings.

Excerpt from Flavio Caroli, *Post-Astrazione* (catalogue), Milan, 1986. Translated by Angela Kerley

PRUSSIA, 1987
Oil on canvas
170 × 160

(Photo) Silvia Massotti

Born Christchurch, New Zealand, 1945

Lives and works in Auckland

Maria Olsen is a painter with sculptural interests. Her earliest exhibited works were pastel drawings and egg tempera paintings, delicate and exquisitely coloured, which had a three-dimensional quality. Usually of small objects (bones, cotton reels, fragments of material) arranged in niches or on ledges, they were like offerings at a shrine. Each object was imbued with its own private history. In 1980 she made an image in clay based on one of these drawings and moved increasingly towards producing sculptural reliefs of rounded, wrapped and bandaged forms. A number were shown in her 1983 exhibition at RKS Art, Auckland. Olsen's nurturing experiences as a mother and of working with crippled children, and the effects of her two pilgrimages to India were among the particular impulses informing these works. Typical was *Rabia* (named after an Indian woman saint), which had a simple triangular, totemic presence; another, *Pimpalgaon*, hung from the wall as a very open and irregular grid. It referred to the organic nature of life in a small Indian village. These reliefs, in which archaeological rediscovery and spiritual continuity are coupled with everyday frailty, set the pattern for her subsequent work.

It is usual for Olsen to be involved simultaneously with a variety of media as she explores an idea from a number of different perspectives. Accordingly, for *ANZART in Edinburgh* (1984) the artist contributed recent pastel drawings of bone-like configurations and two reliefs, *Frill* and *Threshold*. Rudimentary, with an organic presence, they had an androgynous quality alluding to the Hindu linga-yoni. They pointed towards the possibility of restoring a state of equilibrium to our essential being, a reconciliation of the spiritual and temporal, of female and male, of ancient wisdom and contemporary knowledge. Her philosophical and humanitarian concerns are also tempered by whimsy and humour: 'I try and start with the idea that I think is the most ridiculous, perhaps the one that I find could embarrass me, the one I find most intriguing.' Comparison with Philip Guston's late canvases, which blend a sense of the ludicrous with tragedy, could be made readily, but Olsen is much more inward-looking, visualising internal ideas rather than manifestations of worldly existence. Similarly, the tactile and often 'absurd' structures of Eva Hesse and Harmony Hammond suggested connections with a strand of American feminist art.

By 1985 Olsen's reliefs increased in scale, becoming weighty tumescent entities. Termed 'bone stacks', the principal shapes are built up over a fibreglass base with layers of linen and other fabric soaked in gesso. Pigments suspended in rhoplex, a translucent acrylic base, have been applied in layers and provide a viscous surface. Traces of luminous colour, pinks and yellows, reds and blues, emerge at intervals from a predominantly sombre whole. Matching the wrapped and moulded forms, there are no precise boundaries to these painted marks. What is important are the emotional resonances set up in the surface treatment, between translucency and opacity, between what is hidden and what is revealed. The image contained by these shifting marks simultaneously appears as flesh and stone, witnessing a state of what one observer earlier described as 'a momentariness, and a momentousness'.[1]

Olsen derives her imagery almost entirely from imagination and memory and she rejects too rational an interpretation of it. Like R. M. Rilke, a poet she particularly admires, she pays attention to the inner states of our consciousness, searching for and struggling towards that intuitively felt moment where feelings and layers of meaning coalesce and are given visual presence. Her on-going interest in literature from both East and West and an extensive study of Jungian theory enriches the discoveries she makes in the course of her work.

The *Bone Stack* chosen for this exhibition is closely allied to two other painted reliefs, *Embrace* (Centre for Contemporary Art, Hamilton) and *Bone Stack with Ladder* (National Art Gallery, Wellington). They are organic mounds reminiscent of prehistoric menhirs, of objects which invite religious veneration. Through their commanding physical presence they are memorable. More recently Olsen has focused on the symbol of the cauldron, another image with archetypal roots: 'I see these bone stacks as metaphorical in the same way as the cauldrons are. They are meant to represent the dolmen idea.'

Cauldrons first appeared in pastel drawings of 1985 and subsequently developed into dense, sombre paintings on unstretched canvas, which at first glance link her approach to that of Anselm Kiefer or Enzo Cucchi. Yet it is Olsen's denial of the ego that separates her from neo-expressionist art. Her vast cylindrical cauldrons in dream-like vistas have a transformative character which, like the bone stacks, invites multiple interpretations.

One particular source for the image was an early lithograph of hot pools, termed 'cauldrons' in the thermal region of New Zealand's central North Island. The idea gained resonance for Olsen after her reading of such books as Erich Neumann's *The Great Mother, an Analysis of the Archetype*: 'For the cauldron is not only a vessel of life and death, renewal and rebirth, but also of inspiration and magic.'

Contrary to some readings of her work as 'misanthropic' and imbued with 'deep angst', Olsen does not see them negatively in any way. Through her explorations, in particular of the last three years, she has become much more interested in the feminine psyche. Not that the artist consciously aligns herself with feminist theory, nor indeed with any particular contemporary Western art movement. Her strongest links are with Jung and his archetypal symbolism. Rather than suggesting charnel houses, the bone stacks with their constituent parts struggling to embrace also celebrate a union of the anima and animus. Similarly, her images of cauldrons with disparate objects afloat (cotton reels, a truncated column, bones) may invite an analogy with the steaming vats of human existence. But they are also circular vessels within which one's dreams and collective histories spiral outwards in a medium which finally spills over as pure water, an elemental flowing.

Anne Kirker, 1987

1. Spens, 1984.

SKY, 1985
Pigment emulsion and paintstick on paper
87 × 141

(Photo) Elspeth Collier

His communicative art began with the performance of 'Bracelet', which he first gave in 1979. The structure of this performance is both simple and direct. He visits an unfamiliar country as a traveller, hoping to see villages and hamlets off the normal sight-seeing circuit. He asks the people he meets if he may take their photographs, asking them at the same time to put on a metal bracelet. Sometimes he can't get what he wants to say across, at other times he is refused from the outset. Only when he has obtained a person's assent does he press the shutter. On the bracelet are printed words extracted at random from English language newspapers, colour names, the units of various different currencies, etc. After taking a photograph, he notes carefully on a card matters such as the subject's name, age, occupation and the date.

In these 'Bracelet' performances conducted in India (1979), the Philippines (1981), Thailand (1982) and China (1984), Orimoto turns the tables on the nature of the photographic record and attempts to gain an ever firmer hold on the essence of what he refers to as 'communication'. The discrepancy between his appeal and people's reactions, and the dual significance of the bracelet as an object which both 'links' and 'binds' (its metallic lustre puts one in mind of handcuffs), give to this performance a sharply defined sense of linkage and depth.

Since 1983 Orimoto has also been evolving another performance event entitled 'Ear-Pulling'. This is a highly sophisticated performance in comparison with the simple acts of communication involved in 'Bracelet'.

Seven or eight earrings are attached to one ear of a man or woman. The earrings are each linked by pieces of metal on which are engraved related works such as 'Since', 'Always', 'Then', or 'Chinese', 'Irish', 'Greek'. A length of thread is then stretched from the tip of each piece of metal to form a fan shape as if to pull the ear outwards.

As was also the case with the 'Bracelet' performances, the English words engraved on the bracelets or pieces of metal would seem to suggest for Orimoto both the possibilities and impossibilities of communication by means of language. For the mountain tribesmen of Thailand with no knowledge of the English language, these letters are merely meaningless shapes. However, for us, as we look at these photographs of people wearing the bracelets, the distance between the meaning of the words and the people with the words attached to their bodies strikes us with the shock of the unexpected as well as appearing somehow humorous.

In the case of an 'Ear-Pulling' event, the person whose ear is being pulled is unable to see for himself the words attached to his ear. He is enclosed in a complex of words assailing his body. But the meaning of these words remains in a limbo outside his range of vision, forever unseen. The suggestion here seems to be that even highly physical acts, such as that in 'Ear-Pulling', can never be conducted on a level totally separate from that of language.

It will be very interesting to see how Orimoto develops his performances in the future: will he emphasise the aspect of the act itself, or will he attempt to create an elaborate visual device based on the scope of the photographic image?

Orimoto's activities are stretching the possibilities of photography in an unusual way that other Japanese photographers have paid little attention to. Of course, Orimoto is an artist whose work cannot be merely confined within the framework of photography, but there can be no doubt that his work will prove to be a major stimulus to photographers. Border lines are only created as a result of being overstepped or deviated from. Similarly, the sphere of photography will no doubt begin to take on a new aspect through encounters with 'travellers' such as Orimoto.

Kotaro Iizawa

PULL TO EAR, 1977/87
Photographs, each 61 × 43

MODERN LIFE

We absorb the image, the glistening body-form, that *is* and will continue to be the *life-source*, the centrifugal axis to our attentions. We squint. We screw+tin-eyes but it is a dying, dying sun that lays a pale blanket over our point of conjecture, that turns the mud-pool into a Great Gilded Dish, flat'n'round. We skirt the perimeter, lifting our eyes up from the central mystery only to reaffirm that We Are Still on Solid Ground. We are.

> Nick Cave (fragment from sleeve-text of *From Her to Eternity*, 1984)

It is mistaken to think, like Baudrillard, that we have reached a kind of Golden Age. We are still on cold soil. Modernism was a new Stone Age: an era of modern megaliths and Stonehenge, of land art. Then man discovered fire. A deluge of painter's fire gutted modernism. The Iron Age has now dawned, the era of metal sculpture, of Deacon, Cragg, Houshiari, Visch, Oudendijk . . . The age of cold materials, forged hot. The beginning of a Culture. It is an urban culture: the post-modern romanticism of the tiled city garden. The jungle has made way for the asphalt jungle. Streets and tenements, crammed to bursting-point, are empty, their crowdedness making real contact impossible. Only burglary is the order of the day; so are collisions on congested pavements. The frequency of this sort of highly unpleasant occurrence calls for the cultivation of a thick skin to protect the vulnerable individual like armour. This also prevents anything from getting out; all the warmth stays inside. Individual capacities dwell in the core but are not exploited—the individual may be 'full' but, because it is nobody's business, appears to be just as empty as the tiled courtyard.

And yet it is not true that not a single trace of emotion can be observed. It is less felt than smelt: an aggressive odour, an invisible component of the exhaust fumes of the metallic arsenal, the essence of locomotion.

Aggression as an instrument: both a weapon and a tool for tackling the city. A possible interpretation for Sonja Oudendijk's sculptures of 1985/86, I think. What is more, the context is absorbed into the interpretation. By this I mean that the presentation space of a gallery or museum is transformed into a studio, seeing that instrumentarium occupies a fixed place on the walls—indicated by the painted shadows of the objects. The equipment is ready for use. And yet it looks useless; at any rate its function is not apparent. It is as if the things were once used and no longer have any function: they are in evidence as signs, recalling former exploits, like scars.

In that sense Oudendijk's work is linked to an old tradition of meaning in sculpture: sculpture as a Monument—in this case to contemporary history. But these 'monuments' do not glorify historic events; they are just as factual, intrinsically amoral, as the actual event. Cold, harrowing scars.

Works of 1986/87 may be seen as similar monuments. They are an almost cartographic rendering of the contemporary environment: locations consisting of palisades, sometimes closed, sometimes with openings, surrounding a courtyard. Oddly enough it is not the walls that mark the fixed spot, but the empty courtyard that establishes the place: the colour is painted directly on the floor. The courtyard is nothing but a patch of colour, a 'glistening body-form', a central mystery. Some courtyards have no colour of their own, the colour being on the outside, between two settlements. The painted area becomes a coloured track, a taut highway gliding past the houses. The forms are empty and in one of Oudendijk's most recent works even reduced to closed facades shielding the emptiness. There is no ground to tread on, the façades are uninhabitable. All that is left is the endless road, the only attachment in an otherwise totally detached environment. This kind of black-and-white proposition—the friction between Nick Cave's 'mud-pool' and 'Great Gilded Dish'—a proposition of cold facts in the face of unattainable, burning ideals, is in my opinion characteristic of the post-modern romantic attitude.

Two films made by Jim Jarmusch in the early eighties, *Stranger than Paradise* and *Permanent Vacation*, are, I think akin to Oudendijk's sculpture. In the latter film young Allie Parker roams from house to house, only to find out that 'the inhabitants are all the same, except the rooms have different ice-boxes'. He is unable to relate to anyone. And yet he has an ideal, voiced in the title of the song 'Somewhere over the Rainbow'. At the end of the film he leaves New York for Paris, in pursuit of his ideal—though realizing that he is 'a tourist on permanent vacation'.

Sonja Oudendijk's sculpture sheds a light on the situation. No mysteries about what is at the heart of the sculptures: by tilting them and fixing them on the wall, Oudendijk provides a clear view. Whether the interiors are empty, or the patch of colour on the wall suggests a certain 'habitability', remains a mystery.

Where everything is so ice-cold, there must be a source of heat somewhere. There are no two ways about it; the emphatic presence of the one makes you painfully aware of the equally emphatic absence of the other. There is no sentimentality; the asphalt does not melt. We Are Still on Solid Ground.

Cold fire.

We squint. But we still see something—empty façades, yes. No hollow phrases.

Marja Bosma
Translated by Ruth Koenig

UNTITLED, 1987
Wood, rubber, metal paint
30 × 120 × 235

(Photo) Edo Kuipers

GIULIO PAOLINI

Born Genoa, Italy, 1940

Lives and works in Turin

Giulio Paolini's *L'Altra Figura* (1984) is a complex example of Arte Povera, post-modern scepticism and formal elegance. Unlike some earlier politically critical work, this shows a classical attitude to presentation. Two identical casts of a classical head mirror each other, gazing sightlessly as if over the shoulder at 'The Other'. Between them on the floor lie the shattered remnants of a third copy. In some respects the shattered image is like the reflection in the lake where Narcissus pined. Obsessed with the reflected image of his own face, he was unable to fondle it, for each time he reached out to the image the ripples in the water broke it hopelessly into fragments.

Man has sought to control his environment through idolatry. In the age of the multiple copy, reproduction and simulation, the possibility of the absolute image becomes impossible. The fragments of antiquity are like the fall of Icarus, who attempted to enter the realm of Apollo and got burnt, then fell broken into the sea.

Unlike much critical art in the 1980s, Paolini employs profoundly poetic imagery with a minimal elegance which provides viewers with a stage upon which to act out their own interpretations.

Tony Bond, 1987

L'ALTRA FIGURA, 1984
Plaster
183 × 250 × 190
Collection: Art Gallery of New South Wales

Born Sydney, Australia, 1945

Lives and works in Sydney

SWINE FEVER (THE PATCH)/
THE HISTORY OF PHOTOGRAPHY

To see oneself (differently from in a mirror): on the scale of History, this action is recent ... Odd that no one has thought of the disturbance (to civilisation) which this new action causes. I want a History of Looking. For the Photograph is the advent of myself as other: a cunning dissociation of consciousness from identity. Even odder: it was before Photography that men had the most to say about the vision of the double. Heautoscopy was compared with an hallucinosis; for centuries this was a great mythic theme. But today it is as if we repressed the profound madness of Photography: it reminds us of its mythic heritage only by that faint uneasiness which seizes me when I look at 'myself' on a piece of paper.

Roland Barthes, *Camera Lucida*, Fontana, London, 1984

In *Camera Lucida* Barthes aligned the genesis of photography more closely to theatre than to painting. Out of the *camera obscura* emerged the arts of perspective, photography and the diorama, three arts of the stage. Noting the original relation of the theatre to the cult of the Dead, Barthes described photography as a kind of primitive theatre, a *Tableau Vivant*, a 'figuration of the motionless and made-up face beneath which we see the dead'.[1] In a close and comparable way Mike Parr's black boxes and slot installations, which have preoccupied him intensely over the past decade, have provided dark theatrical insights onto a charred other self. And at the same time the self-image, which has figured in all his series of drawings, stretched into anamorphic contortions, and rendered by incisive gestures and nervous lines, has continually reiterated that surprise and fear felt during the moment of discovery when the self is first perceived as something outside one's interior consciousness.

Parr's play with the Lacanian puzzle of posing the self through an image of the other carries with it all the intrigues of difference and equivalence. As theatre, it is portentous. The repetitions of portraits can be seen advancing into the future, accelerated by the very rhetoric of drawing and reproduction into the decay of death. Parr's photodeath. Out of the charcoal of drawing and the black dust of the photocopier comes a body of portraiture in which, as Bernice Murphy notes, 'Parr asserts a *dialectics of absence*: through incessant reconstitution of his self-image, a process of self-erasure, rather than self-presence, gains an ascendant implication.'[2]

In anticipation of his new installation, *Swine Fever (The Patch)/ The History of Photography*, Parr proposes a corridor whose separate halves would function as a kind of close, double vision. It is a corridor where the constrained space between two long, wall-mounted installations would nullify any possibility of viewing the work with detachment and distance. Instead, says Parr, 'the spectator is caught in the crossfire between two zones'—a structure reminiscent of the bifurcated vision and the dialogues between representational modes in Parr's other work.

On one side of the corridor is *Swine Fever (The Patch)*, a large drawing where the white paper functions as an intangible space upon which portraits are suspended. The portraits are 'shorted out' by their difficult, ambiguous location. They are squashed, distended, overlaid into layers which are forced back into an infinity of space. For Parr it is a kind of drawing which has its origins in photography. Like Niepce's early experiments with

photography, where grains and blurs of tone try to fix the shape and presence of things, the drawing is a series of 'patches' across a field of endless holes, full of visual noises and disinformation. Parr here invokes Lacan when he speaks of psychotic hallucinations as attempts to patch over holes in the fabric of reality. The mind stitches the rent material together, but always provisionally, never completely.[3]

Set within the tight, narrow arena of the corridor, the drawing makes a critical issue of focal distance. The heads are tangled and enmeshed, like a *maelstrom* of decentred forms. 'If you get too close,' says Parr, 'there is no portrait.' But on the other hand the narrow limits of the space are a resistance to correctly focused reading. The spectator is forced by the wall and the image to sense an inevitable imbalance, a feeling of incongruity and incompletion, which Parr gives an autobiographical reference: 'It is a one-armed, somnambulistic, tightrope situation.'

On the opposite wall to this drawing is *The History of Photography*. Cantilevered out from the wall, and forming a solid, extended horizon, just below eye level, the *History of Photography* consists of two of Parr's long, charred chipboard 'slot' machines, clenched together in a tight sawtooth embrace. The two slots lock into one, forming a scorched, savage object. The strangely hybridised viewing apparatus of the slot/camera box here undergoes further transformations. It seems to become a mechanical trap, or something beastlike, the head of a dog.

With their burnt black geometry, Parr's objects are always evocative instruments, machines for metaphor. But in quite a literal way Parr also presents each piece as an account of his body: 'The body acts as a point of leverage to gain access to the work, and for the viewer to "complete" it.' In the new work are physical reminders of other recent installations, such as the stressed shaft of his 1987 *(Measurement) The Self-Portrait Machine*, with its aperture leading the viewer into its dark length, or the interiority of the silent black hole of *The Polar Sea (In the Wings of the Oedipal Theatre, Part 3)*, of 1986.

There are connections, too, with the way that photography penetrates the body in Parr's early filmed performances. We recall the relentless gaze of an inquisitive camera eye into the artist's mouth, while it is painfully crammed with the spears of unignited matches: the act of photography becomes both the metaphor and the means for a cathartic moment of self-measurement and knowledge.

Parr's *History of Photography* suggests complex passages through his own history of self-observations and investigations. His repeated processes of self-imaging wrestle with obsessive dualities of identity and consciousness. But with so many double-takes and shifts to disturb its mechanisms, this project of individual history vociferously resists its own measure, and abrades resolution.

Bruce Adams, 1987

1. Roland Barthes, *Camera Lucida*.
2. Bernice Murphy, 'Mike Parr', *The Australian Bicentennial Perspecta* (catalogue), Art Gallery of New South Wales, Sydney, 1987.
3. See Bice Benvenuto and Roger Kennedy, *The World of Jacques Lacan*, Free Association Books, London, 1986.

SWINE FEVER (THE PATCH), 1987
Girault pastel and charcoal on Tamaroll paper
243 × 408

Born Garessio, Italy, 1947

Lives and works in San Raffaele, Piemonte

First of all one pays heed to the virgin wood where a gust of wind is contained in the continuous flux of leaves dominated by the logic of the wind, taut, busying itself in the hollow spaces of quietude, privileged negatives of the moving form which in its repetition tends to sculpture—the closed eyelids, the torpid body upon an ancient bed, the neck's nape drowning in the foliage and the open mouth and breath submerged in the mound of leaves—run over by a blast of wind they produce the sound, they are useless nourishment, the flowing sap produces the leaves, prolongs the earth and lets go the bark, in place of the wood, which is engulfed by a gust of wind, becoming the instrument of sound—elements formed in the air, for the air, in habitual contact with the wind, modelled by the wind, transported by the wind. Gone over again by the hand of man, they repeat the contours, the eddies, the tiny whirlpools, the rippled presence of the wind. In order to repeat the wind, the leaves get back themselves.

Excerpt from Giuseppe Penone, *Penone* (catalogue),
Stedelijk Museum, Amsterdam, 1980
Translated by Angela Kerley

I COLORI DEI TEMPORALI, 1980/87
Bronze, copper, iron
300 × 135 × 115

Unfortunately for me, or perhaps fortunately, I make use of things the way I want to. How sad for a painter who loves blondes not to be able to put them in a painting because they don't harmonise with a basket of fruit. How horrible for a painter who hates apples to be forced to use them all the time because they go well with the carpet. I put whatever I please in my paintings.

There was a time when paintings proceeded towards their final result in successive stages. Each day brought something new. A painting was a sum of additions. For me, a painting is a sum of destructions. First I make a painting, then I destroy it. But in the end nothing is lost, the red taken from one place turns up somewhere else.

It would be quite interesting to record photographically not the stages of a painting, but its metamorphosis. It might then be possible to reconstruct the paths the brain takes to make its dream a reality. But the most interesting thing that would be revealed is that there is no fundamental change in the painting. The initial vision remains practically intact, in spite of outward appearances. I often think of light and shade. When I put them in a painting I proceed to 'break them up' by adding a colour that creates an opposite effect. If the painting then is photographed, I realise that what I introduced to correct my first idea has disappeared and that essentially the image captured by the photograph corresponds to my original idea preceding all the transformations to which I subjected it.

A painting is never thought out and decided upon ahead of time, because it is subject to changes in thinking while in process, and when it is finished it continues to change, according to the feelings of whoever looks at it. A painting lives its own life just like a person. It undergoes the changes that daily life subjects it to. And this is natural, because a painting can only live through the man who looks at it.

I would like to reach a point where no one could see how one of my paintings has been made. Why? I want my paintings above all to contain emotion.

When one begins a painting one always meets with temptations. One must distrust these, destroy one's own painting, and do it over many times. Even when the artist destroys a beautiful creation, he doesn't really do away with it, but rather changes it, condenses it, makes it more essential. The completed work is the result of a series of discoveries which have been eliminated one by one. Otherwise one runs the risk of self-admiration. And for me, I do not sell anything to myself!

In reality one works with very few colours. When they are put in just the right place, the illusion is created that there are a great many.

Abstract art never gets beyond painting. So what's the excitement? There is no such thing as abstract art. You have to start from somewhere. You can completely remove any appearance of reality but the idea of the object will somehow have left its ineradicable sign: because it is the object that has touched the artist, that has excited his ideas, that has stirred his emotions. In the final analysis, ideas and emotions are rooted in his work. They are an integral part of it even if their presence is not evident. Whether he likes it or not, man is an instrument of nature, which imposes its character and its appearance on him. In my paintings of Dinard and the ones of Pourville, I expressed practically the same vision, but you can see the difference between the atmosphere of those done in Brittany and those done in Normandy, and you can recognise the light of the cliffs of Dieppe. I didn't copy that light, I didn't even pay it much attention. I was simply immersed in it. My eyes saw it, and my unconscious registered its vision, and then my hands passed on my sensation. You can't go against nature. It is stronger than the strongest man! It is simpler to go along with nature. We can allow ourselves certain liberties, but only in the details.

Moreover, there is no such thing as figurative or non-figurative art. Everything appears to us in the form of a figure. Even in metaphysics ideas are expressed through figures, so obviously it would be absurd to think of a painting without figuration. A person, or an object, or a circle are all figures, and they act on us in a more or less intensive manner. Some are closer to our own feelings, with the result that they elicit emotions that appeal to our own emotional faculties. Others appeal more directly to the intellect. It is well to accept them all. My mind needs emotions just as much as my senses. Do you think I am interested in the fact that this painting represents two people? These two people once existed but now they exist no longer. The sight of them gave me an initial emotion but slowly their real presence became blurred, and they became for me a fiction, and then they disappeared, or rather, they were transformed into general problems. For me they are not two people any more but only forms and colours, you must understand, that still express the idea of two people and that still keep the vibrations of their existence.

The artist gathers emotions from everywhere: from the sky, from the earth, from a piece of paper, from a passing form, from a spider's web. And it is exactly because of this that you can't make distinctions between things, because they're not stratified by class. You must take what you can use where you find it, but not from your own work. It would be revolting for me to copy myself, but I don't hesitate to take what I want from a portfolio of old drawings.

Excerpts from Mario di Micheli, *Scritti de Picasso (Writings of Picasso)*, Feltrinelli, 1964

I treat my paintings just like I treat things. I paint a window just as I look through a window. If that open window doesn't suit my painting, I draw a curtain and shut it, as I would do in my room. You must act in painting as you do in life . . .

There ought to be an absolute dictatorship . . . a dictatorship of painters . . . a dictatorship of one painter . . . to suppress all those who have betrayed it, to suppress the cheaters, to suppress the tricks, to suppress mannerisms, to suppress charms, to suppress history, to suppress a heap of other things. But common sense always gets away with it. Above all, let's have a revolution against that! The true dictator will always be conquered by the dictatorship of common sense . . . and maybe not!

Excerpts from Christian Zervos, *Conversation avec Picasso (Conversation with Picasso)*, Cahiers d'Art, 1935

WEEPING WOMAN, 1937
Oil on canvas
56 × 46
Collection: National Gallery of Victoria, Melbourne. Purchased by the Art Foundation of Victoria
with the generous assistance of the Jack and Genia Liberman Family and Donors of the Art Foundation of
Victoria

MARGARET PRESTON

Born Adelaide, Australia, 1875

Died Sydney, 1963

Australia . . . has ignored a fine simple art that exists at her own back door. It has to learn what this art could do to help clear up the minds of our people and give them a national culture that I have given many years of my life to the study of this aboriginal art.

Margaret Preston, quoted in *Studio*, vol. 124, 1942

Aboriginal painting was for years an inspiration to Margaret Preston but, unlike many who have been affected by it but whose admiration took the form of superficial imitation, Margaret Preston completely assimilated many of their characteristics of design and incorporated them in her highly individual works— usually of native flora and landscapes.

Her design is always bold, vigorous and inventive, while the colour is based on a subtle and sensitive observation of the Australian bush.

Margaret Preston was one of the first to take Aboriginal paintings seriously as works of art, and her superiority over other adaptors or imitators lies in the fact that she regarded the study of their art not so much as an end in itself but as a means to a better understanding of nature, or of those aspects of it which could be described as specifically Australian.

Her paintings are essentially decorative in aim but, like all good decorative paintings, they have a firm backbone of knowledge formed from close study and keen observation.

James Gleeson, 'Margaret Preston', *Australian Painters: Modern Painters 1931–1970*, Lansdowne Press, Sydney, 1971

Margaret Preston was Australia's foremost woman painter between the wars, a period when many of the best Australian artists were women. 'Their art was remarkably pure; painting was done for pleasure and from inner necessity, not often for money or for fame.'[1]

Talented, adventurous and certainly the most vociferous of the women artists, Preston differed from her compatriots in her strident demands for recognition—not simply for her own art but for the many theories she held about Australia's artistic atrophy. Her single, urgent plea was for a truly indigenous national art for this country, liberated from 'Grandpa G. Britain'[2] and the threat of internationalism, by a study of Aboriginal art. Her spirited crusade was partly the expression of her 'broad and bursting personality', as her friend Hal Missingham once put it,[3] and also an outcome of the tenacity bred in her by experience . . .'

Artists are in the business of making ideas visible and as ideas change, or experience informs them with new interpretations or details, so their visual expression shifts—sometimes radically, sometimes imperceptibly. Margaret Preston met life head-on, in spite of the 'bad growing pains' it gave her, and thus her work is the record of a genuinely creative and adventurous artist. It underwent radical transformations in the shift from realist to Post-Impressionist, to 'primitive' in inspiration—so much so that it

might seem, at times, to be the work of three different people. Certain points, however, remained stable: principally her ability to hold the viewer within the dynamic design of the picture plane and her unequivocal commitment to the image, which makes her work always a statement, never just a suggestion.

Her dynamic character required many different forms of expression in a career that spanned over seventy years. Her childlike enthusiasm for new ideas and new forms of expression was helped along by a powerful ego, which demanded constant experiment and constant challenge in order that Preston maintain her own high standards of aesthetic commitment. The question of which of her periods is the most successful will be answered by different generations of people according to their individual tastes. Her still-life paintings and wood-cuts of Australian flora and fauna will continue to delight by their freshness, grace and vigour, while the ultimately unresolved spirituality of her Aboriginal-inspired work will also continue to attract and intrigue. As the artist herself said, 'The ladder of art lies flat, not vertical'.[4] Her attempts to map out the principles of decorative design in her work were interpreted in a uniquely Australian way, as was her attempt to create a truly indigenous art-form based on Aboriginal art. She was, above all, a communicator, not content that art occupy a passive role in people's lives but demanding that it excite, enliven and engage.

Excerpts from Elizabeth Butel, *Margaret Preston, The Art of Constant Rearrangement*, Penguin Books and the Art Gallery of New South Wales, 1985

1. Daniel Thomas, 'Introduction' in *Treania Smith Collection*, Painters Gallery, Sydney, 1985.
2. Margaret Preston, 'Australian Artists Versus Art', *Art in Australia*, 3rd Series, no 26, December 1928.
3. Hal Missingham, 'Margaret Preston', *Art and Australia*, vol. 1, no 2, August 1963.
4. Margaret Preston, 'From Eggs to Electrolux', *Art in Australia— Margaret Preston Number*, 3rd Series, no 22, December 1927.

The trajectory of her earlier career typifies those of a generation of remarkable Australian artists, while her art of the 1920s in its clarity, colour and dynamism stands as that generation's highest achievement. But even more significantly, Preston forms a model beyond the inter-war era, and is exceptional in the history of Australian art. Far from the norm of an early summit and slow decline, her career represents a series of peaks, varied in elevation and import. These are a function not just of her energy, but of her unremitting attempt to help forge a national culture.

Excerpt from Ian North, 'Margaret Preston, Model of an Era', *The Art of Margaret Preston*, Art Gallery Board of South Australia, 1980

GREY DAY IN THE RANGES, 1942
Oil on hardboard
51 × 50.7
Collection: Art Gallery of New South Wales

Born Washington, DC, USA, 1941

Lives and works in Chicago

One of Puryear's essential dialogues has been with Minimalism, which he encountered as a graduate student at the Yale Art School. Puryear has learned from the Minimalist sense of precision, economy and proportions. He admires Donald Judd's 'cogency of thought'. And the power of Puryear's work, like Richard Serra's, has a great deal to do with spatial imagination. Like Serra, Puryear has the ability to make sculpture that is known by the body before it is articulated by the mind. Puryear's gestures and armatures can be experienced as extensions of skin and bones.

But Puryear rejects the dogmatism of Minimalism, its resistance to associations and its rejection of craft. The impersonal working methods are what made him realise that he was 'absolutely not a Minimalist'.

He explains: 'The hand means too much to me. The risk-taking in the process of building and making something means too much to me. I never did Minimalist art, I never did, but I got real close . . . I looked at it, I tasted it and I spat it out. I said, this is not for me. I'm a worker. I'm not somebody who's happy to let my work be made for me and I'll pass on it, yes or no, after it's done. I could never do that.'

In short, Puryear is very definitely a post-Minimalist, and he is a key bridge between the 1960s and 1980s. In his ability to work privately and publicly, to make sculpture for himself, driven by his obsessions, and to make work that is accessible to the public, he has managed to combine a traditional view of sculpture as something made by an individual working in the studio, and a view of sculpture as something made in collaboration with others for a community.

In some artistic and academic circles, the idea of the heroic individual, creating himself from scratch, has been fiercely attacked. One reason so many artists have their work fabricated is that its impersonality and often its smooth reflecting surfaces tend to call attention not to the individual artistic self, but to conditions surrounding the work.

Puryear believes both in anonymity and in the self. He is drawn to folk artists. 'I have a certain kind of nostalgic belief in anonymity,' he says. 'I mean these folk artists who spend their whole lives working without even knowing that they're artists, and they have this kind of compulsion. Somehow there's a part of that that I take a lot of solace in.'

But he also believes that art can come only from the individual. 'I taught for two years at Fisk, which is a black college in Nashville,' he said, 'and there were times when I found it hard, or a struggle, let's say, to encourage students to find themselves, because they were so busy being members of a group.

'My encouragement was to find the you in there. That's what's going to have to make the art; not your history, not your culture. Those things are reflected. They're never going to go away. That's in your nature. It's in who you are. But there's a you in there that's even more crucial than that, and you've got to find it and you've got to release it.'

Excerpt from Michael Brenson, 'Maverick Sculptor Makes Good', *The New York Times Magazine*, 1 November 1987

SEER, 1984
Painted wood and wire
198 × 132.7 × 114.3
Collection: Solomon R. Guggenheim Museum, New York. Purchased with funds contributed by
Louis and Bessie Adler Foundation Inc., Seymour M. Klein, President

I have no pleasure in works of art, for I always see at once the weak points in a picture, at any rate if I have any sympathy for the object. In other cases my attention strays and I am quite incapable of concentrating my glance on the picture. To hide these weak spots and to cover them up one after the other until I can no longer see them has led me to overpainting; in other words, love and the urge for perfection. I wanted to turn them into even finer works of art; everything else is pure speculation. In the meantime I noticed that there was no end to the weak spots even if the picture is quite black; then overpainting forms a new visual structure of its own, and again there are weak points, black in black. Thus I never stop working on my own pictures. I am plagued by a permanent dissatisfaction while the fortunate lovers of art can still take delight in the underlying, invisible parts.

It was with these words that Rainer began his 'self-commentary' in the catalogue of his retrospective in the Hamburg Kunstverein (1971). A few lines later he predicted that, when confronted with the exhibition ready for showing, he would be overcome by fear, shame and a mania for improvement. These comments reveal the conflict which Rainer has been converting into creative energy for almost thirty years. He himself appears to attach no value to continuity in the sense of steady development, then he confesses that he is not striving at 'producing any homogeneous, consistent work'. But perhaps it is just this continuity of effort that produces the consistency from which all the phases and abrupt dialectical transitions of his activity derive their common base.

Rainer's comment in the Hamburg catalogue clearly denotes the difference between his faculty for vision and experience and the harmless delectation which the 'fortunate art lover' can permit himself. He suffers from his work. In contrast to modern work-immanent maxims of judgement, he bases his standard of evaluation not on the picture itself but on a virtually pre-existent idea of perfection which acts as a permanent challenge to him at his work. This viewpoint betrays hubris and obsession. It is in this way that an artist would express himself who has nothing other than his own artistic self-realisation in mind. Is this supposition correct?

In order to determine the kind of perfection which Rainer wants to attain, we must measure its quality alongside the conceptions which it generally evokes. This leads to two exemplary positions of the artist, each of which aims at a definite type of perfection.

These are known to us from mythical and historical tradition. In both cases the artist senses the limits of his creative potential and tries to circumvent them. In the one case he discovers the discrepancy between the pure idea and its material implementation—a deficit with which the theory of art has been occupied since Plato—and in the second case he complains that his pictures lack the full vitality of living creatures and belong to a world of make-believe—from this deficit stems Prometheus' attempt to usurp for himself the privileges of the gods.

As a general rule this dissatisfaction takes hold of two diametrically opposed types of artists and accordingly produces as a result in the one case, the icon (as the visible image of spirituality), in the second case the attempt to let art merge into life. Distance as opposed to lack of distance. The purist who wishes to free himself from the taint of the material will try, through the medium of strict form refinement, to penetrate into the taboo zone of the idea and ideality to satisfy his need for perfection. As a contrast, he who is driven by the urge for a fuller, more vital tangibility will leap over all aesthetic barriers.

Rainer is an exception, for in his activity these two contrary impulses merge into one another. The urge for sublimation, for utmost concentration on the 'idea', led to 'overpaintings'; the ambition for spontaneous, undeviating recording of psychophysical events and actions made him turn to body language. It is decisive that both impulses are firmly knitted together and that they do not stand under aesthetic auspices.

———

. . . It is only since Rainer has begun to use 'body language' that he has been able to capture the tension between the covered and the uncovered form.

Limits such as perfection and completion indicate a formal *non plus ultra*. But Rainer has nothing of this sort in mind. He is not aiming at a maximum achievement of points. His hubris is directed against and not towards aesthetic perfection. We remember how he was overcome by fear and the urge for change in the face of the completed work. On one occasion he called the overpaintings 'exercises in mortification'. We do not hesitate to include the religious-ascetic core of this statement in our interpretation. By continually mortifying it, he keeps his work alive; Rainer ritualises the practice of art into sacrificial death which promises life, for the Christian theme of the Redeemer's death he uses a visible parable. Fear, mania for change and the urge for mortification force Rainer to perpetuate the creative process. Thus the urge for perfection is denied fulfilment since his fear of the finished product causes Rainer to imagine ever new mistakes, shortcomings and deficiencies. He cannot permit the umbilical cord to be severed. Not only is the arbitrariness of his own independent aesthetic product suspect in his eyes, because therein the artist claims the arrogant right of saying, 'See, it was good'—Rainer thinks absolutely in transaesthetic categories, i.e. for him the final form is the dawning of a final phase, in other words an eschatological dimension. We maintain that for him artistic activity constitutes healing, and therefore becomes part of the process of salvation, for it leads men from 'alienation to reconciliation'. From the theological point of view, history (in the words of Karl Löwith) is a movement, running as one great diversion, which in the end reaches the beginning again 'by constantly repeated acts of indignation and devotion'.

Rainer's intellectual development aims away from alienation to reconciliation. It is not directed towards an autonomous work, but persists in the process of innovation, in the search for ever new starting points. After Rainer has lifted the idea of perfection out of the sphere of the materially tangible and measurable and transcended the way into a religious expectation of salvation, he makes its effective inaccessibility (in the 'overpaintings') the theme of his art. He has realised that what irritates him in the 'weak points' is not any formal defect which can be remedied, that the verdict 'bad' does not apply to the creative quality, or the species 'artist' but to man who as an artist suffers from his distance from God and continually gives proof of this in the act of creation. Rainer has been demonstrating for thirty years an act of creation whose great persistence makes visible the fissures and cracks, the injuries and ailments of that seriously wounded creature, man. It is in this visualisation that lies the healing process.

Excerpts from Werner Hofmann, 'Beyond Beautifulness', *Biennale di Venezia* (catalogue), 1978

THE CRUCIFIED BEAR, 1985/87
Oil on wood, application
171 × 121

(Photo) Galerie Ulysses, Vienna

Tony Danyula (Liyagawumirr)

Daypurryun (Liyagawumirr)

David Malangi (Manharrngu)

Neville Gulaygulay (Manharrngu)

Johnny Dhurrukuyu (Manharrngu)

Jimmy Wululu (Gupapuyngu)

George Milpurrurru (Ganalbingu)

Dorothy Djukulul (Ganalbingu)

Charlie Djurritjini (Ganalbingu)

Neville Nanytjiwny (Liyagalawumirr)

Jimmy Mamalunhawuy (Malarra)

Paddy Weibunanga (Rembarrnga)

ABORIGINAL MEMORIAL

Since 1788 at least several hundred thousand Aboriginals have died at the hands of white invaders. Some time ago an elder artist in Ramingining brought me several videotapes belonging to his dead son. Not having a video-cassette recorder, he wanted to play the tapes and show me. The son and the artist were and are very close to me. The tapes were battered and dust-ridden. I hesitated to run them through my machine but our relationship and my curiosity made me play them. His son had been a member of the Northern Land Council Executive and, in the course of his work contacts, had been given some more 'political' videotapes as background briefing for himself and the community. One of these was a copy of a John Pilger documentary called *The Secret Country*. In the opening precis of the program he talked of the decimation of a tribal group who owned the land on the Hawkesbury River in New South Wales and who died 'to the last man, woman and child defending their country'. He continued that, throughout the land in every country town, there was an obelisk to those who had fallen in this war or that, but nowhere was there a memorial to these first Australians who died defending their country.

In the course of my work as Art Adviser, the major role is to make the outside world more aware and appreciative of Aboriginal art and culture. Some works of art are visually accessible to 'white eyes'; however, others aren't and are difficult to place. The Hollow Log Bone Coffin was one of these. During the sixties, when Aboriginal art was 'discovered', installations of so-called 'totem poles' were popular, though rarely placed in the prominent places that they deserved. Then, although a gradual growth in Aboriginal art appreciation crept up during the seventies, this was in the main to do with paintings, with the Western Desert school of 'dot and circle' leading the way. Sculpture, generally referring to bird and other animal life pieces, was also sought after; however, works as uncompromising as the Bone Coffins were still hard to place. The problem was to change people's perceptions of Aboriginal sculpture and art in general. A 'tour de force' was needed.

This cynically commercial venture lurked in the back of my mind until the Pilger program crystallised these thoughts. During the day-to-day business of the Art and Craft Centre in Aboriginal communities, a series of regular exhibitions is planned and run. Art is a way of recording history, aspirations and feelings of the period. Art is a communication medium that often transcends language barriers. The aim is that themes, concepts and ideas of Aboriginal culture are carried within each exhibition, which is visually accessible to the general viewing public. During the Bicentennial year in 1988 most Aboriginal organisations and many white ones are boycotting the celebrations. Many white artists have withdrawn their works from Bicentennial shows. As a commercial enterprise set up to ensure returns to artists, it was realised that any boycott decisions would have strong economic consequences. The bind was to present Aboriginal culture without celebrating—to make a true statement.

In north-eastern Arnhemland present-day Aboriginal people carry on many age-old ceremonies and rituals. One of these is the Hollow Log or Bone Coffin ceremony. When a person dies, the body is washed, painted with relevant totemic designs, sung over and mourned. Some time later the bones of the deceased are recovered and distributed to relatives in a small ceremony. After a period, which may be years, the relatives hand over the bones to ceremonial leaders for them to hold a Hollow Log ceremony. A log hollowed out naturally by termites is found, cleaned and painted with relevant designs like the body amidst singing and dancing in a special camp for those completing the ritual. The bones are cleaned, painted with red ochre and placed in the log in special dances. When a set series of songs and dances has been completed, the log is carried and danced into the main public camp and stood upright. It is then left.

Full-size versions minus the bones are made and sold today as sculptures. These works are art pieces in their own right. Originally being living trees, the installation is like a forest—an Aboriginal artistic vision of the forest and landscape. In the original ceremony each Pole would contain the bones of deceased people, embodying the soul. Each tree in this new forest would contain symbolically the spirit of a deceased person. The forest, the environment is us; we are the environment. Each Hollow Log is ceremonially a Bone Coffin, so in essence the forest is really like a large cemetery of dead Aboriginals, a War Cemetery, a War Memorial to all those Aboriginals who died defending their country. Two hundred Poles were commissioned to represent the two hundred years of white contact and black agony.

In south-east Australia many well-documented massacres of Aboriginal people have occurred since 1788. Many of these were covered up and forgotten (buried) as reported in Pilger's program, and thus the name *The Secret Country*. In northern Australia present-day distortion of history continues still. It is widely touted that Aboriginals there were and are treated differently and did not suffer as other Aboriginals did from white contact. Thus they have no reason to feel betrayed, deprived and angry as those southern blacks and Queensland Aboriginals are. Though many benevolent acts were carried out, similar massacres were occurring in Arnhemland around the turn of the century about the time of similar incidents in other parts of Australia. This is still 'secret history' for most of Australia.

There is currently an upsurge in interest in Aboriginal art by the Australian public and overseas visitors. A large part of this is a result of the tourist boom sweeping the country. In other parts of the world where the particular indigenous art has become the flavour of the month, it has often led to attempts to exploit it commercially to the nth degree. The resultant pressure on artists to produce has led ultimately to a collapse or emasculation of the art form. Aboriginal art is now under incredible strain to fulfil white wishes of their culture. Certainly different factions have tried to lead the art this way and that. Whether they truly represent Aboriginal cultural aspirations is questionable. Beyond these schisms and distractions Aboriginal artists and art have sustained their resilience in the face of these demands and continued to survive, convert the white community and make real statements.

John Mundine, Art Adviser, Ramingining

(Photo) Fenn Hinchcliffe

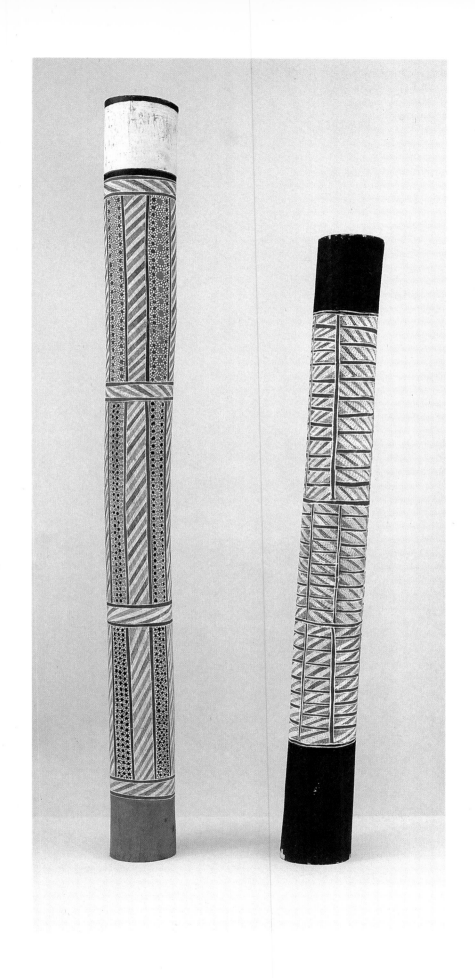

THE ABORIGINAL MEMORIAL (200 HOLLOW LOG BONE COFFINS), 1987/88
Wood and ochres
Collection: Australian National Gallery

Born London, England, 1955

Lives and works in Sydney

TAMING THE SPECTRUM, No 4, 1987
Cibachrome photograph
Seven parts, each 89 × 89 (framed)

(Photo) Michael Richards

GERHARD RICHTER

Born Dresden, German Democratic Republic, 1932

Lives and works in Cologne

Over forty paintings by Gerhard Richter produced during 1986 offer a forceful visual statement, individually and as a group. If some works are large in scale and others closer to easel size, all are imposing by virtue of their thick, colourful surface. Natural tones of red, blue, yellow and green predominate, with the addition of orange or violet in a few instances, as well as black. All works possess a similar striking appearance, yet each is different with respect to the densely applied quality of its multiple layers of paint. Through vibrant colour and the unfettered appearance of their handling, the paintings, all abstract, declare a freedom of expression that gives the impression of control and abandon simultaneously.

An underlying consistency of approach to painting unites a varied and seemingly inconsistent method of working on Richter's part. Since the beginning of his career twenty-five years ago in 1962, Richter has continuously changed the overt subject matter of his paintings and since 1968 has alternated between the creation of figurative and abstract works. From the start he has shifted from one mode of painting to another: from works with realistic imagery to works with no recognisable subject matter, from glossy paintings with colour rectangles to subdued, matt grey works to his most recent abstractions. For the last decade Richter has mainly devoted himself to the creation of abstract works, although landscapes and still lifes sometimes intervene. He maintained in an interview two years ago, however, that the 'abstract works are my presence, my reality, my problems, my difficulties and contradictions'.[1] They are, in short, the artist's primary concern . . .

From 1968 to the present he has dealt with the conventional genres, including the nude, the portrait, the landscape, and the still life, as well as with total abstraction. Each new work or series of works demonstrates the idea that painting, paradoxically, is everything, by, in essence, being about nothing outside of itself. Richter tends to avoid the word 'painting' so as not to confuse the specific subject matter of a painting with the matter of painting in general. 'A picture shows nothing, just a picture',[2] he maintains. In order to liberate all categories of painting from a false dependence on an elusive reality and, by extension, from recourse to prior solutions to painting, Richter has sought to remove himself from the content of the work. As he has stated: 'I want to understand what is . . . I want to avoid all aesthetics, in order not to have obstacles in my way and not to have the problem of people saying, "Well, this is how he sees the world. This is an interpretation."'[3] And, furthermore: 'I refuse to see the world in a personal way . . . and the way of painting is irrelevant.'[4] To this end, Richter succeeds in distancing himself from established representation or expression by revising traditional methods of the artistic decision-making process . . .

With *Construction*, 1976, Richter initiated the series of Abstract paintings. He already had painted purely abstract pictures by 1968, including a series of Colour Streaks that evolved from the direct but impersonal smearing of paint on canvas without reference to a model. As in the case of the Colour Charts and the Grey paintings, the Colour Streaks represent 'nothing' since they refer only to the characteristics that define their own visual presence.

The Abstract paintings of the last decade exhibit a more extensive investigation which specifically concerns the question of paint application, not as a reflection upon a process, but as a reflection of painted and painterly fact. Until 1980 works in this series were based on photographs taken by the artist of some of his smaller, painterly sketches and enlarged as images for depiction. By means of the intermediary photograph, Richter insured the impersonality of his rendition so that brush work and painterly application become their own self-referential subject matter. One step removed from the original painted surface, the Abstract paintings present a compelling visual directness.

According to the artist, his most recent Abstractions aim at even greater directness than before. Without a prior model or preconceived idea of how they might turn out. Richter reworks their many layers—destroying and rebuilding areas of paint with spatula and brush—until a resolute, homogeneous structure, quite literally, surfaces. The paintings of 1986 appear richer and more complex, more 'informal and less clear',[5] to use his words, more detailed and more diffuse. They convey no message, but 'tell something,'[6] as Richter points out in his statement for the 1982 *Documenta* catalogue:

'If we describe an event or give an account or photograph a tree we are creating models without which we would be animals.

'Abstract paintings are fictive models because they show a reality that we neither can see nor describe, but whose existence we can surmise. This reality we characterise in negative terms: The unknown, the incomprehensible, the infinite, and for thousands of years we have described it with ersatz pictures with heaven, hell, gods, devils. With abstract painting we created a better possibility to approach that which cannot be grasped or understood, because in the most concrete form it shows 'nothing'. Accustomed to recognising something real in pictures, we rightly refuse to recognise only colour in all of its variety as the represented and instead allow ourselves to see the ungraspable, that which was never seen before and which is not visible. This is not an artful play but a necessity because everything unknown frightens us and makes us hopeful at the same time. Of course, figurative painting has that transcendental character too. The less 'function' representation has the more forcefully it shows the mystery because every object as part of an incomprehensible world embodies this. This explains, for example, the growing fascination for fine, old portraits. Therefore, paintings are better the more intelligent, the more beautiful, the more mad, the more extreme, the more evident, the more incomprehensible their way is of showing this incomprehensible reality in a simile. 'Art is the highest form of hope.'[7]

Abstract rendition in Richter's recent paintings points to the illusionary character of the painted canvas. In contrast to the work of two other well-known German artists, Joseph Beuys and Anselm Kiefer—the one of a slightly older generation, the other a little younger—Richter makes no claims for painting beyond its own, if equally illusory, reality. All three artists share the belief that art is the single greatest instrument of change. However, whereas the sculpture of Beuys incorporates themes of escape and survival by his use of objects and materials connected with the War, and whereas Kiefer brings to his painting a re-examination of national and moral values in the later aftermath of the War, Richter comments on the human condition with respect to the potential for (artistic) change without direct reference to the social situation. Each painting by Richter within a series is different, as are the separate series one from another, yet all are similar insofar as they participate in the redefinition of painting.

Excerpts from Anne Rorimer, 'Gerhard Richter: the Illusion and Reality of Painting', *Gerhard Richter. Paintings* (catalogue), Marian Goodman Gallery, Sperone Westwater, New York, 1987

1. Dorothea Dietrich, 'Gerhard Richter: An Interview', *The Print Collector's Newsletter*, vol. XVI, no 4, September/October 1985.
2. Bruce Ferguson and Jeffrey Spaulding, 'Gerhard Richter', *Parachute*, Fall 1979.
3. Rolf Gunter Dienst, 'Interview', *Gerhard Richter*, Venice.
4. Dienst.
5. Telephone conversation with the artist, February 1987.
6. Dietrich.
7. Statement in *Documenta 7*, vol. 1, Kassel, 1982 (translated from German by Stefan Germer).

CLAUDIUS (604), 1986
Acrylic on canvas
311 × 406

M A R K   R O T H K O

Born Dvinsk, Russia, 1903

Died New York City, 1970

Rothko by 1949 had enlarged and neutralised his forms, allowing colour to breathe. Colour does not allude to landscape, as it had only a few years before, nor is it any longer a secondary element which supports shape. Colour has come to stand for form. Absolutely crucial to his colour expression is Rothko's paint handling, which evolved from his Surrealist watercolours. It is basically a water-colour technique translated into oil. Paint is soaked into the very fibre of the canvas, so that colour seems dematerialised, a characteristic effect of Rothko's most successful late work. The intensity and warmth of hues (he often favours yellow, orange, violet, red) and an extreme sensuousness of pigment would seem to be at odds with this quality of dematerialisation. But Rothko's colour is full of contradictions. He frequently remarked he did not wish colour to be accepted at face value, asserting that dark paintings could be more cheerful than light ones, bright colour more serious than deep hues. Rothko's goal was to make colour both area and volume, emotion and mood, at once palpable and disembodied, sensuous yet spiritual. For colour represents something larger than its own sheer physical presence. Rothko has come to think of colour as the doorway to another reality.

Rothko himself said that he was not interested in colour for its own sake. Nor did he want to be labelled—and limited—as an abstract painter. 'I'm not interested in relations of colour or form . . . I'm not an abstractionist.'[1] He explained that colour was important to him as a vehicle to express 'basic human emotions—tragedy, ecstasy, doom . . . The people who weep before my pictures are having the same religious experience I had when I painted them. And if you, as you say, are moved only by their colour relationships, then you miss the point.'[2] Rothko had always sought to convey these basic emotions—but he had formerly done so through expressionist figures, dream-like subway scenes and, finally, mythic and Surrealist imagery. But it is only in his painting of the 1950s and 1960s that he achieves 'the simple expression of the complex thought' as he distils the meaning of his earlier work into colour; colour which is the vessel for transcendental meaning.

Though Rothko limited his forms and restricted his number of colours, his intention was to enhance rather than reduce the expressive possibilities of his painting. To suggest multiple levels of meaning he had first to strip away extraneous detail, just as the Surrealist poets and painters divested the object of conventional associations. Once this purification has taken place and imagery has been renovated, the viewer is permitted new kinds of associations, in Apollinaire's words, 'numerous interpretations that sometimes contradict each other'.[3] In these often contradictory layers of interpretation, Rothko expresses rich content. Formal reductivism thus gave rise to expanded meaning for Rothko as for other artists of his generation.

In a painful, often tortuous process of transformation, Rothko purified his painting by purging it of many of the European models he admired and learned from. He now expressed the metaphysical meaning of his Surrealist works without any recourse to the forms, symbols or allusions of his earlier canvases. References to the external world are subsumed into disembodied colour, as Rothko attains a synthesis of the physical and spiritual. In this respect, it is interesting to note Rothko's admiration for the Italian Primitives, in particular Fra Angelico, who represented the beauty of both spiritual and physical worlds in their religious paintings. That Rothko was able to achieve this synthesis with the rigorously limited means he allowed himself is all the more remarkable. In these pure, reduced, transcendent works, Rothko makes the concrete sublime.

. . . in the last two years of his life Rothko produced an astonishing and prolific body of work. These were in acrylics, a medium which Rothko chose because he was attracted to their fast-drying qualities—he was able to make one painting a day. Some were canvases but the majority were extraordinary paper pieces, among the most exquisite work he had done . . .

The new acrylics are simplicity itself: in most of them two dark planes—either brown or black on grey—are surrounded by a narrow white border. The borders were of extreme importance to Rothko, who constantly readjusted their proportions in relation to the inner configurations. Imagery, mood and meaning are vastly different from his work of the 1950s and early 1960s. The glowing colours of the earlier paintings are replaced here by deeper, quieter hues; the rectangles, which formerly floated, are denser, more stable, because of the more opaque quality of the acrylics. Rothko's preference for horizontal divisions within vertical canvases and configurations is replaced by an insistence upon horizontal divisions of horizontal supports. Where the vertical called to mind architecture, the horizontal alludes to landscape. The doorways to a higher reality created before the Houston Chapel were still redolent with sensuous colour and form: there was in them an equilibrium between two states of existence: the spiritual and the physical. The new works, however, speak entirely of another, transcendent world, of a painter who has crossed a threshold into the far side of reality.

These landscapes of the spirit bear a certain resemblance to paintings by Caspar David Friedrich, such as *Monk by the Sea*. Both artists stand in awe of the spirit, both use nature to express that spirit. Friedrich, of course, felt it necessary to incorporate a human element in the figure of the monk; Rothko has long since banished all allusions to the human form. Specific references to beach, sea and sky are also unnecessary for Rothko. He conveys all of his meaning through gesture and in the way the darker, heavier top mass meets the lighter, usually smaller area of grey below. The two planes are painstakingly adjusted and readjusted; between them is a band which appears to be a flicker of light. Often, especially in the paper pieces, this luminosity is Inness-like. The weight and texture of the canvas create a heavier, darker presence than the paper does. In both paper pieces and canvases, however, Rothko is moving towards darkness. '. . . the abstract idea is incarnated in the image . . . But this is not to say that the images created by Rothko are the thin evocations of the speculative intellect; they are rather the concrete, the tactual expression of the intuitions of an artist to whom the subconscious represents not the farther, but the nearer shore of art,' wrote the author of the preface to the catalogue of Rothko's one-man exhibition at Art of This Century in 1945. By the end of his life Rothko had moved beyond such concepts in his painting. No longer is his art earthbound, sensual, corporeal. He had attained a harmony, an equilibrium, a wholeness, in the Jungian sense, that enabled him to express universal truths in his breakthrough works, fusing the conscious and the unconscious, the finite and the infinite, the equivocal and the unequivocal, the sensuous and the spiritual. Now he had left behind all that spoke of the carnate, the concrete. He had reached the farther shore of art.

Excerpts from Diane Waldman, 'The Farther Shore of Art', *Mark Rothko: A Retrospective*, Solomon R Guggenheim Museum, New York, 1978–79

1. Selden Rodman, *Conversations with Artists*, New York, 1957.
2. *Ibid.*
3. Quoted in Anna Balakian, *Surrealism: The Road to the Absolute*, New York, 1959.

UNTITLED (BLACK ON GREY), 1970
Acrylic on canvas
203.5 × 175.5
Collection: Solomon R. Guggenheim Museum, New York. Gift of The Mark Rothko Foundation, Inc. 1986

(Photo) David Heald

Born Melbourne, Australia, 1939

Lives and works in Melbourne

PUTTING THE 'F'

BACK INTO ART

Fabian, fable, fabric, fabricate, fabulous, facade, face, facet, facetious, facial, facile, facilitate, facility, facing, facsimile, fact, faction, factious, factitious, factitive, factor, factory, factotum, facultative, faculty, fad, faddy, faddish, faddist, fade, faggot, Fahrenheit, fail, failing, failure, fain, faint, fair, fairness, fairing, fairly, fairway, fairy, faith, faithful, faithfully, faithless, fakir, falcon, falconer, falconry, falderal, fall, fallacious, fallacy, fal-lal, fallible, fallability, fallow, false, falsity, falsehood, falsetto, falsify, falsification, falter, fame, famed, familiar, familiarity, familiarize, family, famine, famish, famous, fan, fanatic, fanatical, fanaticism, fanciful, fancy, fanfare, fanforanade, fang, fantasia, fantastic, fantastically, fantasy, far, far-fetched, far-sighted, farce, farcical, fardel, fare, farewell, farina, farinaceous, farm, farmer, farrago, farrier, farriery, farrow, farther, farthing, farthingale, fasces, fascinate, fascination, fascism, fascist, fashion, fashionable, fast, fasten, fastidious, fastness, fat, fatal, fatalism, fatalist, fatalistic, fatality, fate, fated, fateful, father, fatherhood, fatherland, fatherly, fathom, fathomless, fatiguing, fatling, fatten, fatty, fatuous, fatuity, faucet, fault, faultless, faulty, faun, fauna, favour, favourable, favourite, fawn, fay, fealty, fear, fearful, fearless, fearsome, feasible, feasibility, feast, feat, feather, feathery, feature, featureless, February, feckless, fecund, fecundity, fed, feed, federal, federate, federation, fee, feeble, feed, feel, feeler, feeling, feet, foot, feign, feint, felicitate, felicitation, felicitous, felicity, feline, fell, fellah, fellow, felon, felony, felonious, felt, female, feminine, femininity, feminism, feminist, fen, fence, fencing, fend, fender, fennel, ferment, fermentation, fern, ferocious, ferocity, ferous, ferret, ferric, ferrous, ferrule, ferrel, ferry, fertile, fertility, fertilize, fertilization, fertilizer, ferule, fervent, fervency, fervour, fervid, festal, fester, festival, festive, festivity, festoon, fetch, fetching, fete, fetid, foetid, fetish, fetich(e), fetlock, fetter, fettle, feu, feud, feudal, fever, feverish, few, fewness, fey, fez, fiasco, fiat, fib, fibber, fibster, fibre, fibrous, fibrafic, fibrafication, fichu, fickle, fiction, fictitious, fiddle, fiddlestick, fiddler, fiddling, fidelity, fidget, fidgety, fie, fief, field, fieldwork, fiend, fiendish, fierce, fiery, fife, fifer, fifteen, fifteenth, fifth, fifty, fiftieth, fig, fight, fighter, figment, figuration, figurative, figure, filament, filbert, filch, file, filial, filibeg, filibuster, filigree, filagree, fill, fillet, fillip, filly, film, filmy, filter, filtration, filth, filthy, fin, final, finale, finality, finally, finance, financial, financier, finch, find, fine, finesse, finger, fingering, finical, finicking, finish, finite, finnan, fiord, fjord, fir, fir-tree, fire, firearm, firebrand, fire-brigade, firedamp, firedog, fire-engine, fire-escape, fire-fly, fire-irons, fireman, fireplace, fireproof, firework, firing, firkin, firm, firmament, first, firstly, firth, frith, fiscal, fish, fisherman, fishery, fishmonger, fishy, fission, fissure, fisticuffs, fit, fitful, fitment, fitter, fitting, five, fives, fix, fixedly, fixity, fixture, fizz, fizzle, flabbergast, flabby, flabbiness, flaccid, flag, flagstone, flagellant, flagellate, flagellation, flageolet, flagon, flagrant, flail, flair, flake, flaky, flamboyant, flame, flaming, flamingo, flan, flange, flank, flannel, flannelette, flap, flare, flaring, flash, flashy, flask, flat, flatten, flatter, flatterer, flattery, flatulence, flatulent, flaunt, flautist, flavour, flavouring, flaw, flawless, flax, flaxen, flay, flea, fleck, flecker, fledge, fledged, fledgling, flee, fleece, fleecy, fleet, fleeting, Flemish, flesh, flesher, fleshly, fleshy, flew, flex, flexible, flexibility, flick, flicker, flier, flight, flighty, flimsy, flinch, fling, flint, flinty, flip, flippant, flippancy, flipper, flirt, flirtation, flit, flitch, float, floatation, flock, floe, flog, flogging, flood, floodlight, floodlighting, floor, flop, floppy, flora, floral, floret, florid, florin, florist, floss, flossy, flotilla, flotsam, flounce, flounder, flour, floury, flourish, flout, flow, flower, floweret, flowery, flown, fly, fluctuate, flue, fluency, fluff, fluffy, fluid, fluke, flummery, flung, fling, flunkey, fluorescence, flurry, flush, fluster, flute, flutist, flutter, fluty, fluvial, flux, fly, foal, foam, fob, focal, focus, fodder, foe, foetus, fog, foggy, fogy, fogey, foible, foil, foist, fold, folder, foliage, folio, folk, follow, follower, following, folly, foment, fomentation, fond, fondle, font, food, fool, foolery, fool-hardy, foolish, foolscap, football, footing, fop, foppish, for, forasmuch, forage, foray, forbear, forbearance, forbid, forbidding, force, forceful, force-meat, forceps, forcible, ford, fordable, fore, forearm, forebode, foreboding, forecast, forecastle, focsle, foreclose, forefather, forefinger, forefoot, forefront, foreground, forehead, foreign, forejudge, foreknow, foreknowledge, foreland, foreleg, forelock, foreman, foremast, foremost, forenoon, foreordain, forerunner, foresail, foresee, foreshadow, foreshore, foreshorten, foresight, forest, forestall, forester, forestry, foretaste, foretell, forethought, forever, forewarn, foreword, forfeit, forfeiture, forgather, forgave, forgive, forge, forgery, forget, forgetful, forget-me-not, forgive, forgiveness, forgiving, forego, fork, forlorn, form, formless, formal, formalize, formality, formation, formative, former, formerly, formic, formic acid, formidable, formula, formulary, formulate, formulation, forsake, forsooth, forswear, fort, forte, forth, forthcoming, forthright, forthwith, fortification, fortify, fortitude, fortnight, fortnightly, fortress, fortuitous, fortunate, fortune, fortune-teller, forty, fortieth, forum, forward, forwardness, fossil, fossilize, foster, fought, fight, foul, foully, found, foundation, founder, foundling, fount, fountain, four, fourteen, fourth, fowl, fowler, fox, foxy, fraction, fractional, fractious, fracture, fragile, fragility, fragment, fragmentary, fragrance, fragrant, frail, frailty, frame, franc, franchise, Franciscan, frank, frankincense, franklin, frantic, fraternal, fraternity, fraternize, fraternization, fratricide, fraud, fraudulence, fraudulent, fraught, fray, freak, freakish, freckle, free, freebooter, freedom, freehold, freeman, freemason, freeze, freight, freightage, French, frenzy, frenzied, frequency, frequent, fresh, freshen, fret, fretful, friable, friar, friary, fricative, friction, Friday, friend, friendly, friendship, frieze, frigate, fright, frighten, frightful, frightfulness, frigid, frigidity, frill, frilled, fringe, frippery, frisk, frisky, fritter, frivolous, frivolity, frizz, frizzle, fro, frock, frog, frolic, frolicsome, from, frond, front, frontage, frontal, frontier, frontispiece, frost, frosty, froth, froward, frown, frowzy, froze, frozen, freeze, fructify, frugal, frugality, fruit, fruiterer, fruitful, fruitless, fruition, frump, frumpish, frustrate, frustration, fry, fuchsia, fuddle, fudge, fuel, fugitive, fugue, fulfil, fulfilment, fulgent, full, fuller, fullness, fully, fulmar, fulminate, fulness, fulsome, fumble, fumbler, fume, fumigate, fumigation, fun, function, functionary, fund, fundamental, funeral, funereal, fungus, funicular, funnel, funny, fur, furbelow, furbish, furious, furl, furlong, furlough, furnace, furnish, furniture, furrier, furrow, furry, further, furthermost, furthest, furtive, fury, furze, fuse, fusible, fuselage, fusil, fusilier, fusilade, fusion, fuss, fussy, fustian, fusty, futile, futility, future, futurity, fuzz, fuzzy.

Statement by the artist, October 1987

PUTTING THE 'F' BACK INTO ART, 1987
Oil and enamel on linen
Three panels, 213.3 × 548.6

ANNA MARIA SANTOLINI

Born Milan, Italy, 1951

Lives and works in Milan

GIORGIO VERZOTTI: Your works, including these last canvases that we're looking at, speak to us of energy, of gesturing, of strength— more than anything else, this strange quality, strength.

ANNA MARIA SANTOLINI: It is said at times that my work is virile, and that seems funny to me. Also out of place. What does it mean to say masculine or feminine, what do these value categories say of a work? I think that in my work is realised the famous 'Don't seek, find' and I find this strength in me. It seems to me a given fact, it doesn't scare me, it's not a problem. To work in art means to express a complexity, an interiority; in order to express you need concentration and therefore physical strength, an accumulation of tension.

GV: Certainly you couldn't tell if these works had been done by a man or a woman. But I don't want to make a point of the question of the feminine. You could say that out of this illustrated energy, these moving figures alluding to another dimension, an urgency in whose name the composition is articulated, something signals and takes form. In your first works there was a recall to myth, explicit at times, so much so I think I can call this dimension the 'divine'.

AMS: In whose name the form is rendered visible, materialised.

GV: Across a flux, a transmigration of signs. From the invisible to the visible, in the most immediate way possible, with the gesture. Really the rendering is visible in the work, the surrendering of the invisible and the revealing of it, the form is caught in this act, in the moment of its originating. But it is a genesis that, in making itself evident, trails behind itself the sign, that sign that belongs to the myth, to that origin and that depth. It trails behind it the greatest possible number of attributes and tries in the fullest way possible to make sense.

AMS: For this reason the work that I have completed in the end can be nothing if not profoundly ambiguous. Polyphonic, polysemic, open, I would like to say, effusive. The strength comes as a consequence, and also mitigates control of me regarding the sign. There is vehemence, there is also an awakened body state. I paint listening to music, I move myself, I overburden myself physically, even until I drive myself a bit crazy . . . I find a way of forcefully entering into communication with what I'm doing, of finding a moment of maximum concentration. I am not methodical in my work, I accumulate tension and I work with energy. It isn't a trance but a transfer across which something is made concrete outside of me. I search for evocative factors, every artist has his own technique of evocation. Mine is not confessional, I don't want to lose the emotive burden but stay present on the rational level, on the alert. The work is realised when I feel that these principles are really present. I work between balance and confrontation. There are parts of the painting I do with my left hand, to trick the right, to distract me from myself.

GV: Do you paint fast?

AMS: It's bizarre. There are paintings that I finish incredibly quickly, feverishly, and others that take months; there is no middle way. In the beginning there is always an impulse like a volcano, then a lot of the paintings I leave. Each of my works, as you can see, consists of stratifications, needs different sedimentations. Even after months I intervene with modifications.

GV: Paintings without centre, without time, potentially unfinishable.

AMS: Each one I feel as part of an interminable fresco, of which I capture a fragment from time to time. This doesn't mean that I think I've never finished a painting. Only that things that come to me do so across tension, like magnetic fields. I stop things, I apprehend them, not thanks to a state of quietude but on the contrary to a state of passion. In fact, it's quite true that there is some eroticism in my paintings.

GV: The phenomenon, then, induces the phenomenology of a humoral subject, which expresses itself with its lower parts, albeit with passion. Something that is not formalised in a graceful and winning language but that, just in case, assumes a tone of aggression. There seems to me to be a negative significance at work, denying, anti-economical, in eroticism. In your previous works we saw soft, slow movements that outlined a sort of positive genesis of the form, a constructive journey towards the finished form, even if not *a prioristic*, even if bonded to the organic. In the paintings that we have in front of us the language of energy, of split levels, of corners, these almost mechanical elements undo the form. They are suspended between the organic and the *a prioristic*.

AMS: By now, there is everything in the work. There is no longer a going towards; it loses sense to speak of evolution in these terms. I don't know what you mean by negation, I would say that in the work something happens, indeed, everything happens and the work is entirely this happening, this everything that shows itself completely every now and then. There are some interpenetrations, superimpositions, a seething forming of itself, and an annihilation, a disturbance, something highly dramatic.

GV: However, it is not simply a question of 'whatever happens, happens', there is some reasoning, some distance. To some extent the dimensions of the canvases predispose them to this dramatic urgency, the work is never redundant, it's indeed almost sober. Then, the absence of colour and the prevailing choice of white and black mitigates against redundance. Each work is complete in the sense that it possesses its own interior rhythm, turned inward, that doesn't overflow with vitality.

AMS: Certainly I don't allude to tribal dancing with my signs, even though I do represent a battle for the form carried out on the level of the passionate, and the rational, intellectual. Painting is substantially intellectual. However, by way of the two principles of black and white, I want to say that in the end the whites win. As carriers of light they resolve the conflict.

Excerpt from Giorgio Verzotti, 'Anna Maria Santolini', *Flash Art*, no 136, December/January 1986/87
Translated by Angela Kerley

DEDALUS: OPERA BALLET, 1987
Tyres, aluminium, iron, copper
Installation, 120 × 250 × 500

(Photo) Salvatore Licitra

Born Hall/Tirol, Austria, 1960

Lives and works in Vienna

Although the monochrome technique emphasises the substance of the picture, the works by Eva Schlegel derive their main effect from the immaterial quality of the painting, setting the surface now and then in subtle, emotional vibrations that penetrate into depth and volume. In contrast to these colour-dimensional nuances, the plaster pictures sealed with graphite confront us with the hard, object-like element, without, however, losing their painted touch.

They intrigue by their multiple appearance: reflexes change with the movement of the onlooker, the undefinable shimmering of the polished graphite, sometimes looking like a metal surface, the magic of the black colour or the undecodable structure of the uneven body surface suggesting distant archaic messages, or is there a mysterious glow somewhere in the depth of the picture? All these impressions are evoked by a simple technique: instead of the usual colour, plaster is applied to a clamped metal sieve (canvas). After smoothing, the plaster surface is gradually sealed with graphite in a strenuous drawing process. Two contradicting experiences are felt when working the material and being guided by it; the making disappear by covering (negation) on the one hand, and the making appear of hidden elements (negation of the negation). Only the graphite skin brings out the surface structure of the plaster, only physical covering gives birth to the psychic character of the neutral body. The physical strain of the sealing procedure is reflected by the hardness of seemingly cool metal. However, this effect is immediately questioned by the softness of the plaster surface. In addition, the imaginary quality of the indefinite colour space deploys its effect with increasing dimensions.

Painting in this context goes beyond the immaterial weightless quality of the monochrome surface and—in contrast thereto—beyond the accentuation of the object as such towards the third dimension and invites the onlooker to a direct physical and meditative interaction.

Markus Brüderlin
Translated by Suzanne Krenn-Papasian

FIVE CUBES, 1987
Graphite on plaster
Five cubes, each 100 × 100 × 30

Born San Francisco, USA, 1939

Lives and works in New York City

There is no general rule as to which formal properties suffice to determine the structure of a relation. I have chosen certain conditions (rules that I have made up) that reveal themselves in the logic of the procedure.

Limitations of weight, physical properties and materials cannot be imagined.

As forces tend toward equilibrium the weight in part is negated.

There is a difference between definite literal fixed relationships, i.e. joints, clips, gluing, welding, etc, and those which are provisional, non-fixed, 'clastic'. The former seem unnecessary and irrelevant and tend to function as interposed elements.

The perception of the work in its state of suspended animation, arrested motion, does not give one calculable truths like geometry, but a sense of a presence, an isolated time. The apparent potential for disorder, for movement, endows the structure with a quality outside its physical or relational definition.

Statement by the artist, *Art Now: New York*, vol. 3, no 3, New York, September 1971

Richard Serra is an artist whose sculpture shows all the signs of a powerful grasp of the world historical process, particularly of the situation of labour in it. His art takes a contradictory stance to labour, which at once epitomises the tension in its current condition, and, with a visionary accuracy, resolves that tension. The visionary is a dialectician, reconciling real opposites, with the utopianism of the reconciliation ultimately as real as the opposites. In modern labour leisure and work are unresolved, and the pressures for their resolution are greater than ever. It is these pressures that change their identity, our sense of their meaning—that create a dialectical reversal that is crystallised by what occurs in the experience of Serra's sculpture. Such experience, as Serra's landscape pieces emphasise, with their demand for peripatetic participation—carrying that traditional demand of sculpture to an extreme, so that moving within the work is the only way of moving around it—is part of the integrity of the sculpture . . .

From the start Serra's sculpture was directly conscious of and responsive to the work process. It took its entire identity and energy from specific work. I know of no sculpture that can compare with his early sculpture's effort to define itself so insistently in terms of the work process, that takes such care to be nothing but its work. In this he outdoes Abstract Expressionism, which was always too bound to the search for symbols to take itself completely seriously as a work process. By being so exclusively—sublimely—a work process, Serra's sculpture achieves a social destiny, for it comes to codify the relentlessness of the labour process in industrial society, the sense of no alternatives to that process and so the sense of it as *the* work process. This leads to a sense of the work process as in and of itself the process of freedom. Work time is seen to be free time—the only time in which humanity is truly free, truly itself, for work time is the only time when it shows its power. For it involves, simultaneously, confrontation with natural reality and social reality, the dialectical transformation of both through the same work.

Donald B. Kuspit, 'Richard Serra, Utopian Constructivist', *Arts Magazine*, vol. 55, no 3, November 1980

Among the other 'wall props' in the Pace Gallery show there is one called *Keystone* that is built with three identical steel plates, each sixty inches square and three inches thick. Like most of Mr Serra's sculptures, it seems to be virtually impossible to photograph. Scale, texture, small but fundamental departures from flatness—all prove to be shy of the camera.

Keystone is predicated, for instance, on the slight forward tilt of the two lower elements and the huge flat upward thrust of the top one. Noting that tilt, we may wish to read the piece as a schematic torso—navel to upper thigh—of the kind that Brancusi brought to perfection. But this is Brancusi plus pity and terror. As we calculate the possible height of the entire figure, we feel ourselves in the presence of a vast definitive fragment that doubles as a complete work of art. Gone, too, are the plinths of yesteryear. Mr Serra uses the floorboards in such a way that we almost believe that the piece is free to move around and might step forward to claim us as its kin. Altogether, the sculptures at Pace are among the finest of our time.

John Russell, *New York Times*, 9 October 1987

KEYSTONE, 1987
Hot rolled steel
Three plates, each 152.4 × 152.4
Collection: Solomon R. Guggenheim Museum, New York. Purchased with funds contributed by Stephen and Nan Swid

SEVERED HEADS

Tom Ellard, born Sydney, Australia, 1962

Stephen Jones, born Sydney, Australia, 1951

Both live and work in Sydney

Severed Heads have plied their trade in various incarnations in various boxes over the years. Some of these boxes have been full of drunken angst-ridden yobs with catfood in their hair. Others have contained well-dressed gentry with a correct art viewing stance, hand on jaw, which is slack, three to four feet from the object of admiration. Sometimes a bit of both. We've noticed that despite providing a consistent entertainment, the reactions can vary enormously. In Calgary and Brussels they all ran around bumping into each other, in Ljubljana they spat, in London they walked out, while at one show in Sydney 1,200 watts of public address was insufficient to wake one chap in the front row.

This should be no surprise to any performer. Audiences are very potent organisms, which is why artists have to work so hard to make up for it. Standing on raised platforms in sequined boots, hurling around huge inflatable sexual organs while various stage props explode in various colours and so on. The whole façade crumbles the moment a patron yells, 'boring!'.

I once had the opportunity to chat with a high-ranking American record company executive. I asked why Severed Heads had so far escaped much commercial success. 'You haven't got THE LOOK,' he said. Well, Stephen and I are not slow. As Stephen has considerable experience in video production, we intensified the creation of our LOOK. A large video screen dominates the stage, the unfortunate reality hidden in the darkness stage left. Often the singer's head is portrayed, pumped up and colourised, reproportioned and pimples concealed by computer analysis. Even better, we can deflect attention onto something incongruous or utterly abstract. This leaves the patron with a chance to exercise some personal vision and with a share of the applause. It also avoids having to make the best of a bad job, for example, I think the picture reproduced here is much nicer than the singer's face, don't you?

Anyway, we are continuing to think of ways to improve our presentation, which often means thinking of ways to remove our presence from the whole entertainment process. In the long run, that means allowing the patrons to run the whole show and our video work offers a likely way of achieving just that. For one thing, other tactics are far less promising in that there are never enough sequined boots to go around. A few cameras, wires and funny boxes will do the trick more nicely.

Allow us to demonstrate the stage that we have reached in this research. Although at the time of writing the exact specifications of the installation are unclear, the idea is to build a system that is an audience to its audience. It will observe the activities of the people observing its activities. While you are entitled to your opinion of the worth of the work, remember that the work is entitled to its opinion of you. You might be entertaining but are you art? As for Stephen and myself, we'll pull a fast one and only describe the process in meta-language.

During the time of the Biennale we've planned a few live performances where the usual tactic of big-screen-small-people will apply. Some people call these dead performances, but anyway. The music and vision on these nights will pertain to records that we sell in shops, the wages of art being far short of the wages of commerce. All are invited to attend but please not to spit.

Tom Ellard, Sydney, 1987

HOT WITH FLEAS, 1987
Videotape

VIVIENNE SHARK LeWITT

Born Sale, Australia, 1956

Lives and works in Melbourne

THE OMEN, THAT WASCALLY WABBIT, 1987
Oil on linen
61 × 71

(Photo) Terence Bogue

DAVID SMITH

Born Decatur, Indiana, USA, 1906

Died Albany, Vermont, 1965

I believe that my time is the most important in the world—that the art of my time is the most important art—that the art before my time has made no immediate contribution to my aesthetics since that art is history, explaining past behaviour, but not necessarily offering solutions to my problems. Art is not divorced from life. It is dialectic. It is ever changing and in revolt with the past. It has existed in the minds of free men for less than a century. Prior to this, the direction of art was dictated by minds other than the artist for exploitation and commercial use. The freedom of man's mind to celebrate his own feeling by a work of art parallels his social revolt from bondage. I believe that art is yet to be born and that freedom and equality are yet to be born.

If you ask why I make sculpture, I must answer that it is my way of life, my balance, and my justification for being.

If you ask for whom do I make art, I will say that it is for all who approach it without prejudice. My world, the objects I see are the same for all men of good will. The race for survival I share with all men who work for existence.

Statement by the artist, made at a forum held by the *New York Herald Tribune* and the New York City Board of Education, 19 March 1950

The material called iron or steel I hold in high respect . . . What it can do in arriving at a form economically, no other material can do. The metal itself possesses little art history. What associations it possesses are those of this century: power, structure, movement, progress, suspension, brutality.

I follow no set procedure in starting a sculpture. Some works start out as chalk drawings on the cement floor, with cut steel forms working into the drawings. When the structure can become united, it is welded into position upright. Then the added dimension requires different considerations over the more or less profile form of the floor drawing assembly.

Sometimes I make a lot of drawings using possibly one relationship on each drawing which will add up in the final work.

Sometimes sculptures just start with no drawing at all . . . My drawings are made either in work books or on large sheets of linen rag. I stock bundles of several types, forgetting the cost so I can be free with it. The cost problem I have to forget on everything, because it is always more than I can afford—more than I get back from sales—most years, more than I earn . . . When I'm involved aesthetically I cannot consider cost, I work by the need of what each material can do. Usually the costly materials do not even show, as their use has been functional.

The traditions for steel do not exist that govern bronze finishes, patinas, or casting limits. There are no preconceived limits established as there are for marble, the aesthetics of grain and surface or the physical limits of mass to strength. Direction by natural grain, hand rubbing, monolithic structure, or the controls of wood do not apply physically or traditionally to steel . . .

I do not accept the monolithic limit in the tradition of sculpture. Sculpture is as free as the mind, as complex as life, its statement as full as the other visual mediums combined. I identify form in relationship to man.

Excerpt from notes for 'David Smith Makes a Sculpture', *Art News*, January 1969

People wanting to be told something, *given the last word*, will not find it in art. Art is not didactic. It is not final; it is always waiting for the projection of the viewer's perceptive powers. Even from the creator's position, the work represents a segment of his life, based on the history of his previous works, awaiting the continuity of the works to follow. In a sense a work of art is never finished.

My concept as an artist is a revolt against the well-worn beauties in the form of a statue. Rather I would prefer my assemblages to be the savage idols of basic patterns, the veiled directives, subconscious associations, *the image recall* of orders more true than the object itself, resulting in vision, in aura, rather than object reality.

Excerpt from a speech given at Williams College, Williamstown, Massachusetts, on 17 December 1951

CUBI XXVII, 1965
Stainless steel
282.9 × 222.9 × 86.4
Collection: Solomon R. Guggenheim Museum, New York

(Photo) Robert E. Mates

FREEDOM

Freedom for the masses means both Liberty and Bondage.

Freedom is only accessible to rare human beings endowed with inventiveness and imagination, who are capable of creating their own worlds (like artists who transform the visible world into their own reality). It is accessible to individuals who have enough willpower to consider themselves their own makers and to take responsibility for their own doings, and who, while courageous, are at the same time aware of the danger: like someone standing on the brink of a precipice who perceives the discrepancy between the risk involved and his own fallibility.

Those rare individuals also manifest their courage in opposing the society's indifference and hostility, and in contending the distorted and misshapen mediocrity known as culture.

My aim hereof is exquisitely clear.

Ordinary people who are unable to comprehend the whole scope of life, people devoid of their own will who always need somebody to guide them and whose docility makes them only law-abiding— such people are doomed to voluntary or involuntary *submission.*

The unique individuals can transform people who are tied to the commonplace reality; they can teach them that common things may turn uncommon, and that the insignificant may acquire significance.

Certain people are endowed with latent or dormant inner powers which need some stimulant to be activated, like certain substances in which a proper catalyst provokes rapid chemical reactions.

There is no dividing line between capable and incapable persons, just as there is no clear division between good and bad people.

People shape the reality and are, in turn, themselves shaped by it; by critically examining the reality, a new reality (or an unreal reality) is being created. (1974)

ART AND REALITY

When an old reality wears off and is withdrawn from circulation like a used coin, to be replaced by a new reality, art inevitably offers a mirror-like reflection of this perpetual process of transition.

Art never slows down its steps to stroll into an emotional desert of restful contemplation, or to re-tread its former course.

It is therefore impossible to produce a permanent or MODEL ART: a kind of art that, like a street car, would continuously circle the same track.

Whenever artists attempt to establish canons or conventions, these never last long, and are soon replaced by new canons and conventions which take on ever new shapes.

Art helps us to break into the house of true reality—to pierce the mist of everyday greyness which artists perceive as an illusory or a deceptive reality.

Living in a state of inexplicable agitation hides a truth which the artist's inner eye is able to perceive, noticing, at the same time, something deeper than purely visual beauty. (1975)

A visit to a small provincial town whose ubiquitous decay and disorder gives one pleasure and helps to discern beauty and to regain creative vein.

Muddy ground, a puddle of rottenly opalescent water reflecting houses, trees and clouds, leaking roofs, stained walls, heaps of stones, bricks, weeds and logs in gardens; all these things generate a desire to find order in chaos.

Owing to our sensitive eyes
    a fleeting moment may leave its permanent trace,
      some order be discovered in a chance event.

While watching a cinematic succession of dilapidated gardens our perception of reality generates the feelings of exaltation and tension, transforming our vision into a flat view with no perspective or space; one starts to perceive the world in geometrical terms, its proportions distorted and distances altered, curves turning into straight lines and straight lines curving, colours ceasing to mark objects and acquiring a dramatic harmony which expresses one's state of mind.

Everything becomes incomprehensible: a topsy-turvy world.

After deliberating for a long time how to convey these states of mind in a painting, I finally decided that the above impressions and the resulting pattern can be expressed by means of parallel lines— once straying away, then crossing each other—encompassing nothingness; beginning with a number of rapidly drawn rhythmical lines, then reduced to clusters or individual lines, and ending with a couple of carefully balanced lines. (1976)

Statements by the artist

Galerie Zak, Paris, 1929
Standing, from left: Henryk Stażewski, S. Grabowski, Schumoff; sitting: A. Zamoyski, Michel Seuphor, W. Chodasiewicz-Grabowska, J. Brzekowski, Piet Mondrian, F. Henry

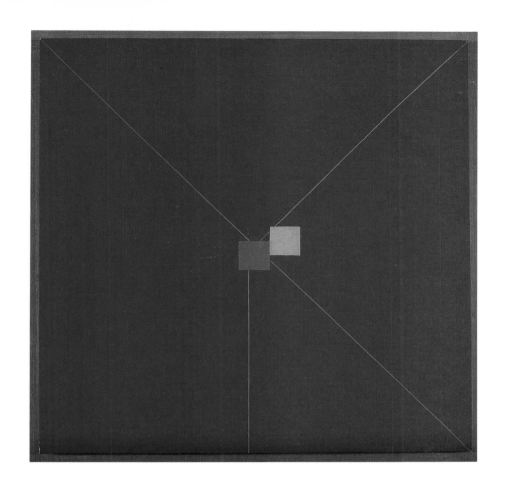

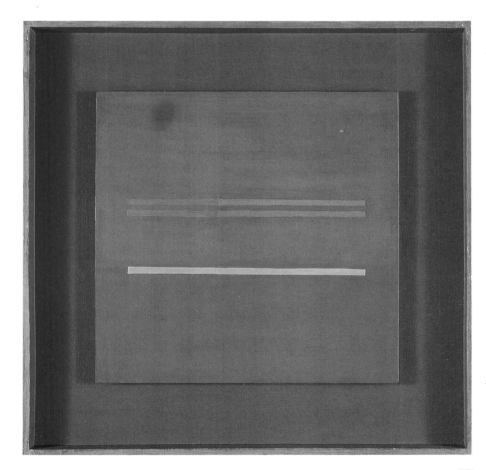

COLOUR A, 1980
Acrylic, hardboard, wood
64 × 64

(Photo) Mariusz Lukawski

COLOUR B, 1980
Acrylic, hardboard, wood
44 × 44

(Photo) Mariusz Lukawski

GARY STEVENS
CAROLINE WILKINSON

Gary Stevens born London, England, 1953

Lives and works in London

Caroline Wilkinson born Edinburgh, Scotland, 1951

Lives and works in London

If the Cap Fits is in two parts. Each part has a distinctive character. The first part is sculptural, the second makes reference to pantomime. The first part ends with the performers unable to get into another piece of clothing, the second begins as if this process had continued impossibly. I think of myself as a sculptor negotiating the theatre.

My work is informed by the vaudeville tradition and its development into cinema. Many of the jokes and much of the appeal of early silent film comedies was based on the inference of a mind and its nature through the behaviour of the protagonist. The performers/characters were curious thinking objects and their performance drew a distinction between the subject as a conscious agent and a person as an object, be it psychological, historical, social, economic, physical, etc. My world doesn't attempt to imitate those comedies but to reinvent that tradition and its representations. The result, on the surface, looks primitive and funny.

In *If the Cap Fits* the performers are presented from the beginning as guilt-stricken and self-conscious. There is a suggestion that they share some domestic space but they do not know what their relationship to each other is. The problem is not dressed as a situation that has biographical or psychological antecedents. The possibility of a dramatic relationship is precluded. Instead of a drama the stage silts up and the movement of the piece develops like some hysterical symptom. They never become human. The performance is a flowering of this problem.

The performance is set in an environment that suggests security, a living room. The rug is then pulled out from under their feet. They are models of people that regard themselves with an inexpressible incomprehension.

Gary Stevens, 1987

———————————————

The dramatic tensions which exist within *If the Cap Fits*, Gary Stevens's most recent performance, are what make it compelling. Funny—tragic, theatrical—sculptural, familiar—bizarre, the audience is stretched between a variety of extremes. On stage for one and a half hours, Stevens and his partner, Caroline Wilkinson, attempt to establish a relationship between their continually shifting identities. Who are they? Husband and wife, brother and sister, lovers or partners in crime? Gary Stevens and Caroline Wilkinson? At once, actors in domestic drama and self-conscious performance artists, they suggest a line between illusion and reality which is erased even as it is drawn.

In the first few minutes of the performance, we are introduced to a table and a chair—two pieces of furniture which complement one another and provide an analogy for the relationship between the two performers. An unpretentious, humble chair. A snooty, elegant table. For a moment, they are seen to possess the personalities which Stevens and Wilkinson project onto them— then they are seen to be inanimate. Just a table and a chair. Like Stevens and Wilkinson, they simultaneously play the Sartrean roles of Beings In Themselves and Beings For Themselves. Wilkinson later tells a charming fairy story which accounts for the table's creation of itself. *Causa sui*, like God! Pieces of ordinary furniture are transformed by extraordinary leaps of the imagination. And then they are props again—devices which reveal and disguise the identities of the two performers.

Stevens finally moves from behind the chair to begin the 'costume drama'—an almost slapstick routine in which he and Wilkinson loot the chest of drawers behind them to discover what seems like an inexhaustible supply of trousers, jackets and dresses. One after the other, trousers are put on over trousers, jackets over jackets, dresses over dresses until, eventually, Stevens and Wilkinson stand confronting each other, ridiculous and fat. Their attempts to embrace are foiled. Clothes, which are supposed to make the man, bury him—Wilkinson thrusts her hand through Stevens' gaping fly, only to discover another fly. What could be an aggressively passionate gesture is not felt. These ironies are hilarious, heart-rending and all too human.

The relationship between the two performers is never established—on the contrary, the question of their identities becomes increasingly complicated. Towards the end of the performance, Stevens actually leaves the stage to join the audience and is called back by Wilkinson, only to forget what he has to say. Like a bad dream, the drama grinds to a halt, incapable of resolution. How are questions of identity resolved? How can anyone be sure that a mask won't slip only to reveal another mask? A groping hand may never reach the passion that it seeks—only layers and layers of clothing. Perhaps a cap only fits on another cap. *If the Cap Fits* finishes as it has to. Unresolved. There is no character who steps in, like Monsieur Poirot, to tell everybody who they are and what they've done. Instead, there are two confused, embarrassed people on stage who have run out of lines—and an audience that has been profoundly moved.

Jonathan Watkins, *Art Monthly*, December 1986/January 1987

IF THE CAP FITS, 1986
Performance work

ANDRZEJ SZEWCZYK

Born Katowice, Poland, 1950

Lives and works in Kaczyce Górne

'F. Kafka's Letters to F. Bauer' are written in lead on oak-wood. I started to work on them in autumn 1981.

The script is symbolic. It symbolises sadness.

GREY is a colour devoid of eroticism, devoid of music.

Lead has an essentially temporal quality and contains all the transformations of the Cosmos, of the ageing materials of which it formerly consisted.

Lead is poisonous. To me it always has a lethal ring.

Finally, mention is due to the poetic quality of lead, its homely beauty of FEAR AND SADNESS. Lead is the ideal metal of epitaphs to be written in.

Every copy is a small, private wailing wall.

Statement by the artist, 1987

MEMORIALS OF F. KAFKA'S LETTERS TO F. BAUER, 1983
Lead on wood
Two pieces, each 17 × 30 × 4.5
Two pieces, each 15 × 22 × 4.5

(Photo) Tadeusz Rolke

MEMORIALS OF F. KAFKA'S LETTERS TO F. BAUER, 1983
Lead on wood
Installation at Foksal Gallery, Warsaw, 1984

(Photo) Tadeusz Rolke

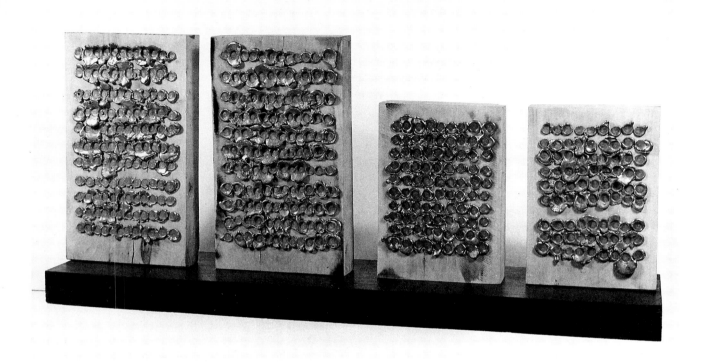

IMANTS TILLERS

Born Sydney, Australia, 1950

Lives and works in Sydney

Imants Tillers' new works using vitreous enamel on steel may surprise those familiar with his canvas board paintings of recent years. Not, perhaps, because they involve different materials, or that two works are floor pieces, but because of their visual simplicity. Starting with his single-image, charcoal on canvas board works of 1981–82, Tillers' paintings have become progressively more densely associative, technically complex and monumental in scale. Despite continually making reference to pre-existing images, these works have a look that is unmistakably Tillers. One irony of the paintings in the present Biennale—some of which make no direct use of appropriated imagery—is that they are less instantly recognisable as Tillers' work than his canvas board paintings.

A good look reveals that the two modes of work are actually far from discontinuous. The most apparent continuity concerns the enamelled steel plates comprising the floor pieces. They are similar in size to the canvas boards, and thus fit easily into Tillers' ever expanding system of individually numbered units (which he compares to pages in a book), at last count totalling 16,374. Individual works consist of a designated number of units which, when assembled, form a grid. In the canvas board paintings several grids may fill various functions at once; the scaling up of images, the superimposition of layers, and the demarcation of spaces additional to those of the basic grid. Distinguished from its use in a modernist tradition culminating in conceptualism, Tillers' grid is not a reductive principle, but a pictorial device for the multiplication of images, surfaces and spaces.

In the new Biennale paintings, however, a reductive principle appears to have returned, especially in the two floor pieces. Geometry reasserts itself in these works, which create regular patterns through repetition and thematic variation, always respecting the flatness of the grid. Has Tillers capitulated; do these works represent an abandonment of the critical themes of his earlier work in deference to the rather tired metaphysic of the grid?

If this question is suspended for a moment, the answer may become clearer when we consider the material evolution of the vitreous enamel paintings. Industrial materials, hard edges and high gloss finishes indicate a technological process in their manufacture. If these works are referred to as 'paintings', it is certainly not on the basis of any verifiable brush stroke or stylistic signature. But the artist is closer to the process of production than one might expect. The technology is, in fact, simple. Glass and pigment are sprayed onto steel panels, then heated to the point at which they fuse. Tillers cuts cardboard stencils through which the glass and pigment are sprayed in successive layers. Unlike a silkscreened surface, the layering of enamel is here visible—as are irregularities of colour and surface arising from the individual painting of each panel. Marks that trace the coming into being of a work relate to a constant theme in Tillers' art, the critique of metaphysics. What Nietzsche termed an art of 'metaphysical comfort'[1]—images whose 'present perfection' eclipses any thought of their having a history—is undermined in Tillers' art where what is painted always carries a trace of how it was produced.

Although Tillers' floor pieces are reminiscent of works from the sixties and seventies based on the mythic power of the grid, they are peculiarly different. Rhetoric that empowered the grid in conceptual art often celebrated it as a kind of floating signifier; a value-free, neutral form without content or prejudice. Tillers' works, compared to those of Carl André (conceptualist and creator of the best known grid-related floor pieces) are at once alluding to the latter and covering new ground.

Whereas André's sculptures may be stepped upon, Tillers' brittle enamel surfaces are far too fragile to be put into foot service. At the same time there is something familiar about these determinedly non-utilitarian 'rugs'. This may be because the manufacturer of these enamel panels supplies road signs to the Victorian government, which use precisely the same colour (streetsign blue), lettering and steel-plating as Tillers' floor pieces. André's 'checkerboards' tend to be smooth and pavement-like, Tillers' are breakable, glassy, reflective and loaded with references—not only to the method of their making, but to a specifically urban object, the street sign, (whether this connection is made or not, the pieces may remind one of a variety of urban and domestic items). Added to these are references made by words in the pieces themselves. For example, 'Anomaly' and 'Nobility' are names of streets that border the manufacturer's factory, mapping it onto another kind of grid altogether! Still, *Anomaly Nobility* is hardly a lesson in the bizarre streetnames of industrial suburbia. In a cognitive sense, the systematic repetition of two similar sounding words teaches us very little. If anything, literal meaning is disrupted in the play of sounds and forms.

Disruption notwithstanding, there is no missing the moral import of references in the floor pieces to nobility and virtue. One can sense the yearning for an age in which truth and beauty were proper concerns of painting, a neo-classical longing that captivates artists, like de Chirico, in whom the decadence of modern man is most deeply felt. The ethical crisis of recent art is addressed in Tillers' wall-mounted painting *Red Square*—a work created after Mel Ramsden's *Secret Painting* (1967–68). The humour of Ramsden's ultimate conceptual painting is far more sceptical than rapturous, announcing the final absurdity of a painting whose content remains invisible, known only to the artist. Tillers' own appropriation carries this absurdity one step further, but his use of the image is more particular. It is only in our society, where the sacred and the secular have been irrevocably and officially separated, that secret paintings are an absurdity.

In the early seventies, only a few years after Ramsden refused to tell, Aboriginal sand painters of the Western Desert at the Papunya settlement began to depict, using western materials, their traditional images. The content of these first paintings was sacred and secret, not to be disclosed to the uninitiated. But the relative permanence and portability of acrylic on canvas meant that the uninitiated did see the sacred paintings, causing a crisis within the Aboriginal community. The crisis was resolved with the realisation that this form of painting could only continue without its making reference to sacred meanings, and that is the basis on which it has continued. Tillers has drawn attention to an inescapable irony; in one (decadent Western) culture the secrecy of art is announced precisely when there is nothing to keep secret, in another (authentic Aboriginal), the secrets worth keeping are briefly revealed with the introduction of western techniques. Clearly, the addition of vitreous enamel paintings to Tillers' artistic repertoire does not signal a retreat from the critical concerns central to his recent work. In these paintings for the Bicentennial Biennale, Tillers explores a Nietzschean paradox of which the tribal elders have long been aware: The more the perfumed fragrance of meaning is dispersed and evaporated, the rarer will be those who can still perceive it.[2]

Nicholas Baume, 1987

1. Friedrich Nietzsche, *Human, All Too Human*, trans. M. Faber with S. Lehmann, University of Nebraska Press, 1984, p. 162.
2. *Op. cit.*, p. 217.

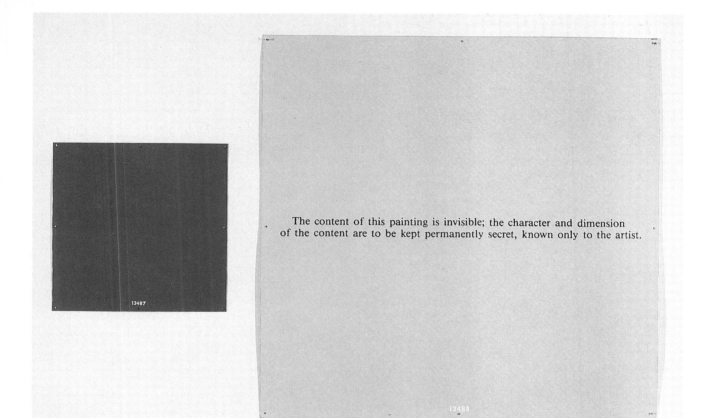

The content of this painting is invisible; the character and dimension of the content are to be kept permanently secret, known only to the artist.

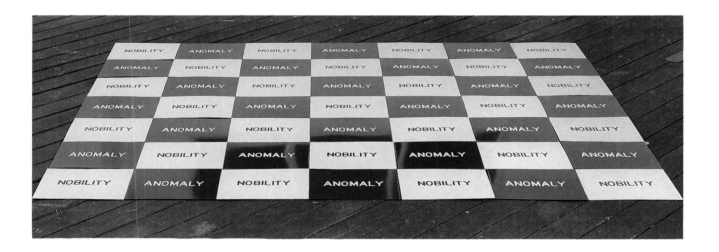

SECRET PAINTING/RED SQUARE, 1987
Vitreous enamel on steel
Two panels, 53.3 × 53.3 and 122 × 122

ANOMALY NOBILITY, 1987
Vitreous enamel on steel
Forty-nine panels, 195.5 × 249

(Photo) Fenn Hinchcliffe

The language of this art was the body. And when had the body last been seen? Rainer Maria Rilke, *Rodin*, 1946

I came to understand that wholeness for modern sculpture has been the conceptual wholeness of geometry, imposed from outside and at a distance. But the wholeness of the Venus of Willendorf is experienced internally, in the hand which holds and enfolds it. Construction affirms the separateness of parts, touching minimally at ends and edges. The Venus is not only the paradigm of fullness, but of the unified and inseparable relation of part to whole: each part is a reflection of the whole, while physically compact with and continuous with the whole: its wholeness issues from its invisible centre. The relation of the whole object to the enclosing hand suggests a scale of relationships for sculpture from the pinch of finger and thumb through the grasp of the hand, the embrace of one or both arms, to the walked and implied embrace of the whole body around the object. This in turn might suggest a conception of the human body itself, not as a discreet arrangement of joined and interactive parts, but as a system in which each part is at once itself and replicates the whole, both in form and action, along a progressive scale of physical connectedness; thus the finger is a whole in itself, an image of the entire body, and part of the hand; the hand has the same relation to the arm, the arm to the torso, the torso to the complete body, the body itself to the surfaces of the environment. Rilke had pointed out how Rodin had liberated the wholeness of the human body from the representation of its physical completeness, but the sculptors who followed Rodin and reacted against him took his invitation to develop the fragment as a thing in itself, separate from the body. In consequence we are hardly aware of the potentially inexhaustible order of part-whole relations within the body, and in its dynamic relation to the environment—through gravity for example.

If the potential of this field of work seems limitless, there are dangers also, two notably: on the one hand the danger of inertia, of ending with a meaningless lump of matter, without movement, life or presence. This is the danger of staying too long with the sculpture, of working it to death. On the other hand, the danger of stopping too soon, of not allowing the sculpture to develop beyond a point where it can too easily be identified with a familiar external reality. Any unusual mass in nature, a hill, cliff or rock is given a name to quiet the anxiety its inexplicable presence might otherwise arouse. So the sculptor is tempted to hold and refine a particular reading, either because he has started with it, or because it has presented itself early and seemingly inescapably. If the likeness, the association, is so strong as to exclude all other readings, and to overwhelm an identification with the object as substance, behind or beyond any reading, then the sculpture fails. If the desire to identify the disturbing and unfamiliar is a constant of human nature, the opportunity to resist identification is part of the legacy of early modernism that could too easily be forgotten.

Because the pieces in this exhibition have the title *Horse*, and the memory of the horses of the Elgin Marbles was part of their beginning, there is the possibility that the public response will not go beyond a literal reading of the image. But if these are horses' heads they are also human knees or elbows or shoulders, or torsos or whole figures; or perhaps no nameable image at all, something unthinkable and monstrous. To reassure myself I have sometimes characterised these shapes as simply the embodiment of the voids of my earlier work; but that embodiment is no simple process. It brings to the light much that I would rather not see and acknowledge as mine. It took me many years to accept Rodin, and I still have an uneasiness about his sculpture that I never experienced with that of Degas: but I now see this as a strength, the acceptance of the awkward, the ugly and disfigured, as the consequence of modelling, which at its purest is the direct transmission of energy from the human body into matter, without mediation of tools, without censorship of eye or brain.

Statement by the artist in *William Tucker, Recent Sculptures and Monotypes* (catalogue), Annely Juda Fine Art, London, 1987

Probably not even the artist himself could explain why, sometime in the early 1980s, he experienced a great hunger for the thinglike mass that the art of the modeller creates. Perhaps it was a simple matter of surfeit. After all, there have been astonishing stylistic shifts in the twentieth century that can only be accounted for as the craving for change that comes after an overabundance of any kind. The century had seen the art of sculpture increasingly condensed until, as Tucker himself showed, it was sometimes the mere wisp of a hairfine line floating into infinity. Now Tucker needed the other experience: he coveted the sense of life that drags itself up, struggles from its stern magnet, the ground, to unknown realms of feeling. He wanted to take a lump of matter and shape it, pull it, so that it rose and stood in the world, a thing. Some of the experiments with plaster in the early 1980s would take on the lineaments of figures struggling into resistant spaces. They sprang forward or back into anthropomorphic gestures. In the *Guardians* there were distinct allusions to the thrust of bodies; true torsion that might have been mined from the substance of Michelangelo's slaves. The *Gymnasts* that followed were still more suggestive. Tucker embodied gestures, or rather, made physical metaphors that suggested gestures, while holding the objects to the ground by their enormous implied weight. These pieces lunging into space were scarcely larger than a man, but they had all the implications of massive, even monumental sculpture. They spoke of deep intuitions. Effort. Resisting gravity is no mean feat. They struggled up like Beethoven's Grosse Fugue, that jarring, scraping ascent to the crescendo: life-likeness. The shock of these lumpy presences and the extremist nature of the analogue to human emotions brought Tucker to the brink of an outright figurative art. But the 'aspiration' of which he had once spoken is larger. Tucker created presences that overwhelmed their designated space; jostled them and shaped them, and gathered up in their being references that range far wider than merely the human figure in his upright contest with the forces of nature.

Excerpt from Dore Ashton, 'William Tucker's Aspiration', *William Tucker, Gods: Five Recent Sculptures* (catalogue), The Tate Gallery, London, 1987

TETHYS, 1985
Bronze
188 × 119.3 × 162.5

(Photo) Sarah Wells

Tuckson had great admiration for what he called Pollock's 'going on for ever' paintings.

His own childhood drum set, his love of the endless, ecstatic improvisations in jazz are related qualities. In his last years he played Beethoven, Mozart, Bach over and over again, furious with envy of music: 'The buggers, listen to it—how do they do it?'

Yet he had a sharp awareness of the brevity of things. He told Joe Szabo, 'Life's too short to bother with philistines'. He often observed that most painters have been better when young, especially in Australia. He had been racing against death all his life—by painting so hard, by keeping so close to the energy sources in new art and in his fellow artists—and his early death was not out of character.

In the context of Australian art, with whom should he be compared?

Aboriginal art had first been admired by Margaret Preston, but although Tuckson respected her for bringing Aboriginal art to our attention, he was not influenced by her Aboriginal-style paintings of the 1940s. He noted that her work was excellent within a 'decorative' style, and by implication that it lacked emotion. Tuckson was influenced by Aboriginal art in less obvious ways than Preston. Margaret Tuckson says it first interested him for its casual way of filling an area, the lack of worry about shapes spilling over outlines. He said it was too easy if you used a lot of colour and his deliberate limitation of colour both in the scribbly, earth-textured period and in the red, black and white period may have something to do with Aboriginal art. So also might the fine linearism of his scribbly period.

But the influence of modern painting was surely more important than that of Aboriginal art. Picasso, Klee, Dubuffet, and to a lesser extent Pollock and De Kooning, were the formative influences.

He must be considered in the context of other Australian pioneers of Abstract Expressionism in the late 1950s, with artists like Ralph Balson, John Passmore, John Howley, John Olsen, Elwyn Lynn and, slightly later, Michael Taylor. They also were more influenced by Europe than America, but unlike Tuckson many Australian abstract expressionists remained painters of Australian landscape. Only Balson was purely non-figurative. In Tuckson it is the figure, not the landscape, which maintains a ghostly presence, occasionally as a just-recognisable face, always as an insistence on his own physical process of making the work, and in the last paintings as emphatic verticality.

Watteau's *Gilles* prompted the most lyrical dissertation Tuckson ever gave me on a single painting. It is a full-length, life-size man in white satin, standing straight, his round face gazing directly at the spectator. Though not a self-portrait, Watteau clearly identified himself with this image. Tuckson had a similarly poignant sense of being present in his own work, as well as a Watteauesque tenderness with shimmering white surfaces.

When impersonal Hard-edge painting swept Australia in the late 1960s, Tuckson resisted masking-tape and, for someone so interested in new art, it was a kind of crisis to have to fight against a new style. His solution, in the paintings of the 1970s, looks less like a reflection of the then current Lyrical Abstraction than a return to the more austere contemporaries of Pollock, like Barnett Newman, whose verticals are often an abstract sign for Man.

And in spite of his extreme sensitivity to all new art movements he was not eclectic. He was painting only about himself. A linear expressiveness is found in all his works.

Although he might have pretended to dismiss James Gleeson's reviews of his two exhibitions as 'Just words', Tuckson really liked them very much. James Gleeson ('The travail of painting', *Sun-Herald*, 22 April 1973) should have the last word: 'What he is on about is the act of painting. His pictures are about what it feels like to paint a picture—and as Tuckson feels it, a large part of it is agony.

'Making a painting or indeed any kind of art is a kind of birth. There is labour involved . . . Tuckson isn't interested in the art that conceals the effort. He shows the making of a painting with all the travail fully exposed, without prettification or pretence that it hasn't hurt; there is something almost shocking in the completeness of the exposure . . .

'In the end he triumphs because he does communicate his urgency through the painting. The pictures become a point of contact.

'The viewer who takes the risk of opening himself to these works will be rewarded by a rare glimpse of the emotional and physical costs of creativity.'

Excerpt from Daniel Thomas, Introduction to *Tony Tuckson 1921–1973* (catalogue), Watters Gallery, Sydney, 1982, first published in *Tony Tuckson 1921–1973: memorial exhibition* (catalogue), Art Gallery of New South Wales, 1976

WHITE LINES (HORIZONTAL) ON RED, 1970/73
Acrylic on hardboard
183 × 137.5
Collection: National Gallery of Victoria

The tremendous energy released by a bolt of lightning is potential energy. Latent in the atmosphere, inverse charges build up within the mounting storm clouds until a critical threshold is reached, and in an instant (about one tenth to half the speed of light) hundreds of thousands of volts of electrical energy are discharged, the stream of electrons forcibly burning a path through the non-conducting air, often jumping the gap between sky and earth.

And all this in a moment, in a time narrower than our tiniest thought, yet the image of lightning, in addition to leaving a momentary afterimage on the retina, is forever imprinted in the mind's eye of all who have ever experienced an electrical storm. We realise that we have seen this image before and are constantly seeing it as the diverse forms of nature continue to reveal their deeper common origins. We see the tree against the grey November sky; we see the river and its tributaries from an airplane window; we see the array of blood vessels in the body or web of the brain's interconnecting nerve cells in a medical film, we sense a thought as it grows and branches out in our minds and lives.

The axis of the lightning bolt is the vertical, it travels along the line connecting heaven and earth. It is the same axis on which the individual stands when he or she walks out onto the great plain under the dome of the sky. It is the line that connects the ground they stand on to the deepest layer of time-lines in the geological strata of the earth far below, visible in the slice of the canyon wall. It is the path which the tree reveals as it stands and which is already contained in its seed. It is the same along which the tree at the centre of the world grows, the 'axis mundi' described by Eliade, Campbell, Jung and others in their *re*-searches and reintroductions of that which we already have known into our newly conscious contemporary minds.

In our horizontal models of time and movement, our image of the sediments of time, our expressions of 'down' through history and 'up' through evolution, the vertical pole becomes the continuous present, the connecting thread, the simultaneous, perpetual 'now' that we are living at this instant and have always lived. It is the single point which, when displaced becomes the line, becomes the surface, becomes the solid forms of our world and minds, and which, without the imparted energy of movement (time) or the direction of movement (space) becomes the point once more, a process incremented by our breath as we each recapitulate its great form in the course of our individual journey.

There was a moment in pre-history when a large animal slumped down with its last breath and thoughts to leave its bones in the earth that the researcher is carefully sifting through in the fossil pit. There was a moment when the Cro-Magnon artist lifted the pigment-dipped natural fibre brush to the walls of the cave that one now enters with electric light to view the image of the ancient bison on its walls. There was a moment when your father died, and his before that, and the same moment when the impulse and attraction between two human beings fused into the one that is yourself, as you will do/have done so many times in the past. There is a moment when the newborn first lets out a cry into the dry air, when the pressure of light first falls on the virgin surface of the new retina and is registered by some pattern of nerve impulses not yet fully 'understood'. There is a single moment when the flash of insight bursts into your unguarded mind, when all the pieces fall together, when the pattern is seen or the individual element uncovered . . . when the breath of clarity opens the mind and you 'see' for the first time in a long while, remembering what it was like again as if suddenly jolted from sleep. There is a moment when a single neuron fires in the darkness within the brain, when a threshold is reached and a tiny spark jumps the gap that physically separates one cell from another, doing the same shimmering dance when the heat of the flame touches the skin or a deep memory replays on the surface of the mind. There is a moment, only truly known in anticipation before it happens, when the eyes close for the last time and the brain shuts down its circuits forever (the end of time). There is also the moment of recognition, the return of the familiar, the second-time perception that releases the latent energy and excitement of the first. It can be in a face, in a landscape, in a desire. Then there is the moment of awareness of the other, embodied in the physical separation of mother and child, and restated from the first conceptualisation of persons and objects in a space outside the skin, to the first encounter with an animal in the wild. The power of the gaze crystallises these moments, and the eyes become the conduits of the exchange of energies between the organism and the environment, between the observer and the observed. A line of sight can just as easily slice through the separation between subject and object as it can define it.

As the gateway to the soul, the pupil of the eye has long been a powerful symbolic image and evocative physical object in the search for knowledge of the self. The colour of the pupil is black. It is on this black that you see your self-image when you try to look closely into your own eye, or into the eye of another . . . the largeness of your own image preventing you an unobstructed view within. It is the source of the laughter that culminates the staring game that young children play, and the source of the pressure that a stranger feels on their back in public as they turn to meet the eyes they know are there. It is through this black that we confront the gaze of an animal, partly with fear, with curiosity, with familiarity, with mystery. We see ourselves in its eyes while sensing the irreconcilable otherness of an intelligence ordered around a world we can share in body but not in mind.

Black is a bright light on a dark day, like staring into the sun, the intensity of the source producing the darkness of the protection of the closed eye. It is the black we 'see' when all the lights have been turned off, the space between the glowing electron lines of the video image, the space after the last cut of a film, or the luminous black of the nights of the new moon. If there is a light there, it is only the light searching in the dark room, which, limited by the optical channel within its beam, assumes there to be light everywhere it turns.

Notes by the artist for Laserdisc, BETA/VHS, *I Do Not Know What It Is I Am Like*, published by Voyager Press and The Contemporary Art Television Fund, 1986.

I DO NOT KNOW WHAT IT IS I AM LIKE, 1986
Videotape, colour, stereo sound

(Photo) Kira Perov

267

JEFF WALL

Born Vancouver, Canada, 1946

Lives and works in Vancouver

LUMINESCENCE

ELS BARENTS: The technological form of back-lit transparencies is a sort of 'super-photography'. It relates to aspects of mass spectacle as well as to bureaucratic ways of presenting information. Your metal boxes emit a light which makes the images very absorbing, and because the photography is so clear we are invited to look at the pictures very closely. But at the same time, they seem to be immaterial projections that can be seen just as well from a distance. Despite their very realistic subject matter, the transparencies have a dreamlike presence. The intensity of colour and light and the large scale of the works creates a dimension that's hard to describe. I know you place great importance on the interconnections between different technologies that create this effect, and also on the interconnections between these technologies and the art of painting, which you admire tremendously. How did you develop this set of connections for yourself?

JEFF WALL: I hadn't been to Europe for four or five years since I lived there in the early seventies. Then in 1977 I went back for a holiday with my family. Among other museums, I visited the Prado for the first time and looked at Velazquez, Goya, Titian. I remember coming back to Vancouver and thinking once again how powerful those pictures were, how much I loved them. And also, how they contained innumerable traces of their own modernity.

But I also felt that it was impossible to return to anything resembling the idea of the 'painter of modern life', as Baudelaire termed it. And yet I think that in many ways for modernism that's a fundamental term, 'the painter of modern life'. Because there is no more appropriate occupation. It's a complete occupation because the art form, painting, is the greatest art form and the subject is the greatest subject. But, as I said, I felt very strongly at that time that it was impossible, because painting as an art form did not encounter directly enough the problem of the technological product which had so extensively usurped its place and its function in the representation of everyday life. It's interesting because of course this was just at the time when a lot of young artists were rediscovering painting. I remember being in a kind of crisis at the time, wondering what I would do. Just at that moment I saw an illuminated sign somewhere, and it struck me very strongly that here was the perfect synthetic technology for me. It was not photography, it was not cinema, it was not painting, it was not propaganda, but it has strong associations with them all. It was something extremely open. It seemed to be the technique in which this problem could be expressed, maybe the only technique because of its fundamental spectacularity. That satisfied the primary expectation of the product of technology, which is that it represents by means of the spectacle.

I think there's a basic fascination in technology which derives from the fact that there's always a hidden space—a control room, a projection booth, a source of light of some kind—from which the image comes. A painting on canvas, no matter how good it is, is to our eyes more or less flat, or at least flatter than the luminescent image of cinema, television, or the transparencies. One of the reasons for this is that the painting or the ordinary photograph is lit with the same light that falls in the room and onto the spectator him- or herself. But the luminescent image is fascinating because it's lit with another atmosphere. So two atmospheres intersect to make the image. One of them, the hidden one, is more powerful than the other. In a painting, for example, the source or the site of the image is palpably in front of you. You can actually touch the place where the image comes from, where it is. But in a luminescent picture the source of the image is hidden and the thing is a dematerialised or semi-dematerialised projection. The site from which the image originates is always elsewhere. And this 'elsewhere' is experienced, maybe consciously, maybe not, in experiencing the image. Rimbaud said, 'Existence is elsewhere', and Malevich once wrote, 'Only that which cannot be touched can be sacred'. To me, this experience of two places, two worlds, in one moment is a central form of the experience of modernity. It's an experience of dissociation, of alienation. In it, space—the space inside and outside of the picture—is experienced as it really exists in capitalism: there is always a point of control, of projection, which is inaccessible. It is a classical site of power. I see it as an analogue of capitalist social relations, which are relations of dissociation. We are permitted to play the game of transformation of nature, the great festival of metamorphosis, only by going through capital, by being subjected to the laws of capital. For example, you can't turn seeds into plants without going through, or into, capital. Ask any farmer. Something becomes inaccessible to us as we work on it. Thus we are both in the game and separated from it at the same time. The technological product, as we currently experience it from within capitalism, recapitulates this situation in its experiential structure, which gives us something very intensely and at the same time makes it remote.

Furthermore, the fascination of this technology for me is that it seems that it alone permits me to make pictures in the traditional way. Because that's basically what I do, although I hope it is done with an effect that is opposite to that of technically traditional pictures. The opportunity is both to recuperate the past—the great art of the museums—and at the same time to participate with a critical effect in the most up-to-date spectacularity. This gives my work its particular relation to painting. I like to think that my pictures are a specific opposite to painting.

Excerpt from Els Barents, 'Typology, Luminescence, Freedom: Selections from a conversation with Jeff Wall', *Jeff Wall: Transparencies*, Schirmer/Mosel, Munich and Rizzoli, New York, 1987

THE OLD PRISON, 1987
Cibachrome transparency, fluorescent light, display case
74 × 246.5 × 20.5

STEVES FARM, STEVESTON, 1980
Cibachrome transparency, fluorescent light, display case
74 × 246.5 × 20.5

Born Pittsburgh, Pennsylvania, USA, 1928

Died New York, 1987

It is appropriate, I think, to memorialise Warhol in the medium of metaphysics, for he functioned at every stage as an instrument of philosophical demonstrations, even if he was never conscious of the theorems he proved or disproved. Whatever he did must accordingly be appreciated on two levels of history, one of them extremely deep, so that a second, philosophical story must be told when the first, or art-historical, story has been told. On the surface level of history, he was, of course, in the great first generation of Pop artists which, on the deep level of the philosophical history of art, broke every rule its immediate predecessors, also great artists, had sought to hammer in to the ruling definition of art, proving that the denial of a definition of art is itself a definition of art. Artmaking in New York in the 1950s transpired in a mist of romantic theorising and an almost religious celebration of what one might call the blood and flesh of painting, namely the material stuff of art. The drip, the swipe, the smear, the scrub of paint, the stroke, the swag, the slash, the spatter were vested with an intensity of meaning that ordinarily attaches only to sacramental gestures. And abstraction was dogmatised with such ferocity that artists carried the thrill of heresy in their hearts when they in secret believed in The Image. It was a dour, puritanical period when artists walked Tenth Street in their paint-streaked garments to demonstrate their oneness with their art, and gathered at The Club to shout themselves out over minute questions of orthodoxy. The Pop artist used this creed as a sort of punch-list, violating systematically every point of dogma, and the sense of exhilaration that exploded in the art world when this was achieved is an index of liberation. From then on everything was permitted, and when Roy Lichtenstein produced an *image* of a brush-stroke, embellished with pictures of drips and splatters, imprisoned in outlines as sharp as if printed and rendered in comic-book colours, it became plain that the theories of Abstract Expressionism belonged to the history rather than the philosophy of art. To have demonstrated that was a philosophical act.

Because of the slurried surfaces of Abstract Expressionist painting, it was urgent, in making a revolutionary transit from abstraction to realism, to select a subject or set of subjects as antithetical to expressionist treatment as possible. After all, such traditional subjects as the female form, the landscape or the still life all had a history of expressionist presentation. It was a stroke of genius to use the hard, the mechanical, the instantly recognised objects of commercial reality for this purpose—the soup can, the ketchup bottle, the Coke bottle, the cereal box—or the more familiar effigies from the comic-strip world—Mickey Mouse or Nancy. It does not matter which came first—the subject or the style—and of course there would be transitional works, like an expressionist Nancy, for example. Jasper Johns abandoned expressionism late, and there is a story that Warhol showed his mentor, the filmmaker Emile de Antonio, two soup-can paintings, one of them expressionistically brushy and the other mechanical and linear, not knowing which direction to take. His early Dick Tracy and his Popeye initially used the *maniera* of expressionism superstitiously, as it were, as if it were dangerous to abandon it; but it would have become plain, sooner or later, as it was immediately plain to de Antonio, that the revolution could be achieved only by employing a style as nearly mechanical as the subjects themselves—the printed label, the industrially produced container. And though this could be done by cultivating a certain dexterity—by stifling the impulse to expression by disciplining the hand—the question emerged of what the point of this any longer was: why not just take over the methods of mechanical reproduction themselves? Indeed, the mechanical means became as integral to the work as the free brush stroke had been in the repudiated works.

And with this, something remarkable was achieved: first, the insertion into pictorial space of objects heretofore unredeemed and perhaps unredeemable for art—tomato-soup cans where saints and madonnas once flourished; second, a mode of presentation so mechanical, by contrast with painterly, that mechanical reproduction was itself elevated to the vocabulary of expression; and finally, by making the products of commercial art the subject of high art, the blurring of the invidious distinction between the two in such a way that the highly successful commercial artist, Warhol himself, was able to achieve the status of a highly successful high artist without changing a thing. Warhol rose to the top by turning the art world inside-out and upside-down, rather than by attempting, like, say, Gauguin, to turn *himself* inside-out and upside-down. It was a triumph of artistic will scarcely paralleled in the history of art, and all the more astonishing because his motives were openly crass: he wanted to be rich, a famous artist, a superstar. Pop! 'Isn't that the sound,' we might imagine him saying when asked for its definition, 'a bubble makes when it bursts?'

Once the mechanical, and hence the precisely repetitious, had become the form and substance of the new art, the barriers were removed against its mass production, so that the artwork could be a kind of industrial product and the studio itself a kind of factory. Warhol instantly grasped all the components in an entire new system of the arts, and it is characteristic of him that he made the move into mass production for a crass motive and managed to achieve a philosophical triumph. By transforming art, he transformed the entire relationship between reality and art, making reality an internal feature of art itself . . .

Warhol generated intellectual energy, always, by disregarding and hence erasing boundaries that separated what one would have supposed to be logically distinct orders of things, and allowing them to explode into one another through conceptual collapse. It was part of his cunning to have used the most banal mechanisms of artistic expression—the home movie camera, the Polaroid, the paint-by-number canvas board—and by the zero degree of intervention to have raised to consciousness the irrelevant prejudices of aesthetics . . .

Excerpts from Arthur C. Danto, 'Who was Andy Warhol?',
ARTnews, May 1987

Of all these artists, Warhol took the most radical steps to redefine the place of art within the continuum of culture. In the first waves of what could be termed a post-modern sensibility, during the 1950s, there had been a steady erosion of the vanguard artist's traditional elitist position, but it was Warhol who most decisively accepted mass culture as an arena of concern every bit as compelling as the privileged angst of the fine-art specialist. Warhol claimed to 'like' everything, and in doing so he tore down the barriers between art and life with a shocking finality. In laying claim to this populist aesthetic, he demonstrated an intuitive grasp of the semiotics of power in a capitalist democracy, for by liking everything, he made it clear that he finds everything to be alike. For Warhol (and he shows us this in every aspect of his work), all cultural objects, high and low, share an identifying similarity: they are merely tokens of exchange, endlessly reproducible signs of wealth and power.

Excerpt from Thomas Lawson, 'The Future is Certain',
Individuals: A Selected History of Contemporary Art 1945–86,
Museum of Contemporary Art, Los Angeles, Abbeville Press,
New York, 1986/88

DOUBLE LAST SUPPER — JESUS, 1985
Acrylic on canvas
304.8 × 670.6

A new wave of historians, writing about Australia, has observed that our relationship to space and place is central to our sense of ourselves. Our accomplishment as a people has become our sense of conquering the land. Very much the antipodean, Caroline Williams is engaged in using landscape to define a sense of self, to define mankind's relationship to nature and its equivocal history, and most importantly, to define a relationship to the traditions of depicting landscape. Since the seventeenth century, when landscape painting came of age, artists have been intent upon making the landscape symbolise a fairly impressive range of spiritual, emotional, moral and imaginative states. In keeping with the best of this tradition, Williams' art is at once intelligent, accessible and satisfying to look at.

The pictures for which Williams has become known in recent years in Australia and her native New Zealand dwell on the gap between culture and nature. In a previous series this is evidenced in witty, ironic pictures in which bewigged eighteenth century gentlemen stride proprietorially across antipodean prospects. Their presence is at once serious and ridiculous. As a gesture of intent these gentlemen are sometimes observed measuring the land either with instruments or by stride. That they do so in the elegant, vivid frockcoats of eighteenth century European civilisation, as though they have escaped from a Stubbs or a Reynolds and are determined not to appear discomforted, seems to us preposterous. Though this is undoubtedly an apt way of characterising the nature of colonisation, it is precisely because they have stepped out of eighteenth-century landscape painting and into Williams' panoramic sweep of weather-troubled wilderness that their rituals are made surreal. So while ideas of the sublime in landscape are evoked, and are indeed essential to Williams' conception, it is irony that prevails. In some earlier pictures Williams depicts similarly attired figures carrying a cross—the making and breaking of civilisation is here attested to, and clearly this is a male province.

In the later works seen here, the sense of place portrayed by landscape has become less specific, temporally as well as spatially. The figures have disappeared, and the sweeping vistas which conjured the uncolonised lands give way to brooding landscapes of craggy mountainous terrain and skies portentous of weather. The landscape might be any wild, lonely and romantic place. These images are distinguished by the dark, uneasy presence of archaeological remains or monolithic intrusions. For Williams there never was a golden age, no Claudian evanescent glow bathes these landscapes, nor are the archaeological remains remotely classical. Certain atmospheric qualities in the earlier pictures, especially in the luminous handling of skies and the generally sombre hues of the shadowed earth, already suggesting the romantic landscapes of the late eighteenth and nineteenth centuries, are now more clearly in the service of a genuinely romantic, even gothic sensibility. Like the *Capricci* of Piranesi, especially the Prison series, Williams conjures a mythic sense of the past. Man's vaulting ambition is doomed to defeat by nature, though the grim but picturesque reminders survive.

Though all these paintings are enriched by our knowledge of history and its images, the meaning in each is perfectly clear. With many artists meaning can only be attained cumulatively—in modern parlance, we can only 'read' an individual painting after exposure to part or all of the artist's oeuvre. The allegory which Williams employs is not dependent on an idiosyncratic mythology, though it may well contain such elements. Nor is it dependent upon careful explanation.

Williams cut her teeth on paintings in the grand manner. New Zealand, like Melbourne, is well-endowed with eighteenth century British paintings. One particular painting, much in the manner of Richard Wilson, hung in her father's club. It was vast, commanding and beautifully crafted—epic and permanently impressive in her artistic development.

Her paintings are romantic in that they deal with the sublime (with grandeur, decay and the forces of nature) and they are also moral in that Williams imbues the terrible with a sense of man's destructive intrusions. All the paintings are strikingly evocative and atmospheric. They touch our imaginative and sensuous response to landscape and man's presence in it. There is nothing arbitrary, gratuitous or effete about these pictures as there is with much neo-romantic painting. They sit solidly within a long, vivid and varied history of landscape painting.

Elizabeth Cross

PAINTING, 1987
Oil on canvas
147 × 176.4

FRED WILLIAMS

Born Melbourne, Australia, 1927

Died Melbourne, 1982

Almost everything in Williams's art derives from direct contact with the motif. For over thirty years his working week has contained at least one day spent painting *en plein air*. Gouache or watercolour are his media or, more frequently in the 1970s, oil sketches, and there are occasional drawings. During holidays or visits to specific painting sites, Williams may paint daily for a fortnight or more directly from nature.

Gouache series painted directly from nature are frequently seen as complete in themselves, not as studies to be worked up into full-scale paintings at a later date. The gouaches themselves may be reworked in the studio. Similarly, the oil sketches made on the spot may remain as a series and not receive further working. This is particularly true of the early 1970s when Williams began to sketch more consistently in oil. The oil sketches form a repertoire of motifs, a quarry of experience, from which he selects and draws at will, sometimes even making a composite work from different sketches. Even when a series has begun, Williams will return to the motif in nature, making further studies to amplify his earlier experiences and retain the freshness of his inspiration. In some instances, Williams actually etches the subject before painting it as he did in 1965 in a number of major works such as the Oval and Circle Landscapes. The etchings and prints generally come at the end of the creative cycle and are the codification of the work, its lasting memory.

Thus the relationship of Williams's experience of the landscape to final work is a complex and variable one. Underlying all this is a common and constant search for formal invention. Although known as a landscape painter, he is that only in a particular sense: his art draws more continuously on landscape motifs than on anything else. For he rarely paints a 'view' of the landscape, nor is the character or feature of a given place of particular interest to him. Thus, in the 1960s, a Lysterfield landscape could be virtually interchangeable with a You Yangs landscape. The same units of form, the same palette, even similar compositions, could encompass both. Likewise, he is rarely interested in capturing atmospheric effects. Although at different stages he has frequently adopted an aerial point of view, few landscapes are as consistently airless as those of Fred Williams.

Williams's aim and goal, the strategy of his art, is to realise fully the pictorial form occasioned by the motif in the landscape. His chief efforts as a painter are spent clarifying and elaborating the pictorial structure suggested to him in that direct contact and experience of nature. Although many of his oil sketches and gouaches are miracles of observation, their purpose is to furnish further pictorial possibilities. What he makes, not what he sees, is the centre and focus of his activity—although what he makes always proceeds from what he has seen.

It is incorrect to see this process as 'abstracting from nature', a process that brings in its train the perverse judgement that the landscape element has held Williams back, that he is somehow not prepared to go 'all the way' into abstract painting. What Williams does is work at the motif until he becomes so familiar with it, possessing it so intimately that the forms given to him in the landscape become as natural and personal to him as handwriting. The process of his art, its slow period of gestation from initial experience to finished painting, is essentially one of transforming his experience of the landscape into a handwritten code.

The character of Fred Williams's art depends on its constant recourse to nature—its variety and diversity constantly renew his art. Of all his generation, Williams has understood most clearly, and acted most strenuously upon, the knowledge that paintings are made with paint, not with ideas or concepts, not with myths or legends, not from the imposing theme or the ambitious thought. It is not his experience, but the translation of that experience into paint that makes up his art.

Excerpts from Patrick McCaughey, *Fred Williams*, Bay Books,
Sydney, 1980

UPWEY HILL, 1966
Oil on canvas
112 × 127

RENATE ANGER
UNTITLED, 1986
Egg tempera on cotton
Two pieces, 350 × 155
Courtesy of the artist

UNTITLED, 1986
Jute
6 pieces, 210 × 80 × 2
Courtesy of the artist

TOM ARTHUR
THE ENTIRE CONTENTS OF A GENTLEMAN'S
ROOM—THE LOCATION OF MEANING, 1988
Mixed media installation
540 × 480 × 720
Courtesy of the artist

RICHARD ARTSCHWAGER
WEAVING, 1987
Acrylic on celotex and wood
157 × 136 × 10
Courtesy of Leo Castelli Gallery, New York

GIANNI ASDRUBALI
NEMICO, 1987
Acrylic on canvas
223 × 190
Courtesy of the artist

NEMICO, 1987
Acrylic on canvas
350 × 230
Courtesy of the artist

NEMICO, 1987
Acrylic on canvas
230 × 165
Courtesy of the artist

FRANCIS BACON
STUDY FROM THE HUMAN BODY, 1949
Oil on canvas
147 × 134.2
Courtesy of National Gallery of Victoria,
Melbourne

RALPH BALSON
UNTITLED, 1961
Enamel on hardboard
76.4 × 137.3
Courtesy of Art Gallery of
New South Wales, Sydney
Gift of Dr Pearson, 1984

NON-OBJECTIVE ABSTRACT, 1958
Oil on composition board
137.2 × 152.4
Courtesy of National Gallery of Victoria,
Melbourne

CONSTRUCTIVE PAINTING, 1950
Oil on composition board
120.8 × 121
Courtesy of National Gallery of Victoria,
Melbourne

BALTHUS
NUDE WITH CAT, 1949
Oil on canvas
65 × 80.5
Courtesy of National Gallery of Victoria,

Melbourne
Felton Bequest

MAX BECKMANN
SOLDATENKNEIPE (SOLDIERS' PUB), 1948
Oil on canvas
55.5 × 85
Courtesy of Staatsgalerie, Stuttgart

AFTERNOON, 1946
Oil on canvas on plywood
89.5 × 133.5
Courtesy of Museum am Ostwall,
Dortmund

OLD WOMAN IN ERMINE, 1946
Oil on canvas
150.5 × 80.5
Courtesy of Art Gallery of
New South Wales, Sydney

MICHAEL BIBERSTEIN
UNTITLED (DIPTYCH), 1987
Acrylic on linen and acrylic on wood
180 × 160 × 5
Courtesy of Galeria Marga Paz, Madrid

UNTITLED (DIPTYCH), 1987
Oil on canvas and acrylic on wood
35 × 58 × 4
Courtesy of Galeria Marga Paz, Madrid

UNTITLED (DIPTYCH), 1987
Oil on canvas and acrylic on wood
34 × 55 × 3
Courtesy of Collection Ruefli, Switzerland

UNTITLED (DIPTYCH), 1987
Oil on canvas and acrylic on wood
38 × 64 × 3
Courtesy of Lydia Megert Gallery, Berne

ROSS BLECKNER
SINISTER BEND, 1987
Oil on canvas
274.3 × 182.9
Courtesy of Perry Rubenstein, New York

HOSPITAL ROOM, 1985
Oil on linen
122 × 101.6
Courtesy of Steven and Diane Jacobson,
New York City, and Mary Boone Gallery,
New York

CHRISTIAN BOLTANSKI
ARCHIVES: DETECTIVE, 1987
Photographs, metal biscuit boxes, electric
lights
400 × 1000
Courtesy of The Ydessa Art Foundation,
Toronto

PIERRE BONNARD
LA SIESTE, 1900
Oil on canvas
110 × 131
Courtesy of National Gallery of Victoria,
Melbourne
Felton Bequest

PETER BOOTH
BANSHEE, 1986
Oil on canvas
152 × 127
Courtesy of University of Melbourne Art
Collection

PAINTING, 1986
Oil on canvas
167 × 244
Courtesy of Heide Park and Art Gallery,
Melbourne

MARIE BOURGET
FOUR TABLEAUX, 1987
Silkscreen on plastic
4 works, each 120 × 100
Courtesy of the artist

HAUT RELIEF, 1985/87
Six framed works under glass, each 20 × 60
One work in painted iron, 167 × 60 × 20
Courtesy of the artist

ARTHUR BOYD
BATHERS AND PULPIT ROCK, 1984/85
Oil on canvas
244 × 457
Courtesy of Queensland Art Gallery,
Brisbane

CEMETERY II, 1944
Oil on cotton gauze on cardboard
51.3 × 63.2
Courtesy of Australian National Gallery,
Canberra.
The Arthur Boyd Gift 1975

LOVERS IN A BOAT, 1944
Oil on cotton gauze on cardboard
50.6 × 63
Courtesy of Australian National Gallery,
Canberra.
The Arthur Boyd Gift 1975

BUTTERFLY MAN, 1943
Oil on muslin on composition board
55.5 × 75.5
Courtesy of Heide Park and Art Gallery,
Melbourne

CRUCIFIXION (THE KITE), 1942
Oil on muslin on cardboard
55.4 × 68.7
Courtesy of Heide Park and Art Gallery,
Melbourne

GEORGES BRAQUE
BARQUE SUR LES GALETS, 1959
Oil on canvas
24 × 42
Courtesy of Galerie Maeght, Paris

LES CHAMPS (CIEL BAS), 1956
Oil on canvas
27 × 45
Courtesy of Galerie Maeght, Paris

LA PLAINE I, 1955/56
Oil on canvas
20 × 73
Courtesy of Galerie Maeght, Paris

PAYSAGE À LA CHARRUE, 1955
Oil on canvas
34 × 64
Courtesy of Galerie Maeght, Paris

JULIE BROWN-RRAP
TRANSPOSITIONS: THE INVISIBLE BODY, 1988
Mixed media
Courtesy of Mori Gallery, Sydney

GRADIVA/GRAVIDA—PHILOSOPHIES OF THE
BOUDOIR, 1985/86

Photo-emulsion, acrylic, oil on canvas on three-ply
Two panels, each 122 × 183
Courtesy of Eva and Tom Breuer

GÜNTER BRUS
DER SELBSTMENSCH, 1987
Crayon on paper
Series of five, each 106.5 × 80.5
Courtesy of private collection, Düsseldorf

MICHAEL BUTHE
LE DERNIER SECRET DE FATIMA, 1986
Oil and silver on canvas
200 × 460
Courtesy of the artist

LE DERNIER SECRET DE FATIMA, 1986
Oil and gold on canvas
200 × 460
Courtesy of the artist

GENEVIÈVE CADIEUX
LA BLESSURE D'UNE CICATRICE OU
LES ANGES, 1987
Photo enlargement, gouache, paper and
wood frame
Two elements, 297 × 231 × 17 and
300 × 300 × 9
Courtesy of Galerie René Blouin, Montreal

SARAH CHARLESWORTH
GOLD DIGGERS (DIPTYCH), 1987
Laminated Cibachrome prints with
lacquer frame
Two interlocking panels, each 101.6 × 76.2
Courtesy of private collection

BUDDHA OF IMMEASURABLE LIGHT
(DIPTYCH), 1987
Laminated Cibachrome prints with
lacquer frame
Two interlocking panels, each 101.6 × 76.2
Courtesy of private collection

HANNAH COLLINS
WHERE WORDS FAIL COMPLETELY, 1987
Gelatin silver prints mounted on canvas
Two panels, 244 × 167.6 and 244 × 305
Courtesy of the artist

THIN PROTECTIVE COVERINGS II, 1986
Gelatin silver print mounted on canvas
670 × 366
Courtesy of Matt's Gallery, London

ROBERT COMBAS
LE BEAUJOLAIS NOUVEAU EST ARRIVÉ, 1986
Acrylic on canvas
235 × 302
Courtesy of Galerie Yvon Lambert, Paris

LA BASSE COUR À GERMAINE TAILLEFER,
LA GROUPIE DU CURÉ, 1986
Acrylic on canvas
205 × 230
Courtesy of private collection, Paris

BACCHANALE, 1985
Acrylic on canvas
200 × 338
Courtesy of Galerie Yvon Lambert, Paris

NEIL DAWSON
RIPPLES 2, 1988
PVC, rigid foam, carbon fibre, epoxy resin,
stainless steel wire

450 × 600 × 0.3
Technical associate Bruce Edgar
Courtesy of the artist
Located in the gardens of the Art Gallery of
New South Wales

WILLEM DE KOONING
TWO TREES ON MARY STREET . . .
AMEN!, 1975
Oil on canvas
203.2 × 177.8
Courtesy of Queensland Art Gallery,
Brisbane

WOMAN, 1950
Oil on canvas
163 × 117.5
Courtesy of the permanent collection of
Weatherspoon Art Gallery, University of
North Carolina, Greensboro
Lena Kernodle McDuffie Memorial Gift

RICHARD DEACON
LISTENING TO REASON, 1986
Laminated timber
226 × 609 × 579
Courtesy of Marian Goodman Gallery,
New York

ART FOR OTHER PEOPLE No 4, 1982
Black cloth and steel rods
30.5 × 183 × 30.5
Courtesy of Art Gallery of
New South Wales, Sydney

MARCEL DUCHAMP
LA BOÎTE EN VALISE, 1936/68
Mixed media
74 × 174 × 142
Courtesy of Musée National d'Art
Moderne, Centre Georges Pompidou, Paris

WHY NOT SNEEZE ROSE SÉLAVY?, 1921
Reconstructed by Galleria Schwarz, Milan,
1964; no 4 from an edition of 8
Painted metal birdcage, marble cubes,
thermometer and cuttlebone
12.4 × 22.2 × 16.2
Courtesy of Australian National Gallery,
Canberra

LILI DUJOURIE
UNTITLED, 1987
Water sculpture/fountain installation
360 × 160 × 210
Courtesy of Foundation for Independent
Art-Historical Research (St. OKO),
Holland

L'AURORE, 1987
Marble and plaster
250 × 650 × 120
Courtesy of Joost Declercq, Gent

LESLEY DUMBRELL
FOXGLOVE (TRIPTYCH), 1987
Acrylic on canvas
Three panels, each 213.3 × 152.4
Courtesy of Art Gallery of
Western Australia, Perth

AZZURUM, 1987
Acrylic on canvas
198 × 198
Courtesy of Christine Abrahams Gallery,
Melbourne

RICHARD DUNN
ONE HUNDRED BLOSSOMS—
THE STUDIO, 1988
Charcoal and pastel on paper, timber
construction
250 × 60 × 600
Courtesy of the artist

ONE HUNDRED BLOSSOMS (DETAIL), 1988
Charcoal and pastel on multiple sheets of
paper, each 76 × 56
Dimensions variable, each panel 76 × 112
Courtesy of the artist

BRIAN ENO
MORE DARK THAN SHARK
Videotape, 1985
Colour, stereo, PAL
Courtesy of Opal Ltd

Book compiled by Brian Eno and Russell
Mills, Faber and Faber, London, 1986

Interview with Russell Mills
Video clip
Courtesy of the artist

LUCIANO FABRO
NUDE DESCENDING A STAIRCASE, 1987
Marble
6 × 45 × 180
Courtesy of Christian Stein Gallery,
Milan/Turin

IAN FAIRWEATHER
TORTOISE AND TEMPLE GONG, 1965
P.V.A. on board
144.7 × 190.5
Courtesy of the Collection of James Fairfax

MONSOON, 1961/62
Synthetic polymer paint and gouache on
cardboard
98 × 188.5
Courtesy of Art Gallery of
Western Australia, Perth

HELMUT FEDERLE
GESCHWISTER SCHOLL, 1987
Acrylic on canvas
275 × 175
Courtesy of the Ludwig Collection,
Neue Galerie, Aachen

GREAT WALL, 1986
Oil on canvas
280 × 180
Courtesy of the Fredrik Roos Collection,
Zug

NAME WITHOUT M, 1980
Acrylic on canvas
204 × 304
Courtesy of the Banque Hypothécaire du
Canton de Genève, Geneva

BILL FONTANA
ACOUSTIC VIEWS, 1988
A live sound portrait of Sydney Harbour
and surrounding environments. Realised
with technical support from ABC Radio
through its program *The Listening Room*.
Transmitted from the facade of The Art
Gallery of New South Wales.

KATHARINA FRITSCH
UNTITLED, 1987/88
Aluminium and polyester
240 × 100 × 100
Courtesy of the artist

GÉRARD GAROUSTE
UNTITLED, 1987
Oil on canvas
200 × 180
Courtesy of the Galerie Liliane et Michel
Durand-Dessert, Paris

UNTITLED, 1987
Acrylic on on canvas
220 × 180
Courtesy of the Galerie Liliane et Michel
Durand-Dessert, Paris

UNTITLED, 1987
Oil on canvas
200 × 235
Courtesy of the Galerie Liliane et Michel
Durand-Desert, Paris

ROSALIE GASCOIGNE
ROADSIDE, 1988
Wood and aluminium strip
125 x 122
Courtesy of the artist

GOLDEN WEDGE, 1987
Wood and aluminium strip
122 x 168
Courtesy of the artist

TIGER TIGER, 1987
Reflective material, wood, aluminium strip
Two pieces, each 112 x 112
Courtesy of the artist

ISA GENZKEN
GUARDINI, 1987
Concrete and steel
226 x 81 x 46
Courtesy of the artist

KUSS, 1987
Concrete and steel
228 x 98 x 61
Courtesy of the artist

SCHÖNBERG, 1986
Concrete and steel
136 x 75 x 50
Courtesy of the artist

GODBOLD & WOOD
CAPTIVE, 1987
Mixed media installation
112 x 104 x 68.5
Courtesy of the Richard Pomeroy Gallery,
London

FRANZ GRAF
UNTITLED, 1987
Watercolours, lime, ink on canvas
110 x 220
Courtesy of Galerie Nächst St Stephan,
Vienna

UNTITLED, 1987
Pencil on transparent paper
Series of six pieces, each 46 x 34
Courtesy of Galerie Nächst St Stephan,
Vienna

PETER HALLEY
TWO CELLS WITH CIRCULATING
CONDUIT, 1987
Day-Glo acrylic, Roll-A-Tex on canvas
197 x 350.5
Courtesy of the Dakis Joannou Collection,
Athens

EITETSU HAYASHI
Special performance on Wadaiko
(traditional Japanese drums)
Broadwalk Theatre, Sydney Opera House
Presented as part of 'Close-up of Japan',
Sydney, 1988, sponsored by The Mitsui
Public Relations Committee

JOY HESTER
WOMAN IN FUR COAT (SELF PORTRAIT),
c. 1957
Brush and ink
36.8 x 26
Courtesy of Georges Mora

LOVERS II (LOVERS ON YELLOW
GROUND), 1956
Brush and ink on ink wash on watercolour
on paper
75.9 x 50.5
Courtesy of Australian National Gallery,
Canberra.
Gift of Mrs Robert Dulieu 1981

LOVE II, 1949
Charcoal, brush and ink, blue pastel,
gouache
31.4 x 25.3
Courtesy of Lyn Williams

FACE II, 1947/48
Brush and ink and wash on paper
30.5 x 24.1
Courtesy of Janine Burke

ROGER HILTON
UNTITLED (NUDE), 1974
Gouache, pastel and pencil charcoal on
paper
26 x 40
Courtesy of Ray Hughes, Sydney

RECLINING NUDE WITH FLOWERS, 1973
Charcoal and gouache on paper
39 x 56
Courtesy of Colin and Kay Lanceley

OI YOI YOI, 1963
Oil on canvas
152.4 x 127
Courtesy of the Trustees of the
Tate Gallery, London

TAISHI HIROKAWA
SONOMAMA SONOMAMA, 1982/86
Gelatin silver prints
Each print 50.8 x 40.6
Courtesy of the artist

JENNY HOLZER
Untitled with selections from THE LIVING
SERIES, TRUISMS and THE SURVIVAL
SERIES, 1986
Electronic moving message unit, red diodes
12.7 × 73.6 × 5
Courtesy of Barbara Gladstone Gallery,
New York

Untitled with selections from THE LIVING
SERIES, TRUISMS and THE SURVIVAL
SERIES, 1986
Electronic moving message unit, red diodes
12.7 × 73.6 × 5
Courtesy of Barbara Gladstone Gallery,
New York

Untitled with selections from TRUISMS, THE
LIVING SERIES and THE SURVIVAL
SERIES, 1986
Electronic moving message unit, red diodes
12.7 × 73.6 × 5
Courtesy of Barbara Gladstone Gallery,
New York

Untitled with selections from TRUISMS, THE
LIVING SERIES and THE SURVIVAL
SERIES, 1986
Electronic moving message unit, red diodes
12.7 × 73.6 × 5
Courtesy of Barbara Gladstone Gallery,
New York

Selections from TRUISMS, 1985
Electronic moving message unit, red diodes
16.5 × 308.6 × 10
Courtesy of Barbara Gladstone Gallery,
New York

More SURVIVAL, 1985
Electronic moving message unit, red diodes
17.8 × 89 × 10
Courtesy of Barbara Gladstone Gallery,
New York

Selection from TRUISMS, 1985
Electronic moving message unit, red diodes
14 × 77.5 × 10
Courtesy of Barbara Gladstone Gallery,
New York

Selections from THE SURVIVAL
SERIES, 1983/84
Electronic moving message unit, yellow
diodes
16.5 × 154.3 × 10
Courtesy of Barbara Gladstone Gallery,
New York

Selections from THE SURVIVAL SERIES, 1983
Electronic moving message unit, red diodes
16.5 × 308.6 × 10
Courtesy of Barbara Gladstone Gallery,
New York

REBECCA HORN
BLINDFOLDED BINOCULARS, 1986
Metal motor binoculars
400
Courtesy of the artist

ROBERT HUNTER
PAINTING NO 6, 1987
Acrylic on board
122 × 244
Courtesy of the Baillieu Myer Collection of
the Eighties, Melbourne

PAINTING NO 9, 1987
Acrylic on board
123.2 × 244.3
Courtesy of the Collection of Michael and
Elizabeth Wardell

PAINTING NO 4, 1987
Acrylic on board

122.5 × 244.5
Courtesy of private collection

TOSHIMITSU IMAÏ
JAPANESE GARDEN INSTALLATION, 1988
Special installation composed of paintings,
Japanese banners and flags, pampas grass,
rocks and gold leaf
Presented as part of 'Close-up of Japan',
Sydney, 1988, sponsored by The Mitsui
Public Relations Committee
Located in the Sculpture Court, Art Gallery
of New South Wales, Sydney

AUTUMN GRASSES IN SUMMER, 1987
Acrylic and mixed media
210 × 540
Courtesy of the artist

MUSASHINO, 1986
Acrylic and mixed media
210 × 540
Courtesy of the artist

AUTUMN, 1957
Oil painting
193.9 × 130.3
Courtesy of the Tokyo Metropolitan Art
Museum, Tokyo

IRWIN
FOUR SEASONS, 1988
Oil, zinc, wood, metal
Four paintings with bases of old doors,
450 × 200 × 30
Courtesy of the artists

WAS IST KUNST, 1984/88
Mixed media with oil painting
Twelve works from series of twenty,
from 53 × 56 to 110 × 70
Courtesy of the artists

MICHAEL JOHNSON
BUJI, 1986
Oil on linen
198 × 426.7
Courtesy of the Robert Holmes à Court
Collection, Perth

FRONTAL TWO, 1968
Acrylic on canvas
210 × 195
Courtesy of the James Baker Collection,
Museum of Contemporary Art, Brisbane

ANSELM KIEFER
GLAUBE, HOFFNUNG, LIEBE, 1984/86
Emulsion, acrylic, shellac on
photodocument paper on linen with lead
280 × 380
Courtesy of Art Gallery of
New South Wales, Sydney.
Part of the Mervyn Horton Bequest Fund.

YGGDRASIL, 1985/86
Emulsion, acrylic, shellac on canvas and
lead
220 × 190
Courtesy of private collection

ASTRALSCHLANGE, 1985/86
Emulsion, oil, shellac, acrylic on canvas and
traces of burning
190 × 220
Courtesy of private collection

EDWARD & NANCY REDDIN KIENHOLZ
HOLDIN' THE DOG, 1983/84
Mixed media
203.2 × 170.2 × 66
Courtesy of Cliff and Mandy Einstein

THE LAST BUFFALO FROM WORLEY, 1984
Mixed media
102.9 × 57.2 × 152.4
Courtesy of Barry and Gail Berkus

YVES KLEIN
ARMAN, 1962
Portrait relief
175 × 95 × 26
Courtesy of Musée National d'Art
Moderne, Centre Georges Pompidou, Paris

ROBERT KLIPPEL
THE TRAIN, 1987
Painted wood sculpture
226 × 415 × 152
Courtesy of Watters Gallery, Sydney

JANNIS KOUNELLIS
UNTITLED, 1987
Steel, wood, stone, cloth, paint, gas burner
and smoke
Twelve panels, each 201 × 91
Courtesy of Anthony d'Offay Gallery,
London

BARBARA KRUGER
UNTITLED (I'M JUST LOOKING), 1987
Lenticular photograph
58.4 × 127
Courtesy of the private collection of Carol
and Paul Meringoff

UNTITLED (GOD SAID IT, I BELIEVE IT,
AND THAT SETTLES IT), 1987
Plastic letters, felt on aluminium
150 × 51 × 35.6
Courtesy of Rhona Hoffman Gallery,
Chicago

UNTITLED (I WILL NOT BECOME WHAT
I MEAN TO YOU), 1983
Photograph
213.3 × 122
Courtesy of Emily and Jerry Spiegel

UNTITLED (WE HAVE RECEIVED ORDERS
NOT TO MOVE), 1982
Photograph
182.8 × 122
Courtesy of the collection of Arthur and
Carol Goldberg

NIKOLAUS LANG
PETER IN THE SKY–DEDICATED TO PUTTAPA
BOB, UNCLE BERT AND GARY FOLEY–
IMAGINARY FIGURATIONS NO 6, 1987
Cross-section of 'coloured sands' deposits
(calico, glue on stick framework), Maslin
Sand Quarry
210 × 340 × 28

OCHRE AND SAND: DEDICATED TO THE
VANISHED TRIBES OF THE FLINDERS RANGE
AND ADELAIDE AREA, 1987
Ochre and sand displayed on paper
6 × 600 × 504

MARIA LASSNIG
DUODRAMA, 1987
Oil on canvas
200 × 205
Courtesy of Galerie Heike Curtze,
Vienna and Dusseldorf

TISCHRUNDE, 1986
Oil on canvas
200 × 195
Courtesy of Galerie Heike Curtze,
Vienna and Dusseldorf

ATLAS, 1984
Oil on canvas
260 × 200
Courtesy of Schömer Gesellschaften,
Klosterneuburg

FERNAND LÉGER
LES CINQ TOURNESOLS, 1953
Oil on canvas
92 × 73
Courtesy of Musée National Fernand
Léger, Biot

THE BICYCLE, 1930
Oil on canvas
64.8 × 50.8
Courtesy of Art Gallery of
New South Wales, Sydney
Gift of Mrs H.V. Evatt, March 1966,
in memory of Dr H.V. Evatt

LES CONSTRUCTEURS, 1920
Lithograph
35.5 × 29.2
Courtesy of private collection, Melbourne

INGEBORG LÜSCHER
UNTITLED, 1987
Wood pulp, paste, plaster, cardboard, iron,
sulphur
15 × 51 × 28.5
Courtesy of the artist

UNTITLED, 1987
Wood pulp, paste, plaster, cardboard, iron,
sulphur
40 × 14.5 × 25
Courtesy of the artist

UNTITLED, 1987
Wood pulp, paste, plaster, cardboard,
sulphur
6.5 × 39 × 22.5
Courtesy of the artist

UNTITLED, 1987
Wood pulp, paste, plaster, cardboard,
sulphur
10 × 30 × 27.5
Courtesy of the artist

LEN LYE
RAIN TREE, 1978
Acrylic on canvas
275.6 × 185
Courtesy of Len Lye Foundation,
New Plymouth

EARTH, 1978
Acrylic on canvas
62.8 × 185
Courtesy of Len Lye Foundation

BLADE, 1962/76
Stainless steel, motor, timing mechanism,
formica, chipboard, cork
206 × 91
Courtesy of Len Lye Foundation

FOUNTAIN, c. 1959
Stainless steel, motor, painted steel, wood
284 × 160 × 160
Courtesy of Len Lye Foundation

HILARIE MAIS
THE GRID, 1987
Wood
190 × 190 × 6
Courtesy of Wollongong City Gallery

GRID II, 1987
Wood and oil paint
230 × 230 × 6
Courtesy of the artist and Roslyn Oxley9
Gallery, Sydney

DOORS/THE MAZE, 1986/87
Wood, oil paint, and chain
204 × 223 × 9
Courtesy of the artist and Roslyn Oxley9
Gallery, Sydney

HENRI MATISSE
POLYNÉSIE LA MER, 1946
Collages on paper
197 × 310
Courtesy of Musée National d'Art
Moderne, Centre Georges Pompidou, Paris

COLIN McCAHON
THE LARK'S SONG (a poem by
Matire Kereama), 1969
PVA on two wooden doors
Each door 81 × 198
Courtesy of Auckland City Art Gallery,
New Zealand

HERE I GIVE THANKS TO MONDRIAN, 1961
Oil on hardboard
121.5 × 91.5
Courtesy of the Auckland City Art Gallery,
New Zealand

SIX DAYS IN NELSON AND
CANTERBURY, 1950
Oil on board
87.5 × 112
Courtesy of the Auckland City Art Gallery,
New Zealand

VICTOR MEERTENS
FALCHION, 1988
Galvanised iron, galvanised iron primer,
wood
332 × 135 × 142

LOCOMOTIF, 1987
Galvanised iron, galvanised iron primer,
wood
344 × 94 × 144

DIAPASON, 1987
Galvanised iron, galvanised iron primer,
wood
335 × 101 × 160

A BUTTATA, 1987
Galvanised iron, galvanised iron primer,
wood
386 × 97 × 148

GERHARD MERZ
DANTEUM, 1987
Pigment on canvas
Three paintings, 90 × 350 × 10
Courtesy of the artist

FRANÇOIS MORELLET
PAR DERRIÈRE (À 2) (LA GÉOMÉTRIE DANS
LES SPASMES), 1986
Acrylic on canvas
Two paintings 200 × 200 and 400 × 100
Courtesy of Galerie Liliane et Michel
Durand-Dessert, Paris

"69", 1986
Acrylic on canvas
Two paintings, each 100 × 400
Courtesy of the artist and Galerie Liliane et
Michel Durand-Dessert, Paris

ROBERT MORRIS
UNTITLED, 1987
Encaustic and silkscreen on aluminium
panel and painted cast fibreglass
256.5 × 315
Courtesy of Leo Castelli Gallery, New York

OLIVIER MOSSET
SMACK, 1986
Oil on canvas
200 × 210
Courtesy of Galerie Emmerich-Baumann,
Zürich

UNTITLED, 1975
Acrylic on canvas
203.2 × 213.3
Courtesy of Galerie Emmerich-Baumann,
Zürich

NATSU NAKAJIMA &
MUTEKI-SHA
SLEEP AND REINCARNATION from
EMPTY LAND
Performance work
Dancers: Yukio Waguri and
Yuriko Maezawa
Broadwalk Theatre, Sydney Opera House
Presented as part of 'Close-up of Japan',
Sydney, 1988, sponsored by the Mitsui
Public Relations Committee

HERMANN NITSCH
Painting action
Commissioned by the Australian Biennale

JOHN NIXON
SELF PORTRAIT (NON OBJECTIVE
COMPOSITION), nos 1–10, 1980/88
Enamel, oil, acrylic and objects on various
supports
Ten paintings, each approximately 65 × 75

SIDNEY NOLAN
BURIAL OF BURKE, 1985
Oil on canvas
Triptych, each panel 183 × 160
Courtesy of the artist

DIMBOOLA, 1944
Ripolin enamel on canvas
63.8 × 76.5
Courtesy of National Gallery of Victoria,
Melbourne.
Presented by Sir Sidney and Lady Nolan

RAILWAY GUARD, DIMBOOLA, 1943
Ripolin enamel on canvas
77 × 64
Courtesy of National Gallery of Victoria,
Melbourne

FLOUR LUMPER, DIMBOOLA, 1943
Ripolin enamel on strawboard
76 × 63.5
Courtesy of National Gallery of Victoria,
Melbourne

GIANFRANCO
NOTARGIACOMO
UNTITLED, 1987
Oil on canvas
200 × 300

UNTITLED, 1987
Oil on canvas
200 × 300

LE NOSTRE DIVERGENZE, 1971/83
Coloured plasticine
Twenty sculptures, each 60 high
Courtesy of Galleria La Salita, Rome

MARIA OLSEN
VESSEL
Oil on muslin on canvas
163 × 216
Courtesy of the Ministry of Foreign Affairs,
Wellington,
New Zealand

BONE STACK, 1985
Papier maché
215 × 184 × 25
Courtesy of the Victoria University of
Wellington Art Collection

SKY, 1985
Pigment emulsion and paintstick on paper
87 × 141
Courtesy of Michael Volkerling and
Ruth Harley

TATSUMI ORIMOTO
PULL TO EAR, 1977/87
Photographs, each 61 × 43

SONJA OUDENDIJK
UNTITLED, 1987
Wood and metal paint
Five parts, 50 × 360 × 50
Courtesy of the Stedelijk Museum
'De Lakenhal', Leiden, Netherlands

FROM V TO P '81 CAL, 1987
Wood, steel, metal paint
Eight parts, 120 × 260 × 40
Courtesy of Galerie Hans Gieles,
Amsterdam

UNTITLED, 1987
Wood, rubber, metal paint
30 × 120 × 235
Courtesy of Galerie Hans Gieles,
Amsterdam

NATURAL SETTING, 1987
Wood, rubber, metal paint
Sixteen parts, 200 × 300 × 26
Courtesy of Galerie Hans Gieles,
Amsterdam

GIULIO PAOLINI
L'Altra Figura, 1984
Plaster
183 × 250 × 190
Courtesy of Art Gallery of
New South Wales, Sydney

MIKE PARR
The History Of Photography and
Life After Death (Battery Man), 1988
Wall relief, chipboard
45 × 600 × 70

Drawing, charcoal, Girault pastel, and
acrylic on Tamaroll paper
228 × 600
Courtesy of the artist

GIUSEPPE PENONE
I Colori Dei Temporali, 1980/87
Bronze, copper, iron
300 × 135 × 115
Courtesy of Christian Stein Gallery,
Milan/Turin

PABLO PICASSO
Weeping Woman, 1937
Oil on canvas
55 × 46
Courtesy of National Gallery of Victoria,
Melbourne.
Purchased by the Art Foundation of
Victoria with the generous assistance of the
Jack and Genia Liberman Family and
Donors of the Art Foundation of Victoria

MARGARET PRESTON
Aboriginal Glyph, 1953/58
Gouache stencil on black paper
34.5 × 28.5
Courtesy of Art Gallery of
New South Wales, Sydney.
Gift of the artist 1960.

Still Life With Shells, 1956
Oil on canvas
39 × 44.1
Courtesy of Sir James and Lady Cruthers,
Perth

Fish, 1949
Colour stencil on black card
24.8 × 32.4
Courtesy of The University of Melbourne
Art Collection.
Gift of Professor Brian Lewis 1970.

Grey Day In The Ranges, 1942
Oil on hardboard
51 × 50.7
Courtesy of Art Gallery of
New South Wales, Sydney

MARTIN PURYEAR
Seer, 1984
Painted wood and wire
198 × 132.7 × 114.3
Courtesy of Solomon R. Guggenheim
Museum, New York. Purchased with funds
contributed by Louis and Bessie Adler
Foundation Inc., Seymour R. Klein,
President

ARNULF RAINER
The Crucified Bear, 1985/87
Oil on wood, application
171 × 121
Courtesy of the artist

Cross With Rest Of Fur, 1985/86
Oil on wood, application
211 × 80
Courtesy of the artist

Snake-Pit, 1986
Oil on photograph on wood
80 × 120
Courtesy of the artist

Snake-Pit, 1986
Oil on photograph on wood
80 × 120
Courtesy of the artist

Death Mask, 1984
Oil on photograph on wood
80 × 60
Courtesy of the artist

Death Mask, 1984
Mixed media on photograph
60 × 50
Courtesy of the artist

RAMINGINING
ARTISTS COMMUNITY
The Aboriginal Memorial (200 Hollow
Log Bone Coffins), 1987/88
Wood, ochres
Courtesy of Australian National Gallery,
Canberra

JACKY REDGATE
Taming The Spectrum, 1987
Cibachrome photographs
Seven parts, each 89 × 89 (framed)
Courtesy of Mori Gallery, Sydney

GERHARD RICHTER
Claudius (603), 1986
Acrylic on canvas
311 × 406
Claudius (604), 1986
Acrylic on canvas
311 × 406
Courtesy of Galerie Rudolf Zwirner,
Cologne

MARK ROTHKO
Untitled (Black On Grey), 1970
Acrylic on canvas
203.5 × 175.5
Courtesy of Solomon R. Guggenheim
Museum, New York.
Gift of The Mark Rothko Foundation, Inc.
1986

Black, Orange On Maroon (#18), 1963
Oil on canvas
175.5 × 163.5
Courtesy of Solomon R. Guggenheim
Museum, New York.
Gift of The Mark Rothko Foundation, Inc.
1986

GARETH SANSOM
Putting The 'F' Back Into Art, 1987
Oil and enamel on linen
Three panels, 213.3 × 548.6
Courtesy of the artist

ANNA MARIA
SANTOLINI
Autoritratto, 1987
Iron, copper, aluminium, Murano glass
100 × 70 × 40
Courtesy of the artist

Dedalus: Opera Ballet, 1987
Tyres, aluminium, iron, copper
Installation, 120 × 250 × 500
Courtesy of the artist

Quasi Un Disegno Bianco, 1987
Mixed media on canvas
100 × 250
Courtesy of the artist

EVA SCHLEGEL
Untitled, 1987
Graphite on plaster
100 × 125
Courtesy of the artist

Untitled, 1987
Graphite on plaster, oil on plaster
Two parts, each 20 × 20

Untitled, 1987
Graphite on plaster, oil on plaster
Two parts, each 20 × 20

RICHARD SERRA
Keystone, 1987
Hot rolled steel
Three plates, each 152.4 × 152.4
Courtesy of Solomon R. Guggenheim
Museum, New York. Purchased with funds
contributed by Stephen and Nan Swid

SEVERED HEADS
Chasing Skirt, 1988
Audio-visual work

VIVIENNE SHARK
LeWITT
Untitled, 1988
Oil on linen
56 × 41
Courtesy of the artist and Roslyn Oxley9
Gallery, Sydney

Untitled, 1987
Oil on linen
41 × 56
Courtesy of the artist and Roslyn Oxley9
Gallery, Sydney

The Omen. That Wascally Wabbit, 1987
Oil on linen
61 × 71
Courtesy of the artist and Roslyn Oxley9
Gallery, Sydney

DAVID SMITH
Cubi XXVII, 1965
Stainless steel
282.9 × 222.9 × 86.4
Courtesy of Solomon R. Guggenheim
Museum, New York

HENRYK STAŻEWSKI
Colour A, 1980
Acrylic, hardboard, wood
64 × 64
Courtesy of Muzeum Sztuki, Lodz

COLOUR B, 1980
Acrylic, hardboard, wood
44 × 44
Courtesy of Muzeum Sztuki, Lodz

COLOUR C, 1980
Acrylic, hardboard, wood
44 × 44
Courtesy of Muzeum Sztuki, Lodz

GREEN COMPOSITION, c. 1957
Oil on canvas
46 × 61
Courtesy of Muzeum Sztuki, Lodz

GARY STEVENS &
CAROLINE WILKINSON
IF THE CAP FITS, 1986
Performance work
Wharf Studio, Pier 4/5, Walsh Bay

ANDRZEJ SZEWCZYK
MEMORIALS OF F. KAFKA'S LETTERS TO
F. BAUER, 1983
Lead on wood
Two pieces, each 17 × 30 × 4.5
Two pieces, each 15 × 22 × 4.5
Courtesy of Muzeum Sztuki, Lodz

IMANTS TILLERS
SECRET PAINTING/RED SQUARE, 1987
Vitreous enamel on steel
Two panels, 53.3 × 53.3 and 122 × 122
Courtesy of the artist and Yuill/Crowley
Gallery, Sydney

ANOMALY NOBILITY, 1987
Vitreous enamel on steel
Forty-nine panels, 195.5 × 249
Courtesy of the artist and Yuill/Crowley
Gallery, Sydney

VITREOUS VIRTUOUS, 1987
Vitreous enamel on steel
Forty-nine panels, 195.5 × 249
Courtesy of the artist and Yuill/Crowley
Gallery, Sydney

WILLIAM TUCKER
HORSE X, 1986
Bronze
89 × 91.4 × 53.3
Courtesy of the artist and David McKee
Gallery, New York

TETHYS, 1985
Bronze
188 × 119.3 × 162.5
Courtesy of the artist and David McKee
Gallery, New York

TONY TUCKSON
WHITE LINES (VERTICAL)
ON ULTRAMARINE, 1970/73
Synthetic polymer paint on hardboard
Two panels, 213.5 × 244
Courtesy of Art Gallery of
New South Wales, Sydney.
Gift of Annette Dupree 1976

WHITE LINES (HORIZONTAL)
ON RED, 1970/73
Acrylic on hardboard
183 × 137.5
Courtesy of National Gallery of Victoria,
Melbourne

BILL VIOLA
I DO NOT KNOW WHAT IT IS I AM LIKE, 1986
Videotape, colour, stereo sound, 89 minutes
Courtesy of Electronic Arts Intermix,
New York

JEFF WALL
THE BRIDGE, 1980
Cibachrome transparency, fluorescent
light, display case
74 x 246.5 x 20.5
Courtesy of the Canada Council Art Bank

STEVES FARM, STEVESTON, 1980
Cibachrome transparency, fluorescent
light, display case
74 x 246.5 x 20.5
Courtesy of the Labatt Collection, Toronto

THE JEWISH CEMETERY, 1980/86
Cibachrome transparency, fluorescent
light, display case
74 x 246.5 x 20.5
Courtesy of the Mackenzie Art Gallery,
University of Regina

ANDY WARHOL
SELF PORTRAIT (9), 1986
Acrylic and silkscreen on canvas
203 x 203
Courtesy of National Gallery of Victoria,
Melbourne.
Presented by the National Gallery
Women's Association

DOUBLE LAST SUPPER - JESUS, 1985
Acrylic on canvas
304.8 x 670.6
Courtesy of Galerie Hans Mayer

CAROLINE WILLIAMS
PAINTING, 1987
Oil on canvas
147 x 176.4
Courtesy of private collection

UNTITLED NO 6, 1987
Oil on canvas
191 x 250
Courtesy of Roger David Stores Collection

PAINTING, 1987
Oil on canvas
191 x 250
Courtesy of National Gallery of Victoria,
Melbourne

FRED WILLIAMS
STRATH CREEK FALLS V, 1979
Oil on canvas
152 x 182.6
Courtesy of Lyn Williams

HORSEMAN IN LANDSCAPE, 1968
Oil on canvas
152.7 x 183.6
Courtesy of National Gallery of Victoria,
Melbourne.
Presented by the National Gallery Society.

YOU YANGS LANDSCAPE, 1967
Oil on canvas
183 x 152.5
Courtesy of National Gallery of Victoria,
Melbourne

UPWEY HILL, 1966
Oil on canvas
112 x 127
Courtesy of private collection, Melbourne

BIBLIOGRAPHY

RENATE ANGER
Dorothée Bauerle, *Renate Anger: Antworten* (catalogue), Künstlerhaus Bethanien, Berlin, 1987. Peter Winter, *Renate Anger: Arbeiten 1984–85* (catalogue), Galerie Kammer, Hamburg, 1986. *Renate Anger: Malerei* (catalogue), Kunstverein Bremerhaven, 1982.

TOM ARTHUR
Urszula Szulakowska, 'Put your Face on the Burning Sand—peripheral ambience and kinetic integrity in Tom Arthur's assemblages and installations', *The Entire Contents of a Gentleman's Room* (catalogue), University of Melbourne Gallery, Melbourne, 1987. Tom Arthur/Tony Maniaty, 'Interview', *The Entire Contents of a Gentleman's Room* (catalogue), University of Melbourne Gallery, Melbourne, 1987. Jonathon Holmes, *On Site* (catalogue), Tasmanian College of Art, Hobart, Tasmania, 1984. Tom Arthur/Tony Maniaty, *Goodbye Carpet, Goodbye Small Door* (catalogue), Newcastle Region Art Gallery, 1983. Robert Lindsay, 'An Assembled View of Sculpture', *Anything Goes, Art in Australia 1970–1980*.

RICHARD ARTSCHWAGER
Jean-Christophe Ammann, *Richard Artschwager* (catalogue), Kunsthalle Basle, 1985. Coosje Van Bruggen, 'Richard Artschwager', *Artforum*, no 22, September 1983. Armstrong, Cathcart & Delahunty, *Richard Artschwager's Theme(s)* (catalogue), La Jolla Museum of Contemporary Art, La Jolla, California, 1979. Roberta Smith, 'The Artschwager Enigma', *Art in America*, no 67, October 1979. Marjorie Welish, 'The Elastic Vision of Richard Artschwager', *Art in America*, no 66, May–June 1978.

GIOVANNI ASDRUBALI
F. Menna, 'Gianni Asdrubali', *Nuova Prearo Editore*, February 1987. F. Menna, 'L'opera d'arte e la costruzione del nuovo', *Flash Art*, May 1987. R. Barilli, 'Qui c'è aria di nuovo', *L'Espresso*, August 1986. S. Sereni, 'L'artista torna allo studio', *Panorama mese*, December 1985. M. Bondino, 'Gli artisti nuovi nuovi', *Epoca*, 19 July, 1985.

FRANCIS BACON
Andrew Forge, Dawn Ades, *Francis Bacon* (catalogue), Tate Gallery, London, 1985. Michael Peppiatt, 'Francis Bacon: the Studio as Symbol', *Connoisseur*, September 1984. Masanori Ichikawa, *Francis Bacon: Paintings 1968–82*, National Museum of Modern Art, Tokyo, 1983. Mel Gooding, 'Francis Bacon: Full Face and in Profile', *Arts Review*, 25 November, 1983. David Sylvester, *Interviews with Francis Bacon*, Thames & Hudson, London, 1975 (revised edition 1980).

RALPH BALSON
Bruce Adams, 'Metaphors of Scientific Idealism: The Theoretical Background to the Painting of Ralph Balson', in Anthony Bradley and Terry Smith (eds) *Australian Art and Architecture: Essays presented to Bernard Smith*, Oxford University Press, Melbourne, 1980. James Gleeson, 'Ralph Balson', *Australian Painters: Modern Painters 1931–70*, Lansdowne Press, Sydney, 1971.

BALTHUS
Sabine Rewald, *Balthus* (catalogue), Metropolitan Museum of Art & Harry N. Abrams Inc., New York, 1984. Germain Viatte, 'Balthus', *Aftermath: France 1945–54* (catalogue), Barbican Art Gallery, London, 1982. Jean Leymarie, *Balthus*, Albert Skira, Geneva, 1978. Jean Leymarie, *Balthus, dessins et aquarelles*, Galerie Claude Bernard, Eds du Chêne, Paris, 1971.

MAX BECKMANN
Carla Schulz-Hoffmann & Judith C. Weiss (eds) *Max Beckmann Retrospective* (catalogue), Munich, 1984. 'Max Beckmann', *The Moderns* (catalogue), Art Gallery of New South Wales, Sydney, 1984. Hans Belting, *Max Beckmann—Die Tradition als Problem in der Kunst der Moderne*, Berlin, 1984. Matthias Eberle, *Die Nacht—Passion ohne Erlösung*, Frankfurt, 1984. *Max Beckmann, Aquarelle und Zeichnungen 1903–50* (catalogue), Kunsthalle Bielefeld, 1977. Erhard & Barbara Göpel, *Max Beckmann, Katalog der Gemälde* (catalogue in 2 vols), Berne, 1976.

MICHAEL BIBERSTEIN
Aspekte der jungen Schweizer Kunst (catalogue), Städtische Galerie Regensburg, 1981. Willard Holmes, *Michael Biberstein, Jörg Renz, Jürg Stäuble* (catalogue), Art Gallery of Greater Victoria, B.C., Canada, 1980.

ROSS BLECKNER
Gianfranco Mantegna, 'The Ellipse of Reality, Ross Bleckner', *Tema Celeste*, April/May 1987. Jeanne Siegel, 'Geometry Desurfacing: Ross Bleckner, Alan Belcher, Ellen Carey, Peter Halley, Sherrie Levine, Philip Taaffe and James Welling', *Arts Magazine*, no 60, March 1986. Gary Indiana, 'Light and Death', *The Village Voice*, 12 February, 1986. Donald Kuspit, 'Ross Bleckner', *Artforum*, no 22, April 1984. Peter Halley, 'Ross Bleckner: Painting at the End of History', *Arts Magazine*, no 56, May 1982.

CHRISTIAN BOLTANSKI
Content (catalogue), Hirschhorn Museum & Sculpture Garden, Washington, 1984/85.

PIERRE BONNARD
Germain Viatte, 'Pierre Bonnard', *Aftermath: France 1945–54* (catalogue), Barbican Art Gallery, London, 1982. Jean Clair, *Bonnard*, Henri Screpel, Paris, 1975. Franco Russoli, *Pierre Bonnard*, Purnell & Sons Ltd, London, 1967. Antoine Terrasse, *Bonnard*, Albert Skira, Geneva, 1964. André Lhote, 'Le Bouquet de Roses', *Pierre Bonnard*, Eds du Chêne, Paris, 1944.

PETER BOOTH
Michael Brenson, 'Art: Vision of Australia in Peter Booth's Works', *New York Times*, 10 January 1986. Gary Catalano, 'Peter Booth: A Painter of Our Time', *Australia: Venice Biennale 1982*, Visual Arts Board, Sydney, 1982. Jennifer Phipps, 'Peter Booth', *Flash Art*, no 105, December 1981/January 1982. Frances Lindsay, 'Peter Booth', *Art and Australia*, vol. 16, no 1, Spring 1978. Grazia Gunn, *Peter Booth. Paintings & Drawings 1968–1976* (catalogue), Monash University Gallery, Melbourne, 1976.

MARIE BOURGET
A. Rochette, 'The Post-Beaubourg Generation', *Art in America*, June 1987. John Russell, 'A New Wave of French Artists at the Guggenheim', *New York Times*, 12 October 1986. Lynn Gumpert, *A Distanced View* (catalogue), The New Museum of Contemporary Art, New York, 1986. L. Dennison, *Angles of Visions: French Art Today* (catalogue), Solomon R. Guggenheim Museum, New York, 1986. M. Nuridsany, 'Dans la lumière de Marie Bourget', *Art Press*, no 88, January 1985.

ARTHUR BOYD
Ursula Hoff, *The Art of Arthur Boyd*, Andre Deutsch Ltd, London, 1986. Sandra McGrath, *The Artist and the River: Arthur Boyd and the Shoalhaven*, Bay Books, Sydney, 1982. Christopher Tadgell, *Arthur Boyd Drawings 1934–1970*, with a Foreword by Laurie Thomas, Secker & Warburg, London, 1973. Imre von Maltzahn, *Arthur Boyd—Etchings and Lithographs*, Lund Humphries, London, 1971. Franz Phillip, *Arthur Boyd*, Thames & Hudson, London, 1967.

GEORGES BRAQUE
'Georges Braque', *The Moderns* (catalogue), Art Gallery of New South Wales, Sydney, 1984. John Golding, *Georges Braque*, Purnell & Sons Limited, London, 1966. Maurice Gieure, 'Réflexions', *Georges Braque*, ed. Pierre Tisné, Paris, 1956. Dora Vallier, *Braque, La Peinture et Nous*, Cahiers d'Art, XXXIX, 1953. André Breton, *Le Surréalisme et la Peinture*, Editions Gallimard, Paris, 1928.

JULIE BROWN-RRAP
George Alexander, 'Julie Brown-Rrap', *Australian Bicentennial Perspecta* (catalogue), Art Gallery of New South Wales, 1987. Ingrid Periz, 'Reading a Thief's Journal', *Photofile*, vol. 4, no 2, Winter 1986. Catriona Moore, 'Dangerous Liaisons', *After Image*, vol. 14, no 2, September 1986. George Alexander, 'Persona and Shadow', *On The Beach*, no 6, Spring 1984. John Delacour, 'Julie Brown's Disclosures—In Context, Out of the Biennale', *Art Network*, no 7, Spring 1982.

GÜNTER BRUS
Dieter Ronte, 'Günter Brus', *Der Überblick* (catalogue), Museum Moderner Kunst, Vienna, 1986. *Günter Brus/Arnulf Rainer* (catalogue), Hamburger Kunsthalle & Ritter Verlag, Klagenfurt, 1986. Günter Brus, 'Aus dem Arbeitsheften August–Dezember 1985', *Der Ausblick* (catalogue), Galerie Heike Curtze, Düsseldorf & Vienna, 1986. Barbara Catoir, 'Schönheit—Genuss der Selbstverdammung', *Trunkene Triebe* (catalogue), Galerie Heike Curtze, Düsseldorf & Vienna, 1983. Günter Brus, *Bild-Dichtungen* (catalogue), Whitechapel Art Gallery, London, 1980.

MICHAEL BUTHE
Jan Hoet, *Michael Buthe—Inch Allah* (catalogue), Museum van hedendaagse Kunst, Gent, 1984. *Sculpture from Germany* (catalogue), Independent Curators Incorporated, New York, 1983. Stephan von Wiese, *Michael Buthe—Skulptura in Deo Fabulosa*, Verlag Silke Schreiber, Munich, 1983. Stephan von Wiese, 'Les Mythes Individuels de Michael Buthe', *Art Press*, no 52, October 1981. Annelie Pohlen, 'Michael Buthe—Museum Folkwang Essen', *Flash Art*, no 98–99, 1980.

GENEVIÈVE CADIEUX
Reesa Greenberg, 'In Praise of Lumières', *C Magazine*, Toronto, December 1986. Donatella Verzura & Gregorio Magnani, 'Lumières: Perception-Projection', *Flash Art International*, no 131, December 1986. Charles Hagen, 'Lumières: Perception-Projection', *Artforum*, New York, November 1986. Philippe Evans-Clark, 'Lumières: perception-projection', *Art Press*, no 108, Paris, November 1986. Philippe Evans-Clark, 'Messages sent in the Medium of Light', *The New York Times*, New York, August 17 1986.

SARAH CHARLESWORTH
David Clarkson, 'Sarah Charlesworth Interview', *Parachute*, December 1987. Jeremy Gilbert-Rolfe, 'Where do Pictures Come From? Sarah Charlesworth and the Sexual Development of the Sign', *Arts*, December 1987. Dena Shottenkirk, 'Imaging the Other', *C Magazine*, Spring 1987. Paul Bob, 'Cutting up Culture', *East Village Eye*, June 1984. David Deitcher, 'Questioning Authority', *After-Image*, Summer 1984.

HANNAH COLLINS
Paul Smith, 'Terminal Culture? The British Edge', *Art in America*, September 1987. Stuart Morgan, *Under the Sign of Saturn* (catalogue), August 1987. Stuart Morgan, 'Antidotes to Madness?', *Artforum*, June 1986. Michael Philipson, 'Antidotes to Madness?', *Artscribe*, June 1986. Maureen O'Paley, Introduction to *Antidotes to Madness* (catalogue) Riverside Studios, April 1986.

ROBERT COMBAS
Démosthènes Davvetas, interview, *Robert Combas, Peintures 1985–86* (catalogue), capc Musée d'art Contemporain de Bordeaux, Bordeaux, & Stedelijk Museum, Amsterdam, 1987. Giovanni Camuffo, *Robert Combas, Lavori 1982–86* (catalogue), Galleria Il Capricorno, Venice, 1986. Patrice Bloch & Laurent Pesanti, 'Combas', *Fiac Magazine*, October 1985. Didier Moiselet, 'Entretien avec Robert Combas', *Halle-Sud*, no 8, 1985. Ben, Cornand, Marcos, Millet, Pailhas & Perdriolle, *Combas 84* (catalogue), ARCA, Marseille, 1984.

NEIL DAWSON
T.L. Rodney Wilson, 'Neil Dawson', *Aspects of Recent New Zealand Art: Sculpture 1* (catalogue), Auckland City Art Gallery, 1986. Michael Spens, 'Monet not Maori: Art in New Zealand', *Studio International*, no 198, 1985. Peter Leech, 'Visuality in visual art: Neil Dawson', *Art New Zealand*, no 36, 1985. Jim & Mary Barr, in Anthony Bond (ed.), *Australian Perspecta* (catalogue), Art Gallery of New South Wales, Sydney, 1985. Peter Leech, 'Elusive objects: recent work by Neil Dawson', *Art New Zealand*, no 25, 1982.

WILLEM DE KOONING
Henry Geldzahler, Introduction to *Willem de Kooning: Abstract Landscapes 1955–63* (catalogue), Larry Gagosian Gallery, New York, 1987. Cummings, Merkert & Stoulling, *Willem de Kooning: Drawings, Paintings, Sculpture* (catalogue), Whitney Museum of American Art, New York, 1983. Diane Waldman, *Willem de Kooning in East Hampton* (catalogue), Solomon R. Guggenheim Museum, New York, 1978. Harold Rosenberg, *Willem de Kooning*, Harry N. Abrams, New York, 1974. Thomas B. Hess, *Willem de Kooning* (catalogue), Museum of Modern Art, New York, 1968.

283

RICHARD DEACON
Joshua Decter, 'Sculptural Transgressions: Observing Paradigms of Cultural Experience', *Juxtapositions: Recent Sculpture from England and Germany* (catalogue), P.S.I., The Institute for Art and Urban Resources, Inc., New York, 1987. Marjorie Allthorpe Guyton, 'Richard Deacon, Serpentine Gallery', *Arts Review*, 25 October 1985. Judith Russi Kirscher, 'Tony Cragg, Richard Deacon', *Artforum*, Summer 1985. Richard Francis, *Richard Deacon*, Tate Gallery Publication, March 1985. Lynne Cooke, 'Richard Deacon at the Riverside Studios', *Art in America*, November 1984.

MARCEL DUCHAMP
Anne d'Harnoncourt & Kynaston McShine (eds), *Marcel Duchamp* (catalogue), Museum of Modern Art, New York, and Philadelphia Museum of Art, Pennsylvania, 1973. Pierre Cabanne, *Dialogues with Marcel Duchamp*, Viking, New York, 1971. Cleve Gray (ed.), 'Marcel Duchamp, 1887–1968', *Art in America*, vol. 57, no 4, July/August 1969. Arturo Schwarz, *Marcel Duchamp*, Fabbri, Milan, 1968. John Cage, '26 Statements re Duchamp', *Art and Literature*, no 3, Autumn/Winter 1964.

LILI DUJOURIE
Sakias Bos, *Lili Dujourie* (catalogue), Fonds Régional d'art Contemporain des Pays de la Loire, 1987. *Falls the Shadow* (catalogue), Hayward Gallery, London, 1986. *A Distanced View* (catalogue), The New Museum of Contemporary Art, New York, 1986.

LESLEY DUMBRELL
Ted Gott, 'The Female Unique', *Backlash* (catalogue), National Gallery of Victoria, Melbourne, 1986. Irena Zdanowicz & Patrick McCaughey, *Colour and Transparency. The Watercolours of Lesley Dumbrell, Robert Jacks, Victor Majzner*, National Gallery of Victoria, Melbourne, 1986. Ron Radford, *Recent Australian Painting: A Survey 1970–83* (catalogue), Art Gallery of South Australia, Adelaide, 1983. Grazia Gunn, 'Lesley Dumbrell', *Art and Australia*, vol. 18, no. 1, 1980. Geoffrey de Groen, 'Lesley Dumbrell interview: When every second artist will be a woman', *Conversations with Australian Artists*, Quartet, Melbourne, 1978.

RICHARD DUNN
Meaghan Morris, 'Intrigue', *Sighting References*, Artspace, Sydney, 1987. Susan Morgan, 'Great Expectations: The Sixth Biennale of Sydney', *Artscribe*, January/February 1987. Thomas Wulffen, *Kunstforum*, January/February 1986. Terence Maloon, 'Richard Dunn', *5/5: Fünf vom Fünften*, DAAD Galerie, Berlin, 1985. Donald Kuspit, 'Australian Drawings at CDS', *Art in America*, March 1985.

BRIAN ENO
'Brian Eno: Breaking Barriers', *Designers Journal*, London, October 1987. Karl Lippegaus, *Die Stille im Kopf: Interviews und Notizen über Musik. More Dark than Shark*, Faber & Faber

LUCIANO FABRO
Luciano Fabro (catalogue), ARC Musée de l'Art Moderne, Paris, 1987. *Luciano Fabro* (catalogue), Fruitmarket Gallery, Edinburgh, Umberto Allemandi & Company, Turin, 1987. Germano Celant, *The Knot, Arte Povera*, Umberto Allemandi & Company, Turin, 1985. J. De Sanna, *Fabro*, Essegi, Ravenna, 1983. Luciano Fabro, *Aufhänger*, König, Cologne, 1983.

IAN FAIRWEATHER
Peter Gant & William Nuttall, *Ian Fairweather: Paintings and Drawings 1927–70* (catalogue), Niagara Galleries, Melbourne, 1985. Murray Bail, *Ian Fairweather*, Bay Books, Sydney, 1981. Nourma Abbott-Smith, *Ian Fairweather: Profile of a Painter*, University of Queensland Press, 1978. James Gleeson, 'Ian Fairweather', *Australian Painters: Modern Painters 1931–1970*, Lansdowne Press, Sydney, 1971.

HELMUT FEDERLE
Donald Kuspit, 'New Geo and Neo Geo', *Artscribe*, September 1986. Ingrid Rein, 'Helmut Federle, Galerie Nächst St. Stephan', *Artforum*, September 1986. Wilfried W. Dickhoff, 'Im Gespräch mit Helmut Federle', *Wolkenkratzer Art Journal*, June 1986. Max Wechsler, 'Helmut Federle: Die Anmassung der Bescheidenheit', *Wolkenkratzer Art Journal*, June 1986. Markus Brüderlin, 'Interview mit Helmut Federle', *Kunstforum*, no 81, October/November 1985.

KATHARINA FRITSCH
Julian Heynen, *Elefant* (catalogue), Kaiser Wilhelm Museum, Krefeld, 1987. Jutta Koether, 'Katharina Fritsch', *Artscribe International*, May 1987. L. Gumpert, *A distanced view* (catalogue), The New Museum of Contemporary Art, New York, 1986. M. Jochimsen, *Junge Rheinische Kunst* (catalogue), Sophia, 1986. Katharina Fritsch, 'Friedhöfe', *Kunstforum International*, vol. 65, no 9, 1983.

GÉRARD GAROUSTE
Laurent Busine, *Gérard Garouste, Les Indiennes* (catalogue), Ed. Lebeer-Hossmann, Brussels, & Palais des Beaux-Arts, Charleroi, 1988. Froment, Giudieri, Risset, Couderc, *Gérard Garouste, Peintures de 1985 á 1987* (catalogue), capc Musée d'art contemporain de Bordeaux, 1987. Bernard Blistène, 'Gérard Garouste: hors du calme', *Galeries Magazine*, no 21, Paris, October/November 1987. Catherine Francblin, 'L'art est un jeu de Monopoly', *Artpress*, no 118, Paris, October 1987. Bernadette Martial, 'Gérard Garouste, fragments sur la sculpture', *Malerei, Painting, Peinture*, no 4, Munich, May 1987.

ISA GENZKEN
Joshua Decter, 'Sculptural Transgressions: Observing Paradigms of Cultural Experience', *Juxtapositions: Recent Sculpture from England and Germany*, (catalogue), P.S.1, The Institute for Art and Urban Resources, Inc., New York, 1987. Rudi H. Fuchs, *Isa Genzken, Gerhard Richter* (catalogue), Galleria Pieroni, Rome, 1983. Bruno Corà, 'Isa Genzken *Twin*', *A.E.I.U.O.*, vol. III, no 6, Rome, 1983. Paul Groot, 'Isa Genzken', *Kunstforum International*, Bd 62, Cologne, 1983. Renate Puvogel, 'Isa Genzken-Wolfgang Nestler-Horst Schuler', *Das Kunstwerk*, vol. XXXV, no 2, Stuttgart, 1982.

GODBOLD & WOOD
Adrian Searle, 'Under the Sign of Saturn', *Artscribe International*, November 1987.

Godbold & Wood, *Levate* (edition of ten books), September 1987. Stuart Morgan, 'Godbold & Wood', *Under the Sign of Saturn* (catalogue), August 1987. Jonathan Watkins & Kate Bush, *Child of Our Time/The Vacant Centre*, Richard Pomeroy Gallery, London, July 1987. Jonathan Watkins, 'Artangel, Chisenhale, Godbold & Wood', *Art Monthly*, May 1987.

PETER HALLEY
Peter Halley, 'Notes on Abstraction', *Arts*, Summer 1987. Sarah Kent, 'Smart Art', *Time Out*, 9–16 September 1987. Joshua Decter, 'Peter Halley', *Arts*, Summer 1986. Michele Cone, 'Peter Halley', *Flash Art*, February/March 1986. Jeanne Siegel, 'The Artist Critic of the Eighties: Peter Halley and Stephen Westfall', *Arts*, September 1985.

JOY HESTER
Janine Burke, *Joy Hester*, Greenhouse Publications, Melbourne 1983. Charles and Barbara Blackman, 'Joy Hester—Her Art', *Art and Australia*, vol. 1, no 18, Spring 1980. Janine Burke, *Australian Women Artists, 1840–1940*, Greenhouse Publications, Melbourne, 1980. Barrie Reid, 'Joy Hester, Draughtsman of Identity', *Art and Australia*, vol. 4, no 1, June 1966. Barrie Reid (ed.), *Modern Australian Art*, Museum of Modern Art, Melbourne, 1958.

ROGER HILTON
David Nicholson, 'Roger Hilton', *Artscribe*, no 34, March 1982. Roger Hilton, *Night Letters and Selected Drawings*, selected by Rosemary Hilton, Newlyn Orion Galleries Limited, 1980. Alan Green, 'Every Artist is a Con-Man', interview with Roger Hilton, *Studio International*, no 187, London, March 1974. Peter Fuller, review of 'Roger Hilton: Paintings and Drawings 1931–1973', Serpentine Gallery, London, *Connoisseur*, no 186, London, May 1974. Alan Bowness, 'Roger Hilton', *Cimaise*, no 63, Paris, January/February 1963.

TAISHI HIROKAWA
Taishi Hirokawa, *Sonomama sonomama*, Ryuko Tsushin Co. Ltd, Tokyo, 1987.

JENNY HOLZER
Dan Cameron, 'Jenny Holzer', *Tema Celeste*, no 10, March 1987. Colin Westerbeck, 'Jenny Holzer', *Artforum*, vol. 61, May 1987. Jean-Pierre Bordaz, 'Jenny Holzer and the Spectacle of Communication', *Parkett*, no 13, 1987. Bruce Ferguson, 'Wordsmith, An Interview with Jenny Holzer', *Art in America*, vol. 74, December 1986. Jeanne Siegel, 'Jenny Holzer's Language Games', *Arts Magazine*, December 1985.

REBECCA HORN
Dan Cameron, 'Horn's Dilemma: The Art of Rebecca Horn', *Arts Magazine*, November 1987. Eleanor Heartney, 'Sighted in Münster', *Art in America*, no 9, September 1987. Germano Celant, 'Isolation Cells', *Individuals* (catalogue), Museum of Contemporary Art, Los Angeles, 1986.

ROBERT HUNTER
Field to Figuration: Australian Art 1960–86 (catalogue), National Gallery of Victoria, Melbourne, 1986. *Subject of Painting* (catalogue), Art Gallery of New South Wales, Sydney, 1985. *Australian Perspecta* (catalogue), Art Gallery of New South Wales, 1983.

TOSHIMITSU IMAI
Tetsuya Nakamura & Toru Hamada (eds), *Imai*, Matrix Japan SA, Tokyo, 1987. Takeyoshi Miyazawa (ed.), *Imai: Ka-Cho-Fu-Getsu*, Bijutsu Shuppan-sha, Tokyo, 1985. Hideo Kaido (ed.), *Imai*, 1975.

MICHAEL JOHNSON
Terence Maloon, 'Michael Johnson', *Michael Johnson, Paintings 1968–86* (catalogue), University of Melbourne Gallery, 1986. Elwyn Lynn, 'Seven abstract painters with resilient spirit', *Australian*, 9 July 1986. Terence Maloon, 'Who's afraid of abstract art?', *Sydney Morning Herald*, 28 June 1986. Ron Radford, *Recent Australian Painting: A Survey 1970–83* (catalogue), Art Gallery of South Australia, Adelaide, 1983. Ronald Millar, 'Understanding colour—the return of Michael Johnson', *Herald*, Melbourne, 8 April 1982.

ANSELM KIEFER
Robert Kleyn, 'Anselm Kiefer', *Tema Celeste*, April/June 1987. Paul Taylor, 'Café Deutschland', *Art News*, no 85, April 1986. Jean Fisher, 'Tale of the German and the Jew', *Artforum*, no 24, September 1985. Donald B. Kuspit, 'Transmuting Externalization in Anselm Kiefer', *Arts Magazine*, no 59, October 1984. Johannes Gachnang, 'New German Paintings', *Flash Art*, no 106, February/March 1982.

EDWARD & NANCY REDDIN KIENHOLZ
Robert L. Pincus, *On a Scale that Competes with the World: The Art of Edward Kienholz and Nancy Reddin Kienholz* (dissertation), University of Southern California, 1987. Colin Gardner, 'Edward and Nancy Reddin Kienholz at L.A. Louver', *Artforum*, January 1987. Robert Silberman, 'Imitation of Life', *Art in America*, March 1986. Wystan Curnow, 'Humane Conditioning', *Studio International*, no 1007, 1984.

YVES KLEIN
Yves Klein, 1928–62: A Retrospective (catalogue), Institute for the Arts, Rice University, Houston, 1982. Thomas McEvilley, 'Yves Klein: Messenger of the Age of Space', *Artforum*, vol. 20, December/January 1981–82. Brian O'Doherty, 'The Gallery as Gesture', *Artforum*, vol. 20, December/January 1981/82. Pierre Restany, *Yves Klein le Monochrome*, Paris, 1974.

ROBERT KLIPPEL
James Gleeson, *Robert Klippel*, Bay Books, Sydney. Gary Catalano, *The Years of Hope: Australian Art and Criticism 1959–68*, Oxford University Press, 1981. Ken Scarlett, *Australian Sculptors*, Nelson 1980. Graeme Sturgeon, *The Development of Australian Sculpture 1788–1975*, Thames and Hudson, 1978. James Mollison, 'The Australian Collection', *Art and Australia*, January 1977.

JANNIS KOUNELLIS
Lynne Cooke, 'Luminous Penumbra', *Jannis Kounellis* (catalogue), Anthony d'Offay

Gallery, London, 1986. Diane Waldman, *Transformations in Sculpture*, Solomon R. Guggenheim Museum, New York, 1985. Floriana Pique, 'Jannis Kounellis: Christian Stein/Turin', *Flash Art*, no 116, March 1984. Jamey Gambrell, 'Jannis Kounellis at Sonnabend', *Art in America*, no 71, May 1983. Robin White, 'Interview with Jannis Kounellis', *View*, no 1, 1979.

BARBARA KRUGER
Jean Baudrillard, 'Untitled', *Barbara Kruger* (catalogue), Mary Boone/Michael Werner Gallery, 1987. Carol Squires, 'Diversionary (Syn)Tactics: Barbara Kruger has a Way With Words', *Art News*, February 1987. Thomas McEvilley, 'Barbara Kruger', *Artforum*, Summer 1986. Kate Linker, 'Barbara Kruger', *Flash Art*, no 121, March 1985. Andy Grundberg, 'Pictures That Poke Fun at Power', *New York Times*, 1 April 1984.

NIKOLAUS LANG
Philip Jones, 'A Craving for Ochre', *Nikolaus Lang: Sand and Ochre* (catalogue), South Australian School of Art, Adelaide, 1987. Armin Zweite, 'Nikolaus Lang', *Documenta 8* (catalogue), Kassel, 1987. *Requisiten* (catalogue), Städtische Galerie, Nordhorn, 1980. Nikolaus Lang, *Australisches Tagebuch* (catalogue), Aargauer Kunsthaus, Aargau, 1979. Günter Metken, 'Nikolaus Lang', *Farben Zeichen Steine*, Westfälischer Kunstverein, Münster, 1978.

MARIA LASSNIG
Maria Lassnig, Edition Ritter, Klagenfurt, 1985. Harald Sterk, *Austrian Portraits*, Edition Christian Brandstätter, Vienna, 1982. Peter Gorsen, 'About her Self-Portraits', 1978. *Body-Awareness Paintings* (catalogue), 1970. *Unfigurative Malerei* (catalogue), Klagenfurt, 1952.

FERNAND LÉGER
'Fernand Léger', *The Moderns* (catalogue), Art Gallery of New South Wales, Sydney, 1984. Peter de Francia, 'Fernand Léger', *Paintings, Gouaches, Drawings and Prints* (catalogue), Edward Totah Gallery, Milan/London, 1983. Edward F. Fry, 'Léger and the French Tradition', *Fernand Léger* (catalogue), Albright-Knox Art Gallery, Buffalo, New York, 1982. *Fernand Léger* (catalogue), Musée des Arts Décoratifs, Paris, 1956.

INGEBORG LÜSCHER
Lisa Licitra Ponti, 'Quattro frammenti per Ingeborg', *Domus*, no 654, Milan, October 1984. Annemarie Monteil, 'Ingeborg Lüscher in Genf', *du*, no 6, Zürich, 1984. André Kamber, 'Ingeborg Lüscher' (catalogue), Kunstmuseum Solothurn, 1982. Annemarie Monteil, *Ingeborg Lüscher oder die Verbindung von Leben und Kunst* (catalogue), Galerie Dany Keller, Munich, 1982. Elisabeth Kübler & Keto von Waberer, *Zorn und Zärtlichkeit*, Galerie Maeght, Zürich, 1980.

LEN LYE
Wystan Curnow & Roger Horrocks, 'Len Lye, selected writings', *Figures of Motion*, Auckland University Press, 1984. 'Len Lye Issue', *Art New Zealand*, no 17, 1980. *Len Lye: A Personal Mythology* (catalogue), Auckland City Art Gallery, 1980. Michael Dunn, 'Len Lye in New Zealand', *Art and Australia*, vol. 16, March 1979. Ray Thorburn, 'Ray Thorburn Interviews Len Lye', *Art International*, vol. 19, April 1975.

HILARIE MAIS
Bruce Adams, 'Myths Trapped on Canvas', *Sydney Morning Herald*, 2 May 1987. Maggie Gilchrist, 'Male Monoliths, Female Icons', *Art and Australia*, November 1985. Ursula Prunster, 'Transformations', *Third Australian Perspecta*, Art Gallery of New South Wales, Sydney, June 1985. Graeme Sturgeon, *Australian Sculpture Now* (catalogue), 2nd Australian Sculpture Triennial, November 1984. Terence Maloon, 'A discreet message about discreteness', *Sydney Morning Herald*, 1 September 1984.

HENRI MATISSE
'Henri Matisse', *The Moderns* (catalogue), Art Gallery of New South Wales, Sydney, 1984. J. Jacobus, *Matisse*, Milan, 1974. Henri Matisse, *Propos de Henri Matisse*, Amis de l'Art, October 1951. Henri Matisse, *Les Problèmes de la peinture*, 1945. Henri Matisse, *La Grande Revue*, 25 December 1908.

COLIN McCAHON
Gordon H. Brown, *Colin McCahon: Artist*, A.W. & A.H. Reed Ltd, Wellington, 1984. *I Will Need Words: Colin McCahon's Word and Number Paintings* (catalogue), National Art Gallery of New Zealand, 1984. *McCahon's 'Necessary Protectionism'* (catalogue), Govett-Brewster Art Gallery, New Plymouth, 1977. 'Colin McCahon', *Art New Zealand*, November–January, 1977–78. *Colin McCahon, a survey exhibition* (catalogue), Auckland City Art Gallery, 1972.

VICTOR MEERTENS
'Diversity in Australian Art', *Southbank Show* (catalogue), Queensland Art Gallery, Brisbane, June 1987. Phillis Woolcock, 'King-size show for Brisbane and Japan', *Courier Mail*, Brisbane, 20 June 1987. Graeme Osborne, 'Unusual collaboration of art forms', *Age*, Melbourne, 17 March 1987. Gary Catalano, 'Angel of a human environment', *Age*, Melbourne, 11 March 1987. Gary Catalano, 'A tale of two Victors', *Age*, Melbourne, 7 May 1986.

GERHARD MERZ
Ludwig Rinn, *Documenta 8* (catalogue), Kassel, 1987. Klaus Ottmann, 'Gerhard Merz', *Flash Art*, 1987. Bazon Brock, 'Die Schönheit ist ein Köter, der der Wahrheit hinterherläuft', *Von hier aus*, Düsseldorf, 1984.

FRANÇOIS MORELLET
Colliard, Douroux, Morellet, *François Morellet: La géométrie dans les spasmes, géométrie, figures hâtives* (catalogue), La Consortium Dijon, 1986/87. Blistène, Millet, Oxenaar, *Morellet* (catalogue), Musée National d'Art Moderne, Centre Georges Pompidou, Paris, 1986. Bernhard Holeczek, François Morellet, *François Morellet—Neue Arbeiten* (catalogue), Galerie M, Bochum, 1985. Jan van der Marck, Charlotta Kotik, *François Morellet: Systems*, Albright Knox Art Gallery, Buffalo, New York, 1984. Bernhard Holeczek, François Morellet, *François Morellet, Werke 1976–83* (catalogue), Joseph-Albers-Museum, Bottrop, 1983.

ROBERT MORRIS
Edward F. Fry, 'Robert Morris in the 1980s', *Robert Morris: Works of the Eighties*

(catalogue), Museum of Contemporary Art, Chicago, and Newport Harbor Art Museum, 1986. Carter Ratcliff, 'Robert Morris: A Saint Jerome for Our Times', *Artforum*, no 25, April 1985. Nancy Princenthal, 'Robert Morris', *Art News*, no 84, Summer 1985. Matthew Baigell, 'Robert Morris's Latest Works: Slouching toward Armageddon', *Art Criticism*, no 2, 1985. Robert Morris, 'American Quartet', *Art in America*, no 69, December 1981.

OLIVIER MOSSET
Robert Nickas, 'Interview with Olivier Mosset', *Flash Art*, no 132, February/March 1987. Jeffrey Rian, 'Olivier Mosset at John Gibson', *Art in America*, no 9, September 1987. Maurice Besset, *Olivier Mosset* (catalogue), Musée Sainte-Croix, Poitiers, 1985. Alan G. Artner, 'Color-field Painting returns in an impressive exhibition', *Chicago Tribune*, 18 January 1985. Joël Lechaux, 'Olivier Mosset', *Artistes*, Summer 1983.

NATSU NAKAJIMA
Irene Borger, 'Butoh blossoms in Muteki-sha's "Garden"', *Los Angeles Herald Examiner*, 21 September 1987. Lewis Segal, 'Japanese Tradition in "Niwa"', *Los Angeles Times*, 21 September 1987. Anna Kisselgoff, 'Dance that Startles and Challenges is coming from Abroad', *New York Times*, 13 October 1985. Andrea Rowe, 'Eastern dance an intense, fragile study of life', *Citizen*, Ottawa, 25 September 1985. Oscar Moore, 'LIFT Festival', *Plays and Players*, October 1983.

HERMANN NITSCH
Otmar Rychlik, 'Conversation with Hermann Nitsch', *Hermann Nitsch, 20. Malaktion* (catalogue), Wiener Secession, 1987. Hermann Nitsch, *Orgien Mysterien Theater*, März Verlag, Darmstadt, 1969.

JOHN NIXON
Mike Parr, 'Beleagured Transcendence (The Art of John Nixon)', *The Australian Bicentennial Perspecta* (catalogue), Art Gallery of New South Wales, Sydney, 1987. *Tableaux Abstraits* (catalogue), Villa Arson, Nice, 1986. *Australian Art 1960–1986* (catalogue), National Gallery of Victoria, Melbourne, 1986. *Australian Visions: 1984 Exxon International Exhibition* (catalogue), Solomon R. Guggenheim Museum, New York, 1984. *D'Un Autre Continent: L'Australie, le Rêve et le Réel* (catalogue), ARC, Musée d'Art Moderne de la Ville de Paris, 1983.

SIDNEY NOLAN
Brian Adams, *Sidney Nolan: Such is Life*, Hutchinson of Australia, Melbourne, 1987. Gavin Fry, *Nolan's Gallipoli*, Rigby, Adelaide, 1983. Charles Osborne, *Masterpieces of Nolan*, Thames & Hudson, London, 1975. Geoffrey Dutton, 'Sidney Nolan's Burke and Wills Series', *Art & Australia*, September 1967. Elwyn Lynn, *Sidney Nolan: Myth and Imagery*, Macmillan, London, 1967.

GIANFRANCO NOTARGIACOMO
Sergio Guarino, *Gianfranco Notargiacomo* (catalogue), Galleria Peccolo, Livorno, 1987. Caroli, Calvesi, Lux, Mori & Vescovo, *Gianfranco Notargiacomo* (catalogue), Museo Diego Aragona Pignatelli Cortes, Naples, 1983. Luciano Caramel, *Biennale di Venezia*, Venice, 1982. Flavio Caroli, 'Torna l'Informale', *Corriere della Sera*, 1 February 1981. Edith Schoss, 'Around European Galleries', *New York Herald Tribune*, 13 March 1971.

MARIA OLSEN
Alexa Johnston, *Recent New Zealand Art: Sculpture 2* (catalogue), Auckland City Art Gallery, 1986. C. Barton, 'Maria Olsen—New Work', *Art New Zealand*, no 40, 1986. Cheryll Sotheran, 'Six New Zealand Artists for Australia', in Anthony Bond, *Australian Perspecta* (catalogue), Art Gallery of New South Wales, Sydney, 1985. Michael Spens, 'Meaning, Excellence and Purpose: ANZART in Edinburgh', *Art New Zealand*, no 33, 1984. Elizabeth Eastmond, 'Maria Olsen at RKS', *Art New Zealand*, no 26, 1983.

TATSUMI ORIMOTO
'Art Apace', *Dream*, May 1986 'Japan Art Scene', *Art '85*, May 1985. 'News Column— Art', *Shotenkenchiku*, May 1984. 'All That Art', *Bijututecho*, May 1982.

SONJA OUDENDIJK
W. Hayes, 'Zes Beeldhouwers', *Arte Factum*, September 1987. 'Désir du Sud—Étoile du Nord', *Fodor*, no 5–6, September/December 1986. Antje von Graevenitz, 'Sonja Oudendijks ante-chambre', *Archis*, no 7, 1986. Tineke Reynders, 'De Camouflage van Aorta', *Metropolis M*, March 1986. 'Atelierssignalementen: Bart Domburg, Sonja Oudendijk', *Kunstbeeld*, no 7, May 1986.

GIULIO PAOLINI
Anthony Iannacci, 'Markus Lüpertz and Giulio Paolini', *Artscribe*, May 1987. Carolyn Christov-Bakargiev, 'Giulio Paolini', *Flash Art*, April 1987. S. Taylor, 'A Conversation with Giulio Paolini', *Print Collector's Newsletter*, no 15, November/ December 1984. Giulio Paolini, 'Tout Paolini', *Connaissance des Arts*, no 384, February 1984. N. Orengo, 'Interview with Giulio Paolini', *Libri nuovi*, Einaudi, Turin, 1975.

MIKE PARR
Bernice Murphy, 'Babel/Nuremburg (The Photographic Winter) In the Wings of the Oedipal Theatre Part 4', *The Australian Bicentennial Perspecta* (catalogue), Art Gallery of New South Wales, Sydney, 1987. Daniel Thomas, 'The Artists and their Australian Context', *An Australian Accent, Three Artists, Mike Parr, Imants Tillers, Ken Unsworth*, John Kaldor Art Projects 7, P.S.I, The Institute for Art and Urban Resources, Inc., New York, 1984. Suzi Gablik, 'Report from Australia', *Art in America*, vol. 69, no 1, Marion, Ohio, January 1981. Mike Parr, 'Rules and Displacement Activities: Problems of Socialization', *Data Magazine*, Milan, December 1976. Lucy Lippard (ed.), *Six Years: the Dematerialization of the Art Object from 1966 to 1972*, Praeger, New York, 1973.

GIUSEPPE PENONE
Jean-Paul Monery & Christine Poullain, *Giuseppe Penone* (catalogue), Musée de Peinture et Sculpture, Grenoble, March 1986. Jessica Bradley, *Giuseppe Penone* (catalogue), Musée d'Art Moderne de la Ville de Paris, Paris, July 1984. Johannes Cladders, *Giuseppe Penone Ecrits et Dessins* (catalogue), Städtisches Museum Abteiberg, Mönchengladbach, 1982. Germano Celant & Giuseppe Penone, *Identité italienne, l'Art en Italie depuis 1959*, Centre Georges Pompidou, Paris, June 1981. Celant, Penone & Feliz, *Giuseppe Penone*, Museum Folkwang, Essen, 1978.

PABLO PICASSO
'Pablo Picasso', *The Moderns* (catalogue), Art Gallery of New South Wales, Sydney, 1984.

Domenico Porzio & Marco Valsecchi, *Pablo Picasso*, Chartwell Books, New Jersey, 1973. Mario de Micheli, *Scritti di Picasso*, Feltrinelli, 1964. Christian Zervos, *Conversation avec Picasso*, Cahiers d'Art, 1935.

MARGARET PRESTON
Roger Butler, *The Prints of Margaret Preston*, Australian National Gallery and Oxford University Press, Melbourne 1987. Elizabeth Butel, *Margaret Preston, The Art of Constant Rearrangement*, Art Gallery of New South Wales and Penguin Books, 1985. Ian North (ed.), *The Art of Margaret Preston*, Art Gallery Board of South Australia, Adelaide, 1980. Hal Missingham, 'Margaret Preston', *Art and Australia*, vol. 1, no 2, August 1963. Sydney Ure Smith (ed.), *Margaret Preston's Monotypes*, Ure Smith, Sydney, 1949.

MARTIN PURYEAR
Barry Schwabsky, 'The Obscure Objects of Martin Puryear', *Arts Magazine*, vol. 62, no 3, November 1987. Michael Brenson, 'Maverick Sculptor Makes Good', *New York Times Magazine*, November 1 1987. Alan G. Artner, 'Massive work a visual odyssey', *Chicago Tribune*, 17 September 1987. Cindy Kirshman, 'Earthworks Art Sways with its Dimension', *Chicago Tribune*, 3 April 1987. Hugh M. Davies & Helaine Posner, 'Conversations with Martin Puryear', *Martin Puryear* (catalogue), University Gallery, University of Massachusetts, Amherst, 1984.

ARNULF RAINER
Barbara Catoir, *Madness, Ugliness, Destruction and Death*, Munich, 1980. Rudi H. Fuchs, *On Arnulf Rainer* (catalogue), Eindhoven, London, 1980. Dieter Honisch, *Painting in order to end all Painting* (catalogue), Baden-Baden, Bonn, Vienna, 1980. Otto Breicha, *Hirndrang*, Edition Welz, Salzburg, 1980. Hans Aurenhammer, *Totenmasken*, 1978.

JACKY REDGATE
Pam Hansford, 'Work-to-Rule', *Photofile*, Winter 1987. Ross Gibson, 'Jacky Redgate', *The Australian Bicentennial Perspecta* (catalogue), Sydney, 1987. *Sydney Morning Herald*, 11 March 1987. *Afterimage*, vol. 14, no 2, September 1986. *Burlington Magazine*, London, August 1986.

GERHARD RICHTER
Anne Rorimer, 'Gerhard Richter: The Illusion and Reality of Painting', *Gerhard Richter, Paintings* (catalogue), Marian Goodman Gallery, Sperone Westwater Gallery, New York, 1987. Walter Grasskamp, 'Gerhard Richter: An Angel Vanishes', *Flash Art*, no 128, May/June 1986. Stephen Ellis, 'The Elusive Gerhard Richter', *Art in America*, no 74, November 1986. Jürgen Harten, 'The Romantic Intent for Abstraction', *Gerhard Richter Paintings 1962–85* (catalogue), Städtische Kunsthalle Düsseldorf, 1986. Dorothea Dietrich, 'Gerhard Richter: An Interview', *Print Collector's Newsletter*, no 4, September/October 1985.

MARK ROTHKO
Claude R. Cernuschi, 'Mark Rothko's Mature Paintings: A Question of Content', *Arts Magazine*, May 1986. Brian O'Doherty, 'Rothko's Endgame', *Mark Rothko, the Dark Paintings 1969–70*, The Pace Gallery, New York, 1985. Bonnie Clearwater, 'How Rothko looked at Rothko', *Art News*, vol. 84, no 9, November 1985. Diane Waldman, 'The Farther Shore of Art', *Mark Rothko: A Retrospective*, Solomon R. Guggenheim Museum, New York, 1978–79. Peter Schjeldahl, 'Rothko and Belief', *Art in America*, vol. 67, no 2, March/April 1979.

GARETH SANSOM
Robert Lindsay, *From Field to Figuration* (catalogue), National Gallery of Victoria, Melbourne, 1987. Frances Lindsay, *Gareth Sansom* (catalogue), University of Melbourne, 1986. Ron Radford, *Recent Australian Painting, A Survey 1970–83* (catalogue), Art Gallery of South Australia, Adelaide, 1984. Bernice Murphy, 'Recent Paintings in Australia', *Flash Art*, no 110, January 1983. Janine Burke, *Gareth Sansom: Collage* (catalogue), Regional Development Program, Australia Council, Sydney, 1982–83.

ANNA MARIA SANTOLINI
Giorgio Verzotti, 'Anna Maria Santolini', *Flash Art*, no 136, January 1987. Achille Bonito Oliva, *Progetto dolce*, Milan, 1987. L. Caramel, 'Anna Maria Santolini', *Dopo il concettuale, nuove generazioni* (catalogue), Palazzo delle Albere, Milan, 1986. F. Menna, 'Anna Maria Santolini', *La soglia: l'opera d'arte tra riduzione e costruzione*, Comune de Pordenone, 1985. A. D'Avossa, 'Anna Maria Santolini', *Le Arti News*, no 2–3, 1984.

RICHARD SERRA
Rosalind Krauss, 'Richard Serra Sculpture', *Richard Serra/Sculpture* (catalogue), Museum of Modern Art, New York, 1986. *Richard Serra: Recent Sculpture in Europe 1977–85*, Galerie M, Bochum, 1985. Harriet Senie, 'The Right Stuff', *Art News*, no. 83, March 1984. Bois, Krauss, Pacquement, *Richard Serra* (catalogue), Musée National d'Art Moderne, Centre Georges Pompidou, Paris, 1983–84. Weyergraf, Imdahl, Buchloh, Borden, *Richard Serra: Works 66–77* (catalogue), Kunsthalle, Tübingen, 1978.

SEVERED HEADS
Tom Ellard, 'About Severed Heads', *The Australian Bicentennial Perspecta*, Art Gallery of New South Wales, Sydney, 1987. Mark Carey, 'Sparring with the Big Guy', *Ram*, 21 October 1987. Mark Mordue, 'Punishing Pop with Crunching Rhythms', *Age*, Melbourne, 9 October 1987. Loretta Hall, 'A Bizarre Approach to Video Art', *Melbourne Herald*, 8 October 1987. Susan Charlton, 'Severed Heads: the Band of Just Two', *Sydney Morning Herald*, 9 October 1987.

VIVIENNE SHARK LeWITT
Robyn McKenzie, 'Vivienne Shark LeWitt', *The Australian Bicentennial Perspecta* (catalogue), Art Gallery of New South Wales, 1987. Peter Cripps, 'Vivienne Shark LeWitt', *Interviews With*, The Institute of Modern Art, Brisbane, 1986. Robin Barden, 'Love and Fear', *Tension 6*, 1985. Judy Annear, 'The Allegory of Vivienne Shark LeWitt', *On The Beach*, Winter 1984. Robin Barden, 'The End of Civilisation', *Tension 2*, 1983.

DAVID SMITH
Kersting, Kirby & Merkert, *David Smith: Sculpture and Drawings*, Prestel-Verlag, Munich, 1986. Jean Rikhoff, *David Smith, I remember*, Loft Press, Glen Falls, New York,1984. S.E. Marcus, *David Smith. The Sculptor and His Work*, Cornell University Press, Ithaca, New York, 1983. Rosalind Krauss, *The Sculpture of David Smith, a catalogue raisonné*, Garland, New York, 1977. McCoy (ed.) *David Smith*, Praeger, New York & Washington, 1972.

HENRYK STAŻEWSKI
Janina Ladnowska, 'Henryk Stażewski', *Présences Polonaises*, Centre Georges Pompidou, Paris, 1983. *Henry Stażewski* (catalogue), Muzeum Sztuki, Lodz, 1969–70. Henryk Stażewski, 'Ni le classicisme . . .', *Abstraction-Creation*, no 2, 1933. Henryk Stazewski, 'L'homme nouveau sait voir le monde vide d'objets', *Cercle et Carré*, no 1, 1930.

GARY STEVENS & CAROLINE WILKINSON
Gary Stevens, 'Thinking Objects: Aspects of Laurel and Hardy', *Performance Magazine*, no 37, 1987. Jonathan Watkins, 'If the Cap Fits', *Art Monthly*, December 1986/87. Steve Rogers, 'If the Cap Fits', *Performance Magazine*, May/June 1987.

IMANTS TILLERS
Stuart Morgan, *Imants Tillers*, Institute of Contemporary Art, London, 1988. Sandy Nairne, *State of the Art: Ideas and Images in the 1980s*, Chatto and Windus, London 1987. Howard Fox, *Avant Garde in the Eighties*, Los Angeles County Museum of Art, Los Angeles, 1987. Kerry Crowley (ed.), *Imants Tillers: Venice Biennale 1986*, Visual Arts Board of Australia Council, Sydney, and Art Gallery of South Australia, Adelaide, 1986. Daniel Thomas (ed.), *An Australian Accent: Three Artists* (catalogue), P.S.1, New York, John Kaldor, Sydney, 1984.

WILLIAM TUCKER
John Russell, 'Art: New Sculptures by William Tucker', *New York Times*, 15 November 1985. Ron Shuebrook, 'William Tucker', *Artscribe*, no 36, August 1982. Kenneth Baker, 'William Tucker: Meaning vs Matter', *Art in America*, no 65, November/December 1977. Albert Elsen, 'Early Modern Sculpture', *Art Journal*, no 35, Winter 1976. William Feaver, *Apollo*, June 1975.

TONY TUCKSON
Clinton Tweedie, Introduction to *Godfrey Miller, Tony Tuckson, Ken Whisson: Drawings* (catalogue), Burnie Art Gallery, Tasmania, June 1982. Grazia Gunn (ed.) *Tony Tuckson, John Firth-Smith: Two Sydney Painters* (catalogue), Department of Visual Arts, Monash University, Melbourne, June 1975. Sandra McGrath, 'Tony Tuckson', *Art and Australia*, vol. 12, no 2, December 1974. Daniel Thomas & Frances McCarthy, *Recent Australian Art* (catalogue), Art Gallery of New South Wales, Sydney, October 1973. Tom Farrell, 'Making new artists for Australia', *Daily Telegraph*, 22 April 1950.

BILL VIOLA
Julia Brown (ed.), 'Bill Viola: Statements by the Artist', *Summer 1985* (catalogue), The Museum of Contemporary Art, Los Angeles, 1985. Raymond Bellour, 'An Interview with Bill Viola', *October*, no 34 Fall 1985. Dany Bloch (ed.), *Bill Viola* (catalogue), Musée d'Art Moderne de la Ville de Paris, 1983/1984. Bill Viola, 'Sight Unseen—Enlightened Squirrels and Fatal Experiments', *Video 80*, no 4, Spring 1982, San Francisco, California. Bill Viola, 'Will There Be Condominiums in Data Space?', *Video 80*, no 5, Fall 1982. John Minkowsky, 'Bill Viola's Video Vision', *Video 81*, Fall 1981.

JEFF WALL
Els Barents, 'Typology, Luminescence, Freedom: Selections from a Conversation with Jeff Wall', *Jeff Wall: Transparencies*, Schirmer/Mosel, Munich and Rizzoli, New York, 1987. Ian Wallace, 'Jeff Wall's Transparencies', *Transparencies* (catalogue), ICA, London, and Kunsthalle, Basle, 1984. Donald B. Kuspit, 'Looking Up at Jeff Walls's Modern Appassionamento', *Artforum*, vol. 20, no 7, March 1982. Dan Graham, 'The Destroyed Room of Jeff Wall', *Real Life Magazine*, March 1980.

ANDY WARHOL
Arthur C. Danto, 'Who Was Andy Warhol?', *ARTnews*, May 1987. Jole de Sanna, 'Andy Warhol at the Galleria Refettorio della Stelline, Milan', *Artforum*, vol. 25, January 1987. Donald Kuspit, 'Andy's Feelings', *Artscribe*, Summer 1987. Thomas Lawson, 'The Future is Certain', *Individuals: A Selected History of Contemporary Art 1945–86*, Museum of Contemporary Art, Los Angeles, Abbeville Press, New York, 1986. Art & Language, 'Andy Warhol at Anthony d'Offay', *Artscribe*, November/December 1986.

FRED WILLIAMS
Patrick McCaughey, *Fred Williams*, Bay Books, Sydney, 1980. Alwynne Mackie, 'Fred Williams: Abstracted Landscapes', *Art and Australia*, vol. 16, no 3, March 1979. Patrick McCaughey, 'Fred Williams', *Art International*, vol. XVI, no 9, November 1972. James Mollison, *Fred Williams Etchings* (catalogue), Rudy Komon Gallery, Sydney, 1968. Adrian Rawlins, 'Fred Williams', *Art and Australia*, vol. 2, no 3, December 1964.